The Politics
of Energy Conservation

PIETRO S. NIVOLA

The Politics
of Energy Conservation

THE BROOKINGS INSTITUTION
Washington, D.C.

Library of Congress Cataloging-in-Publication Data

Nivola, Pietro S.
  The politics of energy conservation.

  Includes bibliographical references and index.
    1. Energy conservation—United States.   2. Energy
policy—United States.   I. Brookings Institution.
II. Title.
TJ163.4.U6N58   1986   333.79′16′0973   85-48265
ISBN 0-8157-6088-4
ISBN 0-8157-6087-6 (pbk.)

9 8 7 6 5 4 3 2 1

▉▉▉ THE BROOKINGS INSTITUTION is an independent organization devoted to nonpartisan research, education, and publication in economics, government, foreign policy, and the social sciences generally. Its principal purposes are to aid in the development of sound public policies and to promote public understanding of issues of national importance.

The Institution was founded on December 8, 1927, to merge the activities of the Institute for Government Research, founded in 1916, the Institute of Economics, founded in 1922, and the Robert Brookings Graduate School of Economics and Government, founded in 1924.

The Board of Trustees is responsible for the general administration of the Institution, while the immediate direction of the policies, program, and staff is vested in the President, assisted by an advisory committee of the officers and staff. The by-laws of the Institution state: "It is the function of the Trustees to make possible the conduct of scientific research, and publication, under the most favorable conditions, and to safeguard the independence of the research staff in the pursuit of their studies and in the publication of the results of such studies. It is not a part of their function to determine, control, or influence the conduct of particular investigations or the conclusions reached."

The President bears final responsibility for the decision to publish a manuscript as a Brookings book. In reaching his judgment on the competence, accuracy, and objectivity of each study, the President is advised by the director of the appropriate research program and weighs the views of a panel of expert outside readers who report to him in confidence on the quality of the work. Publication of a work signifies that it is deemed a competent treatment worthy of public consideration but does not imply endorsement of conclusions or recommendations.

The Institution maintains its position of neutrality on issues of public policy in order to safeguard the intellectual freedom of the staff. Hence interpretations or conclusions in Brookings publications should be understood to be solely those of the authors and should not be attributed to the Institution, to its trustees, officers, or other staff members, or to the organizations that support its research.

For my father
Costantino Nivola

Foreword

THE energy crisis of the 1970s led to an unusually intense national debate. The two political parties agreed on the need to conserve energy as part of the remedy to the shortages. But deep political conflicts blocked government action on the key means of achieving conservation—reform of energy pricing policies. Though the Congress deregulated petroleum prices in 1981, regulated pricing formulas persist in other energy sectors.

In this book, Pietro S. Nivola examines key legislative decisions of the 1970s and early 1980s on the pricing of crude oil and natural gas, as well as decisions on fuel taxes and electric rates. He explores the influence of interest groups, popular attitudes, and regional rivalries that often delayed or complicated energy-saving price reforms. He also analyzes the roles of government leaders and political institutions in shaping policy.

At the core of the political struggles over energy pricing, the author argues, are contrasting beliefs about the role of government. Congressional debates on the decontrol of oil and gas prices, for example, reflected sharp partisan differences about the merits of government intervention in energy markets. They also reflected a basic dispute over the use of federal energy pricing policy to redress social inequities. These political divisions have distinguished energy policymaking in the United States from that of other industrial democracies and have made the American debate particularly polemical.

Pietro S. Nivola is an associate professor of political science at the University of Vermont and a former guest scholar and research associate in the Brookings Governmental Studies program. He is grateful to a number of scholars who read the manuscript and offered valuable advice. Among the readers were R. Douglas Arnold, Charles O. Jones, Terry M. Moe, Paul J. Quirk, and James L. Sundquist. John E. Chubb, Martha Derthick, Edward R. Fried, William K. Muir, and Paul E. Peterson made especially extensive comments. Robert H. Meyer and Heywood T. Sanders contributed to statistical sections of the analyses, as did Kor Kiley and Carole H. Newman. The author thanks Theresa B. Walker for editing the manuscript, and J. Karl Scholz, Darlene C. Steil, and Sara A. Pozefsky for research assistance. Pamela D. Harris typed the manuscript, and T. Diane Hodges coordinated the entire enterprise.

The research was made possible by a grant from the Ford Foundation, which the author gratefully acknowledges.

The views expressed in this book are the author's alone and should not be ascribed to the persons whose assistance is acknowledged above, to the Ford Foundation, or to the trustees, officers, or other staff members of the Brookings Institution.

BRUCE K. MACLAURY
President

January 1986
Washington, D.C.

Contents

Tables

CHAPTER ONE

Introduction

MANY IRONIES pervaded the past decade's debate about American energy policy. Not the least was that, beneath all the controversy and confusion, the remedy to the energy problem was clear: the nation's demand for energy could best be brought into balance with the supply chiefly through conservation. No other course of action promised to meet the country's energy requirements more dependably, quickly, cleanly, and cheaply.

That fact seemed widely understood—by virtually every important study of the subject, by a broad spectrum of popular opinion,[1] and by public officials. While professional policy analysts touted conservation as a national priority, federal energy administrators accurately asserted that at least 30 percent of the country's energy use was "pure waste."[2] Congressional reports correctly concluded that the possible gains from conservation greatly exceeded those from increased production, and the two main presidential initiatives of the period—Gerald Ford's *Project Independence* and Jimmy Carter's *National Energy Plan*—stressed the innumerable opportunities for energy thrift.[3]

1. American Petroleum Institute, *Two Energy Futures: A National Choice for the 80s* (Washington, D.C.: American Petroleum Institute, 1980), p. 108; and Barbara Farhar Pilgrim, Charles T. Unseld, and Jerome Williams, *The National Study of the Residential Solar Consumer: Decision Factors and Experience* (Golden, Colo: Solar Energy Research Institute, 1981), p. 21.

2. Press release, John C. Sawhill, hearing before the Federal Energy Administration, San Francisco, October 7, 1974; and John L. Moore, ed., *Continuing Energy Crisis in America* (Washington, D.C.: CQ Press, 1975), p. 4.

3. See *Achieving Price Stability through Economic Growth*, Joint Economic Committee, H. Rept. 1653, 93 Cong. 2 sess. (Government Printing Office, 1974), p. 111; Federal Energy Administration, *Project Independence: A Summary* (GPO, 1974), p. 52; and Executive Office of the President, Energy Policy and Planning Staff, *The National*

By 1980 this enthusiasm was reflected in seven elaborate pieces of legislation that had been passed purporting to have conservation as their leading aim. They included the Energy Policy and Conservation Act of 1975; the Energy Conservation and Production Act of 1976; and the National Energy Conservation Act of 1978. At first glance, the breadth of government intervention mandated by these statutes looked impressive. Fuel-economy regulations were imposed on automobiles and envisaged, though never implemented, for new buildings and certain home appliances. Gas-guzzling automobiles were subjected to tax penalties. Electric utilities were urged to help their customers install energy-conserving equipment, to tolerate more on-site generation of power from excess industrial heat (a process known as cogeneration), and to consider new rate designs. Finally, an assortment of grants, loan supports, and tax expenditures was assembled. Federal assistance for conservation investments grew into a multibillion dollar package whose benefits were distributed generously—to households, businesses, schools, hospitals, mass transit systems, local communities, and state governments.

Nevertheless, at bottom these activities bypassed more urgent tasks. Whatever the need for novel regulatory schemes and large-scale subsidies, a serious conservation program required, first and foremost, an appropriate pricing policy. The country, in the era of the energy crisis, was encumbered by a price structure that held the cost of energy below its replacement value and overstimulated demand. Any bold effort to curb consumption had to begin by dismantling this anachronism. A sound agenda called for an end to price controls on domestic crude oil and natural gas, redesign of electric utility rates, and a stiffer excise tax on the key petroleum refined-product, gasoline.

Instead, the government's conservation policy unfolded the other way around. Price reform languished or, at best, progressed sluggishly and unevenly. In its place arrived a collection of sanctions and subventions, juxtaposed with a system of administered prices that vitiated energy savings. Even today, outmoded pricing arrangements linger. Although petroleum prices were fully deregulated in 1981, wasteful pricing formulas still distort other critical energy sectors—most notably, natural gas and electric power. Every year, for example, thousands of industrial firms finance conservation improvements through federal tax credits totaling millions of dollars; at the same time, many of these firms

Energy Plan (Ballinger, 1977), chap. 4.

squander large quantities of natural gas and electricity, partly because the remaining gas price controls and promotional utility rates subsidize their energy accounts.

Conservation and Prices

Like it or not, nothing works better than higher prices to enhance energy efficiency. Why, for example, during periods of comparatively rapid economic growth, were the rates of energy use in the economies of Japan and much of Western Europe lower than those in the United States? The difference had little to do with larger commitments of government aid for conservation or tighter governmental restrictions. (The Germans would bristle at any speed limits, let alone 55 mph, on their autobahns!) Roughly half of the variance could be explained by a combination of geography, income levels, and basic economic mix.[4] But the rest related, directly or indirectly, to price differentials.[5] Skeptics, of course, would cite a host of other reasons—smaller European dwelling units and higher residential densities; less developed public transportation in the United States; more modern industrial facilities abroad; and an American taste for energy-soaking consumer durables. Such objections are deceptive, however, since these other reasons are partially the result of energy prices. Suburban sprawl, large detached houses, two-ton automobiles, inadequate transit systems, fuel-inefficient plants—none of these energy-intensive aspects of the American context are built in as if by magic. In some measure, all are dependent on comparatively cheap gasoline, oil, gas, and electricity.

One might suppose that, with lower ratios of energy use to gross domestic product during the 1970s, the Europeans and Japanese were left with less room for adjustment as prices rose. But between 1973 and 1979, the average annual growth rate of oil consumption dropped nearly to zero in Western Europe and Japan, where, theoretically, there was

4. Joel Darmstadter, Joy Dunkerley, and Jack Alterman, *How Industrial Societies Use Energy: A Comparative Analysis* (Johns Hopkins University Press for Resources for the Future, 1977), p. 163.

5. National Research Council of the National Academy of Sciences, *Energy in Transition, 1985–2010: Final Report of the Committee on Nuclear and Alternative Energy Systems* (San Francisco: W.H. Freeman, 1960), pp. 108–09; and Joy Dunkerley, *Trends in Energy Use in Industrial Societies: An Overview* (Washington, D.C.: Resources for the Future, 1980), p. 110.

less fat to cut.[6] Meanwhile, the voracious appetite for oil in the United States continued to grow, though much less rapidly than it did before 1973.[7] The lesson was clear enough: where consumers paid the world price for oil, magnified by sales taxation, particularly of gasoline, the effect of the postembargo price surge was to drive relatively modest levels of consumption further down. Where government controls partially insulated consumers from the world price, and where gasoline taxes were slight, high levels of consumption declined less dramatically.[8]

Similar patterns prevailed regionally within the United States. Energy in New England, for instance, was more expensive than anywhere else in the country because of the region's dependence on imported oil, which was not subject to direct price regulation. Not surprisingly, in the wake of the 1973 price jump, per capita consumption of both home-heating oil and residual fuel fell sharply, compared with the rest of the nation. Households and industry in New England began conserving fuel at a rate three times better than the national average.[9]

Programs versus Prices

The conservation measures that policymakers in the United States concocted to avoid "rationing by price" were pitched against an estimated $100 billion of stimulus being pumped into demand by way of

6. Barry P. Bosworth and Robert Z. Lawrence, *Commodity Prices and the New Inflation* (Brookings, 1982), p. 116; and Joseph A. Yager, *The Energy Balance in Northeast Asia* (Brookings, 1984), pp. 11, 15.

7. During 1973–79 the gross domestic product (GDP) grew at a slower average annual rate in Western Europe (2.8 percent) than it did in the United States (3.1 percent), accounting in part for the higher U.S. oil consumption growth rate. Yet, in the same period, Japanese GDP growth averaged 4.5 percent, even as its total final demand for energy increased only moderately (an average annual rate of 0.75 percent). In 1973, Japan consumed only 57 percent as much energy for every unit of gross national product as did the United States. By 1980, it used just 43 percent as much. Daniel Yergin and Martin Hillenbrand, eds., *Global Insecurity: A Strategy for Energy and Economic Renewal* (Houghton Mifflin, 1982), pp. 11, 142, 212, 377.

8. I am referring to the period before 1980, that is, before the Iranian crisis administered a second price shock that occurred as the phased deregulation of oil, initiated in mid-1979, was under way. Between 1968 and 1973, the average annual increase in oil consumption was 5.08 percent in the United States. It declined to 2.09 percent from 1973 to 1979. But for Western Europe, the average annual increase, which had been 7.45 percent from 1968 to 1973, plummeted to 0.15 percent over 1973–79. Bosworth and Lawrence, *Commodity Prices and the New Inflation*, p. 116.

9. Edward J. Mitchell, ed., *Energy: Regional Goals and the National Interest* (Washington, D.C.: American Enterprise Institute, 1976), pp. 3, 14.

price controls.[10] In this setting, there was little chance that the conservation measures, whatever their merits, could bring about the desired reduction in the growth rate of energy consumption. The various techniques employed were inherently less effective than the price mechanism for several reasons.

To begin with, improved energy use requires adjustments throughout the entire economy. But the federal government's conservation programs have been segmental, dealing with particular problems, such as homeowners' attics, gas-guzzlers, and oil-fired power plants, resulting in at least two kinds of deficiencies. First, savings resulting from intervention in one sector could induce consumption in another. Grants, tax breaks, and below-market-rate loans encouraged people to winterize their houses, thereby reducing the expense of home heating. But, unlike the workings of a general fuel-price increase, such subsidies have also enabled people to apply the savings in heating toward greater energy expenditures on everything else—not excluding such uses as warmed outdoor swimming pools and motorboats.

Second, large areas of potential savings have been overlooked. Fuel-economy standards, for example, have boosted the gas mileage of automobiles, but until recently the standards did much less to better the performance of vans and light trucks, which compose a quarter of all new vehicles sold annually. Further, unlike a price hike at the gas pump, the regulations cannot moderate the main force behind gasoline consumption—the amount of driving. Since a case can be made that the central imperative of U.S. energy policy in the transportation sector is to address the problem of passenger miles traveled per gallon, not just vehicle miles per gallon, the fuel-economy standards promulgated in 1975 have left much of the job unfinished.[11]

A more energy-efficient society does not spring from some exotic, centrally contrived technological fix. Energy efficiency requires a diffuse, diversified, and sustained series of low-level adaptations. The experience of the 1970s reveals that three things complicate the process: (1) No one is prepared to sacrifice unless, as a minimal condition, everyone else is deemed to be sacrificing as well. (2) If others can be made to shoulder

10. John H. Gibbons and William U. Chandler, *Energy: The Conservation Revolution* (New York: Plenum Press, 1981), p. 153.

11. Robert F. Hemphill, Jr., "Energy Conservation in the Transportation Sector," in John C. Sawhill, ed., *Energy Conservation and Public Policy* (Prentice-Hall, 1979), pp. 80–81.

the burden, why do so oneself, especially if benefits from their labors are shared broadly, regardless of individual action? (3) The concrete details of conservation are worse than inconvenient; they are boring.

These constraints mean that admonitions and exhortations are ineffectual, even during emergencies. In the early stages of the 1973 and 1979 oil crises, federal authorities pleaded for voluntary restraint to mitigate impending shortfalls of gasoline; utilities were urged to seek substitutes for oil; the states were asked to consider various actions; and the public was told to lower thermostats and obey highway speed limits. The response during both episodes was similar. At the end of 1973, gasoline demand went above the level for the same period in the previous year and did not subside until shortages and long gas lines developed in early 1974.[12] Likewise, before dipping later in the year, demand for gasoline during the first part of 1979 vaulted over the level for the corresponding period in 1978.[13] Perverse as these outcomes seem, they were wholly rational. The "free rider" impulse that conditioned individual conservation decisions was mightier than altruism, and the tendency of public attention to wander from the mundane specifics of these decisions (replete with concerns about weather stripping and water heaters, tire pressures and tune-ups, thermostats and thermal underwear) was stronger than any appeal to patriotism. Under a system of replacement-cost pricing, on the other hand, the same obstacles would have proved less refractory: a multitude of conservation opportunities, no matter how prosaic, would have become economic and likely to be exploited widely because the stakes would have been tied not just to some hazy conception of the collective interest but to immediate self-interest.

The snags that hobble campaigns for voluntary conservation also limited the scope of mandatory restrictions. During the 1970s, standby plans were advanced to help manage petroleum demand in the event of supply disruptions. Each time, Congress discarded almost all of the suggestions. Some provisions, such as a ban on nonessential advertising lights proposed in 1979, were mostly ridiculed for yielding only token gains in oil equivalency. Although the notion of restricting lighted advertising was more symbolic than significant, the issue was symptomatic of a more general dilemma: a great many energy-saving ideas were trivi-

12. William C. Lane, Jr., *The Mandatory Petroleum Price and Allocation Regulations: A History and Analysis* (Washington, D.C.: American Petroleum Institute, 1981), p. 35.

13. Ibid., p. 67.

alized, not necessarily because they were not worthwhile, but because individually they appeared petty, even if cumulatively their impact might be substantial.

Other concepts, such as proposals to curtail gasoline sales by closing service stations on weekends, may have sounded less silly. But in these instances, the interests on whom the restrictions appeared to place an immediate cost would insist, for the most part persuasively, that they did not deserve to be singled out, that other spheres were worthier of concern, or at least that the onus of conservation ought to be distributed evenly. To be sure, some groups, such as the tourist industry in the case of gas station closings, were more successful with this strategy than others were (notably, the automotive industry in the fight over gas-mileage regulations). In general, though, politicians toiled inconclusively with coercive limitations on energy use. Typically, they succumbed to protestations from all sides that while the road to conservation had to start somewhere, it was always better to begin somewhere else, or no-where at all unless everywhere at once.

Finally, the reliance on government sanctions and subsidies to rein in demand invited a burgeoning pork barrel. Just as the prospect of federal sanctions triggered evasive action by every targeted interest, the prospect of federal subsidies prompted every imaginable group to stake a claim. Truckers lobbied for extra incentives to pay for windscreens on cabs and trailers. The intercity bus-line industry came remarkably close to getting its axles greased with $1 billion in special tax benefits. Inland barge operators had long enjoyed the advantages of leaving to taxpayers the mul-tibillion-dollar annual expense of constructing and maintaining the waterways; now, by trotting out the argument that barges saved oil, the operators fended off renewed efforts to levy user fees.[14]

Other peculiar players reaped rewards from the logrolling free-for-all in which conservation initiatives were swept up. Several times, opponents of school integration managed to graft antibusing amendments onto major energy bills on the theory that, *mirabile visu*, they would spare fuel.

A defect in almost any program of investment tax credits is that the program may support projects that would be undertaken even without

14. Richard Corrigan, "Lobbyists Are Putting the Blitz on Carter's Energy Program," *National Journal*, vol. 9 (November 26, 1977), pp. 1836, 1837; and David A. Stockman, "The Wrong War? The Case Against a National Energy Policy," *Public Interest*, no. 53 (Fall 1978), p. 41.

government aid. Residential conservation credits for home improvements have illustrated this proclivity, even in an environment of controlled fuel prices.[15] By 1980, items such as storm doors were being financed by the Treasury at a tax loss per barrel of oil saved equal to $91.93 in 1975 dollars.[16]

The potential for similar false economies hung over the system of low-interest loans sponsored by the federal Solar Energy and Conservation Bank, established in 1980. The kinds of investments that qualified, and the degree to which the subsidized loans departed from market rates and time frames, were such that critics feared the bank would be defraying as much as 60 percent of the installation costs of, say, solar hot tubs and barbecues, at an implicit price of at least $70 per barrel expressed in oil equivalents.[17]

In theory, the central virtue of conservation is not just that it moves energy demand toward equilibrium with supply, but that it can do so cost effectively: the entailed resource reallocations should cost the economy significantly less than the volume of energy the nation would otherwise have to acquire.[18] In practice, much of the activity that government policy has underwritten in the name of husbanding energy may

15. The percentages of respondents who said they would invest in energy improvements on their homes if a proposed tax credit were adopted did not differ substantially from the percentages who made such improvements before the credits were enacted, according to *Roper Reports*, 77-5 (mid-June 1977), items 19a and 19b. Inequity is another problem. Unpublished statistics made available by the Treasury Department's Office of Tax Analysis indicated that in 1979, for instance, only 1.14 percent of the tax returns filed by households or individuals with annual incomes under $5,000 claimed conservation credits. The principal beneficiaries of the tax credit subsidy are the middle- and upper-income brackets.

16. Charles River Associates, Inc., *An Analysis of the Residential Energy Conservation Tax Credit: Concepts and Numerical Estimates* (Boston: Charles River Associates, Inc., 1981), pp. 1–6.

17. *National Solar and Energy Conservation Incentives Act*, H. Rept. 625, 96 Cong. 1 sess. (GPO, 1979), p. 96; and *Compilation of the Energy Security Act of 1980, and 1980 Amendments to the Defense Production Act of 1950*, Committee Print, House Committee on Banking, Finance and Urban Affairs, 96 Cong. 2 sess. (GPO, 1980), pt. 3, p. 2204.

18. Comparative cost effectiveness has been the central claim of the case for conservation. See Amory B. Lovins, *Soft Energy Paths: Toward a Durable Peace* (Ballinger, 1977), pp. 6, 21, 22, 35, 51. For excellent empirical research on the question, see Roger W. Sant, *The Least-Cost Energy Strategy* (Carnegie-Mellon University Press, 1979); and the studies of the Lawrence Berkeley Lab in Lee Schipper, "Raising the Productivity of Energy Utilization," *Annual Review of Energy*, vol. 1 (Palo Alto, Calif.: Annual Reviews, Inc., 1976), pp. 481, 493–95, 511. In 1980 one study group found the evidence so compelling, it concluded: "at present it takes considerably less capital to save a Btu than to produce one." National Research Council, *Energy in Transition*, pp. 75, 84.

have flunked this economic test, sometimes embarrassingly.

Prices and Equity

Inevitably, conservation by price raises knotty questions of social equity. Decontrol of oil and gas in particular has proven bitterly controversial. It appeared that huge sums of income would be shifted from millions of consumers to a handful of big oil companies, and further, that the step would engender immensely regressive effects on the distribution of wealth. Higher gasoline excise taxes, in turn, entail horizontal inequities as well as vertical ones (for example, rural states always claim to suffer more than urban states better served by public transit). Even the most seemingly sensible utility rate revisions become entangled in disputes about fairness. Flat rate schedules may seem eminently fair to residential customers who consume little electricity, but are considered unfair by bulk users, to whom the unit cost of delivering electric power is usually lower. A long litany of apparent injustices is linked with energy pricing reform. These concerns, some genuine, some exaggerated, make the issue tempestuous.

The distributive impacts of rising prices are complicated. Oil deregulation, for instance, surely implied large wealth transfers, but these would occur within the petroleum industry (from refiners to producers) as well as between the industry and end users.[19] Additionally, it was simplistic to rant about consumers enriching the oil companies. Both categories included gigantic corporations, and to some extent, the movement of wealth was from one group of stockholders to another. Both categories also subsumed lesser entities—average households on one side, but on the other, thousands of small-scale independent producers who, at the margin, often stood to gain more from domestic price deregulation than did the majors. The multinationals that obtained most of their crude abroad could sell their products elsewhere at world prices. Further, while regulation-induced shortages intensified U.S. dependence on imported oil, the dependence did not necessarily cause sleepless nights for executives or shareholders of firms with extensive foreign operations; they, after all, supplied the imports.

19. In 1978, for instance, the net income transfer from oil producers to refiners, under the petroleum price and allocation controls legislated in 1973 and 1975, was estimated to be almost twice as large as the net income transfer from producers to consumers. Joseph P. Kalt, *The Economics and Politics of Oil Price Regulation: Federal Policy in the Post-Embargo Era* (MIT Press, 1981), p. 216.

In an immediate sense, of course, the weight of higher prices falls more heavily on the poor than on the wealthy, since poor families spend proportionally more of their budgets on direct energy purchases. But this is not the whole story. Indirect consumption of energy increases more sharply with income. Hence, when prices climb, the pattern of total (direct plus indirect) energy costs incurred across income classes is less regressive than commonly assumed.[20] Further, the more important consideration may be the relation of energy outlays to overall household expenditures, rather than nominal household income. (Income data for the poverty-level population are notoriously unreliable. In fact, average spending on energy consumption has been estimated to exceed average monetary income, as reflected in Census Bureau surveys, by a ratio of more than two to one.)[21] Findings can be disparate, depending on the frame of reference. One study found that even counting only direct energy purchases, the lowest-income households devoted approximately 13 percent of their overall consumption expenditures to energy, as compared with 8 percent energy expenditures for the highest-income class. When presented in terms of the percentage of income going to energy outlays, the picture looked drastically different: the high-income group devoted less than 6 percent, whereas the low-income group appeared to give up about 30 percent.[22]

On balance, the situation may still justify some form of compensation. Although the exact degree of regressiveness embodied in foreseeable energy price increases is debatable, the direction is not, and even a mildly regressive effect can be felt keenly at the margin: clearly, the marginal dollar spent on fuel bills makes more difference to the impoverished person than to the affluent one. That being true, however, the preferable approach is through explicit income maintenance programs whose target efficiency, though hardly admirable, is superior to that of price controls.

Even less popular than deregulation have been the periodic attempts to levy national gasoline taxes. Opponents—frequently led by representatives from sparsely populated western and southern states—sometimes seem to depict proposed increases as morally indefensible. But the re-

20. Hans H. Landsberg and Joseph M. Dukert, *High Energy Costs: Uneven, Unfair, Unavoidable?* (Johns Hopkins University Press for Resources for the Future, 1981), p. 33.
21. Ibid., pp. 34–35.
22. James P. Stucker, *The Impact of Energy Price Increases on Households: An Illustration,* P-5585 (Santa Monica, Calif.: Rand Corp., 1976), p. 10.

gions that often complain loudest tend to be the ones in which, comparatively speaking, electric power, oil, or natural gas has flowed at bargain prices.[23] If, in fact, more expensive gasoline hurts inhabitants of these areas disproportionately, that disadvantage is partially offset by lower prices for other forms of energy.

From the standpoint of fairness to the poor, gasoline taxes may be less objectionable than policies that swell the use of costly oil imports or, for that matter, import fees intended to back them out (which were tolerated, if not promoted, by some of the same politicians that decried the inequities in gasoline taxation). Any policy that bolsters petroleum prices as a whole touches all refined-product consumers, including low-income households that use fuel oil for essential functions such as home heating. Gasoline taxes, on the other hand, only affect people who own motor vehicles and who drive them a lot. Virtually every middle- and upper-class suburbanite, irrespective of region, falls into that category; relatively few poverty-level persons do.[24] The much-maligned notion of a vigorous federal tax on motor fuel may be less inequitable than the rhetoric of its detractors makes it sound.

While price instruments beget injustices, so do other options that, at least in the abstract, enjoy wider appeal. Public opinion polls throughout the 1970s indicated that the preferred alternative to gasoline-price increases was administrative rationing. Yet, when Congress debated emergency rationing proposals between 1977 and 1979, it soon discovered that no formula was readily acceptable.[25] Plans that gave each car owner an equal number of rationing coupons were disadvantageous to those individuals who were particularly dependent on cars (for example, rural residents). But plans allocating coupons on the basis of past consumption patterns favored those dependent individuals, permitting them to use as much gas as ever. People who had striven to conserve gasoline (for example, mass transit riders in urban areas who had begun leaving their cars in the garage) were cheated. Plans to allot coupons on the basis of

23. See the data from the U.S. Energy Information Administration, reported in Harold Beebout, Gerald Peabody, and Pat Doyle, "The Distribution of Household Energy Expenditures and the Impact of High Prices," in Hans H. Landsberg, ed., *High Energy Costs: Assessing the Burden* (Washington, D.C.: Resources for the Future, 1982), p. 18.

24. Approximately half of all low-income families in the United States do not own automobiles. Landsberg and Dukert, *High Energy Costs: Uneven, Unfair, Unavoidable?*, p. 29.

25. Daniel Yergin, ed., *The Dependence Dilemma: Gasoline Consumption and America's Security* (Harvard University, Center for International Affairs, 1980), pp. 41–49, 118, 147.

vehicle registrations either deprived licensed drivers who owned no vehicles or encouraged such persons to register clunkers so as to qualify for
allotments. Plans that covered only licensed motorists excluded 26
million unlicensed adults, or motivated many of them to apply for li-
censes solely to redeem their coupons. Plans to dispense redeemable
coupons through the mail risked widespread theft and abuse. But plans
to distribute them at redemption centers would breed long waiting lines,
which, like the gas queues, were likely to be a lot longer in some places
than others. The intricacies of designing a practical and impartial procedure were manifold. As in other efforts to constrain demand adminis-
tratively, the tendency was to haggle interminably about whose ox would
get gored. Predictably, when Congress finally concluded its deliberations
on standby rationing, it settled upon an accommodation that virtually
guaranteed that rationing would never be put into practice.[26]

Nor was there much reason to believe that the status quo was un-
biased, or that its biases were less marked than those stemming from
greater reliance on the market. Who got what under the system of petroleum price and allocation regulations? Big winners, apart from Arab
sheiks, turned out to be crude-oil refiners, certain categories of fuel-
intensive end users situated primarily outside the Northeast, particular
farm lobbies, and some oil jobbers and refined-product marketers. Un-
avoidably, middle- and upper-class consumers fared better in absolute
terms than the working class and the poor, simply because the latter
groups bought less energy. (Families who were well-off consumed an average of 1,000 gallons of gasoline per year, compared with about 400
gallons per year for families who were less well-off. Assuming that in the
1970s the price of gasoline, if unregulated, would have been about $0.50
per gallon higher than the going rate at the pump, the gross annual
subsidy to each well-off family totaled $500, contrasted with $200 for
each less-well-off family.)[27] Moreover, because of the upward pressure
on world oil prices, attributable at least in part to overconsumption of oil
in the United States, American consumers who may have feasted on a
free lunch in the short run paid for it later by way of inflation and losses
in real economic growth.

All of which leaves a final query: what has been more damaging—the

---

26. The emergency rationing plan that finally cleared Congress in 1979 would permit
the president to put rationing into effect if there were a 20 percent shortage of gasoline for
a period of thirty days, but Congress reserved the right to veto the executive order.

27. Gibbons and Chandler, *Energy*, p. 152.

economic distortions wrought by years of misleading energy price signals, or the distributional side effects that would arise from setting those signals straight? Value-free answers are seldom possible when judging complex trade-offs between equity and efficiency. Yet, in this instance, the weight of the evidence seems hard to ignore: less timid use of prices as a method of conserving energy confers great gains in efficiency, gains that have been partially forfeited by a misplaced effort to redistribute income through energy price restraints. Although a great deal continues to hinge on how hardships borne by the poor are redressed, continued underpricing of energy is, at best, a clumsy method of poverty relief.

Beyond Market Prices

In some respects, the real imponderable has not been whether to take American energy prices up to market-clearing levels, but whether to push them beyond. For years, expert opinion has held that prevailing prices, especially for crude oil, do not include the full social costs of using and producing energy. The following arguments are commonly advanced.

For efficient use, prices should reflect the fact that each unit of nonrenewable energy consumed brings the day closer when more costly substitutes must be found. But the marketplace does not adequately weight this long-term replacement cost. Too much of the cost is left to later generations. The market also undervalues the air, water, and land consumed in making and using energy. If environmental impacts are not fully embedded in final prices, too much energy continues to be sought. Additionally, for petroleum, large quantities of which must be purchased abroad, the true economic cost is not the nominal market price, but that price plus an increment (import premium), since expensive marginal imports often cause an upward revaluation of the oil shipments already on stream.[28] And because of the dominance of the volatile Middle East in the world oil market, petroleum prices must take into account the risk of disruptions, with potentially catastrophic economic and political repercussions. Hence, a security premium is implied.

These propositions, focusing on supposed market failures, need to be assessed briefly here, because they bear closely on the politics of energy taxation, which are assayed in this book. Hardest to establish is the theory

28. Thomas C. Schelling, *Thinking Through the Energy Problem* (Washington, D.C.: Committee for Economic Development, 1979), pp. 29–30, 48–49.

that the market does not properly count future costs and benefits of exhaustible resources. Although subsequent generations will bear the costs of developing substitutes for the resources that the current generation depletes, they will also inherit the wealth and technology generated by the current generation through recovery of resources in the present at considerable immediate risk and cost. Even if markets for depletable resources cannot provide recompense in kind for every possible future claim, there is no obvious way of determining the appropriate social rate at which current resource users ought to, in effect, tax themselves for the sake of posterity.

The failure of energy markets to take account of environmental costs is more verifiable. Yet, by the mid-1970s, it was no longer plausible to maintain that extant energy prices incorporated none of the environmental costs of energy acquisition and use. By then, a great deal of legislation was regulating, however selectively, both production and utilization of energy, with the objective of controlling pollution, health hazards, and safety problems. The efficacy of these efforts was sometimes questionable, but the fact that they contributed importantly to higher energy costs was not.

At first glance, surcharges on foreign oil to trim imports, particularly from unstable regions, seem advisable. Upon closer inspection, the idea raises doubts. On the one hand, inordinate importation of crude oil, as facilitated by the regulatory contraptions that mispriced U.S. oil and natural gas in the 1970s, can bid up world prices, so that the marginal burden borne by the domestic economy is understated by those prices. To the extent that the imports come from insecure sources, the United States is also made vulnerable to instability in the world market. On the other hand, policies to reduce imports well below levels set by market forces can strain the economy, without appreciably cushioning it from market disorders. It has never been clear, for instance, that the American balance of payments would be enhanced by drastic import reduction. Nor would such a policy prevent the United States from experiencing part of the global supply shortfall during a serious interruption, to say nothing of the secondary economic shock waves.[29]

American energy autarky would not ease the world's long-term de-

29. Gary Samore, "The Persian Gulf," in David A. Deese and Joseph S. Nye, eds., *Energy and Security* (Ballinger, 1981), p. 107; and Arnold B. Moore, "U.S. Energy Policy in the World Context," in *No Time to Confuse: A Critique of the Final Report of the Energy Policy Project of the Ford Foundation* (San Francisco: Institute for Contemporary Studies, 1975), p. 96.

pendence on the Organization of Petroleum Exporting Countries (OPEC), or at least on its key members in the Persian Gulf. In fact, amid the current spell of sagging international oil prices, U.S. withdrawal from the world petroleum trade could knock OPEC's prices down so low as to put its competitors, such as Mexico or the North Sea, promptly out of business. In the end, by closing down spare productive capacity in secure areas, oil importers might become, once again, as vulnerable as ever to the vagaries of petroleum output in the Middle East.

Finally, two other questions render a suitable price-premium for imported oil excruciatingly hard to estimate: (1) How big should it be in light of expenditures earmarked for defense of the Persian Gulf (and other oil-rich zones) and maintenance of the strategic petroleum reserve? (2) How big should it be after weighing in a unique political cost—that the premium furnishes a pretext for embracing indiscriminately every contrivance aimed at increasing U.S. energy independence?

The second question is especially nettlesome, even though proponents of energy independence seldom acknowledge it. If the hidden price of imported petroleum is posited to be greatly in excess of the posted price, then virtually any crackpot scheme pretending to further self-sufficiency can justify government support. Government funding could extend more than ever, not merely to ill-conceived conservation programs like those mentioned earlier, but also to lavish energy development projects, with billions poured into fast breeder reactors, synthetic fuels facilities, and other commercially unviable enterprises.

In short, energy prices depressed beneath market levels have understated future replacement costs, environmental deterioration, and the implications of relying heavily on imported oil. Whether the same remains true of less regulated markets is not so certain. Thus, while decontrolled prices are indispensable, it is less evident that they ought to be amplified or corrected with import fees, taxes, or other nonmarket pricing tools, especially if corrections must correspond in size to the exaggerated oil premiums imputed by some researchers.[30] Or at least this is true so long as additional considerations are not introduced.

Additional considerations abound, however, and they are crucial. Even if all domestic energy markets were freed from direct price regulation, numerous government policies would continue to warp relative

30. Some analysts estimate the oil-import premium to be well over $100 per barrel. Douglas R. Bohi and W. David Montgomery, *Oil Prices, Energy Security, and Import Policy* (Washington, D.C.: Resources for the Future, 1982), p. 3.

energy prices in other ways. On the supply side, some of these policies have long been transparent: for decades, energy development has bulged with tax shelters, subsidized insurance, off-budget loans, "acquisition" subsidies, and straight infusions of federal funds, totaling over time perhaps a half-trillion dollars.[31] The demand-side distortions (apart from price controls) are less flagrant, but still large. High on the lengthy list are the various government programs that have fostered a dispersed pattern of urban settlement; public planning that has sponsored a fuel-ravaging transportation system; and, of course, the legacy of low-cost energy—thanks, in part, to the production subsidies just noted.

What is to be done to make up for this? In an imaginary world, matters might be rectified by phasing out all forms of government price rigging, not only the direct interferences but also the oblique ones—from limited-liability insurance for the nuclear power industry to mortgage guarantees for suburban homes; from depletion allowances to the highway trust fund; from federal loans for electrification projects to tax-free development bonds for suburban industrial parks; and on and on. In the real world, deregulation in this comprehensive sense is inconceivable, even if coaxed along over many years. What remain are second-best solutions—chiefly, energy tariffs and excises—to countervail the effects of the government's various market stimulants.

Current Implications

The question of energy efficiency and the fuel-price policy decisions at its base no longer arouse the intense concern inspired several years ago. Since 1981, world petroleum prices have retreated, the OPEC cartel appears to have crumbled, and past shortages are a distant memory. The second energy crisis in 1979–80 was so convulsive that in its immediate aftermath U.S. oil imports, and overall consumption, plunged more than most observers thought possible.[32] That dive would not have been as steep without the federal government's gradual abandonment of controls

31. Richard J. Barnett, *The Lean Years: Politics in the Age of Scarcity* (Simon and Schuster, 1980), p. 55.

32. From 1980 to 1981, U.S. oil consumption fell by 6.2 percent, cutting imports of foreign crude and petroleum products by 15.7 percent to 5.7 million barrels a day, the lowest figure since 1972. Youssef M. Ibrahim and David Ignatius, "As Oil Use Declines, Experts See a Slowing in Price Increases," *Wall Street Journal*, January 27, 1982. By the end of 1982, overall domestic oil demand had dropped to 15.3 million barrels a day (compared with 18.4 million barrels a day in 1977). *New York Times*, March 11, 1984.

on domestic crude and partial relaxation of controls on natural gas.[33]

Nevertheless, a critical examination of energy pricing and conservation is still essential. As in the hiatus between 1974 and 1979, reemergence of what has been called a glut psychology may leave the nation unprepared for the next episode of sudden energy stringency, should world events bring another crunch.[34] Amid the euphoria over the conservation revolution of the 1980s are nagging doubts about the extent and permanence of the gains. The national economy is a lot less fuel intensive now than it was before 1979 (by 1982, the energy needed to generate $1 worth of GNP had been slashed by 20 percent),[35] but at least half of the recent decline in energy demand can be attributed not to structural changes but to the protracted economic slump of the early 1980s.[36]

In some end-use categories, the reports on conservation activity are disquieting. For example, residential fuel use in the United States has dropped appreciably since 1979, thanks, in large part, to lowered thermostats and other behavioral adjustments by households.[37] But much newly built housing remains an energy sieve in comparison with the savings attainable at existing construction costs. Sampling about 6,200 new homes, a study by the Tennessee Valley Authority found that even

33. Even under the oil-price controls enacted in 1975, the gap between U.S. and world prices narrowed considerably toward the end of the decade. In 1976, the composite or average U.S. refiner acquisition cost of crude oil was almost 20 percent lower than the price of imports. But by 1978, the difference closed to 14 percent. In April 1979, the Carter administration allowed phased decontrol, extending over twenty-eight months beginning in June of that year. Thanks to that decision, the disparity between the foreign and U.S. composite price was further reduced, to about 10 percent by the end of 1980. Nevertheless, although the persisting price differentials seemed small, their effect on marginal demand was not trivial. For a nation whose consumption of energy in 1979 amounted to almost half the total primary energy consumption of the Organization for Economic Cooperation and Development, marginal differences in demand equal hundreds of millions of barrels of oil-equivalent.

34. Daniel Yergin, "Crisis and Adjustment: An Overview," in Daniel Yergin and Martin Hillenbrand, eds., *Global Insecurity*, p. 16.

35. Douglas Martin, "Energy Shortage Eases Materially, Basic Shifts in Consumption Cited," *New York Times*, March 8, 1982; Gerald W. Bollman and others, "Oil Decontrol: The Power of Incentives Could Reduce OPEC's Power to Boost Oil Prices," *Oil and Gas Journal*, vol. 80 (January 11, 1982), p. 96.

36. With American factories operating at only 60 percent of capacity during the recession in 1982, this was the consensus estimate. "A Split in OPEC: Cheaper Oil Ahead," *Newsweek* (February 7, 1983), p. 51.

37. According to the Department of Energy, Americans cut their home energy use by 17 percent from 1978 through 1980. *New York Times*, December 12, 1982; and *New York Times*, October 11, 1981.

in the throes of the 1979–80 oil-price explosion, most of the units surveyed were still receiving woefully inadequate insulation.[38] In another investigation, Federal Trade Commission inspectors found similar evidence of inefficiency in newly constructed dwellings.[39] Officials were reportedly astonished by these findings. But they shouldn't have been. Most American homes are heated with natural gas, whereas millions of housing units rely on electrical resistance heaters. Gas and electric rates remain substantially regulated. Even as oil prices soared in 1980, the price spike took time to register fully in household heating bills.

Declining gasoline prices since 1981 have caused slippage, once again, in the most problematic energy sector, transportation. At the end of 1983, total gasoline consumption was back up to the level of 1973 (over 104 billion gallons).[40] The amount of driving had increased. Sales of full-sized cars made a spectacular comeback, and total average fuel economy of domestically produced new-car fleets failed to meet federal standards. Despite the celebrated improvement in efficiency of American automobiles since 1973, the trend in the most recent years has been unsettling. During 1979–80, total average fuel economy was upgraded by 2.6 miles per gallon (mpg), chiefly through downsizing and reductions in weight of vehicles. Between 1980 and 1981, the average gain was 1.6 mpg, and in 1981–82, only 1.1 mpg. Then, through 1983, mileage per gallon did not improve at all. While imports achieved an average of 32.2 mpg, the domestic fleet remained at 24.6 mpg—a rating lower than the level recorded by imports in 1976.[41]

Some of this apparent backsliding has to do with a deficiency often overlooked as glut psychology lulls policymakers: the federal government's most noteworthy accomplishment in the field of conservation —deregulation of petroleum prices—has not sufficed to secure long-

38. The results of this unpublished study were reported in the *New York Times*, December 28, 1980. The survey found that 83 percent of the 6,211 new homes inspected lacked adequate attic insulation and 85 percent had no floor insulation.

39. Ibid.

40. U.S. Department of Transportation, Federal Highway Administration, *Monthly Gasoline Reported by States* (GPO, 1983), table MF-33GA; and U.S. Department of Transportation, Federal Highway Administration, *Highway Statistics 1973* (GPO, 1973), tables MF-24, MF-26.

41. Calculated from U.S. Department of Transportation and Environmental Protection Agency published and unpublished data reported in Motor Vehicle Manufacturers Association, *Motor Vehicle Facts and Figures, '83* (Detroit: Motor Vehicle Manufacturers Association, 1983), p. 74.

range efficiency in the use of energy.

Clearly it is inappropriate to depreciate the improvements in energy-saving policy and practice of recent years. But it would be equally foolish to forget that the adjustments were tardy. Delayed decisions, such as the congressional action in 1975 postponing until 1981 the complete decontrol of oil, exacted a toll.

The political impasse over energy price controls, allocation rules, and taxes throughout the 1970s was largely to blame for the domestic shortages of the period, and hence heavily responsible for the rapid rate at which American importation of crude oil increased.[42] For years the United States had been the world's largest consumer of petroleum, but the government's pricing policies helped turn it into the biggest importer.[43] In 1973, and especially in 1979, the relentless pressure on the world market, driven in part by excess demand in the United States, helped set the stage for chaotic price spirals that, as evinced by the supply surplus and price cuts of 1982–1984, carried fuel charges much higher than they would otherwise have gone. Although domestic energy-pricing policies were never a root cause of the past decade's international energy crisis, they did contribute to it by tautening the world oil market.

The global disequilibrium in energy markets, in turn, bore severe penalties. It ran oil prices up 1,200 percent between 1973 and 1983. In the industrialized countries, this upheaval helped to triple the cumulative rate of inflation, double the rate of unemployment, and lower the rate of economic growth by half. (The cost to the economies of the seven largest

42. See Kenneth J. Arrow and Joseph P. Kalt, *Petroleum Price Regulation: Should We Decontrol?* (Washington, D.C.: American Enterprise Institute, 1979), pp. 25–26; Richard Eden and others, *Energy Economics: Growth, Resources, and Policies* (Cambridge University Press, 1981), p. 410; and Edward W. Erickson and others, "The Political Economy of Crude Oil Price Controls," in Walter J. Mead and Albert E. Utton, *U.S. Energy Policy: Errors of the Past; Proposals for the Future* (Ballinger, 1978), pp. 93, 98. On the 1974 crisis, see Richard B. Mancke, *Squeaking By: U.S. Energy Policy Since the Embargo* (Columbia University Press, 1976), pp. 21–44. It has been estimated that by artificially stimulating demand, U.S. price controls may have been responsible for more than a third of the price run-up that accompanied the Iranian revolution in 1979. *New York Times*, September 8, 1981.

43. For example, one component of the oil price and allocation regulations, the refiner entitlements program, sought to average refinery acquisition costs of controlled domestic crude and higher-priced supplies. It is estimated that this subprogram had the effect of subsidizing approximately one-tenth to one-fifth of each barrel of imported oil, accounting for about 375 million extra barrels of imported oil per year. See Arrow and Kalt, *Petroleum Price Regulation*, pp. 14–15.

industrial nations is estimated at $1.2 trillion through 1981. For the United States alone the estimate is $500 billion.)[44] Developing countries suffered payments deficits so acute that their debts continue to rattle the international banking system. When international oil prices shot above market-clearing levels, the immediate response was a worldwide stampede to invest in costly new energy-producing ventures that subsequently faced financial ruin when prices softened. The misallocations of capital associated with the roller-coaster ride in petroleum prices cannot be shrugged off as a necessary cost of normalizing the world energy market; whole nations, such as Mexico, have been pushed to the brink of default in the process.

The political ramifications were also profound. Internationally, the 1970s brought resurgent protectionism, as governments groped to relieve faltering industries in their recession-mired economies. Accentuating the strain among trading partners were begger-thy-neighbor monetary policies aimed at checking inflation, the other malady worsened by oil shocks.

Domestically, following the hysteria that accompanied the sudden shortages and price bursts, politicians reached for extravagant elixirs. First there was the Ford administration's notion of building 200 additional nuclear plants, 250 new coal mines, 150 more coal-stoked generators, 30 major oil refineries, and 20 large synthetic fuel plants.[45] Then came President Carter's draconian coal-conversion plan, later supplemented by a proposal to spend $88 billion on synthetic fuels projects. Even the Reagan administration, which was anxious to repudiate the boondoggles of the past, promptly proposed an ambitious program to revitalize the ailing nuclear industry.[46] Whenever it became apparent that the country could not afford such exploits, or that the programs would not soon relieve the energy predicament even if they were deemed affordable, the sense of helplessness and frustration mounted.

Public trust in governmental institutions was shaken. Policy had done much to create a crisis and to inflame it once it was under way. The gasoline lines of 1974 and 1979, for example, resulted almost entirely

44. Yergin and Hillenbrand, eds., *Global Insecurity*, p. 5; and Martin, "Energy Shortage Eases."

45. Proposed in President Ford's January 1975 energy message, cited in Daniel Yergin, "America in the Strait of Stringency," in Yergin and Hillenbrand, eds., *Global Insecurity*, p. 106.

46. *New York Times*, October 9, 1981.

from federal regulatory actions.[47] Then, amid the economic aftershocks and fanciful legislative nostrums, interminable disagreements ensued as to how repetitions might be prevented. The inability of policymakers to grasp in time the practical solutions that were available left an impression of a paralytic political system, or more precisely, a government whose actions under pressure either were ineffectual or produced the wrong results.

Plan of the Book

Chapters 2 and 3 of this book review the disputes over federal price regulation of crude oil and natural gas, the two fuels that together provide three-quarters of the energy for the American economy. Price-suppressive policies for domestically produced oil and gas have extensive histories, but during the interlude in which the energy crisis climaxed, the critical legislative determinations came in 1975 and 1978, respectively. How those decisions were made, and why, are the intriguing questions.

The fourth chapter takes a look at electricity ratemaking, a facet of the conservation problem that deserves greater national recognition. Although gas and oil price issues have excited greater political passions, the dilemma of utility rate reform will probably remain more intractable.

Because energy efficiency may require more than a new-found faith in market pricing of petroleum and natural gas (and marginal-cost pricing of electric power), chapter 5 reopens the question of energy taxation, specifically of a substantial consumption tax on gasoline—a desirable policy refinement, but peculiarly elusive in the context of American politics.

In probing these issues, I examine the activities of interest groups, the impact of public opinion, and the effect of localism, meaning the influence of geographically based interests such as particular states or regions. Policy management is also assessed, addressing questions of political leadership as well as the complexities of coordinating action in a governmental system that greatly fragments authority. Finally, the role of commanding political ideas, setting the terms in which protagonists define and debate the policy problem, is explored.

47. Richard B. Mancke, "The American Response: 'On the Job Training'?" in *Oil Diplomacy: The Atlantic Nations in the Oil Crisis of 1978–79* (Philadelphia: Foreign Policy Research Institute, 1980), pp. 14–17, 30, 33–40; and Stephen Chapman, "The Gas Lines of '79," *Public Interest*, no. 60 (Summer 1980), pp. 44, 47–49.

All of these are important dimensions of energy policymaking, and each can contribute partial answers to the main puzzle: why have political storms beset the quest to conserve energy, even when an apparently wide consensus recognizes the importance of conservation? A central theme of this book is that although a variety of forces animate the politics of conservation, political convictions, often rooted in party philosophies, are fundamental ones. To be sure, political beliefs and party positions are intertwined with diverse local interests, modes of policy management, and public attitudes. Yet these influences also acquire a momentum of their own. Contrasting ideals of the American Left and Right—roughly differentiating Democrats and Republicans— have crisscrossed the nation's energy quarrels, even as popular sentiments, special interests, local demands, and institutional leadership shift and shuffle.

What the partisan and ideological feuds are; why they fan the strife over deregulation, fuel taxes, and utility rate structures; and how they have stalled needed policy changes are concerns that crop up throughout the book. They compose the central focus of chapter 6.

CHAPTER TWO

Deregulation of Oil

PETROLEUM PRICE controls ended in January 1981. Why did that historic moment arrive so belatedly? Controls had been in place since 1971, long enough to bracket, and aggravate, the two international oil crises of the 1970s. The controls had also persisted much longer than anyone had anticipated. They had begun as part of the Nixon administration's wage and price freeze, invoked to dampen inflation before the 1972 presidential election. Because of refined-product shortages brought on by the freeze and by the Arab embargo, special legislation was soon added to deal with oil prices and supply. The Emergency Petroleum Allocation Act (EPAA), passed in the fall of 1973, provided a statutory basis for continuing temporarily the administrative price regulations already in effect. The act also authorized mandatory allocation of crude oil and its by-products. But the EPAA was intended as a short-run legislative palliative, to meet, as its name denoted, the emergency conditions of 1973–74. The act did not expand existing price ceilings, which covered only 40 percent of the oil bought by Americans, and it would expire in less than two years. In short, as of early 1975, the petroleum industry had not been shoved into a long-term, all-inclusive regulatory regime.

By the end of that fateful year, however, such a regime had come into being. The Energy Policy and Conservation Act of 1975 (EPCA) went far beyond the preceding legislation. Unlike the pricing provisions of the 1973 emergency allocation act, the EPCA slapped lids on all domestic crude and rolled back the initial average price by more than $1 per barrel.[1] The new law stipulated that the average price could be raised

1. Before the enactment of the Energy Policy and Conservation Act, only so-called old oil (from wells in production before 1972) was price controlled. Approximately one-third of all domestically produced crude was classified as new or released oil as of 1975. The EPCA extended controls to this category.

periodically at the president's discretion, but increases above 10 percent were subject to stringent congressional review. Most important, the Energy Policy and Conservation Act extended the pricing requirements and the allocation authority of the 1973 emergency allocation act through the rest of the decade, after which the executive branch could act autonomously to remove them. Of course, decontrol of crude oil might have been achieved in the interim by repealing the law. But that would have required not only a cunning president but also a different Congress—more comparable, perhaps, to the one elected in 1980. Thus, although President Carter was empowered to take the first steps toward decontrol near the end of his term (and in mid-1979, he did begin the phased decontrol that the Reagan administration completed in 1981), his earlier efforts to reformulate the oil-pricing rules ran into an insurmountable difficulty: convincing the Ninety-fifth Congress to undo the edifice that the like-minded Ninety-fourth had just finished erecting.

Gerald Ford's situation had not been analogous. Technically, with the expiration of the Emergency Petroleum Allocation Act in August 1975 (or possibly even earlier), he could have let all petroleum price and allocation regulations wither away, at the stroke of a pen. The decision not to do so, and to enact the Energy Policy and Conservation Act instead, was the pivotal episode in the recent history of American oil-pricing policy. More than any other phase in the development of policy, the adoption of the 1975 energy act set the nation on a course from which there was little chance of turning back—at least not before much precious time had been lost.

Conventional Theories

Several theories have been advanced to explain how support for the Energy Policy and Conservation Act developed during a decisive period in policymaking.

Clientelism

One well-articulated body of thought stresses that prior federal pricing programs—the 1973 emergency allocation act, the Nixon wage-price controls, even the oil-import quotas of the 1960s—had mobilized a clientele with a keen vested interest in perpetuating, if not widening, the government's role in apportioning supplies and managing prices.[2]

Petrochemical manufacturers, coal mine operators, truckers, farmers, fishermen, and other groups with priority status under the Emergency Petroleum Allocation Act had enjoyed guaranteed supply at a controlled fee. Naturally, they fought to retain the privilege. Even more important, independent refiners, who produced little crude of their own and who had to buy it from expensive sources, pressed for continuation of the federal crude-sharing requirements and an entitlements system that equalized access to low-cost (controlled) oil among refineries. The small refiners were the most vocal. They had received preferential treatment in the old mandatory oil import program and continued to do so through the EPAA's special rules that allotted them a disproportionate share of purchasing rights to controlled crude. Finally, the coalition included independent heating oil dealers and gasoline marketers. Many of these distributors relied extensively on purchases in the spot market and from the leading wholesalers; they sought assurances that these supply channels would remain intact. Some marketers—notably the jobbers who operated as middlemen, buying a product from refinery terminals and reselling it through retail outlets at a profit—were also anxious to freeze in the discounts they had traditionally received at the terminal rack. Pressure from this collection of lobbies drove both Congress and the president first to extend the EPAA repeatedly and then to invent an even broader regulatory framework.

Public Attitudes

A different vein of commentary attaches less importance to the influence of special interests than to the role of diffuse preferences: public opinion was decisive.[3] Polls consistently showed that inflation, not energy, was the dominant concern among voters. To the extent they believed an energy problem existed, they directed the blame for it mostly at the big petroleum producers. Because of the public's aversion to higher prices, and to the oil companies, deregulation was unpopular. These attitudes were supposedly so unmistakable that any president seeking a second term, and any member of Congress interested in getting reelected, could ill-afford to overlook them.

2. Joseph P. Kalt, *The Economics and Politics of Oil Price Regulation: Federal Policy in the Post-Embargo Era* (MIT Press, 1981), p. 237.

3. See, for instance, Thomas H. Tietenberg, *Energy Planning and Policy: The Political Economy of Project Independence* (Lexington Books, 1976), p. 110.

Regionalism

Still another school underscores the implications of conflicts along sectional lines. Members of Congress are usually more responsive to their immediate constituencies than to trends in the national mood, and local concerns diverged sharply on the question of petroleum price deregulation. The producing states of the Southwest would prosper if oil prices were uncapped, because the impetus for energy exploration would generate local economic growth, an advantageous shift in regional terms of trade, and bigger state tax bases. Few consuming states would participate in this boom, and many would bear the brunt of the higher heating payments and electric rates. The impact would be especially pronounced in the Northeast, where oil was burned in everything from home furnaces to utility boilers, and where energy in all forms was already least affordable. The entitlements program that sought to average refinery acquisition costs of controlled domestic crude and higher-priced supplies had helped blunt the rising price of oil in the Northeast by subsidizing as much as 20 percent of the cost of each barrel of imported crude.[4] Not surprisingly, most of the region's representatives were not anxious to relinquish this protection.

Elsewhere, the consequences of decontrol would be more mixed. The Northwest, for example, would see price increases, but they would be softened partially by the area's rich endowment of economical hydroelectric power. The Southeast could feel the pinch in utility charges and in the prices of particular petroleum products, like propane and gasoline, but a temperate climate took the edge off space heating bills. The Midwest would suffer a significant price rise, especially since decontrol would discontinue the federal crude-sharing rules that were periodically glutting that part of the country with oil.[5] Still, the region remained on the receiving end of the main interstate natural gas pipelines and hence was a principal beneficiary of cut-rate gas, courtesy of the Federal Power Commission. Although local conditions varied tremendously, overall the political geography did not favor deregulation. The balance of

4. Kenneth J. Arrow and Joseph P. Kalt, *Petroleum Price Regulation: Should We Decontrol?* (Washington, D.C.: American Enterprise Institute, 1979), p. 13.

5. William C. Lane, Jr., *The Mandatory Petroleum Price and Allocation Regulations: A History and Analysis* (Washington, D.C.: American Petroleum Institute, 1981), p. 89. The pattern became even more marked later in the 1970s. See Philip K. Verleger, Jr., "The U.S. Petroleum Crisis of 1979," *Brookings Papers on Economic Activity, 2:1979,* p. 472.

power tilted toward those sections that would experience the costs most acutely—the populous states in the North, where most members of the House of Representatives are elected and where presidential contests are won or lost.

Institutional Leadership

Finally, numerous observers have emphasized that the power of the American presidency was at a low ebb in 1975. Without strong presidential leadership, the drift toward wider governmental involvement in oil pricing could not be reversed. The Watergate scandal and the 1974 congressional elections had delivered large and rambunctious Democratic majorities on both sides of the Capitol. An unelected Republican president, scrambling to stay in office past 1976, had to struggle against these majorities. The Ford administration did what it could to stem the rising tide of congressional regulatory zeal in the field of energy, but in the end Ford surrendered. The Energy Policy and Conservation Act was signed into law for reasons of political expediency—"the promise to give voters cheaper energy," lamented Treasury Secretary William E. Simon, "just before the New Hampshire and Florida primaries."[6]

These four sets of insights are not mutually exclusive, and all of them shed valuable light on the ascension of petroleum price regulation. Nonetheless, the theories do not constitute a complete explanation. The reasons for this are well worth exploring, before any additional perspective can be gained.

Interest Groups

There is little doubt that the immediate beneficiaries of petroleum price and allocation controls were not just diffuse consumers but also narrow commercial interests. Many of them were motivated to defend the status quo and organized to do so. By 1975 several new trade associations serving these participants were renting downtown office space in Washington and retaining full-time lobbyists. Entire law firms flourished by counseling clients on how to exploit the regulations to full advantage. Back in the congressional districts, local businesses protected, or even propagated, by the regulations were reputed to be politically influential. Perhaps the most frequently cited examples were the small re-

6. William E. Simon, *A Time for Truth* (Berkley Books, 1979), p. 86.

finers. Various executive agencies and congressional committees were unusually attentive to these lobbies. The Federal Energy Administration (FEA) and the Senate Interior and House Commerce Committees listened routinely to independent refiners, gasoline retailers, farm cooperatives, and other patrons (and parasites) of oil price and allocation regulations.

Still, the proposition that decontrol in 1975 was stymied primarily by special interests is difficult to sustain, particularly if one looks beyond specific committee deliberations to the overall voting patterns in the House and Senate. Dozens of roll calls on oil pricing were recorded during 1975, but only a handful accurately gauged congressional preferences with respect to decontrol. Samplings of such roll calls appear in tables 2-1 and 2-2, in which the votes on critical bills are analyzed (see appendix A to this chapter, p. 75).

Congressional Voting Patterns

Prominent among the client groups interested in opposing deregulation were small refiners, gasoline jobbers, and heating oil dealers. Supposedly, their influence was critical. But the statistical results shown in tables 2-1 and 2-2 are highly instructive. The presence of neither gasoline jobbers nor small refiners (regardless of how one specifies them) is negatively associated with congressional support for decontrol. Rather, the direction is the other way around: the greater the local percentage of jobbers and minor refiners, the more likely a representative or senator was to vote for decontrol. Only the distribution of heating fuel dealers is consistently related to nay votes on decontrol. What accounts for these findings?

REFINERS. In theory, most of the refining industry would resist the deregulation of crude oil, not only because regulation afforded certain protections but also for basic economic reasons.[7] In practice, the industry was increasingly divided and unsettled politically as conditions in the world market changed and as the government's rulemaking under the EPAA grew more complex. Both the federal entitlements system and the

7. Arrow and Kalt explain refiners' interest in controlled crude prices as follows: "The burden of rising oil prices is particularly severe for one industry—crude-oil refiners. The depressing effects of rising prices on the demand for petroleum products tend to leave current refining capacity underutilized and to discourage industry expansion. Moreover, the depressing effects of rising prices on demand tend to prevent the industry from passing on the full amount of any crude-oil price increases." *Petroleum Price Regulation*, pp. 30–31.

crude-sharing requirements (the so-called buy-sell program promulgated in February 1974) aided some refiners at the expense of others. Firms that had acquired crude oil at costs below the national average were now reimbursing firms with crude-oil costs above the average. The former relinquished more than a cost advantage; depending on the grade of crude they refined, they sometimes watched recipients of entitlements gain much wider profit margins. For example, a company using entitlements to buy higher grades of crude could pay a fixed average price, $5.25 per barrel, for its supplies, but then sell its product at higher prices than a company refining a lower grade. This happened because the controls permitted wholesale price differentials among products from crudes of varying quality, but controls set a single value for the entitlements with which crude could be acquired regardless of quality.[8] Under the buy-sell requirements, in turn, many refiners who had found additional supplies through spot or short-term purchases in international markets, and who had paid world prices, were told to sell any excess quantity to crude-short refiners at the controlled domestic average price. Thus Peter, who took the trouble to stockpile supplies from foreign sources, was punished for his prudence, while Paul, who did nothing to build inventories, was rewarded for his torpor by getting a share of Peter's surplus at a subsidized price. As inequities of this kind mounted, refinery operators scrambled to obtain rule adjustments and dispensations from the Federal Energy Administration. But many also yearned to get the FEA off their backs.

Because an explicit aim of the emergency allocation act was to "preserve the competitive viability" of small and independent refiners (and because regulations treated these firms preferentially to achieve this aim),[9] it is sometimes assumed that the only breach in the refining industry was between large, integrated firms and the numerically superior, small, nonintegrated ones. In reality, the situation was more complicated. Designated small was any refiner with capacity below 175,000 barrels per day. Independents were specified as refiners obtaining less than 30 percent of their crude from company-owned (or "captive") sources. With such liberal definitions, all but 14 refining companies, of about 250 in the country, qualified for entitlements and for special allocations under the buy-sell program, depending on the origin and volume

8. Lane, *Mandatory Petroleum Price and Allocation Regulations*, pp. 127–36. Much of the following discussion of refiners and marketers draws on Lane's analysis.
9. Pub. L. 93–159 (November 27, 1973).

of the crude oil they processed.[10] Consequently, some nonminor oil companies with supply problems were able to obtain acquisition rights over controlled domestic crude, while many of their competitors, large and small, were not. In some instances, truly marginal refiners were forced to sell oil at low prices to companies the size of Standard Oil of Ohio, Ashland Oil, Amerada Hess, and Phillips Petroleum. In short, the image of countless grass-roots refineries basking in the sunshine of the EPAA, while only the big corporations were getting burned, was a fiction. On balance, the emergency allocation act favored smaller refiners over larger ones, but numerous firms in both categories found the regulatory environment inhospitable.

Between 1973 and 1975, a dozen more refiners went into operation, mostly on a modest scale.[11] These facilities, and others that might have gone out of business in an uncontrolled market, were suckled by special regulatory subsidies. In particular, more entitlements were issued to smaller refiners than would have been the case if a policy of equalizing crude-oil costs among all companies had been strictly applied. The result was to lower the average crude-oil costs of minor refiners below that of their bigger rivals. Naturally, the beneficiaries of this bias did not want it to disappear.

Yet the political influence of the bias babies, as they were called in the industry, was diluted by their geographic location. The vast majority were situated near other competitors and, more important, alongside the domestic oil producers.[12] Congressmen from states containing minor refineries that survived (and occasionally thrived) under the EPAA were also pressured by other refining businesses and by hundreds of producers who lobbied for the elimination of controls. In these states, the groups favoring decontrol had gained the upper hand (as the positive signs on the correlation coefficients in tables 2-1 and 2-2 strongly suggest).

10. Neil de Marchi, "Energy Policy under Nixon: Mainly Putting Out Fires," in Craufurd D. Goodwin, ed., *Energy Policy in Perspective: Today's Problems, Yesterday's Solutions* (Brookings, 1981), pp. 452–53.

11. Aileen Cantrell, "Annual Refining Survey," *Oil and Gas Journal*, vol. 71 (April 2, 1973), p. 100; and Aileen Cantrell, "Annual Refining Survey," *Oil and Gas Journal*, vol. 73 (April 7, 1975), p. 98.

12. When the frequency of very small refiners—that is, those with capacity under 30,000 barrels a day—is correlated with the total number of refiners by state, a coefficient of $r = .94$ is obtained. Regressing the number of very small refiners on state crude oil production yields a coefficient of $r = .76$. Data are derived from Cantrell, "Annual Refining Survey," *Oil and Gas Journal*, vol. 73 (April 7, 1975), pp. 100–18. Both coefficients are statistically significant at the .001 level.

MARKETERS. What about petroleum product marketers? Here too cleavages had developed within the industry. The regulatory structure had frozen the pattern of transactions throughout the distribution chain, from the wellhead to the fuel-hose nozzle. At each link, sellers had to sell to the customers with whom they had dealt historically, and prices down the line were likewise pegged to a prior base period. Lucky retailers who had taken deliveries from low-cost suppliers at the time of the freeze continued to get a good deal, with a government guarantee. But other retailers found themselves locked into base-period relationships with wholesalers who (because of differing crude-grades, or other factors) charged them higher prices. The variations showed up in retail rate differentials that were often substantial within the same geographic areas. Particularly among neighboring gasoline outlets, it became common for formerly competitive service stations to experience sharply discrepant margins. The EPAA's gainers and losers thus glared at each other from opposite sides of the street.

The kinds of gasoline distributors that seem to have fared best under the regulations were the nonbranded station owners, especially the chain marketers who purchased supplies from independent refiners.[13] These sizable independent retailers, equipped with storage tanks and trucks, often paid appreciably less per gallon than the average wholesale price when they loaded up directly at the terminals of small, subsidized refineries. Similar regulatory benefits did not trickle down to branded dealers and many jobbers, who took their deliveries exclusively from the major oil companies.[14] Indeed, some trade associations that represented these marketers, and that had pushed the emergency allocation act in 1973, began recommending two years later that the regulations revert to standby status.[15] The marketers were encouraged by explicit assurances from the Federal Energy Administration that suitable standby protecting mechanisms would be sought. This may help explain why many congressmen whose constituents included numerous gasoline jobbers were often somewhat more inclined to favor decontrol than to oppose it. Many of these legislators were also responding to the interests of producers in their regions. Gasoline jobbers, like small refiners, were most common in the oil-rich states of the South and the West.

13. Lane, *Mandatory Petroleum Price and Allocation Regulations*, p. 158.
14. Interview with Michael T. Scanlon, Jr., vice-president, National Oil Jobbers Council, Washington D.C., January 6, 1982.
15. Neil de Marchi, "The Ford Administration: Energy as a Political Good," in Goodwin, ed., *Energy Policy in Perspective*, pp. 511–12.

Heating fuel dealers were the product distributors most unified in support of the price and allocation controls, principally because the regulatory machinery functioned more congenially for them. Adequate distillate stocks, to meet heating needs and to supply agricultural uses and essential services, were a government priority. Refinery yields were therefore controlled to increase distillate output, at the expense of gasoline and other products. This distillate tilt, and the rule that households and industry were to receive 100 percent of their current space heating requirements, ensured fuel-oil dealers plentiful supplies, even during the worst part of the 1974 oil shortage: in February 1974, distillate stocks, unlike gasoline, stood at 31 percent above the previous year's level.[16] Not only did the EPAA work admirably for most heating oil retailers, but they competed for political attention against fewer local antagonists of the law. The preponderance of dealers populated the Northeast and the North Central regions, where producers and other interests disenchanted with the regulatory apparatus were relatively scarce. The upshot was that their representatives in Congress tended to hear, instead of dissonant voices throughout the petroleum industry, fairly uniform enthusiasm for controls from a specific sector. The hypothesis that these representatives voted accordingly is consistent with the roll call data in tables 2-1 and 2-2: concentrations of heating oil dealers correlate negatively with votes for decontrol.

Conclusion

The oil price and allocation controls of the mid-1970s are not easily characterized as just another case of industry-nursing regulation, serving, in this instance, everyone downstream of producers. By 1975 it was clear that the controls were affecting sectors of the petroleum business in diverse, often unanticipated, ways. Some segments of the industry got what they had expected, but others didn't. Rifts developed among refiners and among marketers. This strengthened the position of producers, particularly in areas crowded with all three interests. To be sure, the clients of controls in the industry had business allies on the outside—for example, some big utilities, most airlines, certain farm organizations, and various industrial "priority users" designated in the EPAA. The main point, however, is not that no notable combination of interest groups strove to prevent deregulation in 1975, but that the co-

16. Lane, *Mandatory Petroleum Price and Allocation Regulations*, p. 37.

alition was less unified and intense than it had been during the crisis of 1973.

If this is true, what explained the various privileges extended to particular interest groups long after the passage of the EPAA? The entitlements system, for example, did not commence with the law's enactment in 1973; it became effective in January 1975. The small-refiner bias in the program was also instated in 1975 and furthered by the Energy Policy and Conservation Act in 1976. The answer is more subtle than that these groups wielded clout in Congress. Many legislators and administrators seemed sentimentally receptive to almost any program purporting to help small business. Other legislators were honestly convinced that their regulatory stratagems were improving the competitive viability of the petroleum industry.[17]

Public Opinion

In the fall of 1974, the Gallup poll reported that over 80 percent of the public cited inflation as the country's most important problem.[18]

This was the highest percentage ever recorded, and it was very much on the minds of representatives when, with near unanimity, they voted to prolong the EPAA into mid-1975. Worry about inflation also influenced the Ford administration's nascent strategy for how to proceed with decontrol, strengthening the position of those in the administration who favored an incremental transition instead of an abrupt one. Yet the extent to which public unease about inflation influenced the energy-pricing decisions after 1974 must not be exaggerated. For one thing, the level of concern started to subside markedly at the end of that year. By the following June barely over half of Gallup's respondents viewed inflation as the nation's top problem, and the trend thereafter was downward until it bottomed out at one-third in early 1978. Besides, even as the high cost of living remained a concern, the percentage of people who attributed inflation to energy costs declined steadily until the Iranian crisis sent oil prices soaring again.[19]

17. This theme recurred throughout the congressional deliberations on the Emergency Petroleum Allocation Act. See H.R. Rept. 93–159, 93 Cong. 1 sess., cited in Lane, *Mandatory Petroleum Price and Allocation Regulations*, p. 28.

18. *Gallup Opinion Index*, Report 160 (November 1978), p. 19, tabulates the percentages citing inflation as the nation's most important problem in chronological order for all Gallup surveys since 1939. See also *Gallup Opinion Index*, Report 167 (June 1979).

19. See, for example, the series of Roper surveys on causes of inflation, from October

Perceptions of the Energy Problem

At no point did a majority of Americans believe that the energy situation was very serious.[20] How this perception constrained policymakers, however, is hard to tell. On the one hand, no popular mandate existed to proffer forceful solutions. On the other, if preoccupation with the issue had been more intense, the feasibility of the boldest remedy— conservation through price deregulation—might have been further diminished. For the average citizen, higher fuel costs did not just relate to the energy problem; they were the problem.[21]

The crisis was not regarded as terribly serious because most people did not think it was real. Solid majorities had concluded that shortages and rising prices were contrived, largely by the big oil producers.[22] But though this perception also imbued a segment of congressional opinion, it was far less pervasive in authoritative circles than in the country at large.

As late as 1979, only about 40 percent of the population understood that the year's turmoil in the world oil market had precipitated another genuine energy convulsion in the United States.[23] (This low figure was not unexpected. Almost as many people had not yet realized that the United States imported any oil from abroad.)[24] Mercifully, a poll of the House of Representatives at the time revealed a different mentality: almost 80 percent of the members declined to dismiss the nation's energy troubles as imaginary or invented by the big oil companies.[25] Congress had little stomach for tackling the energy predicament through price

---

1974 through September 1978. *Roper Reports*, 78–9 (November 1978), pp. E37–39.

20. In August 1979, the Gallup poll counted 47 percent agreeing that the energy problem was very serious. That was the highest level to date, and it never went any higher.

21. Yankelovich, for example, found that in 1980, 76 percent of the population defined the energy problem as the high price of energy, whereas only 38 percent defined it as the possibility of shortages occurring before the end of the century. Yankelovich, Skelly and White, Inc., *Corporate Priorities: Data Reference Book* (New York: Yankelovich, Skelly and White, Inc., 1980), p. 592.

22. See the surveys discussed by William Schneider, "Public Opinion and the Energy Crisis," in Daniel Yergin, ed., *The Dependence Dilemma: Gasoline Consumption and America's Future* (Harvard University: Center for International Affairs, 1980), p. 153.

23. Walter A. Rosenbaum, *Energy, Politics and Public Policy* (Washington, D.C.: CQ Press, 1981), p. 80.

24. George Gallup, "Public Cold to Energy 'Crisis' Warnings," *Washington Post*, April 30, 1978; and *Gallup Opinion Index*, Report 157 (August 1978), p. 27.

25. Survey of 352 House members by the *Washington Post*, October 1979.

reform, but not because the lawmakers shared the electorate's conviction that the predicament was a fabrication.

Attitudes toward Oil Companies

Hostility toward the leading petroleum producers ran deep. Year after year, when Americans were asked to find culprits for the energy crisis, no other group or institution was named more frequently. This orientation encouraged some officials to go out of their way to vilify big oil whenever possible, and it led many to distance themselves from policies that smacked openly of "the industry position." At the same time, the popular cant about oil-company intrigue grew so ill-informed and simplistic that only the most cynical or irresponsible politicians could exploit it, or accede to it, fully. Dozens of examples of far-fetched perceptions could be offered, but a Roper poll that identified a cavernous gap between reality and popular beliefs about oil-company profits on gasoline is illustrative; on average, the margins were overestimated by 350 percent.[26] More important, surveys found that theories about oil conspiracy became most prevalent in times of scarcity: the longer the gasoline lines, the more frustration and anger were heaped on the petroleum suppliers.[27] Among federal energy experts and legislators, on the other hand, it was no secret that supply problems had been exacerbated by government regulatory and allocational failures, especially in the case of gasoline. True, most remained hopeful that the price and allocation controls could be fine-tuned to function more satisfactorily in the future. But many also thought that if petroleum were decontrolled, shortages would diminish—and with them, the public's wrath toward the oil industry. Finally, it was possible for nervous congressmen to have it both ways: heed demands for punitive measures against big oil and endorse deregulation. How? By coupling deregulation with firm support for a tough tax on windfall profits.

However virulent the antipathy toward oil companies, it was not always obvious what the voters wanted the government to do about them. Hardly anybody sought a government takeover of the industry. When Roper

26. *Roper Reports*, 77-4 (May 1977), pp. K63–65.
27. In a Gallup poll taken on August 3–6, 1979, the percentage of respondents who believed that the gasoline shortage had been deliberately brought about by the oil companies reached a high of 70 percent. *Gallup Opinion Index*, Report 170 (September 1979), p. 17.

probed this point in December 1975, barely 12 percent of the sample approved of nationalization.[28] Divestiture of the majors, whether vertically or horizontally, failed to receive majority approval in a Harris sample during November 1975.[29] Nor was there any appreciable interest in establishing a public corporation to compete with the largest private firms.[30] Even consent for government regulation was equivocal. Various Harris polls in 1975 left the impression that a relaxation of federal controls (at least under certain assumptions) was favored by large margins.[31] About the clearest signal that Congress got regarding treatment of the petroleum industry was that most people opposed giving oil companies special tax breaks and that a definite majority favored windfall profit taxes.[32]

Views on Deregulation

Where, exactly, did the public stand on deregulation? Some soundings seemed to detect no broad-based objections to the concept. During the summer of 1975 the Harris organization had proclaimed "a complete turnaround" in public preferences. Fifty-four percent were now willing to countenance decontrol.[33] Other surveys reported steady opposition.[34] The discrepancy resulted from the different ways in which pollsters asked the question. Throughout 1975, for instance, Harris's phraseology omitted any mention of the discomforts of decontrol (higher prices) and referred only to its advantages (increased domestic supplies): "Would you favor or oppose deregulation of the price of all oil produced in the United States if this would encourage development of more oil production here at home?" Naturally, this format elicited more positive responses. At the opposite extreme, several polls posed matters in terms

28. *Roper Reports*, 76-1 (January 1976), pp. H42–46. See also *Harris Survey*, May 1975. Harris found that the idea of the federal government taking over the oil companies was opposed by 71 percent of the respondents.

29. *Harris Survey*, November 1975.

30. Two-thirds of a 1974 Roper survey rejected the idea. *Roper Reports*, 74-3 (April 1974), pp. D14–15.

31. According to Harris, a 44–25 percent plurality in November 1975 favored gradual decontrol of oil prices over a three-year period. *Harris Survey*, November 1975. Similar percentages favored deregulation earlier that spring. *Harris Survey*, May 1975.

32. Harris reported 56 percent approval of windfall profits taxation in 1975, even though no mention was made of how revenues would be distributed. *Harris Survey*, November 1975.

33. *Harris Survey*, August 1975.

34. *Roper Reports*, 75-2 (March 1975), p. J26; 77-3 (February 1977); and CBS News/*New York Times* poll, August 1977.

of sacrifices entailed, leaving the benefits unspecified. This approach drew the most adverse reactions. In one instance, citizens were asked whether they would be willing to "let oil and gas prices go up so people will be more careful about how they use fuel." Seventy-six percent replied negatively.[35] The poll that presented the issue in the most balanced fashion was a Roper survey in August 1975.[36] Respondents were asked to choose between two proposals, which spelled out benefits and costs. The results were as follows:

Option	Response
A: Allow increases in domestic oil and gas prices.	32%
Benefit: Greater supplies of U.S. oil, fewer shortages, and less dependence on Arab oil.	
Drawback: Higher prices on gasoline and oil.	
B: Put tight controls on prices of both domestic and imported oil.	46%
Benefit: Lower prices on gasoline and oil.	
Drawback: Some shortages of oil and gasoline and continued dependence on Arab oil.	
Other (don't know, and so on)	22%

This split probably accurately profiled the prevailing disposition: more support for imposing controls than for taking them off, but no conclusive majority either way. The pattern may have differed regionally, but at least nationally, it appeared to give the president and Congress some leeway.

Conclusion

How did national attitudes inform the oil-pricing debate in 1975? The electorate at large was not dispatching the clear-cut instructions it had issued the year before. People were less obsessed with inflation. More than ever, they discounted the energy problem as a whole, though they continued to blame the oil industry for whatever difficulty was perceived. How these persuasions were manifested left a lot of elected representatives more perplexed by public opinion than attuned to it. The voters were blunt on one point: they wanted to see the oil companies pay more taxes. But the public's message regarding how much government regulation was warranted seemed more open to interpretation. Proponents of

35. *Roper Reports*, 77-3 (February 1977).
36. *Roper Reports*, 75-8 (October 1975), p. G15.

price controls in Congress were impressed by polling results that showed a hefty majority of citizens disapproving of price increases to constrict consumption.[37] Congressional critics of controls, in turn, pointed to statistics evincing popular acceptance of deregulation as an inducement for energy exploration and development. Thus one set of combatants fretted over the public's distaste for price deregulation as a means of restraining demand, while the other side downplayed demand-restraint because it viewed deregulation as a means of stimulating production. Perhaps, then, the concern for mass opinion did not serve to preclude decontrol, but it did tend to steer discussion away from the most important rationale for decontrol—conservation.

Localism

The orientations of the members of Congress on energy pricing adhered more tightly to regional and state interests in the case of crude oil than in the case of natural gas. Yet, the defeat of oil deregulation in 1975 was not just a mismatch in which a handful of small producing states in the South and the West was overpowered by a bloc of big consuming states in the North battling higher energy prices. As it turned out, home-state energy conditions did not infallibly predict congressional divisions on price controls.

Despite important geographic variability in the distribution of costs and benefits of alternative oil-pricing policies, in large parts of the country the net effects of deregulated oil prices were likely to be mild or uncertain. In deciding how to vote, many representatives from such regions either took their cues from other sources or made up their own minds. (See appendix B to this chapter for logit analysis estimates of the effects of local energy conditions on the votes of representatives, p. 79.) Furthermore, public attitudes did not form neat regional clusters. The Roper survey of August 1975, discussed earlier, was large enough to permit regional categorization of responses. In several areas—for instance, the Pacific and Mountain states, and the East North Central states around the Great Lakes—respondents seemed so closely divided over the issue of oil-price controls that quite a few local representatives may have experienced considerable difficulty divining the direction of public opinion.

The fact that federal arrangements for allocating refined products won few friends among gasoline dealers and motorists in urban areas in the

37. *Harris Survey*, November 1973; January 1974.

North complicated matters. This failure may have mattered less in the Northeast, where the system was at least satisfying the demands of heating oil dealers and users, but it alienated some potential constituents elsewhere. Ironically, the vagaries of the allocation process during the severe gasoline crunch of early 1974 deposited an inordinate volume of gasoline in a number of states in the West, many of which were coincidentally major oil producers.[38] In so doing, these regulations conferred more benefits on states opposed to the EPAA than on states that had favored it or that were unsure.

Finally, voting decisions turned on ideological considerations that extenuated Congress's normal impulse to follow local pressures.

Other things being equal, local circumstances did determine votes, sometimes decisively. Other things, however, intruded forcefully. Partisanship was one of them. For all the diverse state and regional impacts, oil pricing was a national issue and was debated by many as though broad questions of public purpose, and party principles, were at stake.

Policy Management

Usually, in descriptions of the Ford presidency much attention is devoted to the unusual circumstances that thwarted executive leadership— aftershocks of the Watergate affair; a defiant Congress, dominated overwhelmingly by the opposite party; and an incumbent president preparing to face the national electorate for the first time. Important as these conditions were, it is also useful to recall that the president still wielded powerful prerogatives with which to shape events. The most awesome of these was the capacity to rule, on most issues, with the backing of just 34 of the 535 members of Congress—that is, the ability to prevail by executive veto. Ford was not reluctant to govern this way. During his brief tenure, he successfully vetoed more bills of national significance than did any previous president.[39]

38. Richard B. Mancke, *Performance of the Federal Energy Office* (Washington, D.C.: American Enterprise Institute, 1975), pp. 12–13. When state crude-oil output is regressed on state gasoline allocations as a percent of local need in February 1974, much overlap is evinced: $r = .62, p < .001$. Data sources for this statistic were the gasoline allocation figures reported in Mancke, *Performance of the Federal Energy Office*, pp. 12–13 and the U.S. Energy Information Administration's figures for 1975 state oil production, American Petroleum Institute, *Basic Petroleum Data Book*, vol. 2 (Washington, D.C.: American Petroleum Institute, 1982), table 5b.

39. A. James Reichley, *Conservatives in an Age of Change: The Nixon and Ford Administrations* (Brookings, 1981), p. 323.

The President's Leverage

Nowhere did the veto power, along with certain other presidential resources, open greater opportunities for executive supremacy than in the energy arena (or so it seemed in the first half of 1975). Time was running out on the Emergency Petroleum Allocation Act. Congress would have to reauthorize any controls past August 31, 1975. Ford could then refuse to sign such legislation, and he stood an excellent chance of being sustained in the Senate. (Presidential vetoes are rarely overridden; only 42 of the 1,226 vetoes cast between 1932 and 1976 were overturned.)

It was true that the administration preferred to accomplish decontrol more gradually, and this strategy required a modicum of cooperation from Congress. Undeniably, electoral politics played a part. The presidential campaign was already under way. (Ford began putting in appearances in New Hampshire as early as April 18, 1975.) Oil pricing was already a partisan issue. Lest it become even more so, the White House deemed it prudent to explore avenues to decontrol that would prevent a sudden price fly-up and that would share responsibility with the Democratic Congress for whatever price escalation did occur. More critically, with the economy in deep recession (unemployment hit 9.2 percent in May), few were ready to risk the effects of deregulating oil overnight. Consensus on this point encompassed not just the Democrats, but also the Republican congressional leadership, key oil companies, and, in the administration, the most ardent advocates of market pricing.[40] Congressional acquiescence was desirable to smooth the path of deregulation, since, under the statutory framework, the president could obtain instant decontrol as of August 31, but technically (and rather ironically), he lacked the authority to phase out controls over several months before or afterward. Also, ideally, certain supplementary legislation would be helpful as controls came off. In particular, the administration wanted standby powers to avoid dislocations in particular sectors, such as the refining industry. It also sought passage of a windfall profits tax. Such a tax was essential to gain public consent for decontrol; it could be used to

40. Even Alan Greenspan, the chairman of the Council of Economic Advisers and one of the administration's keenest advocates of decontrol, preferred a gradual phase out of controls rather than an abrupt end to them. Edward Cowan, "New Administration Plan for Oil Price Rise Hinted," *New York Times*, July 22, 1975.

offset decontrol's immediate macroeconomic impact by recycling revenue into the slumping economy.

The administration needed some congressional forbearance and initially seemed well positioned to get it. Under the Trade Expansion Act of 1962, the president could impose import fees on foreign oil. Considerable pressure could be exerted by applying this instrument artfully. The White House could raise the fees and then tantalize Congress with the possibility of lowering them. This was a profitable way of bartering for votes, especially among legislators in the Northeast, whose constituents consumed imported oil. Import fees also threw up a smoke screen behind which to move deregulation. The fuss over the fees would distract attention from deregulated prices, and in any event, decontrol would look less ominous if timed to coincide with removal of the fees.

All this aside, the EPAA appeared to allow the president some room to maneuver. The statute stipulated that, upon submitting a formal proposal to Congress, the executive branch could initiate gradual deregulation, unless disapproved by a simple majority of either house. The latter provision posed a barrier, but not necessarily an insuperable one. The law held that any resolution of disapproval would bind only if adopted within five days. This proviso was no minor detail. Within such a tight time frame, parliamentary rules and procedures could be manipulated (as by a filibuster in the Senate) to stall a floor vote past the deadline. Hence, it was conceivable that a shrewd and determined president could skirt the emergency allocation act's mechanism for congressional review and thus implement plans to pry off price controls. Furthermore, there were signs that an end run of this sort might not meet overwhelming opposition. Although most members of Congress had voted for extensions of the act when forced to decide in recorded roll calls, quite a few of these representatives seemed equally content to let controls fade away if an explicit vote on the question could be avoided. As long as the White House was prepared to assume most, even if not all, of the liability, tacit assent for deregulation was broader than suggested by the final tallies on oil-pricing bills. Finally, if everything else failed, the president might still hold the trump card. The specter of a bumpy return to market prices loomed as of September 1 if Congress chose to repulse all plans for phased decontrol and if the administration blocked efforts to renew the EPAA. In this context, it was possible that congressional obstructionism, not presidential resolve, would be blamed for the impasse.

Stages of the Struggle

Reconstruction of the facts suggests that the battle over petroleum price deregulation in 1975 passed through three stages: (1) the early rounds in which the president not only played his cards skillfully but also made strides toward attaining his objectives; (2) an interlude, roughly between mid-May and the end of July, when the momentum shifted and a deadlock developed; and (3) the months following the August recess, when the administration capitulated. This three-part framework enables one to identify the critical turning points that provide strong clues to underlying causes of the debacle.

PHASE ONE: PROGRESS. The administration launched its offensive in mid-January. Using the State of the Union message to unveil a series of sweeping energy initiatives, Ford served notice that he wished to start dislodging the controls on oil prices that spring. He would also begin adding duties on foreign oil at monthly intervals. An ultimatum to Congress was implicit in this announcement: legislate a suitable cure for the nation's energy ills or swallow the administration's medicine. The immediate response in Congress was to fly in all directions at once. Separate embryonic energy programs began to incubate in several congressional committees simultaneously, as well as among informal clusters of Democratic notables in both houses. Meanwhile, efforts got under way to reduce the president's discretion over import fees and to secure congressional review of the impending administrative steps toward decontrol.

Despite the disarray—and the signs that some of Ford's adversaries were scheming to strip away his main sources of leverage—the administration held a tactical edge. Predictably, there was consternation over the president's intentions, but initially, most of it was diverted toward the threatened tariffs. In February a measure suspending for ninety days any power to increase import fees landed on Ford's desk. The president responded with a blend of determination and magnanimity. He promptly vetoed the bill and then offered a consolation: additional import duties would be deferred until later in the spring, as would further executive action on domestic oil prices, if Congress made headway on an alternative energy package that might provide a basis for compromise. The gesture was widely regarded (notably by key representatives from the Northeast) as a significant concession, and it encouraged a more conciliatory climate on Capitol Hill. Further moves to amend the Trade Expansion Act were called off, and, at least on the House side, activity slackened in the bid to strengthen the legislative veto clause in the EPAA by lengthening the review period. Most significantly, the murky broth of competing energy proposals, bubbling in Congress after Ford's challenge in January, had undergone a distillation. Interest had begun to focus on the deliberations in two key bodies—the House Ways and Means Committee and the House Committee on Interstate and Foreign Commerce. There, initial developments in March and April were giving the administration grounds for optimism.

Strictly speaking, questions of petroleum regulatory policy did not fall within the Ways and Means Committee's purview. Nonetheless, the committee moved to center stage in the unfolding legislative drama. The main reason for this was simple: as every good politician in town realized, the sine qua non for legitimating the deregulation of oil was enactment of a windfall profits tax. Thus, all eyes turned to Ways and Means, where federal tax bills must originate. And early on, the tax-writing panel signaled an apparent willingness to do what was necessary. In the first weeks of March the committee had sketched a draft bill that featured, with various other energy tax provisions, a levy on excess profits accruing to the big oil companies in the event of decontrol.

In the meantime, the House committee with direct jurisdiction over decontrol—Interstate and Foreign Commerce—pondered a response to the Ford program. An obvious problem of coordination with Ways and Means occurred: it was hard to write a bill deregulating oil prices (or to act on the president's proposals) until the final form of the windfall profits tax was established, and vice-versa. Yet, first indications were that the jurisdictional difficulty might be overcome. The leadership of the two committees—Representative Albert C. Ullman, Democrat of Oregon, the new Ways and Means chief, and Representative John D. Dingell, Democrat of Michigan, who chaired the big Commerce Subcommittee on Energy and Power—had agreed to cooperate closely. Each acknowledged the need to move deregulation and tax matters in tandem, and reportedly, both expressed hope that a joint measure would eventually go to the House floor.

That possibility seemed genuine, at least through April. The apparent direction that discussions were taking in Ways and Means evoked praise from minority members of the committee and from the administration. As for the companion bill evolving in Dingell's subcommittee, this too was potentially compatible with the administration's goals on oil pricing. (The version eventually fashioned by the Energy and Power Subcommittee hardly prompted dancing in the streets of Shreveport or Houston, but it did permit a tapered removal of price ceilings—though over a protracted time span—and it exempted from controls roughly one of every three barrels of domestic oil in the interim.) These traces of progress prompted the president to allow Congress still more time to complete its task. Again Ford postponed both a formal presentation of his own deregulation plan and the imposition of more import fees.

Throughout all this, the Senate marched to a different drumbeat—chiefly, that being rapped out by Senator Henry M. Jackson, Democrat of Washington, chairman of the Committee on Interior and Insular Affairs. Jackson, a presidential aspirant in 1975–76, had emerged as the scourge of the oil industry in Congress. The EPAA had been his pièce de résistance in 1973, and repeatedly he reckoned that the law should remain in force. Toward the end of April, his committee was cranking out yet another extension of price controls. Yet, despite Senate passage of such a bill on May 1, indications were that overall Senate support for it was less than wholehearted, and far less than what was necessary to override a presidential veto.

A strategic objective of the Jackson bill was to give Congress thirty days (instead of just five) in which to mull over, and dismiss, any administrative changes in the pricing regulations. This attempt to shackle the president troubled many senators, including ostensible backers of the EPAA. After all, it was one thing to keep Congress off the hook by voting to extend the act every few months, but it was another thing to prevent somebody else (the executive) from ever hazarding decontrol. Hence, the roll call on May 1 was fairly close, 47–36, leaving the impression that the president would still have the final word if ever such legislation were to clear both houses. Since House leaders had decided to table their counterpart to the Senate bill, the antics in the upper chamber did not alarm the administration at this stage.

PHASE TWO: STALEMATE. The first real indications that a compromise with Congress was not in the offing came during the first two weeks of May. The Ways and Means Committee was still drafting its anxiously awaited energy tax package. But the contents were becoming increasingly anemic. In particular, although Ullman continued to allege an interest in reporting out a windfall profits tax, either alongside the rest of the bill or separately, no such tax was being marked up. As this became apparent the White House and its congressional allies grew more apprehensive. On May 9, Representative Barber B. Conable, Jr., of New

York, the ranking minority member on Ways and Means, cautioned that a windfall profits provision was an essential element of the committee's bill. Without it, the whole product seemed pointless to House Republicans and to the administration. The White House was even more emphatic. Press Secretary Ron Nessen labeled the committee's markup vehicle a "marshmallow."[41]

Almost every component of the Ways and Means measure was weakened during the arduous committee proceedings. However, the framers managed to retain enough controversial elements (such as a significant gasoline tax) to arouse potentially ferocious bipartisan resistance on the House floor. In the nature of the case, inclusion of a windfall profits tax, in some fashion, would have enhanced the bill's prospects. The tax had great symbolic significance. Its presence would have communicated a willingness to abandon controls and might have attracted to the Ullman bill a larger bloc of conservative and moderate Democrats, as well as the administration's GOP stalwarts. Despite the administration's numerous hints to that effect, the committee proceeded to shoot itself in the foot: on May 12 it formally voted against sending any windfall profits legislation to the floor.

Whatever the motives for this decision, its consequences were catastrophic. The White House immediately declared its opposition to almost all of the Ullman plan, ensuring the bill's disembowelment on the House floor a few weeks later. Omission of the tax sent an even more damaging signal to the House Commerce Committee, which was in the midst of debating forms of decontrol and other alternatives. On May 15 the full committee chose to repudiate the language approved by its Energy and Power subunit, and began lumbering inexorably down the road of further regulation, at the end of which lay the Energy Policy and Conservation Act.

The demise of the Energy and Power Subcommittee's formula, and the failure to wangle a viable tax bill out of Ways and Means, suddenly left Ford with no tangible basis for discussion with Congress. Trouble lay ahead, with the Senate's latest modification of the Emergency Petroleum Allocation Act waiting to be crossed with the seeds of the Energy Policy and Conservation Act being sown in House Commerce. To stunt this development, and to salvage any hope of peeling away price

41. Albert R. Hunt, "Energy Tax Bill Expected to Clear Panel, Then Stumble in Full House," *Wall Street Journal*, May 12, 1975.

controls before they became permanent, the administration could no longer defer striking at the problem unilaterally. Late in May, in a nationally televised speech, Ford berated Congress for its proclivity to "drift, dawdle and debate forever," dramatizing his point by tearing off pages from a calendar.[42] He then announced a new round of import fees and reaffirmed an intention to draw up his own itinerary for decontrol to be submitted in the near future.

Congressional reaction was almost a replay of that in January. Once again, there were cries of indignation and frantic efforts by the president's principal adversaries to box him in. In June the Democratic leadership in the House dusted off a review-extension measure that had been drafted but shelved several months earlier, and that could be used to match the Senate's bill of May 1. But again, the majorities that eventually adopted legislation along these lines a month later fell comfortably shy of the votes needed to overcome the inevitable Ford veto, which came almost immediately. So in mid-July the decisive showdown between the White House and the Ninety-fourth Congress was at hand.

On Wednesday, July 16, the president put forward formal notice of his deregulation plan. Under his approach the ceiling of $5.25 per barrel for controlled domestic crude—defined as oil from wells that were in production in 1972—would be permitted to rise at 3.3 percent a month through 1977, when the price per barrel would reach $13.50.[43] Starting the next day, the Senate or the House would have until July 22 to exercise a legislative veto. After that, nothing short of new legislation, signed by the president, could stop the plan from taking effect. With the Senate more susceptible to delaying tactics, everything hinged on how quickly the other body could react. But there too, time was short. The Rules Committee would have to convene; it would have to expedite floor debate; the formal resolution of disapproval would have to be printed; and so on. "Under the parliamentary procedures in the House we cannot possibly do it in five days," Commerce Chairman Harley O. Staggers, Democrat of West Virginia, had concluded back in June.[44]

Not so. Hours before the deadline, the resolution tumbled onto the House floor and passed 262–167. On the chance that Congress might not be able to repeat the feat, and that by sweetening the pill he would rally more adherents, Ford threw a counterpunch on July 25. He sent up

42. Ann Pelham, *Energy Policy*, 2d ed. (Washington, D.C.: CQ Press, 1981), p. 35.
43. *New York Times*, July 17, 1975.
44. *Congressional Quarterly Weekly Report*, vol. 33 (June 14, 1975), p. 1257.

a revised proposal, lowering the provisional price ceilings and stretching the phase out over a few more months. By timing the submission on a Friday, when many members of Congress were already leaving town for the weekend, the administration held off a Rules Committee meeting until the following Monday. But then, after two days of dramatic hearings before an overflow crowd that sensed the momentousness of the occasion, the committee again ruled in favor of immediate floor action on a resolution rejecting the administration's plan. A motion to postpone the rule, which could have assured victory for the president, was turned back by one vote in the committee. Now, the full House was again put in a position of having to turn thumbs up or down on decontrol. On July 30, Ford was beaten, 228–189.

From this point on, the routes open to the administration were few and perilous. A disagreeable choice loomed: either to accept the omnibus energy program that had finally taken shape in the House, and perhaps bargain for adjustments on the margins, or to step back, dig in, and mow down with vetoes the waves of congressionally initiated regulatory schemes that might ensue. The second alternative was not infeasible and would have made good policy, except that it implied total, instantaneous decontrol on September 1, with no windfall profits tax or other safeguards to cushion the economic and political shock. Nonetheless, through August there was no evidence that the White House had decided which way to go.

PHASE THREE: COLLAPSE. When Congress gathered again after the August break, the dreaded sunset of the EPAA had finally arrived. To the surprise of some, the day of reckoning proved anticlimactic. The oil industry successfully held domestic prices steady during the first weeks of September, aware that any turbulence could send the administration, as well as Congress, careening back toward regulation, which could be reintroduced with retroactive provisions. But the respite was assumed to be temporary; soon market forces would begin ratcheting prices up. Hence, the congressional campaign to resume controls forged ahead relentlessly.

Meanwhile, time was working against the administration. During the August recess, the members of Congress had gone home to hear from their constituents. They returned more worried than ever about what prices might do soon after controls lapsed. Several senators from rural states—including John C. Stennis, Democrat of Mississippi, Pete V. Domenici, Republican of New Mexico, and Robert J. Dole, Republican of Kansas—who had stood with the president, began to waver after listening to the fears of farmers in their areas. Moreover, on August 28, the governors of sixteen states had weighed in, alarmed that with the emergency allocation act's termination, the president would lose authority to allocate natural gas and propane, which were expected to be in short supply the following winter. At about the same time, two of the biggest oil companies, Gulf and Mobil, joined the chorus of concern about "ending controls in a single step."[45] On top of this, beginning in September, a series of studies appeared that warned of inflationary effects from sudden decontrol. The problem was stressed in a Congressional Research Service report issued on September 3, and then echoed in an analysis by the Congressional Budget Office on September 9 that conjectured that abrupt decontrol could "retard or even abort" the impending economic recovery.[46]

And finally, the first primary elections of the 1976 presidential race were now just a few months away. Ford's popularity rating was sagging. By November, according to the Gallup poll, the percentage of persons judging the president's performance unfavorably exceeded the proportion giving him good marks.[47] This trend suggested that the president's public image of firmness was becoming one of obstinacy and that further jeremiads about the unconstructive behavior of Congress would no longer win public sympathy. Political tremors from New Hampshire convinced some pundits that an early settlement with Congress, which would safely clamp a lid on fuel prices before the February contest, would serve Ford well. In a special election on September 16, the Republicans had failed to retain control of a vacated Senate seat in New Hampshire—an outcome that some quickly attributed to the high price of fuel.[48] Crumbling under these and other pressures, the administration fell into retreat. At the end of September a forty-five-day reinstatement of the EPAA was signed into law and then renewed in mid-November to enable congressional conferees to finish work on the EPCA, whose main building blocks had passed the House on September 23.

45. Rowland Evans and Robert Novak, "Overriding an Oil Veto," *Washington Post*, August 31, 1975; and *Congressional Quarterly Weekly Report*, vol. 33 (August 30, 1975), p. 1898.

46. Albert R. Hunt, "Congress, Ford Likely to Resume Battles in September on Energy and Other Issues," *Wall Street Journal*, August 4, 1975; and David E. Rosenbaum, "House Democrats Win Energy Vote," *New York Times*, September 18, 1975.

47. *Gallup Opinion Index*, Report 125 (November–December 1975), p. 12.

48. Richard Corrigan, "A National Referendum on Energy," *National Journal*, vol. 8 (January 3, 1976), p. 27.

Through the fall, the administration did its best to influence the final form of the legislation, reserving the threat of a veto if the president's views were wholly ignored. Some latitude was preserved in the bill. For example, the Federal Energy Administration was given a relatively free hand to begin raising prices for various petroleum-refined products before 1979; in April 1977, the president could propose a partial exclusion of Alaskan crude from price ceilings; also in 1977, he could start accelerating the rate of increase for domestic crude prices every ninety days, provided Congress gave him permission each time. But in the last analysis, after weeks of bargaining, Ford was staring at a conference report that none of the Republican conferees was willing to sign and that he described as "half a loaf."[49]

For several weeks after the final version of the EPCA became known, a furious struggle swirled at the White House as critics of the compromise mounted a last-ditch drive to dissuade Ford from signing it. Senators John G. Tower, Republican of Texas, Dewey F. Bartlett, Republican of Oklahoma, Clifford P. Hansen, Republican of Wyoming, and others warned the president that western conservatives in the Republican party would flock to his rival for the nomination, Ronald Reagan. Enactment of the Energy Policy and Conservation Act might give Ford New Hampshire, but it would lose him Texas, they prophesied. The Council of Economic Advisers, the Office of Management and Budget, and the Treasury Department urged a veto. Secretary Simon, in particular, was adamant. He even telephoned the president late at night, a few hours before a decision was to be announced, asking to talk about it. "And talk he did," recollected Ford, "and talk and talk some more."[50] Elsewhere, little praise for the bill could be detected. Even some leading liberal newspaper editorials expressed dismay at key parts, particularly the overall oil price rollback the bill decreed. The *Washington Post* termed this aspect pure irresponsibility that would send a dangerously misleading signal to consumers, undercut conservation, and impair the economic health of the country.[51] Despite the late barrage of objections, on the morning of December 22, the EPCA became law.

What justifications were uppermost in the inner councils of the administration? According to Ford's Federal Energy Administration chief,

49. Gerald R. Ford, *A Time to Heal* (Harper and Row and Reader's Digest, 1979), p. 341.
50. Ibid.
51. *Washington Post*, November 19, 1975.

Frank Zarb, there were three.[52] First, controls could not be dumped without some phase-out crutches, such as standby measures to deal with the thinning propane market. "We knew damn well that Congress wouldn't give us those," recalled Zarb, who had handled most of the legislative negotiations for the administration. Second, he and the president's political aides suspected that worse legislation might be in store if the EPCA were vetoed: "Scoop Jackson and company were going to prepare something draconian, to put on the president's desk that summer, just before the election." Third, the Federal Energy Administration was somehow confident that "administrative flexibilities in the bill" provided a "window" through which the executive could start deregulating crude oil ahead of schedule, without congressional interference. But probably the main consideration by this time was expressed by Ford on the day of the signing ceremony. There was, he said, a "temptation to politicize" fuel pricing. "If I were to veto this bill, the debate of the past year would almost surely continue through the election year and beyond."[53]

With hindsight, one can argue at length over these assessments. If certain crutches (for example, a windfall profits tax) were indispensable to decontrol, would Congress have persisted in denying them if the president had stood fast? Would Congress have sallied forth with more draconian legislation to test a certain presidential veto?[54] Were the Energy Policy and Conservation Act's "administrative flexibilities" really so flexible, and was it wise to assume that a president willing to use them would be in office in 1977?[55] Finally, why suppose that the temptation to

52. Interview with Frank Zarb, former head of the Federal Energy Administration, New York City, November 24, 1981.

53. "Statement on the Energy Policy and Conservation Act, December 22, 1975," *Public Papers of the Presidents: Gerald Ford, 1975* (Government Printing Office, 1977), p. 1993.

54. Once decontrol became a fait accompli, Democrats had a strong political incentive to sit back and let the Ford administration stew in its own juice. As one top House Republican recognized in May, "I think when a lot of Democrats look at this [decontrol by administrative fiat], they'll decide it's better politics to let the President do the dirty work and then be able to criticize him." Albert R. Hunt, "Energy-Tax Bill Expected to Clear Panel, Then Stumble in Full House," *Wall Street Journal*, May 12, 1975. Senator Ernest F. Hollings, Democrat of South Carolina, expressed a similar opinion. Spencer Rich, "Senate Democratic Leaders Block Energy Oil Vote," *Washington Post*, September 17, 1975.

55. The administrative flexibilities that Zarb considered promising were the Energy Policy and Conservation Act's provision for ninety-day discretionary price increases (assuming congressional approval). In an interview, however, Milton Russell, a former staff

politicize the issue would diminish with the act's adoption? After all, the Democrats gloated over the administration's reversal ("They've gone from a total decontrol on April 1 to control for 40 months and a roll-back in prices," exulted Senator Jackson).[56] The right wing of the Republican party acquired another gripe in its feud with the incumbent president.[57] And throughout the 1976 election campaign, Jimmy Carter taunted Ford for lacking a comprehensive energy policy, even though that was precisely what the Democratic Congress had arranged.

Whatever the case, the policy decisions of 1975 did not simply reflect infirmity of the presidency under Gerald Ford or paroxysms of political opportunism that blocked sound judgments (although these afflictions were prominent at times). The Ford administration had been genuinely committed to the deregulation of domestic oil prices on a carefully planned basis. It came much closer to accomplishing that goal than many observers, even then, recognized. Partisan jockeying and electoral calculations predominated in the second half of 1975 and were conclusive in the final weeks of the administration's internal debate over the EPCA. But these factors had not been nearly so visible during the earlier stages, either in the White House or in Congress. In the spring, the administration and some congressional leaders had striven to bridge their differences and to construct a sensible petroleum pricing program. Perhaps the administration's worst error was to rule out, for economic as well as political reasons, instant decontrol if a gradual approach failed. But, at least in the first part of the year, congressional rejection of any and all proposals for phased deregulation hardly seemed certain, or even probable. Therefore, it is vital to probe more deeply into what went askew at that juncture, and why.

Political Convictions

The turning point in the 1975 debate on oil pricing was the decision of the House Rules Committee in late July to let the full House consider

---

economist on the Council of Economic Advisers, stressed that the CEA's assessment of this provision was different: The president was placed in the untenable position of having to haggle with Congress every three months to accelerate a rise in oil prices. Interview with Milton Russell, Washington, D.C., May 10, 1982.

56. David E. Rosenbaum, "Congress, Ford Reach an Accord on Pricing of Oil," *New York Times*, November 13, 1975; and Philip Shabecoff, "Gasoline and Fuel Oil Costs Expected to Level Off at First," *New York Times*, December 23, 1975.

57. Shabecoff, "Gasoline and Fuel Oil Costs."

and pass resolutions derailing the president's deregulation plans. If the committee had held up the floor votes on these plans, even for a matter of hours, it is entirely possible that price controls could never have been reauthorized. Under the statutory framework an executive order to deregulate became binding if Congress did not nullify it within the designated review period. To reinstate controls, Congress would have had to enact a new law. Such legislation was not likely to survive a presidential veto. Thus a great deal was riding on what the Rules Committee would do when it gathered on July 18, 28, and 29. The unpublished transcripts of those meetings are fascinating, not just because so much was at stake over a procedural question, but also because they recorded virtually all the political splits and strains that paralyzed domestic petroleum price policy during the 1970s.

The Debate in the Rules Committee

The proceedings began with Representative Clarence Brown, Republican of Ohio, impassionately defending the timetable for decontrol first proposed by Ford on July 16. Brown's discourse was long and methodical, but it was also slanted. The main point of deregulation, he insinuated, was not so much to reduce consumption of energy in the land as "to encourage its citizens to go out and produce." The government had made it "very difficult for them," he continued. Although admittedly the price elasticity of domestic oil output was "more arguable and indefinite" than the elasticity of oil consumption, the real benefit of higher prices was the added inducement to oil drilling.[58]

These views evoked sarcasm from Democrats on the committee. Chairman Ray J. Madden, Democrat of Indiana, immediately contested the claim that petroleum producers had suffered for want of incentives. "The government has not made it difficult for big oil to explore," Madden replied. With the tax shelters available to the industry, he argued, "the oil companies had a free ticket and they were taking the 27.5 percent depletion [allowance] and putting it in their pocket."[59] Later, Representative Joe Moakley, Democrat of Massachusetts, added another objection: too much uncertainty surrounded the proposition that rising prices would soon stimulate domestic oil supplies. Moakley reminded his colleagues that the oil industry, in testimony before the

58. Unpublished transcript, Hearings on H. Res. 605 before the House Committee on Rules, 94 Cong. 1 sess., July 18, 1975, pp. 18, 43–44.
59. Ibid., pp. 43–44.

Senate Interior Committee in 1973, had assured Congress that a field price of $6–$7 per barrel would enable the industry to explore and produce plentifully. The average price of domestic crude was now above that level, yet production kept dropping. What was to ensure that $13.50 per barrel—the latest figure to strike the industry's fancy—would suddenly reverse the trend?[60]

At one point during the deliberations, Al Ullman, the Ways and Means chairman, put in an appearance. Members of the Rules Committee sought a pledge that if the administration's decontrol proposal took effect, the tax-writing committee would complement it with a stern windfall profits measure. Ullman's response was confusing. On one hand, he promised that his committee would "report to the Congress very expeditiously a windfall profits tax."[61] On the other hand, he could offer no guarantees as to how strong the bill would be: "I can't in any way prejudge what the Ways and Means Committee will do." Representative James J. Quillen, Republican of Tennessee, was skeptical. Noting that Ways and Means had been "meeting and meeting and meeting and meeting," Quillen asked Ullman why the committee had not come up with a windfall tax many weeks earlier. Ullman's explanation was that an appropriate tax could not be prescribed until pricing legislation had been cleared and that was the Commerce Committee's job, "not the jurisdiction of the Ways and Means Committee." Minutes before, however, he had conceded that Representative John D. Dingell had been "greatly concerned about the contents" of whatever tax bill Ways and Means would write.[62] This exchange revealed a basic predicament. The Ways and Means Committee felt it could not proceed with a windfall profits tax unless it was "tailored to a specific decontrol bill."[63] Meanwhile, Dingell's Commerce Subcommittee on Energy and Power was reluctant to submit any sort of decontrol bill, much less try to steer one through the full Commerce Committee, without getting a preview of what Ways and Means would feature.

---

60. Unpublished transcript, Hearings on H. Res. 641 before the House Committee on Rules, 94 Cong. 1 sess., July 29, 1975, pp. 219–20. Reports released in April by the American Petroleum Institute and the American Gas Association, regarding the disappointing size of U.S. reserves despite postembargo price increases, added to the doubts. *Congressional Quarterly Weekly Report*, vol. 33 (April 12, 1975), p. 749.

61. Unpublished transcript, Hearings on H. Res. 641, July 28, 1975, p. 61.

62. Ibid., pp. 62, 68, 69.

63. Interview with Albert C. Ullman, former chairman of the House Ways and Means Committee, Washington, D.C., October 21, 1981.

Partly because Ways and Means had deleted a windfall profits provision from its energy tax package back in May, Commerce veered away from deregulation when the issue came to a vote in that committee. Congressman Bob C. Eckhardt, the only Texas Democrat on the Commerce Committee to favor price controls, posed the problem straightforwardly: "How do you know when you write [deregulatory] legislation whether or not a [windfall] tax bill will ever get through the Ways and Means Committee?"[64] The dilemma persisted: Ullman's panel would set to work on a windfall tax if Ford's deregulation plan materialized. But without a windfall tax already in place—providing, as Representative Conable put it, "the political backstop for decontrol"—resistance to the president's proposal would be especially intense on the House floor.[65] "I don't know how in the world we can expect any affirmative action [on decontrol] on the floor," Congressman Quillen told Ullman, "unless we can spell out what the Ways and Means Committee is going to do."[66]

In the course of these reflections, another difficulty surfaced. Some representatives at opposite extremes philosophically were unreceptive to the whole idea of a windfall profits tax, almost irrespective of its form or timing. Eckhardt's comments illustrated the sentiment among liberals: "I don't think it makes sense to increase the price of oil inordinately and to the point where windfall profits are made and then arrogate to ourselves how the money ought to be distributed to various brackets of the society."[67] Eckhardt and others also felt that even a tough windfall profits tax would hardly suffice to combat basic flaws in the structure of the petroleum industry, such as the dominant market shares of the majors and the price-fixing practices of the OPEC cartel. The strict conservatives were no less hostile. Even after the administration's own windfall tax proposal (providing for a substantial plow back of revenue to the oil industry for exploration and production) was explained to Representative Delbert L. Latta, the Ohio Republican declared that neither he nor his constituents were persuaded: "You cannot sell it to them and you cannot sell it to me."[68]

On the last day of its hearings, the Rules Committee took the unusual

64. Unpublished transcript, Hearings on H. Res. 641, July 28, 1975, p. 106.
65. Interview with Representative Barber B. Conable, Jr., Republican of New York, ranking minority member, House Ways and Means Committee, Washington, D.C., May 20, 1982.
66. Unpublished transcript, Hearings on H. Res. 641, July 28, 1975, p. 71.
67. Ibid., p. 105.
68. Unpublished transcript, Hearings on H. Res. 641, July 29, 1975, p. 176.

step of inviting an outside witness, Ralph Nader, to testify. The theme of Nader's remarks was conservation. "Without a doubt," he insisted, "the top priority of Congress today should be saving energy." This was "the quickest new energy source we have," since "40 percent" was being wasted. According to Nader, however, steeper energy prices through removal of controls would do little to reclaim the waste; this inefficacy was "well known."[69] How, then, was energy to be saved? Here Nader's presentation became vague. There would have to be a gradual transition away from the wasteful technology into which the country was locked, but except for a couple of concrete recommendations, such as an endorsement of fuel-economy regulations for automobiles, the impetus for the transition was unspecified.

No one on the committee could have failed to notice the inconsistency in Nader's analysis. Conservation without the pressure of higher prices was a meaningless slogan. Yet even Representative John B. Anderson, Republican of Illinois, one of the panel's most astute advocates of price deregulation, did not raise the right questions. Nader was never asked to back up his assertion that the inelasticities for much existing energy use were well known. Nor was he ever asked to explain how wasteful technology could ever be improved if not by providing the economic incentives for technological change. Instead, the dialogue reverted to other concerns. Anderson, for instance, disagreed with Nader's gloomy assessments about the costs of decontrol to consumers and to the economy. Nader feared that tremendous unemployment and inflation would follow. Anderson, reflecting the opinion of most Republicans, was much more optimistic. In his view, deregulation would probably help stabilize world petroleum prices by reducing reliance on OPEC oil, a thesis also stressed by Congressman Brown at the start of the committee's discussions.[70]

When it was all over, the positions of the members were the same as at the outset. Among Democrats, only one, B. F. Sisk of California, changed his mind and announced that he would now support the president. Then, voting along party lines with only Sisk and Texas Democrat John Young defecting, the Democratic majority unceremoniously approved the rule that allowed the full House to crush on July 30 further administrative initiatives toward regulatory reform of domestic crude-oil pricing.

Four features are worth noting about the arguments that unfolded be-

69. Unpublished transcript, Hearings on H. Res. 641, July 29, 1975, pp. 235–36, 237, 252.

70. Ibid., p. 287.

fore the Rules Committee. First, the dispute over deregulation was characterized by a supply-side bias. Would market pricing produce lots of new barrels of American oil, and if so, how soon? Advocates and critics alike framed the problem in those terms. The effect on the demand side was regarded as secondary. Neither group dwelt on it. The proponents of decontrol seldom spoke of energy saving as their top policy objective, and while the opponents often said it was theirs, they managed to treat conservation and pricing policy as though the two were somehow unrelated. Second, much time was spent debating the macroeconomic consequences of deregulation. While everyone conceded that a hasty return to market prices could have adverse impacts, many Democrats dreaded even the gently graded path to decontrol proposed by the administration. At times their dread reached apocalyptic proportions—Ford's program might "destroy the country," concluded one speaker during a committee session.[71] Third, questions of fairness protruded throughout the discussion. Critics of decontrol, for instance, thought it wrong to allow oil producers to collect huge economic rents, and to tag consumers with much higher oil bills, when the industry had already amassed great wealth through tax privileges extended over many decades. Although rents accruing from deregulation could be recaptured by a windfall profits tax, this solution was not only hard to coordinate legislatively; it was opposed on principle by legislators at both ends of the political spectrum. To the Right, the imposition of virtually any new tax on the petroleum industry, even one accompanying decontrol, seemed tantamount to exchanging one form of regulation for another. On the Left, price and allocation controls were deemed fairer to society than the uncertain distributions of revenues that might follow a windfall levy. Finally, a number of liberal Democrats remained convinced that price and allocation controls were helpful in correcting perceived market imperfections.

One will never know for sure whether the decisions in the Rules Committee and in the House chamber at the end of July 1975 would have been any different if the case for deregulation had been argued differently. The committee's final verdict came by the narrowest of margins, and the House was divided, 228 to 189, when it subsequently vetoed the administration's decontrol plan. Certainly, a few more representatives could have decided to change their votes. The contours of the debate, however, tended to freeze the battle lines. The entire question of oil pricing had turned into a sharply partisan and ideological conflict. (See

71. Unpublished transcript, Hearings on H. Res. 605, July 18, 1975, p. 47.

appendix B to this chapter for quantitative analysis of partisanship and ideology, p. 79.)

The Supply-Side Bias

"The name of the game, as far as energy is concerned, is supply," Minority Leader John J. Rhodes, Republican of Arizona, told the House of Representatives in the final days of 1975.[72] He could hardly have summed up his party's position better. If he had added that the game was a gigantic gamble as well, he would have summarized much of the year's debate in a nutshell. Uncertainty bedeviled the relationship between prices and production, and so the claims of the Republicans and their promarket allies invited controversy. How far consumption would fall with every percentage point increase in price was also something no one could foretell perfectly. But the response of supply was considerably more indefinite than that of demand. Few, including the most partisan deregulators, denied this fundamental fact.

The problem of uncertainty with respect to supply was not a question of figuring out when, if ever, the country would deplete its nonrenewable energy resources. To be sure, oil and natural gas were no longer being found in large underground pools but in dispersed, complex rock formations, where extensive drilling was needed to estimate the quantity present. Even then the estimates were subject to an enormous margin of error. An occasional Malthusian may have felt that, without exact knowledge of how much oil the country had left, price deregulation would be a fruitless experiment. If there was any truth to the notion that all American oil reserves were rapidly running dry, deregulation would yield nothing but higher prices. Most observers, however, did not subscribe to the premise that the nation was about to exhaust all new sources of gas and oil. By 1975, Congress was well aware that experts in the past had grossly underestimated prospective fossil fuel supplies. (The U.S. Geological Survey had concluded in 1891 that there was little hope of finding oil in Texas, and in 1939 the Department of the Interior warned that the domestic crude supply would last merely another thirteen years.) Nearly everyone now acknowledged that the United States was still extraordinarily well-endowed geologically. Large amounts of conventional crude remained in the ground—perhaps as

---

72. *Congressional Quarterly Weekly Report*, vol. 33 (December 20, 1975), p. 2767.

much as 300 billion barrels—and if oil could someday be derived from shale or coal, the potential volume was staggering.[73] The real concern was not the ultimate size of the nation's energy resource base, but rather how much of it could be recovered, how quickly, at any given price.

Not that this simplified matters. Predictions remained unreliable because future oil production would require technological advances with costs as yet unknown. The prices required to commercialize shale development, coal liquefaction, or even certain enhanced recovery techniques in existing fields were mostly conjectural. Even if all needed technologies could be assembled ahead of time, efforts to forecast systematically the price elasticity of crude-oil output were dubious exercises. Any projection would rest on a host of arbitrary assumptions about global market conditions (determined by, among other imponderables, political events abroad and the worldwide availability and price of not only petroleum, but also other fuels).

FACTS AND FIGURES. This is not to say that in 1975 there was a dearth of sophisticated studies for Congress to ponder. Apart from several in-house estimates, the lawmakers had the Federal Energy Administration's forecasts of domestic production under alternative price conditions (the *Project Independence* data compiled in 1974); the published results of an elaborate econometric simulation just completed at the Massachusetts Institute of Technology; and the National Petroleum Council's most recent prognosis, to name a few of the principal reports in circulation.[74] But the findings of this prodigious body of research varied, depending on assumptions and methodology. The Federal Energy Administration, for instance, calculated that a field price of $7 per barrel (in 1973 dollars) could increase petroleum output 6 percent by 1980.[75] Meanwhile, the MIT model estimated that a price in that vicinity would only stabilize the quantity at current levels.[76] To make things worse, even that scenario seemed unrealistic in light of trends that had been evident for some time. Discoveries of new reserves had been slipping since the mid-1950s, well before the advent of price controls. Moreover, by the summer of 1975, controlled domestic crude sold for $5 per barrel, but newly discovered oil, which until the enactment of the EPCA was still unregulated, topped

73. American Petroleum Institute, *Two Energy Futures: A National Choice for the 80s* (Washington, D.C.: American Petroleum Institute, 1980), p. 38.
74. *Congressional Record* (July 16, 1975), pp. 23032–33.
75. Ibid., p. 23032.
76. Ibid.

$12. Yet total domestic yield was now around 8.2 million barrels per day, having peaked at 9.6 million barrels per day in 1970.[77]

Under such circumstances, the skepticism of Joe Moakley during the Rules Committee hearings, echoed by scores of other liberal Democrats, was understandable. There was no solid evidence that decontrol would cause a significant upswing in production, at least in the foreseeable future. On this score, the opponents of decontrol proved to be correct. Even with the unexpected price run-up of 1979 and the abolition of controls a year later, U.S. production did not move toward anything like the levels prophesied by optimists a few years earlier. As of 1980, forecasts had been revised sharply downward. Few observers posited any longer that domestic output could regain its former peak, even by 1990, and some saw a continued decline.[78] These reappraisals were motivated by the deepening realization that the remaining prospects for petroleum development in the United States lay almost entirely in secondary and tertiary recovery from old reservoirs, deep drilling, and synthetic fuels projects, the costs and lead times of which were increasingly unfavorable. Indeed, some oil company officials had begun to wonder aloud whether the industry would be able to arrest the decline in U.S. production, even if crude oil went to one hundred dollars a barrel.[79]

IMPLICATIONS. With its concentration on the hypothetical contribution of decontrol to the national oil supply, the political discourse sank into speculation and sophistry. Repeatedly, the champions of deregulation wheeled out facts and figures purporting to show that the marketplace would work magic with the domestic supply curve. Unregulated prices would lift volume "to the point of surplus"; boost production "by probably 90 or 100 billion barrels"; and by the mid-1980s, raise production by another 2.3 million barrels daily.[80] Doubters would rejoin with their own numerical tricks. Yet another "recent study" would be uncovered, alleging, say, that production costs were well under $3.00 per barrel for already tapped (old) oil and under $5.50 for newly found oil. In other words, costs were far beneath the prevailing market rates—implying that most of the remaining crude in the country could be profitably extracted at those prices.[81] Both sides armed themselves with

77. William Sweet, *Energy Issues: New Directions and Goals*, Editorial Research Reports (Washington, D.C.: CQ Press, 1982), p. 53.

78. American Petroleum Institute, *Two Energy Futures*, pp. vi, vii, 20, 36.

79. Pelham, *Energy Policy*, 2d ed., p. 33.

80. *Congressional Record* (September 10, 1975), pp. 28444, 28445, 28459.

81. *Congressional Record*, daily edition (July 30, 1975), p. H7899.

analysis. But since the truth was anybody's guess, rational analysis did not shape policy positions; more commonly, analysis was summoned up just to embellish preconceptions.

If attention had focused instead on the relation of prices to consumption, fatuous reasoning would still have been rife. A number of freshmen Democrats seated on the House Commerce Committee had convinced themselves either that no significant conservation would result from higher prices or that it was possible to conserve energy by making consumption more efficient without making it more expensive.[82] In March, these theoreticians were joined by dozens of other House Democrats in sponsoring a plan that provided "immediate relief to the average family by reducing utility rates" and "rolling back the price of domestic oil" while, as if by alchemy, also "fostering tough conservation measures."[83] In the meantime, some senators were taking a similar tack, scorning the president's policies for "relying upon the discipline of the market, rather than the self-discipline of the American people, to solve the Nation's energy problems."[84] It is doubtful that mentalities of this sort could be budged, even with clear evidence of energy savings from market pricing.

But for another group that was neither sanguine about the self-discipline of American energy consumers nor hopeful about the outlook for American petroleum suppliers, such evidence should have given pause, especially since it was relatively unambiguous. Unlike production, which kept going down despite the quadrupling of oil prices after the embargo, demand had reacted in the expected fashion. By 1975, the United States was consuming oil at a rate better than 300 thousand barrels per day less than in 1974 and about 1 million barrels per day less than in 1973.[85] Moreover, demand for distillates, rather than gasoline, had led the decline, for a very simple reason: distillate prices had risen about four times faster than gasoline prices during the final four months of 1973.[86] Total consumption began inching up again in 1976 as a world oil glut developed and real prices leveled off. But Congress had finished trouncing all of the Ford administration's deregulation proposals long before that.

82. *Congressional Record*, daily edition (June 5, 1975), p. H961.
83. *Congressional Quarterly Weekly Report*, vol. 33 (March 15, 1975), p. 518.
84. *Congressional Record* (May 1, 1975), p. 12663.
85. U.S. Energy Information Administration statistics tabulated in Pelham, *Energy Policy*, p. 5.
86. Lane, *Mandatory Petroleum Price and Allocation Regulations*, pp. 36, 37, 46.

The trouble was that telling signs of demand elasticity, reflected in longitudinal trends, cross-national data, or comparisons of energy utilization among American regions, were not emphasized in the congressional debate. This was not because most members of Congress were unaware of the signs or didn't believe them. Rather, those who pleaded for deregulation were interested in proving that market prices would produce energy. Demonstrating that prices would also help conserve energy was secondary. "My emphasis," Gerald Ford confessed to James Reichley of the Brookings Institution in an interview several years later, "was on stimulating production of domestic oil and gas through increased price levels, which also hopefully would bring some conservation."[87] William Simon, one of the principal architects of Ford's program, expressed the bias more bluntly. To Simon, energy production was nothing less than the vital life-force of the United States. What of conservation? Conservation was an essential "emergency measure." "But to demand of a giant industrial nation that it conserve energy without simultaneously offering an ultimate rescue plan" was "insanity." The ultimate rescue plan was to "liberate" U.S. energy industries from "the government death grip" under which they were "stagnating and struggling futilely," and to "let exploration and production rip with the profit motive as guide."[88]

Channeled this way, the terms of the debate narrowed the possibility of weaning wavering congressmen away from price controls. Because the concept of conservation by price failed to get a full hearing, opponents of decontrol were able to clutter the agenda with conservation schemes that pretended to be more moderate.[89] Some inventions, such as gasoline rationing coupons and gasless days, were familiar. But others were novel and strange. One bill unfurled by a group of liberals on the Commerce Committee's energy subcommittee called for government-ordered reductions of gasoline stocks, with no price increases and no coupon system.[90] In plain English, that meant a series of long, federally certified fuel-pump lines. Such notions could acquire a substantial following (forty House Democrats formally endorsed the blueprint for gas queues), partly because of the per-

---

87. Reichley, *Conservatives in an Age of Change*, p. 366.
88. William E. Simon, *Time for Truth*, pp. 50, 52, 53, 81, 87, 88.
89. According to Speaker Carl Albert, Democrat of Oklahoma, for example, gasoline rationing, or gasless days, or any other measure Congress may deem advisable would represent a more moderate approach than a policy that would resort to higher gasoline prices to reduce consumption. *Congressional Quarterly Weekly Report*, vol. 33 (January 25, 1975), p. 178.
90. *Congressional Quarterly Weekly Report*, vol. 33 (March 15, 1975), p. 518.

ception that the public would sooner accept any inconvenience than pay
higher fuel prices. Furthermore, the proposed measures were not rigorously
contrasted, warts and all, with the market alternative. When such comparisons were finally drawn, as during the intense congressional inspection of
gas rationing plans submitted by the Carter administration several years
later, the plans sounded a lot less practical and equitable than they did in
the casual rhetoric of 1975. In 1975, however, nonmarket methods of conservation and loose talk of "programs which tap the cooperation and will,
instead of the pocketbooks, of individual Americans" were not forced to
carry an adequate burden of proof.[91] More often, they were bandied about
as though their advantage over rationing by price could be assumed a
priori, rather than regarded as an empirical question.

Economic Effects of Decontrol

The defenders of price and allocation controls did not merely convey
unease when discussing the economic impacts of deregulation. At times
they seemed to be describing thermonuclear war. The consequences would
be "devastating," creating such "chaos" and "catastrophe" and "human
suffering" as to "curl the hair of the people" and "curl their toenails,
too."[92] The recession of 1975 was serious. A succession of congressional
reports—several evaluations by the Congressional Research Service and
the Congressional Budget Office, as well as earlier staff work by the Joint
Economic Committee and the House Commerce Committee—warned of
the perils of deregulation in the current economic slump.[93] The Democrats,
moreover, had every incentive not only to blame the Republicans for the
depression (as Senator Jackson called it),[94] but to contend that the administration's energy policies would make it worse. Yet the language of the
Democrats sometimes seemed so extreme that neither the contents of the
impact studies nor the opportunity for partisan mischief could account for
the emotion.

Indirectly, the advocates of deregulation aggravated the situation. If
the acknowledged aim of deregulation was to make energy use more efficient, rather than to let production rip, a return to market pricing might

91. *Congressional Record* (May 1, 1975), p. 12663.

92. *Washington Post*, May 29, 1975; *Wall Street Journal*, July 31, 1975; *Congressional Record* (July 30, 1975), p. 25851; and *New York Times*, July 15, 1975.

93. *Congressional Record* (July 15, 1975), p. 22762; *New York Times*, July 23, 1975; *New York Times*, September 18, 1975; and *Washington Post*, September 5, 1975.

94. *Washington Post*, May 29, 1975.

have stirred less panic. It was fairly difficult to refute the fact that demand for oil would drop with decontrol. Even if the drop came at the cost of a temporary dip in the rate of economic growth, one could argue cogently that important benefits would soon ensue. By running up a smaller national oil bill, and relaxing the pressure on world prices, market forces would begin easing the rate of inflation, though after an initial jolt. Eventually, the same forces could also alleviate unemployment, as the economy started substituting labor and other factors for expensive energy inputs. Granted, if the market unleashed a sudden upsurge in home-grown energy, similar results were conceivable. Employment in domestic energy industries would climb; costly oil imports would slacken; OPEC prices could crack; and inflation might subside. The first of these two scripts was the less utopian, and it would have helped to recognize that distinction forthrightly. But the decontrollers chanted a different refrain: "the only hope we have for dealing successfully with the energy problem is to encourage production" (Representative George H. Mahon, Democrat of Texas);[95] "the only way we can decrease dependence on foreign oil is to increase domestic production" (Representative James T. Broyhill, Republican of North Carolina).[96] And as long as they spoke this way, their detractors could never be reassured that deregulation was an economic risk worth taking. The prosperity-from-production thesis seemed farfetched, especially since output was stagnating while prices and profits rose.

Unhappily, with certain liberals any plea for market pricing, regardless of its formulation, was likely to remain a *dialogue des sourds*. Some legislators purporting to protect the consumer, for instance, had taken into their heads a mysterious new model of how energy demand behaved. "After you get to a certain point," one of them explained, "the elasticity isn't there."[97] Since that certain point had already been reached, these representatives seemed to think, few additional energy savings would follow decontrol. (According to Congressman Herbert E. Harris, Democrat of Virginia, "The idea that we are going to obtain conservation by $12- or $14- or $15- or $16- or $20-a-barrel oil in this country" was "economic idiocy.")[98] Of course, if no factor substitutions were feasible in the economy as energy

95. *Congressional Record* (July 23, 1975), p. 234378.
96. *Congressional Record* (July 15, 1975), p. 22753.
97. Edward Cowan, "New Administration Plan for Oil Price Rise Hinted," *New York Times,* July 22, 1975.
98. *Congressional Record* (July 15, 1975), p. 22758.

costs climbed, the toll in general price instability and lost GNP could be terrifying. The model, however, lacked any serious experiential basis. With the evidence available to them, free marketers could have taken dead aim at it. And, by training their fire on this question, rather than dissipating most of it in duels over elusive supply projections, the rhetorical excess of their adversaries might have taken in fewer believers. But, as in the colloquy between John Anderson and Ralph Nader, a sustained frontal assault on the myth of inelastic demand did not take place.

Without an emphatic defense of the proposition that major economic adjustments to higher energy costs were practicable and even desirable, the proponents of price reform got drawn into another series of inconclusive statistical skirmishes. Those opposed to decontrol kept stating that even phased decontrol would drag real GNP down by 2 to 5 percent; send inflation 2.4 to 3 percent higher; and throw some 700,000 more people out of work.[99] The Ford administration's allies countered with elaborate calculations indicating insignificant unemployment and, in extremis, merely a one-time, 0.5 percent increase in the rate of inflation.[100] Such chasms could not be bridged by roving the margins of the issue and speculating interminably about the extent of future OPEC price hikes; how the increases would ripple through the domestic economy; whether a windfall profits tax could pass promptly; how recycled revenues from it might infuse purchasing power; and other sundry assumptions with which both sides dressed up their estimates. What could have cut through the confusion was a forceful showing that, in the United States or anywhere else, the relation of energy use to energy prices, and to economic well-being, was flexible.

Failure to Legitimate Decontrol

Officials who went around saying that the main point of deregulation was to provide more incentives for petroleum production were uttering precisely what petroleum producers wanted to hear. This association was no advantage, particularly in the political climate of 1975. Spurred by public mistrust of big oil, consumer-oriented legislators leapt at the

99. Edwin L. Dale, Jr., "President Urged to Keep Oil Curb," *New York Times*, August 6, 1975; *New York Times*, September 10, 1975; and *Congressional Record* (July 23, 1975), p. 24379.

100. David E. Rosenbaum, "Ford Is Rebuffed by House Oil Vote," *New York Times*, July 23, 1975; and *Congressional Quarterly Weekly Report*, vol. 33 (May 24, 1975), p. 1067. The estimates were largely based on calculations by the Council of Economic Advisers. See de Marchi, "The Ford Administration," p. 507.

chance to portray as virtually indistinguishable the interests of free marketers and of the oil companies. The two were working hand in hand, according to Senator Jackson,[101] and were cooking up what Congressman Anthony J. Moffett, Democrat of Connecticut, characterized as "a government-sponsored, industry-backed rip-off."[102] Curiously, instead of striving to shed the stigma, the Ford administration and its friends in Congress talked and acted in ways that cemented it.

For years reformers had battled to abolish the array of tax benefits—percentage depletion, intangible drilling cost deductions, "dry hole" expensing, foreign tax credits—that had accumulated for the petroleum-producing industry over several decades.[103] The consensus among economists was that these shelters were not just a revenue drain and a source of inequity; they were misallocating resources.[104] In early 1975, Congress finally succeeded in eliminating the most controversial subsidy, the 22.5 percent depletion allowance for major producers. An irony of this long-sought revision, however, was that it was achieved almost entirely by liberal Democrats, over the intense opposition of the same coalition that purported to fancy an unfettered market—oil-state Democrats, most Republicans, and the president. Indeed, had its authors not fortuitously attached the reform to a popular income tax reduction measure strongly desired by the administration, a possible presidential veto loomed. A few conservatives were embarrassed by the administration's pose. Secretary Simon, for instance, decried the oil industry's "absurd tax exemptions" as much as he despised the "regulatory shackles" clamped on it.[105] But in general, Republican support for the oil depletion allowance was amazingly broad.[106] (On the key

101. *New York Times*, July 15, 1975.

102. *Congressional Quarterly Weekly Report*, vol. 33 (May 24, 1975), p. 1067.

103. Before the repeal of the depletion allowance (and the advent of new levies on the oil industry, such as the heavy windfall profits tax in 1980), the industry had managed to enjoy a very limited tax liability. It has been estimated that between 1968 and 1972, for instance, seven oil companies—Exxon, Texaco, Mobil, Standard of California, Gulf, Standard of Indiana, and Shell—earned over $44 billion in profits. Yet the companies reportedly paid less than $2 billion in U.S. income taxes, an effective tax rate of 5 percent on earnings. Robert Engler, *The Brotherhood of Oil: Energy Policy and the Public Interest* (University of Chicago Press, 1977), p. 54.

104. See, for instance, Stanley S. Surrey, Paul R. McDaniel, and Joseph A. Pechman, *Federal Tax Reform for 1976: A Compendium* (Washington, D.C.: Fund for Public Policy Research, 1976), pp. 53–58; George F. Break and Joseph A. Pechman, *Federal Tax Reform: The Impossible Dream?* (Brookings, 1975), p. 69.

105. Simon, *Time for Truth*, pp. 52, 73.

106. In the key Rules Committee vote on the question, the committee split perfectly along party lines. Richard L. Lyons, "House Unit Clears Way for Oil Depletion Vote," *Washington*

procedural motion that allowed the rider to be introduced in the House, only 15 GOP members joined 227 Democrats voting to consider the amendment; 199 Republicans tried to sidetrack it.)[107] The Republican stance was also brash. Arizona Senator Paul J. Fannin took a line common among Republicans: repeal of percentage depletion signified an "additional tax burden."[108] The implication seemed to be that the repeal was just another new tax, while the original subsidy was every oil prospector's birthright.[109] Many observers were left with the impression that the promoters of price deregulation practiced a double standard, avowing laissez-faire but voting economic privilege.

That impression was scarcely dispelled by Ford's decision, a few months later, to introduce legislation creating an Energy Independence Authority. Originally conceived by Vice-President Nelson Rockefeller, this new federal corporation was to hand out $100 billion in government loan monies and guarantees to energy companies for projects that the marketplace had refused to underwrite. The Council of Economic Advisers, the Treasury Department, and the Office of Management and Budget had objected strenuously to the scheme, but to no avail. The president, who had venerated fiscal conservatism for all his political life, backed Rockefeller's grandiose proposal anyway. Instantly, the Democrats luxuriated in the role of accusing the Republican White House of plotting "a serious waste of the taxpayers' money" and of being "fiscally irresponsible."[110] They also charged the president with being hypocritical. "One of the elementary contradictions in the proposal," noted Senator Edward M. Kennedy, Democrat of Massachusetts, "is the contrast between the President's expression of fidelity to the free enterprise system, and his proposal to insulate some of

---

Post, February 27, 1975.

107. The key roll call was on adoption of the rule (H. Res. 259) providing for floor consideration of the overall federal tax cut legislation and allowing amendments, including the oil and gas depletion allowance repeal. *Congressional Quarterly Almanac*, vol. 31 (1975), pp. 10H, 11H.

108. *Congressional Record* (May 1, 1975), p. 12669.

109. Several Republicans also concluded that declining oil production could be attributed largely to the reduction in the depletion allowance. Once during the Senate debate, for example, Senator Dewey F. Bartlett, Republican of Oklahoma, said, "We had some 2,700 rigs operating [in 1955]. Today we have approximately 1,750 rigs available to operate but we are only operating about 1,600. Why? Because this body and the other body saw fit to reduce the depletion allowance in such large amounts that the industry was charged an extra $2.5 billion in taxes." *Congressional Record*, daily edition (July 30, 1975), p. S14264.

110. de Marchi, "The Ford Administration," p. 520; and *Congressional Record* (October 8, 1975), p. 32175.

the largest profitmaking enterprises in the Nation from the normal risks of doing business."[111]

There were other elementary contradictions. For example, the president invoked high principle when his veto crashed down on the 1975 strip-mining legislation that had passed Congress overwhelmingly; government intervention here was costly and unsound. Simultaneously, however, administration officials were giving serious thought to a massive aid program for electric utilities that would include bigger investment tax credits; special assistance to firms building or operating uranium enrichment facilities; and, at least on the Federal Energy Administration's wish list, a government guarantee of industry debt. Federal purchases of utility stock, tax-free stock dividends, and even public construction of power plants were also proposed.[112] Presumably, this sort of intervention was costly but sound. (Only the increased tax credits were eventually adopted. The rest of the utility bailout was abandoned, thanks in part to outspoken congressional criticism.)[113]

The only common thread that tied these seemingly inconsistent impulses together was a fixation with maximizing production, in the marketplace and far beyond it, usually in the name of energy independence. "I was convinced that we needed to unbridle the oil companies, that we needed to have a lot of extra drilling, and a lot of wasted money to get this thing really off dead center," Frank Zarb, the former federal energy administrator, said years later.[114] That admission spoke volumes about the way the Ford administration, and most Republicans on Capitol Hill, seemed to view their mission.

Windfall Profits Taxation

Now, if someone is so anxious to unbridle the oil companies, and to throw a lot of wasted money at them for good measure, how can he credibly support a serious tax on oil industry profits? Ford's opponents

111. *Congressional Record* (October 8, 1975), pp. 32175–76.
112. de Marchi, "The Ford Administration," p. 522.
113. Senator Kennedy's remarks on the proposed utility bailout were representative: "The specific subsidy program for electric power generation is unjustified," he told the Senate, because the real reason why utilities were postponing or canceling nuclear and coal-based power plants was mainly "the sharp decline in the demand for electric power. . . . A new subsidy to encourage expansion of electric power generating capacity—especially one that ignores reduced interest rates—could be an extremely wasteful and unproductive use of Federal dollars." *Congressional Record* (October 8, 1975), p. 32176.
114. Interview with Frank Zarb, November 24, 1981.

inevitably asked this question, and the answers they got were not reassuring. Repeatedly, the president called for enactment of a windfall profits tax, but always with a large chunk of the proceeds to be plowed back into energy development—"to encourage maximum domestic exploration and production." After the revocation of percentage depletion, the administration began intimating on several occasions that it would seek a milder tax than the one it had initially put forth.

Without any guarantee that the Republicans would be willing to accept a stiff windfall profits measure, whose receipts would be redistributed widely to consumers rather than returned to the energy industries, Democratic moderates who might have chanced decontrol were unnerved. Redistribution, broad and rapid, was considered essential for three reasons. First, it would act as a macroeconomic stabilizer if deregulated prices depressed aggregate demand severely. Second, it would recapture for consumers more of the enormous income transfer that decontrol bestowed upon oil producers. The feeling of many Democrats was simple: an industry that had been subsidized handsomely by taxpayers over nearly half a century was no longer entitled to retain (or repossess through a plowback) the bulk of unearned income that would now accrue to it from OPEC pricing actions. Finally, there was a strong sense that compensatory steps should be taken to offset the regressiveness of deregulation. Most Democrats suspected that if a windfall tax were imposed at all (which was by no means a certainty), it would scarcely be structured to assist low-income households with fuel bills. From the standpoint of these congressmen, therefore, the safe strategy was to stick with price controls, which, although not specifically designed to aid the poor, supposedly cushioned them along with everybody else from the ballooning cost of energy.

To an important degree, these concerns lay at the core of the political gridlock that developed in the House among the various committees that could have legislated deregulation. Liberals vividly recollected past experience with windfall profits legislation—how in 1973, for instance, President Nixon had urged a tax on excess oil profits as a prelude to decontrol; how under the stewardship of Wilbur D. Mills, Democrat of Arkansas, Ways and Means ended up reporting a bill with a plowback credit so expansive as to allow producers to dodge almost 90 percent of their liability. The liberals also recalled how, despite this generosity, industry lobbyists, oil-state representatives, and conservative Republicans continued to fight the measure tooth and nail. (It ultimately died in the

Rules Committee.) True, the distribution of power was different in the Ninety-fourth Congress. The overall Democratic majority was bigger; the newly enlarged Ways and Means Committee included more members to the left of center; Mills had been deposed as chairman. Whether these changes were sufficient to secure passage of a vigorous tax, however, remained unclear. Five of the twenty-five Democrats on the tax-writing unit were still from big oil-producing states—Texas, Louisiana, Oklahoma, and Kansas. Two others, Phillip M. Landrum of Georgia and Mills of Arkansas, were southern conservatives. When these votes were added to those of the committee's twelve Republicans, liberals remained outgunned.

Although the administration's loyalists—in particular, Barber B. Conable, Jr., of New York, Herman T. Schneebeli of Pennsylvania, and William E. Frenzel of Minnesota—were eager to forge a bipartisan tax bill, it was hard to tell just how far they, and the president, were willing to go. After all, the plowback provision tendered by the administration seemed at odds with the redistributive approach that most Democrats had in mind, and there was no reason to believe that the Republicans were prepared to pass a bill without the provision. To anyone who saw in market pricing mainly a vehicle for conservation, a heavy tax on producers made no difference. But to those who viewed market prices almost exclusively as stimuli for production, such a tax was worse than confiscatory; it could erase whatever incentives price deregulation would create.

Meanwhile, Ways and Means Republicans on the far right—most notably, William R. Archer of Texas, John J. Duncan of Tennessee, and Philip M. Crane of Illinois—stood ready to shred any compromise, convinced that any increase in the oil industry's tax burden would translate into idle drilling rigs.[115] In short, for Democrats who could have been talked into swapping price controls for a levy on oil company profits, the situation in Ways and Means inspired little confidence. Assuming a tax were eventually drafted, its scope was something no one could predict. That is why the Commerce Committee was inclined to wait and see through the spring of 1975 before reporting out parallel legislation. Procrastination by the Commerce Committee then gave an alliance of risk-averse liberals and GOP maximalists an ideal excuse, on May 12, to defer indefinitely the consideration of windfall profits taxation in Ways

115. In committee, these three Republicans had voted against insertion of a windfall profits tax in the House Ways and Means energy legislation on May 12, 1975.

and Means. The uncertainty of the tax plan also explains why Ullman failed to comfort his cohorts on the Rules Committee in July, when that panel weighed the possibility of conceding Ford's final decontrol plan if a suitable tax were sure to follow.

Could the regrettable stalemate have been avoided? Could Ullman have collaborated more closely with the Commerce leadership, particularly Congressman Dingell, to fashion a joint energy-pricing and tax package? In an interview seven years later, the former chairman ruminated much as he had before the Rules Committee on July 28, 1975: "I couldn't make a deal with him [Dingell]. I couldn't give him assurances that my committee would write a tax that was tough enough."[116]

The Price Regulator's Weltanschauung

If a deal had been cut on a windfall profits tax, better progress toward crude-oil deregulation in 1975 would have been possible. But an accord was impeded by more than the insecurity among Democrats about the tax's final attributes. An economic theory anchored the left flank of the Democratic position. If one subscribed to the theory, its logic led ineluctably to direct price and allocation controls—and to the conclusion that taxes on excess profits were only second best.

The notion that "just and reasonable" prices could be imputed to energy on the basis of production costs, rather than values determined by the market, stemmed from thirty-five years of federal price regulation in the natural gas industry and sixty-five years of utility ratemaking by the states. Increases in the market value of oil or gas that greatly exceeded original costs of production (as for gas or oil flowing from old wells, drilled and paid for years earlier) were not fair prices, but rents unrelated to the economic contributions of the producing firms. Since these rents belonged rightfully to society, government could expropriate them, either preemptively through regulation or retroactively through windfall profits taxation. The first method, however, reached farther.

"The energy market is not now, and has not been for many years, a 'free market'," emphasized Senator Jackson.[117] Many liberals agreed. They viewed the petroleum business as an oligopolistic industry in which the market power of a few integrated corporations could rig prices well above costs and squeeze out independent refiners and marketers during

116. Interview with Albert C. Ullman, October 21, 1981.
117. *Congressional Record* (May 1, 1975), p. 12663.

periods of tight supply. To liberals, the emergence of OPEC as an effective cartel in the early 1970s served only to confirm that interpretation. Whether or not OPEC's ascendance had wrested control of the international oil trade from the "Seven Sisters" was irrelevant, since, according to the liberals, the cartel's interventions and the interests of the majors in their domestic operations were congruent.[118]

Supposedly, as world prices soared, big oil would tighten its grip on the domestic market by withholding supplies to inflate the value of existing stocks, and perhaps also to drive smaller competitors out of business. (Why sell today to an independent refinery an inventory worth $5 per barrel that could fetch $15 per barrel next year?) Once plots like these were assumed, price ceilings became de rigueur in order to set expectations straight. (Presumably, there is no incentive to hold back supplies if, on account of government controls, next year's prices are set to stay about the same as today's.) Moreover, to further the "competitive viability" of the industry—to ensure that small independents were not severed from the refining and distribution network—a system of mandatory allocations seemed necessary. For such purposes, windfall profits taxation was a poor substitute. A tax would strip off undeserved earnings after decontrol. But if the need was also to protect small businesses from their supposed predators, the tax would not be enough.

The regulatory doctrine that inspired some Democrats to revive the Emergency Petroleum Allocation Act time and again, and that fed the conceptual undercurrents of the Energy Policy and Conservation Act, was not espoused as dogmatically by the party's majority. If it had been, the party would have tried to mandate price controls forever. Instead, even the EPCA did not stipulate an indefinite extension.[119] But for an orthodox minority, the idea of controls was deeply implanted. Indeed, a number of legislators on the Left continued to grieve for minor refineries, product retailers, gasoline jobbers, and other would-be victims of decontrol, as they were called in the Senate Interior Committee,[120] long after the fears and lamentations of these groups had receded. These lawmakers, well represented on strategic legislative panels, formed an intransigent bloc around which more moderate Democratic leaders could not easily maneuver.

118. See *Congressional Quarterly Weekly Report*, vol. 32 (March 8, 1975), p. 477.
119. However, the Democrats would have preferred to legislate price and allocation controls extending over a full five years. *New York Times*, September 10, 1975.
120. Arlen J. Large and Albert R. Hunt, "Grass-Root Gripes about Cost of Living May Tip Congress for Oil Price Controls," *Wall Street Journal*, September 4, 1975.

Conclusion

An early halt to price controls on domestic crude oil should have topped the agenda for a national energy conservation policy. The time to act was during 1975, when extant regulatory statutes were expiring, no new ones had been locked in, and an administration eager to begin the process was still in power. But the opening through which daylight had poured during the first few months of that decisive interregnum was slammed shut by the enactment of the Energy Policy and Conservation Act at the end of the year. When Jimmy Carter assumed office thirteen months later, he had no desire to arm wrestle with Congress over the periodic (ninety-day) administrative adjustments in price ceilings that the energy act theoretically permitted.[121] Through most of the 1970s, the ceilings stood fast.

As part of its National Energy Plan in 1977, the Carter administration did propose to amend existing law by adding a new tax on crude oil at the wellhead (a so-called crude oil equalization tax), aimed at bringing the retail prices of all petroleum products up to world levels. Because, if the equalization tax had passed, end users would have paid world prices for oil eventually (that is, controlled prices with the tax surcharges were equal to prevailing market prices), the proposal was touted as the functional equivalent of deregulation with a windfall profits tax: with this tax interposed, consumers would face real energy values, but producers would reap no unearned wealth in the process. A tactical virtue of the proposal, from the administration's standpoint, was that it demanded little or no teamwork between the tax writers and other legislative units in Congress. Jurisdictional frictions, like those that bollixed up the House Commerce Committee and the Ways and Means Committee in 1975, would be avoided, since only one piece of legislation (the equalization tax) was required, instead of two (separate pricing and windfall profits measures).

Such subtleties notwithstanding, the tax could not be passed off as deregulation in different garb. As far as the producers of oil were concerned, the field prices they could charge remained tightly controlled. And this was reason enough for Republicans and oil-state Democrats to assail the scheme successfully. Despite House approval of the controversial tax along with most other elements of the National Energy Plan, it died in the Senate Finance Committee, then chaired by the redoubtable Russell B. Long,

121. Interview with James R. Schlesinger, former secretary of energy, Washington, D.C., August 6, 1982.

Democrat of Louisiana. Perhaps more basically, even if the equalization tax had become law, it would not have accelerated appreciably the advent of market, or market-equivalent, oil pricing in the United States. The tax was to nudge consumer prices upward in annual increments, with the last increase scheduled for 1980—a timetable about as drawn out as the one allowed under the EPCA. In sum, prior to mid-1979, when price and allocation controls reverted from mandatory to discretionary status, the Carter administration sought no radical departure from the status quo, and in any case, the changes it did seek were never adopted. With the EPCA on the books, the nation's oil-pricing rules became long-term policy. Institutional inertia barred any significant midcourse correction.

Several factors contributed to the decision in 1975 to string out domestic crude-oil price regulation through the remainder of the decade. Special interests, such as certain independent refiners, gasoline distributors, heating fuel dealers, and farm cooperatives, prospered under the regulations and lobbied to keep them. Also, regional discord smoldered between the few states that stood to gain quickly and unambiguously from decontrol, and the more numerous states in which the net benefits were regarded as null, remote, or uncertain. To restore market pricing, aggressive executive leadership was imperative. Without a popular mandate, the Ford administration labored under numerous handicaps—a severe recession; a presidential election not far off; and a contentious Congress, emboldened by Watergate and by the Democratic sweep of 1974. Yet, more significant than these vicissitudes were the substance and style of the policy debate itself.

In a sense, the debate that raged was the wrong one. To the participants, production, not conservation, was what deregulation was about. Both sides sensed that the American people were more comfortable with deregulation if it promised an energy boom here at home than if it cramped consumption. But there was more to the supply-side expectations than a tendency to reflect public sentiment. At bottom, many proponents of decontrol quietly believed what the head of the Texas Railroad Commission proclaimed loudly—"This country did not conserve its way to greatness. It produced itself to greatness."[122]

The problem with this attitude was that the odds of clasping greatness in the country's remaining oil fields were no longer what they used to be,

122. See Daniel Yergin, "Conservation: The Key Energy Source," in Robert Stobaugh and Daniel Yergin, eds., *Energy Future: Report of the Energy Project at the Harvard Business School* (Random House, 1979), p. 142.

and nobody could forecast how much the chances might improve with deregulated prices. Trend lines—for additions to proven oil reserves, yield per foot drilled, and total output—pointed downward. Hard evidence that this was a passing aberration, wrought principally by price controls, was lacking. Amid the uncertainty, Congress tended to partition itself into two sects—the enthusiasts, who trusted that a new age of American oil abundance would dawn with decontrol, and the pessimists, haunted by visions of dry holes or capped wells even at sky-high prices.

Talk of decontrol's effect on demand was less speculative, but not in vogue. Public opinion did not encourage serious discussion along these lines. Neither did a number of lawmakers on the far Left. For persons who assumed that demand as well as supply was inelastic, it made no difference which way the thrust of the argument ran. Deregulation, they assumed, would be disappointing on both counts. Nonetheless, greater emphasis on the energy-saving potential of market pricing would have turned the policy process down a more constructive path. Price-induced conservation was decontrol's most palpable payoff. Accorded the credit this gain deserved, fewer preposterous proxies might have floated around Congress, distracting attention and dividing the members. The macroeconomic fallout of deregulation might have looked less frightful as well. Finally, conservation by price was hard to champion before an unreceptive public. But as things turned out, it was no easier to sell decontrol by peddling it as a business incentive that, with other special inducements, would get domestic crude gushing again.

Equity was the dominant concern of those who opposed deregulation. The economic hardships facing consumers with low or moderate incomes troubled many liberals. The lingering issue of preferential treatment for the petroleum industry also vexed them. In their opinion, regulation and excess-profits taxation were ways of getting even with a supposedly greedy industry that had been indulged, first by a succession of government goodies (market-demand prorationing, import quotas, tax breaks, and other favors) and now by OPEC's administered prices. Committed chiefly to the goal of producing energy, the supporters of deregulation were often of two minds about the role of government in the energy marketplace: they were quick to relieve the domestic petroleum economy from price controls, but not necessarily from tax expenditures and other subsidies. Thus advocates of regulation felt their prejudices were being borne out. They suspected that decontrol wasn't an authentic quest for market freedom, only another fix for oil companies. And more concretely, if decontrol were to come, a stout tax on windfall profits might not follow. After all, could the same crowd that clung to percentage depletion be trusted to send up a tough tax measure?

These misgivings infused the opposition to decontrol. But in addition, an important nucleus of critics drew inspiration from a well-worn tradition—that of doing battle against natural monopolies, or at least against noncompetitive practices, in the energy sector. First it was utilities; then natural gas pipelines; then gas field markets; and now, almost deterministically, the oil industry.

The congressional majority that rebuffed deregulation grew rigid. Where benefits and costs of a policy are characterized by indeterminacy, as with the elasticity of U.S. crude oil supply under market conditions, legislators tend to burrow deeper into partisan molds. They rely on their ideological instincts in deciding how to vote. The polarization is abetted when long-standing disputes about social injustices or economic biases are reignited—particularly if adversaries behave in exactly the ways that fan the flames of these disputes. And division is abetted further when vocal factions come equipped, as were the hard-core price regulators in 1975, with traditional doctrines that purport to explain the biases or injustices and that prescribe established remedies for them.

Appendix A: Correlations between Local Interest Group Concentrations and Congressional Voting Patterns

In tables 2-1 and 2-2 the votes of the members of Congress by party are correlated, in simple bivariate fashion, with three sorts of independent variables denoting the ecological distributions of key client groups whose interests supposedly lay in opposing deregulation: small refiners, gasoline jobbers, and heating oil dealers.

Simple point-biserial tests, rather than multivariate analysis, are carried out in the tables because my aim here is only to identify the directionality of the various relationships, not to assess the relative strength of specific variables. Owing to multicollinearity between several of the variables, a multivariate approach with these data risks giving misleading results. In these tables, and others throughout this book, the independent variables denoting local conditions are composed of data aggregated by states or, for the specified fuel marketers, by regions.

Table 2-1. *Correlations between Local Interest Group Concentrations and House Votes on Oil Decontrol by Party, 1975*[a]

Item	H.R. 4035, June 5		H.R. 7014, July 23		H. Res. 641, July 30		S. 622, December 15	
	Dem. (253 votes)	*Rep.* (128 votes)	*Dem.* (282 votes)	*Rep.* (140 votes)	*Dem.* (275 votes)	*Rep.* (142 votes)	*Dem.* (261 votes)	*Rep.* (135 votes)
Small refiners in state[b]	.34*	.23*	.29*	.15	.29*	.22*	.33*	.25*
Small refinery capacity in state	.41*	.19*	.36*	.16	.33*	.21*	.39*	.24*
Small refiners as a percent of all refiners in state	.25*	.28*	.13	.19*	.22*	.30*	.23*	.32*
Small refinery capacity as a percent of total refinery capacity in state	.17*	.20*	.08	.18	.10	.23*	.12	.28*
Gasoline jobbers in region[c]	.29*	.39*	.41*	.39*	.35*	.35*	.34*	.43*
Heating fuel dealers in region[c]	−.48*	−.41*	−.50*	−.40*	−.45*	−.36*	−.47*	−.45*

Sources: *House and Senate votes: Congressional Quarterly Weekly Report*, vol. 33 (June 7, 1975), pp. 1198–99; vol. 33 (July 26, 1975), pp. 1642–43; vol. 33 (August 2, 1975), pp. 1726–27; vol. 33 (December 20, 1975), pp. 2822–23; *refineries:* Aileen Cantrell, "Annual Refining Survey," *Oil and Gas Journal*, vol. 73 (April 7, 1975), pp. 100–18; and *jobbers and heating fuel dealers:* National Oil Jobbers Council, *Marketer Profile Survey* (Washington, D.C.: NOJC, 1981).

*p < .01.

a. Dichotomous dependent variable: 1 = a vote for decontrol; 0 = a vote against decontrol.

b. Small refiners are companies with a total capacity of less than 175,000 barrels per day.

c. Based on a 1981 survey by the National Oil Jobbers Council. Although the absolute number of jobbers and heating fuel dealers was different six years earlier, their regional distribution was said to be similar. (Interview with Michael T. Scanlon, vice-president, NOJC, Washington, D.C., January 6, 1982.)

Clearly, states as units of analysis provide, at best, indirect measures of local interests or characteristics of a constituency in the case of House members. Unfortunately, data for the local energy attributes relevant to this study are not compiled or available at the level of congressional districts. The roll call analyses in this book are tests of the influence of home-state characteristics on the voting behavior of representatives and senators, rather than tests, strictly speaking, of the influences of immediate constituencies.

As is so often true in congressional voting, the telltale roll calls on energy bills came on key amendments and procedural issues, not always in the up-or-down votes for a bill's final passage. In this appendix and appendix B, critical roll calls on the following bills are analyzed.

H.R. 4035. A bill in the House to extend for fifteen days from five days the statutory congressional review period in the event of a presidential order decontrolling domestic crude oil or petroleum product prices under the Emergency Petroleum Allocation Act, thus allowing Congress more time to vote a possible resolution of disapproval as the law permitted. This seemingly petty procedural concern—whether to have five days or fifteen—was critical to opponents of decontrol, since they believed that a five-day period would not suffice for either chamber to cast a legislative veto.

H.R. 7014. An attempt by Representative Robert C. Krueger, Democrat of Texas, to reintroduce on the House floor a bill, adopted narrowly by the House Energy and Power Subcommittee but shelved by the full Commerce Committee, that would have gradually decontrolled domestic oil prices contingent upon enactment of a windfall profits tax.

H. RES. 641. The resolution to disapprove President Ford's final plan for gradual deregulation of oil prices through the administrative rulemaking mechanism allowed by the EPAA. Passage of this congressional veto terminated further efforts by the president to inaugurate decontrol by executive order.

S. 622. The final vote on the Energy Policy and Conservation Act conference report—a decisive roll call for both the House and Senate in that Congress was still uncertain at that point whether the president would sign or veto the legislation.

S. 621. A bill similar in purpose to H.R. 4035, except that it sought a thirty-day, instead of fifteen-day, elongation of the congressional review period on the EPAA.

H.R. 4035. The vote in the Senate on a compromise between the

Table 2-2. Correlations between Local Interest Group Concentrations and Senate Votes on Oil Decontrol by Party, 1975[a]

Item	S. 621, May 1		H.R. 4035, July 16		S. 1849, Sept. 10		S. 622, Dec. 17	
	Dem. (50 votes)	Rep. (33 votes)	Dem. (59 votes)	Rep. (38 votes)	Dem. (61 votes)	Rep. (39 votes)	Dem. (60 votes)	Rep. (38 votes)
Small refiners in state[b]	.27	.18	.43*	.15	.45*	.16	.33*	.10
Small refinery capacity in state	.22	.13	.38*	.10	.42*	.16	.31*	.08
Small refiners as a percent of all refiners in state	.27	.26	.25	.24	.18	.29	.09	.23
Small refinery capacity as a percent of total refinery capacity in state	.09	.24	.16	.24	.08	.27	.02	.31
Gasoline jobbers in region[c]	.41*	.77*	.24	.71*	.19	.55*	.29*	.76*
Heating fuel dealers in region[c]	−.30	−.70*	−.42*	−.64*	−.42*	−.57*	−.41*	−.70*

Sources: *House and Senate votes: Congressional Quarterly Weekly Report*, vol. 33 (May 3, 1975), p. 949; vol. 33 (July 19, 1975), p. 1584; vol. 33 (September 13, 1975), p. 1972; vol. 33 (December 20, 1975), p. 2829; *refineries*: Cantrell, "Annual Refining Survey," pp. 100–18; and *jobbers and heating fuel dealers*: National Oil Jobbers Council, *Marketer Profile Survey*.

*p < .01 (two-tailed test).

a. Dichotomous dependent variable: 1 = a vote for decontrol; 0 = a vote against decontrol.

b. Small refiners are companies with a total capacity of less than 175,000 barrels per day.

c. Based on a 1981 survey by the National Oil Jobbers Council. Although the absolute number of jobbers and heating fuel dealers was different six years earlier, their regional distribution was said to be similar. (Interview with Michael T. Scanlon, vice-president, NOJC, Washington, D.C., January 6, 1982.)

original House version of H.R. 4035 and S. 621, which would have amended the EPAA by extending the legislative review/veto period to twenty days.

S. 1849. An attempt by the Senate to override President Ford's veto of a bill extending the EPAA from its expiration date of August 31, 1975, to a new date of March 1, 1976. This vote provided a litmus test for decontrol among senators, between those willing to let the executive initiate the process and those opposed to decontrol by either branch.

Appendix B: Logit Analysis of Congressional Voting Patterns

In tables 2-3 and 2-4 the effects of local energy conditions on congressional votes are estimated in logit models for the same crucial roll calls cited earlier. As expected, the representatives and senators that declined to get rid of price controls came from net consuming states (the states that consumed more oil than they produced): net per capita consumption of fuel oil is negatively associated with votes for decontrol and emerges as a powerful variable in most of the equations.[123] Similarly, there was a discernible tendency for support of decontrol to vary inversely with state fuel and electricity prices. In part, the coefficients may be more often significant for the House because House members, running for reelection every two years, were more jittery about the electoral implications of local energy prices.

Nonetheless, an equally striking feature in most of the equations is the weight of the party affiliations of the legislators. In combination with party, the local energy variables (net consumption of distillate fuel oil, average distillate fuel oil price, and average price of electricity) correctly predict large percentages of votes. But the independent effect of party is

123. Owing to their strong intercorrelation, it was not possible to introduce state per capita distillate consumption and state per capita distillate production as separate independent variables in the same equations. Net consumption constitutes a composite measure. Also, it is misleading to rank the relative strength of each independent variable by comparing the sizes of the respective logit coefficients. The estimated coefficients are unstandardized and reflect standard errors of varying magnitudes. For net consumption per capita, for example, the coefficients tend to be large, not because this variable was necessarily the best overall predictor of how Congress voted, but because the general distribution of its values was complex: while members of Congress from producing states (a fairly small subset of states) tended to vote overwhelmingly for decontrol, there was considerable variability among members from the consuming states—a distribution that generated sizable standard errors. As noted, however, net consumption was the technically sound solution to the multicollinearity problem that arose in the multivariate statistical models employed.

Table 2-3. *Logit Analysis of State Energy Attributes as Determinants of House Votes on Oil Decontrol, with Party Affiliation, 1975*[a]

Item	H.R. 4035 June 5 (381 votes)	H.R. 7014 July 23 (422 votes)	H. Res. 641 July 30 (417 votes)	S. 622 Dec. 15 (396 votes)
Net consumption of distillate fuel oil per capita[b]	−31.9454* (5.643)	−40.0206* (4.385)	−30.5537* (4.977)	−38.5836* (5.288)
Average distillate fuel oil price (residential)	−0.0033* (3.547)	−0.0017* (2.431)	−0.0013 (1.921)	−0.0012 (1.662)
Average price of electricity (residential)	−0.0007* (2.820)	−0.0008* (4.436)	−0.0006* (3.221)	−0.0005* (2.598)
Party affiliation	−4.7161* (10.586)	−3.7871* (10.327)	−3.3539* (10.705)	−2.9778* (10.014)
Chi-squared	287.08	261.92	227.04	202.29
Percentage of votes predicted correctly[c]	84.20	68.60	69.30	71.90
Percentage of votes predicted correctly (party affiliation omitted)[d]	49.20	24.10	36.80	45.40

Sources: *House and Senate votes: Congressional Quarterly Weekly Report,* vol. 33 (June 7, 1975), pp. 1198–99; vol. 33 (July 26, 1975), pp. 1642–43; vol. 33 (August 2, 1975), pp. 1726–27; vol. 33 (December 20, 1975), pp. 2822–23; *oil production and consumption:* American Petroleum Institute, *Basic Petroleum Data Book,* vol. 2 (Washington, D.C.: American Petroleum Institute, 1982), tables 5b, 10b, and 12b (variables use the U.S. Energy Information Administration's 1975 data, and then standardize by 1970 U.S. Census of Population); *distillate fuel and electricity prices:* U.S. Department of Energy, Energy Information Administration, *State Energy Fuel Prices by Major Economic Sector from 1960 through 1977* (Washington, D.C.: Department of Energy, July 1979), table B-1, pp. 75–76, 95–96. Distillate prices are in cents per gallon in 1975; electricity prices are in dollars per kilowatt-hour in 1975.

*$p < .05$.

a. Upper figures in each column are the estimated logit coefficients. Figures in parentheses are t-statistics. Data for the first three independent variables are aggregated by states. The fourth, party affiliation, is a dummy specified: 1 = Democrat; 0 = Republican. The dichotomous dependent variables are specified: 1 = a vote for decontrol; 0 = a vote against decontrol.

b. Net consumption signifies consumption minus production.

c. These are the normalized percentages of prodecontrol votes predicted by the above models (that is, the percentages after subtracting the percentages that would be predicted in a model that had no explanatory variables, other than a constant): $\hat{p} - p_o / 1 - p_o$, where $\hat{p}$ is the overall percentage of correct predictions in the equation, and p_o is the percentage of predictions in an equation with no explanatory variables other than a constant.

d. The normalized percentages of prodecontrol votes predicted by the same models, excluding party affiliation as an explanatory variable.

substantial: omitting it from the various models reduces sharply the shares of prodecontrol votes correctly predicted by the remaining variables. The full results of the equations in tables 2-3 and 2-4, reestimated deleting party affiliation, are tabulated in tables 2-5 and 2-6. In the House roll call of July 30, 1975, the inclusion of party clearly accounts for almost half of the percentage of votes explained by the equation, and in at least one case (July 23, 1975), party is plainly the dominant determinant; excluding it lowers the equation's explanatory power by well over half. In short, the legislative coalitions on oil deregulation were significantly partisan, as well as grounded in perceived state or regional interests.

Table 2-4. *Logit Analysis of State Energy Attributes as Determinants of Senate Votes on Oil Decontrol, with Party Affiliation, 1975*[a]

Item	S. 621 May 1 (83 votes)	H.R. 4035 July 16 (97 votes)	S. 1849 Sept. 10 (100 votes)	S. 622 Dec. 17 (98 votes)
Net consumption of distillate fuel oil per capita[b]	−37.6389*	−77.8345*	−99.3266*	−55.3557*
	(2.116)	(2.726)	(2.511)	(2.601)
Average distillate fuel oil price (residential)	−0.0022	−0.0019	−0.0030	0.0003
	(1.227)	(0.827)	(1.288)	(0.146)
Average price of electricity (residential)	−0.0013*	−0.0015*	−0.0014	−0.0009*
	(2.688)	(2.268)	(1.931)	(2.143)
Party affiliation	−4.3281*	−7.3972*	−8.6354*	−4.7729*
	(4.200)	(4.337)	(3.941)	(5.085)
Chi-squared	55.96	97.01	104.02	77.01
Percentage of votes predicted correctly[c]	65.10	87.70	90.20	84.49
Percentage of votes predicted correctly (party affiliation omitted)[d]	48.80	50.90	55.70	51.70

Sources: *House and Senate votes: Congressional Quarterly Weekly Report*, vol. 33 (May 3, 1975), p. 949; vol. 33 (July 19, 1975), p. 1584; vol. 33 (September 13, 1975), p. 1972; vol. 33 (December 20, 1975), p. 2829; *oil production and consumption:* American Petroleum Institute, *Basic Petroleum Data Book*, vol. 2, tables 5b, 10b, and 12b (variables use the U.S. Energy Information Administration's 1975 data, and then standardize by 1970 U.S. Census of Population); *distillate fuel and electricity prices:* U.S. Department of Energy, *State Energy Fuel Prices by Major Economic Sector from 1960 through 1977*, table B-1, pp. 75–76, 95–96. Distillate prices are in cents per gallon in 1975; electricity prices are in dollars per kilowatt-hour in 1975.

*$p < .05$.

a. Upper figures in each column are the estimated logit coefficients. Figures in parentheses are t-statistics. Data for the first three independent variables are aggregated by states. The fourth, party affiliation, is a dummy specified: 1 = Democrat; 0 = Republican. The dichotomous dependent variables are specified: 1 = a vote for decontrol; 0 = a vote against decontrol.

b. Net consumption signifies consumption minus production.

c. These are the normalized percentages of prodecontrol votes predicted by the above models (that is, the percentages after subtracting the percentages that would be predicted in a model that had no explanatory variables, other than a constant): $\hat{p} - p_o / 1 - p_o$, where $\hat{p}$ is the overall percentage of correct predictions in the equation, and p_o is the percentage of predictions in an equation with no explanatory variables other than a constant.

d. The normalized percentages of prodecontrol votes predicted by the same models, excluding party affiliation as an explanatory variable.

Why did home-state energy characteristics not explain a larger proportion of congressional voting behavior? Much of the answer has to do with the fact that outside the oil-producing Southwest and some states in the Northeast, cohesive, bipartisan delegations were less common than might be expected. The House vote of July 23 on a key deregulation amendment is illustrative. If representatives had been preoccupied exclusively with local concerns or constituency preferences—or if such concerns were so readily identifiable as to be beyond dispute within delegations—one would expect much more solidarity at the regional or state level than the roll call showed. Instead, among representatives from the Pacific states, there was disunity: for every four who voted against

Table 2-5. *Logit Analysis of State Energy Attributes as Determinants of House Votes on Oil Decontrol, without Party Affiliation, 1975*[a]

Item	H.R. 4035 June 5 (381 votes)	H.R. 7014 July 23 (422 votes)	H. Res. 641 July 30 (417 votes)	S. 622 Dec. 15 (396 votes)
Net consumption of distillate fuel oil per capita[b]	−20.4818* (4.208)	−31.5530* (3.870)	−23.0985* (4.027)	−29.9441* (4.359)
Average distillate fuel oil price (residential)	−0.0024* (3.797)	−0.0014* (2.535)	−0.0012* (2.119)	−0.0014* (2.268)
Average price of electricity (residential)	−0.0002 (1.246)	−0.0004* (2.957)	−0.0003* (2.264)	−0.0002 (1.682)
Chi-squared	61.76	79.94	59.27	70.12
Percentage of votes predicted correctly[c]	49.20	24.10	36.80	45.40

Sources: *House and Senate votes: Congressional Quarterly Weekly Report*, vol. 33 (June 7, 1975), pp. 1198–99; vol. 33 (July 26, 1975), pp. 1642–43, 106H-107H; vol. 33 (August 2, 1975), pp. 1726–27; vol. 33 (December 20, 1975), pp. 2822–23; *oil production and consumption:* American Petroleum Institute, *Basic Petroleum Data Book*, vol. 2, tables 5b, 10b, and 12b (variables use the U.S. Energy Information Administration's 1975 data, and then standardize by 1970 U.S. Census of Population); *distillate fuel and electricity prices:* U.S. Department of Energy, *State Energy Fuel Prices by Major Economic Sector from 1960 through 1977*, table B-1, pp. 75–76, 95–96. Distillate prices are in cents per gallon in 1975; electricity prices are in dollars per kilowatt-hour in 1975.

*$p < .05$.

a. Upper figures in each column are the estimated logit coefficients. Figures in parentheses are t-statistics. Data for the independent variables in the equations are aggregated by states. The dichotomous dependent variables are specified: 1 = a vote for decontrol; 0 = a vote against decontrol.

b. Net consumption signifies consumption minus production.

c. These are the normalized percentages of prodecontrol votes predicted by the above models (that is, the percentages after subtracting the percentages that would be predicted in a model that had no explanatory variables, other than a constant): $\hat{p} - p_o / 1 - p_o$, where $\hat{p}$ is the overall percentage of correct predictions in the equation, and p_o is the percentage of predictions in an equation with no explanatory variables other than a constant.

deregulation, three voted in favor. The huge California contingent divided 24–18. The Middle West was almost evenly split, with some important states, such as Illinois, perfectly bifurcated. The Mountain states and the Southeast were more skewed but still far from internally unified. Within individual state delegations, about half lacked consensus inasmuch as a third or more of their members were at odds with immediate colleagues.

The positions of the members of Congress were systematically a function of their party affiliations, and correspondingly, of their ideologies (table 2-7). The statistical findings in tables 2-3 and 2-4 are consistent with this proposition. Simple bivariate correlations also dramatize it. When party is correlated with votes in the four House roll calls analyzed in table 2-3, for instance, coefficients ranging from $r = -.49$ ($p < .001$) to $r = -.67$ ($p < .001$) are obtained. Even stronger is the relationship attained by a somewhat more accurate indicator of ideological orientations, the Americans for Democratic Action's (ADA) ratings of members along a liberal-conservative continuum: using the ADA

Table 2-6. *Logit Analysis of State Energy Attributes as Determinants of Senate Votes on Oil Decontrol, without Party Affiliation, 1975*[a]

Item	S. 621 May 1 (83 votes)	H.R. 4035 July 16 (97 votes)	S. 1849 Sept. 10 (100 votes)	S. 622 Dec. 17 (98 votes)
Net consumption of distillate fuel oil per capita[b]	−26.1695* (2.058)	−32.4105* (2.566)	−31.8906* (2.640)	−32.5130* (2.569)
Average distillate fuel oil price (residential)	−0.0005 (0.428)	−0.0008 (0.688)	−0.0010 (0.893)	−0.0003 (0.248)
Average price of electricity (residential)	−0.0005 (1.759)	−0.0002 (0.621)	−0.0001 (0.262)	−0.0003 (0.916)
Chi-squared	17.96	22.83	23.18	23.47
Percentage of votes predicted correctly[c]	48.80	50.90	55.50	51.70

Sources: *House and Senate votes: Congressional Quarterly Weekly Report*, vol. 33 (May 3, 1975), p. 949; vol. 33 (July 19, 1975), p. 1584; vol. 33 (September 13, 1975), p. 1972; vol. 33 (December 20, 1975), p. 2829; *oil production and consumption:* American Petroleum Institute, *Basic Petroleum Data Book*, vol. 2, tables 5b, 10b, and 12b (variables use the U.S. Energy Information Administration's 1975 data, and then standardize by 1970 U.S. Census of Population); *distillate fuel and electricity prices:* U.S. Department of Energy, *State Energy Fuel Prices by Major Economic Sector from 1960 through 1977*, table B-1, pp. 75–76, 95–96. Distillate prices are in cents per gallon in 1975; electricity prices are in dollars per kilowatt-hour in 1975.

*$p < .05$.

a. Upper figures in each column are the estimated logit coefficients. Figures in parentheses are t-statistics. Data for the independent variables in the equations are aggregated by states. The dichotomous dependent variables are specified: 1 = a vote for decontrol; 0 = a vote against decontrol.

b. Net consumption signifies consumption minus production.

c. These are the normalized percentages of prodecontrol votes predicted by the above models (that is, the percentages after subtracting the percentages that would be predicted in a model that had no explanatory variables, other than a constant): $\hat{p} - p_o / 1 - p_o$, where $\hat{p}$ is the overall percentage of correct predictions in the equation, and p_o is the percentage of predictions in an equation with no explanatory variables other than a constant.

Table 2-7. *Correlations of Party and Ideology with House Votes on Oil Decontrol, 1975*[a]

Indicator	H.R. 4035 June 5 (381 votes)	H.R. 7014 July 23 (422 votes)	H. Res. 641 July 30 (417 votes)	S. 622 Dec 15 (396 votes)
Party[b]	−.67*	−.55*	−.56*	−.49*
Rating by Americans for Democratic Action[c]	−.72*	−.73*	−.70*	−.65*

Sources: *House and Senate votes: Congressional Quarterly Weekly Report*, vol. 33 (June 7, 1975), pp. 1198–99; vol. 33 (July 26, 1975), pp. 1642–43; vol. 33 (August 2, 1975), pp. 1726–27; and Americans for Democratic Action, *1975 Voting Record* (Washington, D.C.: ADA, 1976).

*$p < .01$ (two-tailed test).

a. Dichotomous dependent variable: 1 = a vote for decontrol; 0 = a vote against decontrol.

b. Dichotomous independent variable: 1 = Democrat; 0 = Republican.

c. Continuous independent variable: 0 (perfectly conservative) to 100 (perfectly liberal).

measure, the resulting coefficients range from $r = -.65$ ($p < .001$) to $r = -.72$ ($p < .001$).[124] With great regularity, representatives with the more liberal scores (liberal quotients based on general voting records) rejected decontrol; those with the more conservative ratings supported it.

124. It was not possible to include both party affiliation and ADA scores in the logit analyses in tables 2-3 and 2-4 because of the extremely high intercorrelation (multicollinearity) between these two independent variables. Separate Pearson correlations for the variables in each of the respective House votes are shown in table 2-7.

CHAPTER THREE

Deregulation of Natural Gas

NEAR THE END of the 1976 election campaign, Jimmy Carter put in writing a weighty promise to the governors of Texas, Oklahoma, and Louisiana. "First," Carter vowed, "I will work with the Congress, as the Ford administration has been unable to do, to deregulate new natural gas."[1] A few months later, when he entered office and his aides began fashioning the administration's energy program, deregulation of gas was deleted. Instead, the new president proposed to expand federal price controls for the immediate future. Eventually, after an eighteen-month legislative fracas touched off by his plan, a compromise emerged—the Natural Gas Policy Act of 1978 (NGPA), which turned out to be as problematical as the oil-pricing measure adopted three years before (the Energy Policy and Conservation Act).

Under the NGPA, the nation's premier heating fuel, natural gas, was slated for partial decontrol, with about half of all flowing gas to be turned loose from controls in 1985. But the law was so ungainly that six years after its enactment, Congress was still arguing about whether to permit the act to run its course. There was reason to believe that energy waste and inefficiency would persist even after the transition to a freer market or, worse, that the transition might prove too tumultuous to complete on schedule. No such quandary would have continued to hang over American energy policy if Carter had been able to do as president what he had pledged as a presidential candidate. But in 1977 any chance of

Parts of this chapter draw on my earlier essay, "Energy Policy and the Congress: The Politics of the Natural Gas Policy Act of 1978," *Public Policy*, vol. 28 (Fall 1980), pp. 491–543.

1. Carter's letter to the governors was dated October 19, 1976. *Congressional Quarterly Almanac*, vol. 34 (1978), p. 649.

moving swiftly toward complete market pricing of natural gas fizzled. What went wrong?

Events up to 1978

Unlike price controls on domestic crude oil, federal price regulation of the natural gas industry dates back a generation. The Natural Gas Act of 1938 ordered the Federal Power Commission (FPC) to establish rates for natural gas carried in interstate commerce for resale. At first, the commission regulated only the interstate pipeline companies that purchased gas from producers and transported it to local distributors. However, in 1954 the Supreme Court ruled, in *Phillips Petroleum Corp. v. Wisconsin*, that, according to the Natural Gas Act, sales by producers were "sales for resale" and thus were subject to the commission's jurisdiction. Now the commission would regulate the wellhead (producers') prices of gas sold across state lines. The FPC first responded by setting rates for producers on a company-by-company basis. But later, staggering under an unmanageable backlog of cases, the agency abandoned this approach, and, instead, set areawide ceiling prices, supposedly based on average costs of production in the various producing regions.

The areawide ceilings proved too low. Through the 1960s the average new contract price of gas sold to the interstate carriers slid below the average of unregulated in-state contracts and failed to keep pace with the gradually rising prices of other fuels.[2] The depressed price of interstate gas induced excess consumption, a decline in exploration and development, and unwillingness of producers to commit new finds to out-of-state markets.[3] At the end of the decade, shortages were developing outside the producing states.

The first signs of shortages, arriving when control of the Federal Power Commission was shifting to a Republican administration, prompted a frantic series of regulatory adjustments, climaxed by a decision to replace the cumbersome system of regional rate proceedings with a nationwide lid, which was successively lifted until prices for newly contracted interstate gas more than tripled. But despite the sharp de-

2. An illuminating analysis of this period is found in Paul W. MacAvoy and Robert S. Pindyck, *Price Controls and the Natural Gas Shortage* (Washington, D.C.: American Enterprise Institute, 1975), pp. 13–15.

3. Net domestic production of natural gas peaked in 1973 at 22.6 trillion cubic feet (tcf). Net production then declined until 1977, when it stabilized at 19.45 tcf. *Congressional Record* (September 11, 1978), p. 28649.

parture from past practice, the commission was unable to avert the severe gas curtailments that struck the Northeast and Midwest during the mid-1970s, wreaking economic dislocation and spurring demand for replacement fuels, especially expensive oil and gas imports.

Why the Federal Power Commission's new policies failed to restore adequate supplies, or at least failed to do so right away, became the subject of intense dispute. Some argued that the stimulus was too little too late and that producers remained reluctant to dedicate supplies to the regulated interstate market, since they were still fetching appreciably higher prices on intrastate contracts. Others contended that the rapid progression of higher prices granted from 1967 to 1976 tempted producers to withhold output in expectation of still higher rates, if not eventual decontrol. Still others attributed the shortfalls to the unpredictable direction of federal gas policy. Presidents Nixon and Ford, as well as Carter in his electoral campaign, had called for fundamental revisions in the pricing system. Deregulation bills, dormant in Congress since the mid-1950s, were surfacing again and receiving serious attention. Meanwhile, prices were being raised and regulatory requirements modified, but all at the Federal Power Commission's discretion. No one could be sure that the commission, or the courts, might not reverse the trend later.

Although these views were aired extensively in the Ninety-second, Ninety-third, and Ninety-fourth Congresses, it was the Ninety-fifth that debated them most fully. Gas curtailments had worsened every year since 1971, but in the bitter cold winter of 1976–77, a full-blown national crisis was on hand; thousands suffered as gas shutoffs closed down factories, schools, and residential furnaces.[4] In the weeks following this emergency, a newly inaugurated president placed before Congress a plan in which gas-pricing reform was assigned the highest priority (as opposed to the major energy initiative of the two preceding administrations, in which gas pricing was a secondary concern).

Carter's National Energy Plan stuffed the legislative hoppers with proposals ranging from energy taxes and conservation programs to acceleration of industrial conversion to coal and reorganization of electric utility ratemaking. Recognition that the nation's apparent energy deficit could best be narrowed by linking prices of depletable energy resources

4. Gas curtailments during the winter of 1977 caused 8,900 plant shutdowns and periods of unemployment for about 547,000 workers in the East and Midwest. *Congressional Quarterly Almanac*, vol. 33 (1977), p. 648.

more nearly to their full replacement costs was a common element of some of these proposals. The plan's section on natural gas, however, incorporated this notion grudgingly at best and generally sought to remedy the natural gas problem through more regulation rather than less.

Whatever the reason for the continuing scarcity of natural gas—producer uncertainty, speculative withholding, or only the dual market's perverse incentives—the administration's energy programmers concluded that a statutory extension of price ceilings would ameliorate the shortage. The energy plan's gas provisions were as follows. The extant federal cap of $1.42 per thousand cubic feet (mcf) would be reset at $1.75 per mcf, enabling national rates for newly produced gas to better approximate prevailing prices of the uncontrolled gas sold inside the producing states. To guarantee availability of the fuel nationwide, however, the plan also recommended abolishing the interstate-intrastate distinction; federal controls would now apply to both sectors. The Federal Power Commission already permitted producers to set higher rates for newly produced gas than for gas flowing from existing wells. Now, production qualifying for the maximum price, so-called new gas, would be stringently delineated; to tighten the commission's traditional method of vintaging gas, the National Energy Plan added precise depth and spacing standards for gas wells classified as new. According to the plan, this would stimulate additional discoveries, rather than mere in-fill drilling into existing reservoirs. Under the complex definition, new gas was output from Outer Continental Shelf leases granted after 1977 or from wells in any onshore reservoir discovered after 1977 that were two and one-half miles or more from the nearest existing well, or at least 1,000 feet deeper than the deepest existing well within a two-and-one-half-mile radius.[5] Finally, the price ceiling of $1.75 for new gas would be allowed to rise in step with the Btu equivalent of the average refiner acquisition cost of domestic crude oil. But since the prices of domestic crude oil were subject to controls (and the National Energy Plan explicitly did not propose to tie gas rates to the projected higher prices of its crude oil equalization tax), gas prices were to be kept well below market-clearing levels.

In August 1977 the House of Representatives accepted the Carter natural gas policy with some minor modifications. These included a more liberal definition of new onshore gas, now broadened to include

5. Executive Office of the President, Energy Policy and Planning, *The National Energy Plan* (Ballinger, 1977), p. 53.

output from new wells drilled beyond the plan's locational limits in existing reservoirs, and any output from a newly discovered reservoir. The Senate, however, took a different line. In early October 1977 it adopted a bill leaving the intrastate market exempt from federal regulation and deregulating over a two-year period the price of most interstate gas sold or delivered for the first time after 1976.[6] The Natural Gas Policy Act, hammered out in laborious negotiations that began in 1977 and lasted through the better part of 1978, was a composite of the drastically disparate House and Senate measures.

The Natural Gas Policy Act

From the Senate bill, the Natural Gas Policy Act acquired the goal of gradually releasing newly discovered gas from price controls. The volume of gas involved remains the subject of considerable speculation. Estimates range from a high of 60 percent to as little as 40 percent of total supply in 1985.[7] Whatever the volume, serious problems with the law soon arose from the complicated, segmental decontrol it authorized and from the dilatory phase in of decontrol.

The legislation codified twenty classifications of natural gas, designated according to geological source and location, well distances and depths, dates and destinations of first sales, volumes produced, types of contracts, proprietorship of producing land, and other parameters. One category—encompassing methane gas from coal seams and gas derived from geopressurized brine, Devonian shale, or new wells deeper than 15,000 feet—was to be deregulated within one year of enactment. While this so-called high-cost component was decontrolled in December 1979, other categories were scheduled for decontrol much later—some in 1985, others in 1987—and still others not at all. Excluding the high-cost genre, interim price trajectories were legislated in 1978 for all types of gas, on the assumption that gas prices could be programmed neatly to match oil prices, expected to be around $15 a barrel midway through the 1980s.

SUPPRESSING PRICES. In 1979 the Iranian revolution sent the world price of crude oil rocketing from $13 to $35 per barrel by the start of

6. The Senate bill (hereafter referred to as the Pearson-Bentsen bill) called for regulation of offshore gas only through 1982. Onshore gas was made subject to a ceiling of $2.48 per mcf, expiring two years after enactment. *Congressional Quarterly Weekly Report*, vol. 35 (October 8, 1977), p. 2138.

7. Milton Russell, "Overview of Policy Issues: A Preliminary Assessment," in Edward J. Mitchell, ed., *The Deregulation of Natural Gas* (Washington, D.C.: American Enterprise Institute, 1983), p. 10.

1981. The initial consequence of the unexpected oil-price blowup was to leave average gas prices lagging far behind. As late as the spring of 1982, natural gas on a Btu basis was still slightly under 40 percent of the average crude oil price, roughly the same percentage that prevailed at the NGPA's inception and far beneath the point in oil equivalency (estimated at 70 percent) needed to clear gas markets.[8] In short, the immediate effect of the legislation was to keep natural gas relatively underpriced.

More recently, prices of crude oil and natural gas began to converge rapidly.[9] The world oil surfeit on one side and various forces pushing up the cost of gas on the other combined to close the gap that had existed until 1982. After that, overall underpricing in relation to oil seemed to be a thing of the past, but distortions induced by regulation persisted. Some were familiar, others novel. Price disparities between interstate and intrastate markets remained. But alongside them arose something even more disturbing: signs that natural gas prices, artificially repressed for decades, could swing from submarket to supramarket levels.

While the Natural Gas Policy Act placed certain classes of gas on fairly high price paths, others were locked into extremely low ones. In particular, a wide breach was carved between old gas, committed to interstate commerce before 1977, and various newer vintages. As of mid-1982, for instance, the average price of old interstate gas stood at less than one-half the average for new gas, and less than one-fifth the average for high-cost gas.[10] Pipeline companies with access to large inventories of old gas have enjoyed a decided advantage over carriers contracting for the more expensive (post-1977) varieties. The diverse endowments of cheap gas have spread the burden of higher gas prices unevenly among end users. Local distributors on pipelines with "deep cushions" of inexpensive gas have offered their customers cut-rate supplies, but systems with shallow cushions have been forced to pass through their much higher acquisition costs.

The net effect has been not only inequitable geographically, but also

8. Ibid., pp. 10, 11, 15. See also John W. Jimison and Lawrence Kumins, *The Natural Gas Policy Act: Reform Revisited* (Washington, D.C.: Congressional Research Service, 1981), pp. 7, 12.

9. Between 1978 and 1981 the average price for home-heating gas rose from $2.63 to $4.56 per mcf. In 1982, however, the price hit $5.82—near parity with the equivalent for no. 6 residual fuel oil. *Congressional Quarterly Weekly Report*, vol. 40 (October 30, 1982), pp. 2758–59; and vol. 41 (March 5, 1983), p. 444.

10. Lawrence Mosher, "Rising Natural Gas Prices—A Hard Lesson in Regulatory Miscalculation," *National Journal*, vol. 15 (January 1, 1983), p. 25.

deleterious to energy efficiency. High-cushion pipelines have gained customers whose usage of natural gas is less valued. And some low-cushion systems have forced customers whose gas usage was more valued not into conservation, but into relinquishing gas for alternate fuels.[11] Moreover, the interstate market—the recipient of the largest share of low-cost gas—would keep this edge late into the 1980s, since old interstate gas is the main stock that stays ineligible for decontrol unless current law is amended.[12] Thus, according to Department of Energy estimates, 53 percent of all interstate domestic deliveries will still be price regulated after 1985.[13] Consumers in the interstate sector, whose usage of natural gas was subsidized by price controls for a quarter century preceding the NGPA, will continue to be favored with below-average prices (deducting transmission and distribution markups) until the supply of old interstate gas finally runs out.

MARKET DISORDER. An important reason for the recent movement of gas prices up to oil equivalency was a tendency toward "category creep" —the gradual reclassification of gas by shifting production from lower to higher, more profitably priced categories. But another cause related, again, to unequal price cushions among pipelines. Shortly after adoption of the 1978 legislation, gas purchasers began bidding prices up to the maximum allowed by law. For certain categories, such as gas already deregulated, the sky became the limit. In the spring of 1982, for instance, the price of deregulated high-cost gas averaged around $7 per mcf, far above the mean for other gas sources. Evidence suggested that pipeline companies brimming with cheap price-controlled gas, which could be rolled in with more costly supplies, were in a position to bid extravagantly for uncontrolled gas, thus contributing significantly to its zooming price.[14]

By 1982 concern had arisen that, as partial decontrol unfolded, the inordinate fees for certain gas might ripple out across gas prices generally by triggering indefinite escalator clauses in long-term contracts.

---

11. Russell, "Overview," pp. 23–24; and Robert C. Means, "The Intrastate Pipelines and the Natural Gas Policy Act," in Mitchell, ed., *Deregulation of Natural Gas*, pp. 83–84.

12. Means, "Intrastate Pipelines," pp. 82–83, 90–92, 93.

13. Catherine Good Abbott and Stephen A. Watson, "Pitfalls on the Road to Decontrol: Lessons from the Natural Gas Policy Act of 1978," in Mitchell, ed., *Deregulation of Natural Gas*, p. 58.

14. Abbot and Watson, "Pitfalls on the Road to Decontrol," pp. 58–62; *Natural Gas Policy and Regulatory Issues*, Hearings before the Senate Committee on Energy and Natural Resources, 97 Cong. 2 sess. (Government Printing Office, 1982), p. 150.

(Indefinite escalators base the price in a contract on other contracts in the same vicinity. A common form is a most-favored-nation clause, keying the price to, say, the average of the three highest prices in the area.)[15] Later on, this fear of a sharp general price spike, set off by a chain reaction among contracts with indefinite escalators, was to prove exaggerated. But meanwhile, the price of gas in some areas did overshoot its market-clearing plateau, usually recognized as the burner-tip price of residual fuel oil, even with an excess supply.[16]

Up to a point, the contracts problem could not be considered, strictly speaking, a flaw in the legislation, but had to be considered a separate issue, which lawmakers in 1978 had overlooked. But not entirely. Continued price controls had influenced the nature of long-term contracts. By extending controls, hence constraining pipeline companies from being able to negotiate chiefly on the immediate price they paid for regulated gas supplies, the NGPA motivated the pipelines to compete for gas and sign contracts on other terms, such as oil parity, indefinite escalation, and take-or-pay clauses that would kick in after controls were lifted.[17] Further, the law's elaborate stepladder pricing system, in which some sets of gas qualified for very high incentive prices while others didn't, invited a tendency among producers to drill in the high-priced categories (for example, deep wells). The system also motivated pipelines to bid vigorously for this gas, thus bringing on stream a more expensive mix than anyone had expected at the time of the act's passage, and perhaps more expensive than if all natural gas—old and new, deep and shallow, onshore and offshore—had been decontrolled in 1977.

It might be thought that prices surpassing equilibrium levels scored extra gains in conservation. For natural gas, however, no such consolation was assured. Some gas utilities began experiencing substantial load losses as their important bulk heat customers switched to fuel oil, instead of investing in energy-saving methods at the marginal cost of gas. Fear of falling industrial loads would drive pipelines and distribution companies to allocate a larger share of system costs to remaining customers, often resulting in higher gas bills primarily for residential and

15. It has been estimated that about two-thirds of flowing gas is subject to most-favored-nation and similar price redetermination clauses. Daniel L. White, "The Coming Shock of Natural Gas Price Decontrol," *Public Utilities Fortnightly*, vol. 110 (October 28, 1982), p. 25.

16. *Congressional Quarterly Weekly Report*, vol. 40 (October 30, 1982), p. 2759.

17. This subtle point is brought out in Abbott and Watson, "Pitfalls on the Road to Decontrol," p. 66.

small commercial users, whose demand behavior is the least elastic.[18] The problem was accentuated by take-or-pay provisions in contracts that required pipeline companies to take delivery on, or pay for, as much as 90 percent of their long-range volumes. Wholesalers pinned down with these agreements became especially worried about the financial exposure that would result if their marginal sales—chiefly, gas going under industrial boilers—were to sag. Even more basically, gas prices flying up chaotically raised the possibility of a return to the status quo ante—that is, a political backlash, followed by full reimposition of price controls.[19]

In an eloquent defense of the NGPA, delivered before the Senate on September 11, 1978, the bill's floor manager, the late Henry M. Jackson, Democrat of Washington, assured listeners that the act signified a vast improvement over existing law.[20] He was right, in a sense. The legislation's unification of previously independent inter- and intrastate gas markets and its incentives for increased production, principally of hard-to-extract new gas, were to improve the availability of gas. Quickly, the country's gas shortage was turned into a "bubble." But Jackson also claimed that the law would deal "in a definitive way" with the problem of natural gas pricing.[21] On this point, he was mistaken. More trouble lay in store, including, for a while, the ultimate disorder—prices sprinting wildly in a supply surplus. The Natural Gas Policy Act of 1978 may have been the best gas measure one could expect from the Ninety-fifth Congress. Indeed, it may have been the only type of outcome possible, given the political climate on Capitol Hill. That realization, however, is scarcely comforting, considering the act's shortcomings. Why, after spending so much time and effort on natural gas policy throughout the 1970s, did Congress finish by creating more confusion?

Interest Groups

Because income flows worth scores of billions of dollars are at stake in the politics of natural gas pricing, writers on the subject instinctively stress that particular economic interests in gas regulation overshadow broader partisan or ideological influences. This theme permeates most

18. *Congressional Quarterly Weekly Report*, vol. 40 (October 30, 1982), p. 2759; and Russell, "Overview of Policy Issues" pp. 9, 23.

19. U.S. Department of Energy, Office of Policy, Planning, and Analysis, *A Study of Alternatives to the Natural Gas Policy Act of 1978* (GPO, 1981), p. 12.

20. *Congressional Record* (September 11, 1978), p. 28633.

21. Ibid.

discussions of why the NGPA was adopted instead of fuller and faster decontrol. Like many other federal regulatory programs, the act was seen as a measure devised by and for special interests. Although one could invent about as many variations on the theme as there are lobbies active on the natural gas issue, the principal rendition circulating among liberal critics at the time of the act's passage was that the major oil- and gas-producing firms themselves had cunningly concocted the statute.

The Industry's Lobby

The natural gas industry's most vocal participants in the 1977–78 debate were the small- and medium-sized independents. Their principal trade association, the Independent Petroleum Association of America, promptly called the compromise gas bill a blueprint for disaster.[22] Similar denunciations were not heard among most of the large oil and gas producers. Indeed, some even expressed guarded support. This fairly muted response by the majors was read by some observers as a sign of big oil's complicity in forging the compromise. Thus, Senator James G. Abourezk, Democrat of South Dakota, who led the assault on the bill from the Left, immediately accused Congress of perpetrating "legalized forcible rape" of the American consumer "for the sole benefit of the titans of the oil and gas industry."[23]

One might wonder why, if the titans had played such a winning hand, Congress elected to delay and complicate the process of deregulation, since whatever else producers of all sizes clamored for individually, speedy decontrol was what they wanted unanimously. To this, however, big oil conspiracy theorists would reply, first, that the bill's complexities hindered small producers but not large ones and, second, that much of the complexity reflected a need of the framers to veil their plot behind a smoke screen of consumer safeguards. The surest way to make deregulation politically permissible—that is, to avoid a public outcry over any sudden price jump in the short term—was to slip consumers small doses of the medicine over a long period, rather than force them to take the bitter pill all at once. As Abourezk explained, "That, of course, is the point of the phased aspect of natural gas deregulation. It is the frog-boiled method, fostered by the notion that a 10 percent increase each

22. "Statement of the Independent Petroleum Association of America," San Francisco, California, May 21, 1978, p. 2.

23. "Abourezk Attacks So-Called Compromise on Gas Deregulation Proposal," *Abourezk News Release*, Washington, D.C., May 21, 1978, p. 2.

year until 1985 will go by virtually unnoticed, until the great day comes when total deregulation will be achieved without complaint."[24]

What Really Happened

Viewing the Natural Gas Policy Act as another case of congressional capitulation to the giant oil and gas companies is a perspective not supported by the facts. Examining the proposition is important, however, since it can demonstrate a lot about the relative influence, not only of producers, but of other interest groups downstream of them—pipeline companies, distributors, large industrial customers, and so on.

DISADVANTAGES FOR LARGE PRODUCERS. The costs of complying with the NGPA's requirements could prove especially burdensome to minor producers. The expansion of price controls to include intrastate markets, in which many independents focused their exploration and sold most of their product, was particularly unwelcome. Now, in previously unregulated onshore sites, wildcatters would find themselves subjected to the bill's involved system of price determinations for most newly drilled wells. Prospectors also faced other serious restrictions, such as a provision sharply limiting future price increases for old gas even as existing contracts expired or rolled over. The largest energy companies, on the other hand, were less perturbed by these aspects of the legislation. Increasingly, their domestic drilling activity would center offshore and in Alaska, where gas discoveries are often a by-product of oil exploration and, in any event, flow chiefly to the interstate sector. Such interests were mostly unaffected by the features of the Natural Gas Policy Act that most troubled the gas industry's smaller firms—namely, new regulations governing onshore wells and sales within producing states.

But these considerations hardly justify an inference that the act favored big producers. Other key sections of the statute touched these companies directly, and adversely. The rules pertaining to new gas from the Outer Continental Shelf were the worst restrictions. There, the NGPA stipulated that both old and newly discovered reservoirs remain permanently under price controls if the drilling took place in tracts leased before April 20, 1977. For several majors, this meant that deregulation would not cover most, perhaps all, of their current offshore drilling opportunities. This restriction was so onerous that no one was more excited than the large producers when the Reagan administration

24. Ibid.

began considering basic revisions in the law in 1981.

CONSUMER PROTECTION. Further, there was nothing bogus or duplic-
itous about efforts in the gas bill to shield residential consumers from
steeper prices. Chief among the presumed safeguards, apart from the
slow, segmental phase in of deregulation, was a provision for incremental
pricing. The incremental pricing title, not to be confused with marginal-
cost pricing of local gas or electric utility rates, in the NGPA sought to
establish a federal regulatory procedure so that a larger share of increased gas costs would be shifted to industrial boilers. The mechanism
entailed an intricate accounting system, designed to force pipeline companies and distributors to pass a surcharge onto certain low-priority
users, theoretically resulting in savings for residential customers at the
retail level. The title was never implemented in its entirety. Congress
partially retracted it, after becoming aware that incremental pricing
scarcely provided residential users with any real protection, since
surcharges on boiler-fuel users were inducing reconversions to coal and
fuel oil for bulk heat, thus saddling households with higher, instead of
lower, gas bills.

Though incremental pricing failed to benefit consumers as planned,
its original intent was unquestionably to do so, and the designers advanced a sophisticated rationale for their plan.[25] Their theory was that
by overcharging industrial users, great leverage would be exerted on the
pipelines to shop for the lowest prices among producers. The industrials,
unlike residential customers, were supposedly in a position to restrain a
pipeline company's charges by threatening to shorten or discontinue
high-volume, year-round contracts. Furthermore, the legislators argued
that without this "back pressure," the pipelines would indiscriminately
bid up producer prices. With pipeline rates still regulated after 1985, the
companies would continue to maximize revenues by maximizing
throughput. Vigorous competition to purchase supplies was expected to
drive up prices at the wellhead once controls there were lifted. So, incremental pricing signified more than lip service to consumer welfare. In
principle, incremental pricing was meant to check wellhead prices—
which was precisely why its proponents insisted upon the scheme once

25. Interview with William Demerest, majority counsel, Subcommittee on Energy and
Power of the House Committee on Interstate and Foreign Commerce, Washington, D.C.,
August 4, 1978. See also "Joint Explanatory Statement of the Committee on Conference:
Economic Analysis of [the Natural Gas] Conference Agreement," House Committee on
Interstate and Foreign Commerce, 95 Cong. 1 sess., July 31, 1978, pp. A5–A6.

they conceded to the gradual elimination of direct field price controls.

TACTICAL RESTRAINT. There were also severe limitations on the style and extent of the lobbying led by the large oil and gas corporations. One constraint was their own concern that the cause of deregulation could suffer from a conspicuous campaign waged by big oil. With public suspicion of the oil and gas lobby still strong, zealous intervention by the industry's leading firms could backfire, provoking another round of legislative recriminations and investigations. The eight largest companies were in the throes of the massive antitrust case that the Federal Trade Commission had opened in the wake of the 1973 oil embargo. Several of them were also implicated in a far-reaching Department of Energy inquiry into violations of petroleum price controls. In 1975 the big firms had watched Congress strip large producers of the oil depletion allowance—a move once considered nearly impossible. Later that year, Congress again considered the unthinkable—a measure requiring divestitures by the vertically integrated giants, which was turned back in the Senate by an uncomfortably small margin, 45–54. Though the political atmosphere seemed slightly less charged two years later, Congress was still unreceptive to importunate lobbying by big oil. Congressional reluctance to propitiate the majors was evident again in mid-1977, for example, when the Senate added terms to the Outer Continental Shelf Lands Act that were disadvantageous to big offshore leaseholders.

The oil and gas industry also remembered the setbacks that had resulted from excessive industry pressure during previous gas deregulation battles. In 1956 both houses of Congress had adopted legislation gutting the *Phillips* decision by exempting most producers from the Federal Power Commission's jurisdiction. But with the disclosure that the Superior Oil Company of California had apparently attempted to bribe a senator, President Eisenhower felt compelled to veto the bill, citing the bribery incident as an "arrogant" affront to "the integrity of governmental processes."[26] Two years later, a measure to exempt producers was again introduced, this time with the president's full support. The bill died in committee, however, after a *Washington Post* story told of a $100-a-plate dinner organized by Texas oilmen in "appreciation" of the House Republican leadership's efforts on the bill's behalf.[27] More recent experience with pressure politics—in particular, attempts to sway members of Congress through generous campaign gifts, legal and oth-

26. *Congressional Quarterly Almanac*, vol. 12 (1956), p. 472.
27. *Congressional Quarterly Almanac*, vol. 14 (1958), p. 231.

erwise—had also produced mixed results. One of the Seven Sisters, Gulf, was caught red-handed in 1972, having unlawfully contributed tens of thousands of dollars. Moreover, the contributions did not seem to deliver consistently the votes they were supposed to secure. For example, in an important roll call on a 1974 emergency energy bill, vetoed by President Nixon because it contained requirements for an oil-price rollback, five of the thirteen senators who had reportedly received large sums in 1972 from executives of the top nine oil companies voted to override.[28]

Consequently, inasmuch as the larger firms renewed their drive for more favorable natural gas legislation in 1977–78, they resorted increasingly to circuitous tactics, such as attempts to mobilize allied interests at the grass-roots level, rather than badgering members of Congress directly. Through a coordinating organization named the Natural Gas Supply Committee, third parties at the state and district levels were urged to exert influence on their representatives.

THE REFORM COALITION'S RISE AND FALL. This strategy became feasible because, for the first time, an extraordinary collection of outside groups previously uncommitted, or even partial to price controls, now sided with the gas producers. In earlier debates, the usual proregulation phalanx of labor and consumer organizations had been joined by most mayors and governors, leading newspapers, the coal industry, public utilities who surmised that low prices would stimulate consumption and, hence, wider rate bases, numerous industrial users, commercial customers, and agricultural interests reliant on gas for feedstocks. This time, key farm groups, and the principal trade associations representing commercial-industrial purchasers, were convinced that a reliable supply even at high deregulated prices was preferable to continuing shortfalls at low controlled prices. The National Coal Association, realizing that rising gas prices could deepen coal's penetration of the bulk-heat market, now stood foursquare for prompt decontrol. So did the National Governors Conference, on a 34–5 vote. Media opinion leaders, including the *Washington Post* and the *New York Times*, sounded increasingly sympathetic. Adding their names to the coalition were some surprising entries. The NAACP, for instance, moved into the producing industry's corner, noting that price regulation, shortages, and unemployment were causally related.[29] Finally, the oil and gas industry, from wellhead to burner tip,

28. John L. Moore, ed., *Continuing Energy Crisis in America* (Washington, D.C.: CQ Press, 1975), p. 90.

29. Richard Corrigan, "The NAACP and National Energy Policy," *National Journal*, vol. 10 (March 18, 1978), p. 438.

was solidly united. Stuck with the huge costs of underutilized capacity during the chronic curtailments of the mid-1970s, pipeline companies and distributors closed ranks with producers, convinced that deregulation was the only sure way to replenish supplies.

One might suppose that a lobby composed of such a broad spectrum of interests would have scored nothing but decisive victories in Congress. In fact, although the coalition could claim some success as time wore on, the Natural Gas Supply Committee's most critical test came early in the legislative struggle—and there it lost.

When the Carter administration announced its National Energy Plan in April 1977, the oil and gas industry learned, to its dismay, that the president was proposing not a program of deregulation as his earlier campaign statements had suggested, but indefinite controls extending to all sectors, intrastate as well as interstate. The energy plan's gas pricing conditions were so disagreeable to almost all producers that the industry's initial priority was to knock out the whole proposal before it could gain headway in Congress and, however sweetened by compromise, become law. To do this, the gas lobbyists had to strike a mortal blow in the House of Representatives, where deliberations on the National Energy Plan would begin. Lobbying activity throughout the late spring and early summer of 1977 zeroed in on swing votes in the House Interstate and Foreign Commerce Committee, which held jurisdiction over gas regulatory matters. Nineteen of the forty-three committee members were considered worthwhile targets, and eight of these were singled out for special emphasis.

Yet when the showdown came, on July 14, the committee rejected deregulation, choosing instead to report the National Energy Plan's approach. Only seven of the nineteen supposed industry sympathizers dissented from this decision, and among the eight most-lobbied members, only three did. The industry did not fare much better on the House floor. On August 3, a deregulation amendment cosponsored by Representative Robert C. Krueger, Democrat of Texas, Clarence J. Brown, Jr., Republican of Ohio, and Timothy E. Wirth, Democrat of Colorado, was beaten back, in favor of a slightly modified version of the administration's plan.[30]

30. The defeated deregulation amendment, referred to throughout this chapter as the Krueger-Brown bill, defined new gas as gas from newly discovered reservoirs or gas newly sold and delivered if not already under long-term contract. New gas onshore was to be decontrolled after April 20, 1978; new gas offshore, after April 20, 1982.

Later, industry forces did recover in the Senate a good deal of the ground they had lost in the House. In the fall, after a bruising Senate floor fight, the proponents of decontrol managed to ram through a measure crafted to their liking by Senators James B. Pearson, Republican of Kansas, and Lloyd M. Bentsen, Democrat of Texas. But the earlier defeat in the House proved fatal. For months, conferees had to search for a formula that would reconcile two incompatible policies—the Pearson-Bentsen deregulation bill passed by the Senate and the extension of price controls originally approved by the House.

In the end, the compromise that tried to fuse together these polar opposites left the Natural Gas Supply Committee unable to take a clear position.[31] Previously unified blocs in the industry's camp were now split. The farm lobby, for instance, found itself torn between the American Farm Bureau Federation, which decided to oppose the bill, and the National Grange, which backed it. Similar cracks developed among gas-purchasing manufacturers. Within the gas industry, the consensus that had prevailed in 1977 was shattered. The American Gas Association, representing large interstate pipelines, chose to endorse the bill. Clearly, some of these carriers recognized that they might acquire in the NGPA the best of both worlds, increased consignments of gas to the interstate sector, but without the instant fly-up in prices expected under quick, complete decontrol. But the gas association's endorsement belied profound differences of opinion among the pipeline companies, depending on their service areas, contractual arrangements, vertical integration, and so on. Among independent producers, the Independent Petroleum Association of America condemned the compromise, but the Independent Gas Producers' Committee applauded it. (The Independent Gas Producers represented operators who were drilling at depths below 15,000 feet, and whose production therefore qualified for instant decontrol.) The leading oil and gas companies went in different directions. Some—such as Standard Oil of Indiana, Sun Oil, Amoco, Conoco, Marathon, Getty, and Pennzoil—affirmed their opposition. Others—Exxon, Gulf, Shell, Mobil, Arco, Phillips, and Union Oil of California—either remained neutral or professed mild approval.[32]

---

31. Richard Corrigan, "Natural Gas Vote Is Symbolic Carter Test," *National Journal*, vol. 19 (September 9, 1978), p. 1426.

32. *Congressional Record* (September 11, 1978), p. 28644; *Congressional Record* (September 12, 1978), p. 28864; and *Congressional Quarterly Weekly Report*, vol. 36 (September 16, 1978), p. 2453.

Some big companies that supported (or, rather, chose not to fight) the natural gas compromise did so for reasons peripheral to the substance of the legislation. Several in this group had interests so varied and complex that a strong stand against the bill, for all its shortcomings, would have been rash. Although all gas producers stood to gain enormously from faster, more liberal deregulation of field prices than was contemplated under the natural gas bill, some companies were much less sensitive than others to the act's prolongation of controls. Many big, fully integrated companies could shift profits from price-controlled wellheads to uncontrolled downstream product lines, such as petrochemicals. Also, in the event of continued shortages, the multinationals were in a position to compensate for lower profits from conventional domestic gas production by being the suppliers of high-priced substitutes—liquefied natural gas, synthetic natural gas, and, of course, imported oil. Such considerations hardly inspired the majors to greet the new law enthusiastically, but resistance seemed increasingly quixotic, especially as prospects for a much more favorable bill evaporated.

Several of the largest firms stood to lose more from a brawl with the administration over its long-sought gas compromise than they could conceivably gain from defeating the bill. Given the scope of their operations, and thus the many spheres in which Department of Energy decisions would affect their interests, these companies took care not to antagonize the administration gratuitously. Exxon, for example, could not easily assail the NGPA—a bill on which the secretary of energy had staked his reputation—and then return confidently to the department for, say, another $120 million federal subsidy like that spent on the company's coal-to-oil pilot plant in Baytown, Texas.

Conclusion

The architects of the 1978 bill succeeded in wooing an assortment of interested parties by extending to them selective benefits, both inside the legislation and apart from it. In the years following enactment, some of these groups—for example, deep-gas producers, stripper well owners, lucky pipelines, and so forth—became entrenched clients. Indeed, their dependency on the regulatory apparatus that was created became a serious roadblock to subsequent reform.

However, the Natural Gas Policy Act was certainly not the brainchild of the business interests that it regulates. The salient point about the role of the oil and gas lobby in the legislative confrontation of 1977–78 is this: the industry went into battle with a united front and a definite preference; swift and thorough removal of price controls was what it wanted. But the industry came away divided and, for the most part, disappointed; slow, sectoral decontrol was what it got.

Public Opinion

Legislative behavior is influenced by the desire of members of Congress to be reelected. When the electorate's signals are clear, they are hard to ignore. But, as in the debate on oil pricing two years earlier, popular attitudes on gas deregulation in 1977 were less transparent than commonly supposed.

The fanfare accompanying the announcement of Carter's energy program aroused expectations that the government would do more than proselytize about "the moral equivalent of war." As the months went by, impatience mounted over legislative delay, and Congress, not the administration, was faulted.[33] The mood, however, was not easy to interpret in a concrete sense. Although voters wanted Congress to act on the energy problem, they continued to consider the problem fairly unimportant. In the spring of 1977, the president's various televised appeals had managed to convince 35 percent of the public that energy was one of the country's most pressing issues. But the following winter, only 20 percent rated energy as a top problem, and by late August 1978, the sentiment was down to 17 percent.[34]

What is more, even if voters viewed Congress, the institution, as dilatory and evasive on the energy issue, this did not mean that most members of Congress, as individuals, were being tarred with the same brush. It is possible that a few senators, whose seats were up in 1978, chose to climb aboard the natural gas compromise to deflect accusations of having obstructed progress toward a national energy policy. But in general, support for the NGPA among members seemed to have little to do with whether they were up for reelection. In the decisive Senate roll call of September 27, 1978, for instance, among the members who were in the midst of election campaigns, nineteen voted for the bill (59 percent), but thirteen voted against it (41 percent). This was not appre-

33. CBS News/*New York Times* poll, August 1977; CBS News/*New York Times* poll, January 1978; and Dick Kirschten, "Turning the Public Off," *National Journal*, vol. 10 (August 5, 1978), p. 1296.
34. Kirschten, "Turning the Public Off," p. 1296.

ciably different from the way the remaining senators broke out: thirty-eight members who were not, so to speak, endangered species voted yea (57 percent), and twenty-nine (43 percent) voted nay.[35] Finally, though the public seemed to demand some sort of legislated solution, what sort of solution was not at all clear.

Ambiguities abounded. On one hand, surveys regularly showed widespread approval of the president's handling of energy policy as a whole.[36] On the other hand, several recommendations in the National Energy Plan, many of which implied a tighter federal regulatory grip, ran against the grain of mass opinion. The prevailing view on economic regulation now favored fewer controls rather than more. For example, a CBS poll taken in January 1978 discovered that 58 percent of those interviewed agreed with the statement, "The government has gone too far in regulating business and interfering with the free enterprise system." In 1964 only 42 percent had replied that way to a similar query.[37] Moreover, the public had finally begun to recognize that government regulation of energy prices was at least partially responsible for shortages. Seven out of every ten respondents in a CBS survey during April 1977 held this view.[38]

At the same time, attitudes on the narrower question of whether to deregulate natural gas were especially confusing in at least two respects. First, they appeared unstable. A Harris survey in February 1977, for instance, turned up a 51 percent majority endorsing a hypothetical new federal law that would gradually deregulate gas over a twenty-six-month

35. There is no record of how the House divided on the Natural Gas Policy Act because the House ultimately voted on this measure along with the rest of the 1978 energy legislation all at once. The House roll call of October 13, 1978, which will be used elsewhere in this chapter, came on a procedural question, which, however, was a clear test of House sentiment on the natural gas bill. See *Congressional Quarterly Weekly Report*, vol. 36 (October 21, 1978), pp. 3092–93. The vote involved a crucial motion by Representative Richard Bolling, Democrat of Missouri, the effect of which was to keep the gas conference report in a package with the other (often less controversial) parts of the overall energy bill. By ensuring a single vote on the energy package as a whole, rather than permitting roll calls on separate sections as was the case on the Senate side, the prospects for House passage were greatly enhanced. If a separate vote had been held on the NGPA, that portion of the National Energy Act might well have been dumped.

36. *Gallup Opinion Index*, Report 143 (June 1977), p. 14; Richard Corrigan, "Higher Prices: Problem or Solution?" *National Journal*, vol. 9 (July 2, 1977), p. 1050; CBS News/*New York Times* poll, August 1977, results of a Harris poll, reported in James T. Wooten, "Carter Making Plea on Energy to Public," *New York Times*, November 8, 1977.

37. CBS News/*New York Times* poll, January 1978.

38. CBS News/*New York Times* poll, April 1977.

period.[39] Harris reported a majority of 56 percent favoring decontrol when the question was prefaced with the comment: "Many people in the energy field agree that deregulating oil and natural gas prices would encourage companies to explore for and develop new oil and natural gas supplies in the United States." Yet only two months earlier, the same two instruments had yielded rather different results—42 and 43 percent pluralities, respectively, opposed to decontrol.[40]

Second, as always, the polling results depended importantly on how questionnaires were worded. The undefined use of the term *deregulation* contaminated the Harris data. Many respondents were likely to approve something called deregulation so long as they had no idea of what the word meant, except that it would somehow swell supplies. Conversely, pollsters that omitted the term entirely, and phrased their questions colloquially (Should companies be allowed to "increase the price" of gas? Should the price of gas be allowed to "go up"?), inevitably racked up the most adverse answers. Thus, the widely publicized CBS/*New York Times* poll of August 1977 asked: "Would you approve or disapprove of allowing natural gas companies to increase the prices they charge you, so they can pay for the cost of finding more gas?" Only 34 percent of the respondents indicated that they would approve (59 percent said they would not).

Because natural gas is the nation's predominant home-heating fuel, public sensitivity to changes in the price of gas is more pronounced than it is to changes in the price of distillate fuel.[41] Legislators who might have countenanced petroleum price decontrol could ill afford to overlook this distinction between oil and natural gas. That doesn't mean, though, that most of them clung to regulation of the price of gas merely because they were genuflecting slavishly to everybody's preference for economical heat. The popular temper did not always offer lawmakers precise guidance in formulating pricing policy. There were potentially contradictory expectations in the wind (Were people telling Congress to prevent producers from raising prices, but with less regulation?). Although the public's desire for moderation in energy prices was obvious,

39. *Harris Survey*, February 1977.
40. Ibid.
41. Approximately 47 million homes are heated with natural gas. More than half, 55 percent, of residential energy consumption in Btus in 1980 was in the form of natural gas. Electricity was a distant second, with about 25 percent of the total, followed by fuel oil and kerosene, with about 18 percent. U.S. Department of Energy, Energy Information Administration, *Residential Energy Consumption Survey: 1979–80 Consumption and Expenditures, Part 1: National Data* (GPO, 1981), p. 5.

how best to fulfill it—whether by continued regulation or by deregulation—was not.

Localism

The vagaries of national public opinion meant less to members of Congress than did the concerns of narrower constituencies. Many critics would argue that congressional preoccupation with local economic interests limited most discussion of the natural gas question and irreparably damaged prospects for legislating a clear-headed policy. According to this view, what deadlocked Congress, as in the debate on oil pricing, was the antagonism between populous consuming states in the North, intent on keeping energy prices low, and producing states largely in the Southwest, intent on keeping federal regulators out of the region's market. Predictably, the House, in which the first faction was well represented, preferred more federal price restrictions. The Senate, reflecting the strength of smaller western states, leaned toward further deregulation. The resulting standoff finally ended only by policymakers devising, as one commentator put it, a "logrolling monstrosity," crammed with selective favors and blandishments to seduce the necessary majorities.[42]

Undeniably, the defense of local interests by some states added strong spice to the politics of natural gas. In most of the important producer states, the National Energy Plan, to which the House proved receptive, constituted a threat. Through comparatively high wellhead prices in its unregulated markets, the Southwest had financed for years a massive program of exploration and drilling that had yielded abundant in-state supplies. Now, it was feared, all-inclusive federal price rules would permit pipelines feeding the gas-starved Northeast and Midwest to bound in and gobble up any local surplus while the proposed price ceilings would continue to set lower gas rates for interstate consumers.

Voting Patterns

An eclectic coalition emerged in support of the Natural Gas Policy Act. Through various special provisions, engineers of the natural gas compromise were able to dilute the initial dissension that arose on all

42. Robert J. Samuelson, "Carter's Divine Comedy," *National Journal*, vol. 10 (September 2, 1978), p. 1404.

sides and thus ensure passage. Analysis of the pertinent House and
Senate roll calls strongly suggests that the bill managed to blur or
scramble many of the competing demands stemming from regional interests. (See the logit equations in table 3-1, in appendix A to this
chapter, which display the relationships between votes of congressmen
and the key energy attributes of their home states.)

COAL PRODUCERS AND THE NGPA. Some scholars seem to suggest that
important parts of the natural gas bill were designed to serve the interests of coal-producing states and that these states were then sucked
into a consumers' coalition supporting the Carter administration's position.[43] Presumably, the incremental pricing system was the main
portion of the gas compromise that could have appealed to coal operators, hiking the cost of gas as boiler fuel and thus extending coal's
reach into utility and industrial markets. This hypothesis, however, is not
firmly borne out by the evidence. Roll call votes showed that representatives from coal-rich areas were not of one mind when judging whether
their native industry would end up among the big winners under the new
legislation.

TELLTALE VOTES. Excluding the Southwest, most regions experienced
rifts, not only over the NGPA, but also over the earlier legislative proposals, which presented a much clearer test. The Krueger-Brown and
Pearson-Bentsen amendments, for instance, were fairly strong deregulation measures. They threw into sharp relief the basic issue of pricing
policy: whether to decontrol the price of newly produced gas thoroughly
and soon. One could expect local delegations to vote cohesively if their
members were always able to discern specific regional or state interests
regarding gas policy, and if such interests were not open to varying interpretations within the particular states or regions. But apart from the
heart of the Southwest and some states in the Northeast, unified delegations were rare. Krueger-Brown divided almost evenly the representatives
of the Middle West and the Southeast. Even in the Northeast, Krueger-
Brown drew support from roughly one of every four representatives.
Similarly, the Pearson-Bentsen bill did not fracture the Senate along
strict sectional lines, contrary to some expectations. Southwestern senators voted 11 to 1 in favor of the bill, but the margin of victory was
ultimately provided by the support collected elsewhere. Almost a third of
the senators from the Northeast, for instance, sided with the producing

43. See, for example, M. Elizabeth Sanders, *The Regulation of Natural Gas: Policy
and Politics, 1938–1978 (Temple University Press, 1981)*, pp. 170, 191.

states.[44] What is more, during the Pearson-Bentsen floor fight, twenty states found their own pairs of senators in disagreement. These discontinuities cast light on why several home-state energy attributes still failed to predict accurately the political alignment on natural gas pricing, even when, as in the Krueger-Brown and Pearson-Bentsen roll calls, the choice between policy alternatives was stark (see table 3-2, in appendix A to this chapter, for logit analysis of the rates on these bills).

Numerous representatives voted as though the local net benefits of alternative gas policies were often a matter of opinion. Members from states hard hit by curtailments, for example, reasoned in several different ways. Some, primarily senators, were convinced deregulation would stimulate production, reduce scarcity, and stem the migration of local industries to the Southwest, where gas was plentiful. (After all, diminishing industrial loads caused by gas shortages on systems in parts of the Midwest and Northeast were not only costing jobs; they were sometimes responsible for rising residential gas rates, since utilities had fewer bulk users over which to spread their fixed distribution costs.) Others, chiefly House members, still believed the scarcity could be alleviated as readily with price controls as without, or that shortfalls were inevitable regardless of what was done. Even high local gas prices could educe differing points of view. Many members whose states paid most dearly for energy felt that decontrol of gas would add fuel to nothing but the fires of inflation. Another group thought deregulation could vastly expand domestic supplies, diminish dependence on costly substitutes such as liquefied natural gas or imported crude oil, and therefore dampen prices. Lawmakers espousing the second position were not exclusively from the producing states. Plenty represented states that purchased gas and produced none.

Partisanship

Outside the main producing states, voting decisions on gas deregulation followed home-state energy characteristics in ways that were often mixed and irregular. But the prominence of party affiliation in organizing the key congressional divisions stands out unambiguously: 88 percent of the Republicans voted for the Krueger-Brown deregulation amendment, and 74 percent of the Democrats voted against it. In the case of Pearson-Bentsen, 92 percent of the GOP favored the deregu-

44. The Northeast includes the New England states, New York, New Jersey, and Pennsylvania.

lation bill, while 73 percent of the Democratic senators backed away from it.

Policy Management

The most common interpretation of the Natural Gas Policy Act traces malfunctions in the legislative branch to mistakes by the executive. Blame for the awkward legislation, in other words, is placed squarely on the Carter administration. According to this thesis, the administration's strategy on natural gas pricing, indeed, its whole energy initiative, was muddled and misdirected.

The Carter Administration's Errors

As a presidential contender, Carter had seemed to support the concept of gas decontrol. Even before his missives to the governors of three major producing states on the eve of the 1976 election, he had gone on record, in a June presentation to the Democratic platform committee, advocating a five-year experiment in which gas not under existing contracts would be released from controls.[45] Consequently, many were baffled when, the following April, the president recommended a natural gas bill that bore little resemblance to these promises. What changed his mind?

According to critics, a fateful decision had been made, shortly after the inauguration, to draft a comprehensive energy program within three months and to entrust the task to a small staff headed by James R. Schlesinger, then in charge of the White House Energy Policy and Planning Office. The Schlesinger group, huddling in cramped second-floor suites of the Old Executive Office Building, set to work on a plan in an atmosphere of wartime urgency and secrecy. Outside consultation was allegedly stifled. The president, so the critique asserts, was handed a program hastily conceived and thus riddled with inconsistencies, dubious analysis, and grave political miscalculations.

Nowhere, the detractors noted, were the flaws more evident than in the natural gas section of the plan. The rest of the proposal at least followed a policy of raising prices of scarce fuels to hold down consumption. But on natural gas, the plan proposed the opposite: continued ceilings to maintain artificially low prices. Some pundits speculated that

45. *Congressional Quarterly Weekly Report*, vol. 36 (March 18, 1978), p. 713.

Schlesinger, and through him, the president, had been taken in by consumer-minded aides who purportedly populated the energy task force. Other observers found that Schlesinger himself was too aloof and that his "minimal feel for political realities" led him (and so, the president) to misread the latent balance of power in Congress, where the scales, presumably, had begun to tilt in favor of deregulation.[46]

The defense of the energy program by administration officials got off to a bad start. Congressional testimony often seemed ill prepared. For example, Treasury Secretary W. Michael Blumenthal, in an appearance before the House Ways and Means Committee on May 17, 1977, was reported as frequently unable to answer specific questions.[47] Schlesinger too had some embarrassing moments. Before the Senate Energy Committee on May 3, for instance, he was asked to assess the overall economic impact of proposed oil and gas price increases. He replied that he would have to prepare such information.[48] After the hearing, administration officials reportedly conceded in private that in scrambling to unveil the National Energy Plan by April 20, they had not been able to complete adequate economic analysis.[49] Conflicting statements were issued. For instance, within only two days of the energy plan's debut, Office of Management and Budget Director Bert Lance retracted an earlier assertion that the program's effects on the economy would be generally positive.[50] Worse, White House rhetoric grew hyperbolic and confusing. A press conference on October 13, 1977, in which the president angrily accused the oil and gas industry of attempting to stage "the biggest ripoff in history" seemed particularly damaging. Denouncing "potential war profiteering," he declared that the 1973 combined "income" of the industry was $18 billion. The claim was immediately challenged, and later that day an energy department spokesman tried to clarify matters. The president, he said, had meant gross income—that is, annual sale or revenue—not profits.[51]

46. Edward Cowan and others, "Carter Shaped Energy Plan with Disregard for Politics," *New York Times*, April 24, 1977; and *Washington Post*, May 25, 1978.

47. Adam Clymer, "Panel in House Voices Concern on Energy Plan," *New York Times*, May 17, 1977.

48. *Economic Impact of President Carter's Energy Program*, Hearings before the Senate Committee on Energy and Natural Resources, 95 Cong. 1 sess. (GPO, 1977), p. 49.

49. Edward Cowan, "Senators Give Skeptical Reception to Schlesinger Energy Proposals," *New York Times*, May 4, 1977.

50. Steven Rattner, "White House Shifts, Says Energy Plans Won't Aid Economy," *New York Times*, April 22, 1977.

51. James T. Wooten, "Carter Sees 'Rip-Off,' " *New York Times*, October 14, 1977.

As the president boxed himself in with populist appeals that gave the appearance of solidifying an affiliation with hard-line consumer interests, the administration's tactical flexibility waned. Later in the president's term, the media were to characterize the Carter White House as vacillating and indecisive, but during the period in question a different criticism was common: it was said that both Carter and Schlesinger had reputations for intransigence.[52] Their deepening commitments to the consumer lobby and their alleged distaste for compromise, critics charged, made for sour and ineffectual legislative relations. Through much of the debate on the National Energy Plan, the administration's lobbying effort was described as overconfident, lame, negligent, and above all, late in arriving.[53] On the natural gas question, it was commonly believed, the White House did little more in 1977 than threaten time and again to veto any bill containing deregulation. By the spring of 1978, it became obvious that, with midterm elections coming up in the fall, the continuing standstill on natural gas could doom the entire energy bill. Finally, the administration exerted itself to produce an agreement. However, by that time, so the argument runs, only a makeshift solution —one pieced together, as Representative Anthony J. Moffett, Democrat of Connecticut, put it, "in an atmosphere of political hysteria"—was possible.[54]

The Administration's Role in Perspective

This rendition of the administration's role in the events leading to the Natural Gas Policy Act is somewhat simplistic. For all the weaknesses in the Carter energy initiative, in all likelihood the congressional immobility over natural gas pricing and a desultory legislative outcome could not have been easily avoided even if the administration had managed matters differently.

RENEGING ON DECONTROL. Initially, the president had opted to extend

52. *New York Times*, November 11, 1977; and *New York Times*, April 22, 1977.

53. *New York Times*, October 2, 1977; *New York Times*, October 9, 1977; and *Congressional Quarterly Weekly Report*, vol. 35 (October 22, 1977), p. 2236. For a perceptive, scholarly account of the administration's strategy that stresses the inexperience and ineptitude of the White House, see Charles O. Jones, "Congress and the Making of Energy Policy," in Robert Lawrence, ed., *New Dimensions of Energy Policy* (Lexington Books, 1979), pp. 161–78.

54. Albert R. Hunt, "Energy Conferees Are Close to Adoption of Compromise on Natural Gas Pricing," *Wall Street Journal*, May 24, 1977.

price controls rather than push deregulation. However unsound this choice, it was scarcely evident in the spring of 1977 that Carter had joined the weaker side of the contest in Congress. From the administration's perspective at the time, the political realities were plain. For more than a quarter century, repeated attempts to deregulate gas had failed to become law. Only a year before, Gerald Ford, for instance, had called for decontrol of gas as well as oil, but the House of Representatives adopted instead a bill broadening the Federal Power Commission's controls to include in-state gas sales.[55] White House strategists calculated, not unreasonably, that to stand a ghost of a chance on Capitol Hill, comprehensive energy legislation had to secure the Democratic majorities and inspire the Democratic congressional leadership. A package containing gas deregulation was not likely to do this. In fact, in Schlesinger's opinion, such a venture would have resembled "a frontal assault" on long-standing convictions held by the chairmen of the respective House and Senate committees with authority over gas, as well as by Speaker Thomas P. O'Neill, Jr., whose early cooperation on the energy program was essential.[56]

The more prudent strategy was to begin by giving the issue to Representative John D. Dingell, Democrat of Michigan, chairman of the pivotal House Commerce Subcommittee on Energy and Power, and an implacable foe of gas deregulation. Recruitment of several Commerce Committee aides onto Schlesinger's Energy Policy and Planning team abetted the process. These staff members predictably modeled the administration's natural gas proposals after the House bills they had drafted in previous years.

Finally, for many months in 1977, the decision to opt for further regulation appeared to pay off. Under O'Neill's stewardship, the entire energy plan sped through the House largely intact during the summer of 1977. Even when the plan reached the Senate, where stiffer resistance was expected, there was no conclusive evidence that proderegulation forces would command a majority. In the days preceding the first key vote on the issue, a vote on whether to table the Pearson-Bentsen amendment, September 22, 1977, head counts indicated that the outcome would be too close to call. Vice-President Walter F. Mondale found it necessary to be present in the Senate chamber to cast a deciding

55. H.R. 9464, adopted 230–184, February 3, 1976.
56. Interview with James R. Schlesinger, former secretary of energy, Washington, D.C., August 6, 1982.

vote in the event of a tie.[57] Even the gas industry's own trade journal, which scrutinized developments on Capitol Hill with a keen eye, was loath to predict victory for Pearson-Bentsen.[58] In short, as the congressional battle progressed into the fall, the administration still had no reason to believe that its position on natural gas was less serviceable politically than the opposition's counterproposals.

NATIONAL ENERGY PLAN: QUICK AND DIRTY. Much is made of the crash deadline that the White House imposed on the Energy Policy and Planning Office. The rush to submit the plan was responsible for several miscues in the presentation and for some serious blunders in the accompanying technical analysis. At the time, the press did not spot the worst mistake, but students of the period have since brought it to light.[59] In attempting to compare the revenues that would flow to producers under the plan's gas-pricing system with the revenues anticipated under existing law, the Schlesinger task force somehow underestimated the latter projection by some $44 billion. This error subsequently complicated the administration's negotiations during at least one sensitive stage of the gas conference committee's deliberations.

Yet, sloppy handling of technical data and other gaffes may well have seemed to the administration like a price worth paying. The president was able to seize the initiative on the energy problem while he was still riding the crest of popularity and goodwill that christens a new presidency. The generally favorable reception that Carter's early energy messages got from the public, the rising presidential approval ratings at the time, and the relative ease with which most of the National Energy Plan passed the House suggested that the president's instinct—to strike while the iron was hot, even if its edges were rough—had a certain logic.

RHETORIC. Some critics interpreted the Carter administration rhetoric as pandering to the consumer interests that supposedly constituted the principal constituency of the National Energy Plan.[60] In reality con-

57. Adam Clymer, "Senate Keeps Alive Plan to Deregulate Prices for New Gas," *New York Times*, September 23, 1977.

58. *Oil and Gas Journal*, vol. 75 (September 19, 1977).

59. See Michael J. Malbin, "Congress, Policy Analysis, and Natural Gas Deregulation: A Parable about Fig Leaves," in Robert A. Goldwin, ed., *Bureaucrats, Policy Analysts, Statesmen: Who Leads?* (Washington, D.C.: American Enterprise Institute, 1980), pp. 62–87.

60. A well-known piece, forcefully expounding the thesis that antigrowth advocates, with private foundation support, played a decisive role in shaping the Carter administration's early energy planning, is Lewis H. Lapham, "The Energy Debacle," *Harper's*, vol. 255 (August 1977), pp. 58–74.

sumer groups had repudiated the entire energy program within days of its announcement, and judging from the polarity of their views, there was no prospect of mollifying them. On May 18, 1977, Lee C. White, chairman of the Consumer Federation of America's Energy Task Force, branded the Carter proposals regressive and reactionary.[61] A paper issued by that organization discussed the National Energy Plan in what can only be called a Dantean mode; it bore the title "President Carter's National Energy Plan—Paradise for Producers and Purgatory for the Public." Other consumer representatives, public interest organizations, and labor unions reacted along similar lines. Two days after Carter's April energy speech to Congress, Ralph Nader reportedly concluded that the energy plan called for inordinate sacrifice from consumers but not enough from corporations.[62] James F. Flug of Energy Action stated in June that the administration's proposed ceiling price of $1.75 per mcf for new natural gas was "way out of the ballpark."[63] Some time later, William W. Winpisinger, the new president of the International Association of Machinists, was quoted as saying that he was "sick and tired of being hosed to death by the goddamn multinational oil companies" and that his organization had written off Carter as a presidential candidate in 1980.[64]

A more basic aim of the White House speeches, one suspects, was to arouse public opinion, the one resource that any president must mobilize when embarking on a controversial course of action. That the public had been receptive to excoriations of special interests, particularly oil companies, in the past was well known. However, no one had anticipated how difficult it would be in the end to convince people that the energy crisis was serious. And specific things, as opposed to "something," had to be done about it.[65]

---

61. Edward Cowan, "Carter Energy Plan Called 'Regressive,' " *New York Times*, May 19, 1977.

62. *New York Times*, April 22, 1977.

63. *Natural Gas Pricing Proposals of President Carter's Energy Program*, Hearings before the Senate Committee on Energy and Natural Resources, 95 Cong. 1 sess. (GPO, 1977), p. 657.

64. *Washington Post*, April 16, 1978; and Richard Lyons, "Big Union Sniffs at Gas Bill's Backers," *Washington Post*, September 26, 1978.

65. In April–May 1977, Gallup reported that 44 percent of the nation believed that the energy situation was very serious. *Gallup Opinion Index*, Report 143 (June 1977), p. 15. Seven months later, this figure had declined to 41 percent, despite repeated presidential addresses and increasing media attention. *Gallup Opinion Index*, Report 149 (December 1977), p. 17.

The conflicts in Carter's public statements (what he said in April 1977 was not what everybody thought he had said in October 1976) probably damaged the president's image, or credibility, in the long run. In the early rounds of the gas debate, however, the about-face in the president's pronouncements on decontrol did not appear to be a liability and, in fact, may have provided a tactical edge. In one interview, a leading political strategist in the Natural Gas Supply Committee stressed that the unexpected reversal caught the industry off guard, seriously crippling its lobbying offensive during the critical first few months of action in the House.[66]

The Political Topography

Despite notable lapses, the White House lobby was intense, persistent, and in the end, effective. It took painfully long to bear fruit, and the fruit it bore was unappetizing, but that was not for lack of political tenacity, skill, or even leadership. To understand what Schlesinger called the administration's "Long March" for a gas bill, the craggy congressional terrain must be appreciated.

TROUBLE IN THE SENATE. As already noted, the defeat of the administration's bill and the victory of the Pearson-Bentsen substitute in the Senate were by no means foregone conclusions. In fact, if at the end of September 1977 the administration had been able to convert just two more senators, the Pearson-Bentsen amendment would have lost.[67] A measure closer to that passed earlier by the House might then have squeaked through. Nevertheless, unquestionably, events in the Senate were more difficult for the administration to influence than events in the House. The Democratic chiefs in the House—Speaker O'Neill; Floor Leader James C. Wright, Jr., Texas; Caucus Chairman Thomas S. Foley, Washington; and Whips John Brademas, Indiana, and Daniel D. Rostenkowski, Illinois—gave the lower chamber its strongest leadership since the days of Speaker Sam Rayburn. O'Neill and his lieutenants steered the Carter energy program through the House in a manner reminiscent of a disciplined European parliament: deadlines were set on the hearings and markups of standing committees; a special select committee

66. Interview with David H. Foster, executive vice-president, Natural Gas Supply Committee, Washington, D.C., May 26, 1978.
67. Pearson-Bentsen was adopted on a vote of 50–46. Thus, a two-vote switch would have produced a tie, which would then have been broken in the administration's favor by Vice-President Mondale.

was handpicked to coordinate the legislation; and floor action was carefully managed.

Things were different in the Senate, where the procedures, the cast of characters, and the distribution of power gave opponents more room to maneuver. Initially, the Senate Majority Leader, Robert C. Byrd, Democrat of West Virginia, did not embrace the president's energy policy with the same enthusiasm as did O'Neill. Byrd had voted in favor of gas deregulation in 1975, and his first reaction to the Carter administration's energy plan was circumspect: "The President cannot expect every jot and title to be enacted as he proposed it."[68] But even if he had been enamored of the plan, Byrd could not have manipulated the Senate as O'Neill did the House. He could not, for example, call up a rule limiting floor debate and amendments, as the speaker had been able to do by way of the House Rules Committee. And, as it turned out, Senate discussion of the natural gas issue was tortured by, among other things, a nine-day filibuster that left frayed nerves and ill feeling.

Nor could Byrd have helped what went on in the Senate Finance Committee, whose chairman, Russell B. Long, Democrat of Louisiana, had called Carter's plan "an unmitigated disaster on the production side."[69] By contrast, Long's counterpart on the House Ways and Means Committee, Representative Albert C. Ullman, Democrat of Oregon, was sympathetic toward much of the National Energy Plan and also fairly responsive to the House leadership. Although the senior senator from Louisiana and his committee did not have direct jurisdiction over natural gas regulation, he was to cast a long shadow upon the gas deliberations. By holding up resolution of other key parts of the energy package at the conference stage, Long added to the pressure on the administration's forces to give ground. It is difficult to say, exactly what the party leaders, or the administration, could have offered the senator to obtain his backing, or at least his neutrality. From his post atop the powerful Finance Committee, and with unrivaled talent as a parliamentarian, Long could work his will, with or without side deals. To the administration, one thing was certain: gaining Long's consent would have cost much support from liberals, who were already grumbling about what they saw as excessive generosity toward producers in the original energy plan.

68. *Congressional Quarterly Weekly Report*, vol. 35 (December 24, 1977), p. 2635.
69. Richard Corrigan, "Now It's the Senate's Turn on Energy," *National Journal*, vol. 9 (August 20, 1977), p. 1306.

One of the administration's troubled allies was Henry Jackson, who chaired the other key Senate panel, Energy and Natural Resources, through which parts of the energy legislation had to flow. Jackson bore the scars of earlier congressional energy wars, in which he had fought not only for price controls but also for price rollbacks. As a long-standing Senate expert in energy policy, Jackson had strong convictions. Like Long, but for opposite reasons, he distrusted what the adminis-tration had proposed. At first, Jackson felt that the administration's $1.75 new-gas price was extravagant.[70] So, as Jackson was suggesting that the administration press on with other items in the energy program and postpone action on gas, Long was waiting for the gas-pricing question to get settled before moving on to other critical sections of the energy legislation.[71] How the administration could have simultaneously pleased Jackson and Long is a riddle that historians may someday answer satisfactorily, but not that the principals knew how to resolve in the heat of the moment.

Although Jackson eventually came to work closely with Schlesinger on natural gas, during 1977 he and the administration sometimes seemed headed in very different directions. For example, in mid-December 1977, a leading figure in the proderegulation faction on the Senate Energy Committee, J. Bennett Johnston, Jr., Democrat of Louisiana, suddenly came forth with a compromise. In retrospect, Johnston's idea approxi-mated the original Carter position more closely than did the final Natural Gas Policy Act.[72] Nonetheless, the Johnston initiative—which came to be called the Christmas turkey—instantly drew fire, not only from Republicans, who rejected anything short of deregulation, but also from Jackson and other Democrats, who attacked the scheme's cost. The proposal's estimated cost to consumers, at least in direct gas price in-

70. Steven Rattner, "Move to End Debate on Decontrol of Gas Is Begun in Senate," *New York Times*, September 24, 1977.

71. Richard Corrigan, "The Shaky Plans to Deregulate Natural Gas," *National Journal*, vol. 10 (April 1, 1978), p. 523; *Congressional Quarterly Weekly Report*, vol. 36 (April 29, 1978), p. 1039; and vol. 36 (March 11, 1978), p. 631.

72. The Johnston compromise extended federal price controls to the intrastate market and set the price of newly discovered gas at $1.75 per mcf as of February 1, 1978, and then increased it by the rate of inflation plus an extra 4.5 percent annually for the next six years. After that, the price was to be tied to a floating limit of no more than 15 percent a year. Steven Rattner, "Schlesinger Says Jackson Will Help End Gas Deadlock," *New York Times*, January 9, 1978; *Congressional Quarterly Weekly Report*, vol. 35 (December 24, 1977), p. 2631.

creases, ranged below that of the NGPA.[73] Yet Schlesinger's initial efforts to interest Jackson in the Christmas turkey met with little success, though later on the senator agreed to redouble the stalled energy conference's quest for a workable compromise.

To a degree, the administration's troubles with the Senate barons were part of a broader problem: the strong spirit of autonomy that pervaded the Senate in the aftermath of the Nixon years. Through much of the energy debate's first nine months, the Senate's mood verged on sublime indifference, even toward some of the president's most urgent supplications. For example, early in the fall of 1977, the administration was striving to head off a conclusive vote over decontrol on the Senate floor. Shortly before the Pearson-Bentsen roll call, Carter called four presumably suggestible senators to the White House. When the meeting was over, each one—Quentin N. Burdick, Democrat of North Dakota, Wendell H. Ford, Democrat of Kentucky, John H. Chafee, Republican of Rhode Island, and Dennis DeConcini, Democrat of Arizona—headed back to the Capitol and promptly voted against the president.

But the fact that Congress was polarized ideologically over the issue of gas deregulation was the central reason for the administration's difficulties. A quick and simple compromise, among warring factions within the two chambers as well as between the opposing House and Senate majorities, was unimaginable.

The fate of the Christmas turkey illustrated the problem. Whatever Senator Jackson's motives for declining to pursue Senator Johnston's overture, the fact remains that the Johnston proposal could never have attracted a majority of Senate conferees anyway. The numbers were close but unmistakable. No Republican member was prepared to back a formula that did not include deregulation. To the Republicans, the concept of deregulation had acquired great symbolic significance. Higher price ceilings, even vastly higher, were no substitute. Indeed, a plan permitting even the most fabulous price increases under a so-called floating cap would still have been objectionable to Republicans because this was not, strictly speaking, deregulation. Among the Democrats, any formula substantially raising prices, through decontrol or otherwise, would trigger defections from three senators—Abourezk of South Dakota, Howard M. Metzenbaum of Ohio, and John A. Durkin of New Hampshire. Consequently, even if Jackson and other moderates had rallied to

73. *Congressional Quarterly Weekly Report*, vol. 36 (March 11, 1978), p. 632.

its side, the Christmas turkey was destined for decapitation at the hands of the Senate conferees. At best the vote would have been 7–10, with a solid Republican front plus the three Democratic dissidents combining to kill the bill.

This arithmetic impelled Carter, Schlesinger, and Jackson to try a different approach in 1978. Instead of struggling to close the Democratic ranks—which on the Senate side were now hopelessly ruptured by the virtual secession of Abourezk and Metzenbaum—an attempt was made to build a bipartisan coalition around the center. Everyone recognized that this avenue was fraught with risks and complications. To entice Republican support, the compromise had to include deregulation, at some point. But to hold the votes of most Senate Democrats, and to keep the House conferees from bolting, any decontrol had to be abundantly hedged with qualifications like a protracted phase in, incremental pricing to the burner tip, and multiple categorization of gas, designed to ensure that only the "right" sorts of gas would be decontrolled. This balancing act was so delicate that when the conference finally reached agreement in late May 1978, twelve of the twenty-five House negotiators still demurred. Even so, the alternatives were limited. Unhappily, if the Ninety-fifth Congress was to construct any natural gas legislation whatsoever, the May compromise was almost certainly the only prospect.

LIFE IN THE CONGRESSIONAL TRENCHES. Between May and October 1978, the Carter administration drove to win passage of the gas compromise, and one of the tightest legislative jousts in recent history ensued in Congress. The resourcefulness of the White House, which repeatedly salvaged the Natural Gas Policy Act from the brink of defeat, was remarkable. Throughout the Carter presidency, there were examples of the executive's wilted institutional power in the still-inhibiting backwash of the Watergate period. But this was not one of them.

The basic principles of the natural gas bill were no sooner ratified by the conference committee than some sponsors began to get second thoughts. By the time a draft of the agreement, put into legislative language, appeared at the end of July 1978, the second thoughts had swelled into grave doubts, even fundamental objections. To the right of center there were desertions by Representative Joseph D. Waggoner, Jr., Democrat of Louisiana, Senator Johnston, and, for a while, Senators James A. McClure, Republican of Idaho, and Pete V. Domenici, Republican of New Mexico. Johnston's behavior must have been especially puzzling to some of his colleagues. Earlier in the spring, newspapers in

Baton Rouge and New Orleans carried headlines that quoted him extolling the proposed gas bill as a fine compromise and a great victory for Louisiana.[74] By August he had changed his mind. Perhaps the signs of an impending renomination fight had compelled Louisiana's junior senator to switch positions. Johnston's primary opponent, a state legislator named Louis Jenkins, was saying that the natural gas bill would "wreck the oil and gas industry in our state."[75] Some of the administration's erstwhile supporters to the left of center were also becoming undependable. Representative Henry S. Reuss, Democrat of Wisconsin, for example, now chose to heed an outcry from his state's public service commission chairman, who warned that the natural gas legislation would be an economic catastrophe for Wisconsin.[76] By mid-August the administration lacked the necessary signatures to validate the conference report.

THE GUNS OF AUGUST. The conference report was rescued when the president interceded forcefully on August 17. In contrast to some of the earlier White House meetings with wavering members of Congress, this time a late-night session yielded results. Representatives James C. Corman, Democrat of California, and Charles B. Rangel, Democrat of New York, were persuaded to reverse their initial opposition and sign the compromise, while Domenici and McClure were brought back into the fold. Although Schlesinger insisted that there had been no deals in these negotiations, no one could doubt that the administration was now playing political hardball. Despite a White House denial, for instance, it was rumored that McClure's support had been bought by a promise to spend $1.5 billion on nuclear breeder reactor research over the next three years, and $417 million of it in Idaho.[77]

To report out the gas bill was a feat in itself, but to get the full Senate and House to go along with it seemed miraculous. An extraordinary collection of interest groups—including General Motors, U.S. Steel, and the Chamber of Commerce, juxtaposed with the International Association of Machinists, the United Auto Workers, and the

74. *Baton Rouge Morning Advocate*, March 15, 1978; and Kenneth A. Weiss, "Great Louisiana Victory in Gas Legislation," *Times-Picayune*, March 8, 1978.

75. Ibid.

76. William Greider, "High Stakes Argument on Fine Print Ties Up Gas Pricing Bill," *Washington Post*, August 17, 1978.

77. *Congressional Quarterly Weekly Report*, vol. 36 (September 2, 1978), pp. 2396–97; Richard Corrigan, "The Dubious Deal on the Natural Gas Bill," *National Journal*, vol. 10 (September 2, 1978), p. 1402.

AFL-CIO—wanted the legislation stopped. In Congress, an equally queer coalition, made up of conservatives, who were convinced that the NGPA did not deregulate enough, and liberals, who were convinced that it deregulated too much, opposed the legislation. Many of Capitol Hill's celebrities joined the opposition. James Abourezk and George S. McGovern, Democrat of South Dakota, stood alongside Russell B. Long and John G. Tower, Republican of Texas; Edward M. Kennedy, Democrat of Massachusetts, and William Proxmire, Democrat of Wisconsin, stood with Howard H. Baker, Jr., Republican of Tennessee, and Robert J. Dole, Republican of Kansas; and so on. At the end of August, the administration lacked enough votes to pass the bill. Then, only about two weeks later, Majority Leader Byrd made a startling announcement: the gas measure was now virtually over the top.[78] Ten days after that, the Natural Gas Policy Act carried the Senate 57–42.

The tide was turned, in large part, by a series of White House conferences with important business leaders. Though in late August only a handful of business executives could be counted on to back the legislation, in mid-September the Department of Energy was able to supply all senators with the names of scores of major corporations, financial institutions, and trade associations that were backing the bill. Congressional opponents were outraged. Clarence Brown of Ohio accused the administration of having driven companies into submission with "a little straight talk about the realities of doing business in a federally regulated environment."[79] In a letter to a group of corporate officers, Brown charged that Schlesinger had threatened industrial gas users with loss of future Federal Energy Regulatory Commission-approved emergency gas purchases if the legislation failed.[80] When the once audible opposition of various business groups suddenly fell silent, it became clear that the White House was countering special interests with its own potent grassroots campaign.[81]

But the administration's hard-won success in the Senate did not mean that the gas bill's odyssey had ended. All the energy conference reports

78. Fred Barbash, "Natural Gas Measure Almost 'Over the Top' " *Washington Post*, September 17, 1978.

79. *Congressional Quarterly Weekly Report*, vol. 36 (October 21, 1978), p. 3043.

80. Albert R. Hunt, "Senate Begins Debate on Natural Gas Bill Amid Signs Carter Push May Swing Vote," *Wall Street Journal*, September 12, 1978.

81. For a story of how the administration supposedly got the steel industry to "change its tune," see Robert G. Kaiser and J. P. Smith, "Political Dealing Prompts Big Steel's Flip-Flop on Gas Bill," *Washington Post*, September 7, 1978.

now reverted to the House for final consideration. The crux of O'Neill's strategy for moving the controversial gas pricing bill through the House was to keep it bound up with other more popular sections of the Carter energy legislation. If the speaker could force an up-or-down vote on the energy package as a whole, rather than allow roll calls on each of its parts, House passage of the gas act was almost assured. So everything hinged on whether the Rules Committee would grant a rule permitting the single vote. The committee's initial response looked like a fatal blow to the gas bill. The bill's enemies had managed to split the committee's membership evenly, thus blocking the one-vote rule. But once again, the administration struck back nimbly, forcing the committee to reverse itself the next day. One of the panel's members, B. F. Sisk, Democrat of California, apparently came under such withering pressure that his vote was flipped around within a matter of hours. Two others, Shirley A. Chisholm, Democrat of New York, and Gillis W. Long, Democrat of Louisiana, softened their stance and voted "present."

One more cliff-hanger remained. Opponents of the gas compromise tried but failed, by a breathtakingly close vote (206–207), to reopen the possibility of holding a separate roll call on the bill. Finally, with a tally of 231–168, on October 15, 1978, the House enacted the energy package, including the NGPA.

Conclusion

The Natural Gas Policy Act of 1978 was, as Carter accurately characterized it, "one of the most difficult pieces of legislation that the Congress has ever faced."[82] Its passage failed to silence the natural gas debate. The president's signature was barely dry when it became apparent that the titanic struggle had left important issues unresolved. As Senator Metzenbaum warned, these issues would "come back time and again" to haunt Congress.

Nonetheless, the victory was gained against great odds, by sheer determination and considerable political alacrity. Whether another Democratic president would have waged the natural gas war altogether differently and won it more easily is highly debatable. Granted, the Carter administration may have been especially eager to ingratiate itself with congressional Democrats early in the president's term. In the presidential election of 1976 Carter had campaigned as a dark horse, running

82. *Congressional Quarterly Weekly Report*, vol. 36 (September 30, 1978), p. 2616.

against a Washington establishment that included traditional elements of his own party. He was then forced to affirm all the more convincingly his partisan credentials as soon as he assumed office. To work with the Democratic leaders in Congress, their codes and customs had to be respected. Among the customs and codes was habitual hostility toward the deregulation of natural gas.

But there is little reason to suppose that a mainstream Democrat in the Oval Office would have more readily deserted the traditional party position on energy price regulation. Indeed, during 1979, when debate raged inside the Carter White House on whether to permit the Energy Policy and Conservation Act's controls on oil prices to expire the following year, the faction favoring prolongation of controls was led not by Carter or his aides but by the staff of the administration's most venerable party regular—Vice-President Walter Mondale.

Political Convictions

The impasse on natural gas pricing policy, and the final legislative product in 1978, cannot be adequately explained by theories that stress the oil and gas lobby's machinations or that view public opinion, congressional parochialism, or presidential ineptitude as overriding determinants. To throw more light on the question, the nature of the gas deregulation issue must be examined. Three aspects bear scrutiny: (1) empirical uncertainties; (2) the economic "rents" consumers would have to pay; and (3) the sheer length of the legislative dialogue on the subject. These facets tended to deepen a basic political schism, notched in party loyalties and ideological biases, greatly diminishing the chances of settling things neatly.

Uncertainties

During the debate over oil pricing in 1975, congressional advocates of decontrol were interested largely in restoring incentives for domestic production. Elsewhere homage was paid to conservation efforts, but few participants saw conservation as the focal point of the oil-price question. The same was true when the natural gas issue moved to the fore. Indeed, here the emphasis on regenerating production was even greater. In Congress the leading champions of gas deregulation were, for the most part, the same faction eager to deregulate oil. Their outlook was similar, except that additional considerations crystallized their position.

Like oil, only much more so, the conceivable supply of natural gas was vast. The United States Geological Survey, in a conservative prediction, estimated potential reserves of gas to be 70 percent of the cumulative total already found. A more optimistic figure, by the Potential Gas Agency of the Colorado School of Mines, put the possible quantity at about one-and-a-half times the previously discovered total.[83] These orders of magnitude referred to conventional gas, recoverable with known or foreseeable methods and costs. If one added estimates of unconventional sources, such as gas from Devonian shale, tight formations, geopressurized methane, and other geothermal deposits, the potential supply was for practical purposes limitless. So decontrol was regarded as the main step in getting down to the business of unearthing an immense geological treasure.

But another reason for the emphasis on production was that the physical shortages of natural gas differed from those of gasoline and other petroleum-based products. After 1974, the oil crisis abated temporarily, but the gas squeeze drew tauter. Also, the oil crisis was associated with events abroad (the Arab boycott), but the gas crunch was unmistakably a home-spun phenomenon. What were the domestic causes of the shortage? With thousands of households and businesses suffering service interruptions, as in the disastrous winter of 1976–77, it seemed tactless to cite the American consumer's excess demand as a prime suspect; that was like blaming the victim. Consequently, hungry eyes turned to the supply side, where federal regulations were discouraging gas exploration and development. The central topic of debate became whether enhanced production through deregulation would soon fill a perceived gap between gas needs and availability.

Notice that Congress could have spared itself some trouble if the issue had been framed differently. Shortages of any commodity are not gaps that must be filled to meet needs; they are shortfalls of supply with respect to demand. Under market pricing, shortfalls might end solely by way of supply responses, but they *inevitably* vanish through some combination of increased supplies and reduced demand.

NUMBERS GAMES. Because the case for decontrol was left dangling from the uncertain premise of a supply-led return to market equilibrium, a lot of effort was expended trying to estimate the exact size of supply increases under alternative pricing scenarios with varying lead times. In addition to half a dozen outside reports available at the time, Congress

83. *Natural Gas Pricing Proposals*, Hearings, pp. 372, 373.

undertook its own voluminous research. All four of the congressional staff agencies were pressed into service preparing evaluations of natural gas proposals while separate figures were churned out in the models of committee staff professionals. The extensive analysis did not move policymakers closer to informed judgments about natural gas pricing.

Over the years, econometric forecasts of gas production had generated a bewildering range of results. Discrepancies between the real world and the statistically simulated world were glaring, regardless of how independent and well respected the source of the research. At the Massachusetts Institute of Technology, for instance, Paul W. MacAvoy and Robert S. Pindyck had calculated in 1972 that with existing federal regulations a new contract field price of 39.7 cents per mcf by 1974, rising to 54.9 cents per mcf by 1977, could be expected to put 26.6 trillion cubic feet (tcf) of gas on line.[84] But as everyone knew, the Federal Power Commission went well beyond those price levels, bringing newly produced gas up to 42 cents per mcf in 1974 and then to $1.42 per mcf in mid-1976. Yet production in 1977 had not even regained its 1973 peak of 22.6 tcf. Most of the published studies cited in the 1977–78 gas debate showed considerable agreement on how much gas would be forthcoming if the regulatory status quo were to continue. But estimates differed widely about what would happen if new gas were deregulated. For example, the Stanford Research Institute claimed that deregulation would yield more gas annually by 1980 than the Federal Energy Administration foresaw as possible by 1985.[85] New computations by MacAvoy and Pindyck projected more annual output in 1980 even under extant regulations than the Federal Energy Administration and the American Gas Association dared predict for 1985 with decontrol.[86]

Congress's internal inquiries were just as baffling. How, for example, could the Congressional Budget Office conclude that the administration's gas plan, with its extended price caps, would deliver more annual cubic footage of gas than the average annual volume with decontrol projected by Congress's most optimistic free marketers?[87] The fundamental difficulty in these and other studies, of course, was that estimation of supply elasticity was little more than guesswork. The underlying geological conditions and the needed recovery techniques and

84. MacAvoy and Pindyck, *Price Controls and the Natural Gas Shortage*, p. 38.
85. *Natural Gas Pricing Proposals*, Hearings, p. 718.
86. Ibid.
87. Malbin, "Congress, Policy Analysis, and Natural Gas Deregulation," pp. 75–81.

costs could not be perfectly foreseen. Basing estimates on historic trends was a dubious exercise—especially for the natural gas industry, whose behavior over thirty years had been buffeted by government regulatory policies, leaving no record of performance under national free-market conditions. But other methodologies—such as those that rested on current consensus estimates by people in the industry—were not necessarily sounder.

The welter of conflicting statistics did more than leave legislators confused; it thickened an already dense atmosphere of frustration and mistrust. Down the blind alley of formal supply estimations, where subtle changes in key assumptions could mean the difference in multiple trillions of cubic feet of gas production, it was constantly tempting to adjust formulas to fit new circumstances, political and otherwise. Even if the adjustments chanced to be in the right direction, and were warranted by new objective information rather than by tactical needs of the moment, the propensity was to perceive them as politically inspired. In May 1978, for example, the Department of Energy began predicting that phased deregulation, as proposed in the gas compromise backed by the administration, would spur a vital 9 percent increase in output by 1985, reducing oil imports by over 1 million barrels per day.[88] Many in Congress discounted this claim, partly because the administration's forces had spent most of the previous year attempting to prove statistically that deregulation would procure no significant increase in gas whatsoever. Thus when the NGPA reached the Senate and House floors, members on both sides of the aisles repeatedly expressed doubts about the information at hand. The remarks, respectively, of Edmund S. Muskie, Democrat of Maine, who ended up voting for the bill, and of Lowell P. Weicker, Jr., Republican of Connecticut, who voted against it, were illustrative:

Very little . . . is certain about the bill or its consequences, although "facts" are abundant. No one really knows what will happen to energy prices and supplies if we pass the bill, or even if we defeat it.[89]

Tomorrow or the next day, when this very important vote . . . is taken, I can guarantee that there will not be a half-dozen Senators on this floor voting that can understand what it is they are voting on. Nobody knows the consequences of what it is that we are about to either pass or defeat, including those at the Department of Energy, and certainly including those at the White House.[90]

88. *New York Times*, May 26, 1978; and *Congressional Record* (September 13, 1978), p. 29099.

89. *Congressional Record*, daily edition (September 12, 1978), p. S14976.

90. Ibid., p. S14958.

THEORIZING. Amid the uncertainty about the facts, theories of the natural gas supply thrived. Liberal Democrats in both houses latched onto the proposition that price increases above $1.75 per mcf would stimulate little or no additional output. Some simply followed a hunch that gas reserves were nearing exhaustion, but a far more common view was that the producing industry had every incentive to deliberately shut in some of its reservoirs as long as an expectation persisted that prices could continue to rise. More supplies would become available, most liberal Democrats believed, once a stable price ceiling was enforced, thus ending the temptation to withhold gas commitments in anticipation of ever higher prices. Also, by spreading the ceiling to cover all transactions, not just those across state lines, producers would stop diverting gas to in-state markets, where greater profits were still possible.

To an impartial observer, there was no evidence that a lid of $1.75 would suffice to finance costly new exploration and deep drilling, or that mere abolition of the dual gas market would do more than ease temporarily the shortages in various parts of the country. But to the liberal Democrats, there were enough suggestive data on hand to make their contentions sound plausible. The liberals, for instance, frequently pointed out that, even under the existing $1.50 per mcf interstate ceiling price, almost every available drilling rig was in use, that the 11,000 gas wells completed in 1977 were a record, and that additions to proven reserves that year were at their highest level since 1970, when Alaskan reserves were added.[91]

Critics replied that these data masked a more complicated, and disturbing, picture. The vast majority of new wells completed were developmental rather than exploratory, and reserves per foot drilled had declined steadily since 1971.[92] Relatively little drilling was taking place at depths and locations where the bulk of the nation's undiscovered gas was believed to exist. Thus overall U.S. proved reserves of natural gas fell for the tenth straight year in 1977.[93]

But it was one thing to call attention to the observable supply-side trends, another to prove that deregulation would readily turn them around. Further, although frequent inquests had failed to turn up proof

91. *Congressional Record*, daily edition (September 19, 1978), p. S15424.
92. *Natural Gas Pricing Proposals: A Comparative Analysis*, Senate Committee on Energy and Natural Resources, 95 Cong. 1 sess. (GPO, 1977), pp. 11, 13.
93. American Gas Association, *Gas Facts: 1977 Data* (Arlington, Va.: American Gas Association, 1978), p. 1.

that large amounts of gas had been withheld by producers as part of a price-gouging conspiracy, or that the producers had systematically plotted to misrepresent the size of gas reserves, or even that the industry was sufficiently oligopolistic to make collusion feasible, some traces of possible impropriety had accumulated. There was just enough suspicion to keep investigators on the scent.[94] In sum, in debating the prospective impact of higher prices on gas supplies, the blend of fragmentary leads and innuendo was rich enough to sustain competing hypotheses, but never solid enough to give either side a decisive empirical edge. In this fuzzy setting, both camps dug in their heels, talked past one another, and increasingly repaired to partisan postures and ideology.

OPEC. Even if everyone had agreed that the natural gas industry was reasonably competitive and that price equivalency of gas with oil would place a flood of new gas on stream, another uncertainty would have blocked consensus on deregulation: in 1977 it was hard to tell whether an international cartel or market forces were setting the world price of crude oil. At the time, the Organization of Petroleum Exporting Countries (OPEC) seemed quite cohesive. Sooner or later market conditions in the 1970s would have raised the cost of oil substantially, irrespective of OPEC. But the suddenness and timing of the fourfold leap in 1974, and the relative steadiness with which prices were held at their new plateau, suggested that the cartel was ratcheting prices capriciously and then maintaining them effectively.

Hence, as the defenders of the regulatory status quo saw matters, it was bad enough that OPEC could fix the price of oil. But to let natural gas prices follow oil prices was to permit OPEC to control *both*. Deregulation merely meant that gas prices would be "regulated by the OPEC

---

94. The disclosures in mid-1973 by James T. Halverson, a Federal Trade Commission investigator, prompted Senator Philip A. Hart, Democrat of Michigan, chairman of the Judiciary Antitrust and Monopoly Subcommittee, to wonder whether the deepening gas shortage might be a hoax. *Congressional Quarterly Almanac*, vol. 29 (1973), p. 641. Opening a new round of hearings in February 1977, Representative John E. Moss, Democrat of California, chairman of the House Subcommittee on Oversight and Investigations, affirmed that in the past two years his panel had "documented the industry's failure to rework existing gas wells in timely fashion, reported on two glaring examples of underproduction, and disclosed disturbing discrepancies in the reporting of natural gas reserves." *"Behind-the-Pipe" Natural Gas Reserves*, Hearings before the Subcommittee on Oversight and Investigations of the House Committee on Interstate and Foreign Commerce, 95 Cong. 1 sess. (GPO, 1977), p. 1. Finally, during 1977 and 1978 the Federal Energy Regulatory Commission claimed to have prosecuted almost as many violations for "unlawful diversions from certificated service" as the old Federal Power Commission had done in forty years. Sanders, *Regulation of Natural Gas*, p. 182.

Congress, not the U.S. Congress," as Senator Ernest F. Hollings, Democrat of South Carolina, warned.[95]

Critics rejoined by saying that regulation-induced scarcity simply increased dependency on imported oil and gas, but decontrol would promote domestic production, reduce imports, and hence undermine the cartel. An occasional Republican went further, asserting that OPEC prices did reflect true replacement costs and that, in the words of Senator Henry Bellmon, Republican of Oklahoma, "the OPEC cartel cannot make an arbitrary price stick for long."[96] Most Democrats, however, found it easy to scoff at these views, insisting that OPEC's tribute was nothing if not extortionary and that whatever the upturn in domestic gas production, it would never be enough to challenge the producing monopoly's hegemony. In short, were it not for the apparent possibility that natural gas rates could be rigged by oil sheiks, decontrol of gas might have secured a wider audience.

THE WEAK DOLLAR. Another twist was added by the weakness of the American dollar overseas. The precipitous decline of the dollar against European currencies, especially in the summer and early fall of 1978, was an ailment that seemed at first glance easy to diagnose. Officials, both at home and abroad, attributed the problem principally to growing petroleum imports and their effect on the U.S. balance of payments. At the Bonn summit meeting in July 1978, President Carter promised to attack the problem by cutting consumption of foreign oil by 2 million barrels a day within seven years.[97] The pledge was applauded by, among others, French President Valery Giscard d'Estaing, who in an interview with *Le Monde* on July 12 had declared, "At the present time, an important reduction in [U.S.] oil imports is the precondition for an improvement in the world economy.... In my view this is the most important single source of upheaval in the worldwide network of trade and payments."[98] Legislation decontrolling domestic gas prices was touted as a crucial step toward remedying the balance of payments problem and, some believed, toward restoring confidence in the dollar.

The opponents, however, countered with the argument that West Germany, Japan, and Switzerland were all much more dependent on im-

95. *Congressional Record*, daily edition (September 12, 1978), p. S14951.
96. *Congressional Record* (September 13, 1978), p. 29104.
97. Paul Lewis, "Carter Reaffirms His Pledge to Cut Oil Imports of U.S.," *New York Times*, July 17, 1978.
98. *Congressional Quarterly Weekly Report*, vol. 36 (July 15, 1978), p. 1763.

ported oil and gas than the United States was. Yet their currencies were strong. What depreciated the dollar on foreign exchange markets was not an American trade deficit but the country's mounting rate of inflation. And what could be more inflationary, the price controllers asked, than the deregulation of oil and gas? The question, in turn, reopened an old, rambling dispute about how much inflation, if any, deregulation would cause.

The Cost of Decontrol

When it came to assessing the net cost of deregulating gas, figures were once again thrown around in a fashion that mystified and misled many lawmakers. The administration's computations were especially perplexing.[99] An analysis released in May 1977 tried to compare the impacts of various alternatives to a "base case" in which existing regulations would remain unchanged. The base case, however, assumed, unbelievably, that unregulated intrastate gas in 1985 would go for merely $0.70 per mcf. Since the average intrastate gas in 1977 was already around $1.30 per mcf, and was expected to reach at least $2.40 by 1985, the administration's calculus understated by a huge margin the cost of continuing under current law. In fact, the size of the error was put at $44 billion by the staff of Carter's own allies on House Commerce's Energy and Power Subcommittee. This flawed accounting left some members of Congress with the false impression that the statutory status quo would be a much better bargain for consumers than any of the proposals under consideration. Thus, key Democrats on the natural gas conference committee, including Senator Jackson, seemed prepared to table the entire slate of gas-pricing reforms in 1978. Only after the Department of Energy belatedly abandoned the original base case data and began admitting a narrower prospective cost differential between existing law and decontrol did the conference take its first tentative steps toward a compromise.

Some of the cost estimates of deregulation were so disparate that one wondered whether their authors were talking about the same subject. One official evaluation of the Krueger-Brown bill, for instance, judged the measure's additional toll on consumers to be about $57 billion through 1985. Subsequently, it became apparent that the authors of this

99. My discussion of this example draws extensively from Malbin, "Congress, Policy Analysis, and Natural Gas Deregulation," pp. 68–75.

estimate had somehow neglected to subtract the costs of replacing gas with substitutes, the use of which was bound to run higher under continued price controls than if the controls were lifted.[100] At the opposite extreme, some studies weighted replacement costs, or additional expenses such as those attributable to unused pipeline capacity during shortages, so heavily that deregulation would confer on consumers a gigantic savings. One such study concluded that deregulation of new gas offered consumers a net savings of $123.3 billion through 1990, even assuming no transportation cost reduction from increased pipeline use.[101] Sharply discrepant appraisals like these permeated the proceedings in Congress from start to finish. Even as the Senate neared its final vote on natural gas, the coalition fighting the gas conference report claimed the act would add $29 to $41 billion to the nation's fuel bills by 1985. Proponents of the administration's natural gas bill used the House Energy and Power Subcommittee's figure of only $9 billion.

The opposing camps seemed to ascertain the costs of pricing options, not by sifting facts, but by making them up. The great majority of Republicans and oil-state Democrats had convinced themselves that, as far as rates for end users were concerned, decontrol of new gas wellhead prices probably entailed no severe or sudden inflationary effects. To begin with, they stressed, wellhead prices constituted only about 25 percent of the price of gas at the burner tip, with transportation, storage, and other markups accounting for the rest. Second, since the higher-priced new gas would be rolled in with the much greater volume of cheaper gas already flowing, the impact of new-gas deregulation might be so gradual as to be imperceptible from one year to the next. When the partisans of decontrol did acknowledge the possibility of significantly higher prices for consumers, it was quickly added that everyone was in for increased energy prices anyway. If decontrol raised prices, so would further regulation because the resulting shortages would continue to feed demand for costly replacements while also raising unit costs of available gas because of underutilization of transmission facilities with fixed overheads.

None of these considerations impressed the majority of Democrats. To take the lid off new gas in the midst of static or just recently improving supplies, most Democrats warned, was to unleash pent-up

100. Natural Gas Supply Committee, *A Natural Gas Primer*, rev. ed. (Washington, D.C.: Natural Gas Supply Committee, 1977), pp. 10–11; and *Natural Gas Pricing Proposals*, Hearings, pp. 187–88.

101. *Oil and Gas Journal*, vol. 75 (September 26, 1977), p. 42.

demand on a seller's market, guaranteeing an instant fly-up in retail rates. Naturally, matters might be different if decontrol promised vast new supplies, a prompt end to service curtailments, and consequently, no more need for replacement fuels. But only Republicans, and Democrats from oil- and gas-producing states, were convinced that decontrol would work that way in the near term.

Distributive Costs

If, as the Left believed, decontrolled gas prices would smite consumers with ruinous fuel bills and there would be little or no improvement in gas production above the magic threshold of $1.75 per mcf, decontrol signified a multibillion-dollar transfer of wealth to producers. Liberals pounded on the issue: to impose this rent on the consuming public was unjust—and to impose it regressively among consumers was downright reprehensible.

The Bureau of Labor Statistics had recently finished painting a grim picture of the distributional effects of energy price increases.[102] According to the bureau's averages, the poorest tenth of the nation's population spent 29 percent of its income on energy over the year immediately preceding the Arab oil embargo, while the richest tenth spent 3.7 percent. As of July 1975, after the first round of OPEC price hikes had run through the economy, it was estimated that the energy expenditures of high-income households had risen to only 4.6 percent. But households in the lowest income decile were now paying 35.9 percent. Such percentages predated the Energy Policy and Conservation Act's domestic oil-price rollback and also reflected only direct energy outlays, rather than the more complex impact associated with indirect energy costs. Subtleties of that sort, however, never found their way into the debate. The critique of gas deregulation on equity grounds remained as coarse as it was hard-hitting: a lot of people with modest incomes were suffering from OPEC's seemingly arbitrary oil prices, but the hardship would become much more widespread if natural gas, the main heating fuel, were allowed to flare up to the equivalent price of oil.

In principle, the regressiveness of steeper natural gas prices could be softened through the same kinds of relief that had been discussed for petroleum pricing. Every now and then, those who pleaded the cause of

102. See John L. Palmer, John E. Todd, and Howard P. Tuckman, "The Distributional Impact of Rising Energy Prices: How Should the Federal Government Respond?" *Public Policy*, vol. 24 (Fall 1976), p. 549.

gas deregulation would pause to address the question and to venture concrete suggestions. In October 1977, for example, Senator Weicker proposed a nationwide energy stamp program, modeled after the food stamp system. Yet liberal Democrats refused to take seriously this notion of linking decontrol to low-income energy assistance.

Weicker's proposal, authorizing some $100 million a year, was as generous a measure as anyone on the proderegulation side was willing to contemplate. Liberals dismissed such offers as too stingy and narrowly targeted. To them, fair restitution warranted more lavish outlays, since their desire was not merely to aid the poor, but also to compensate society (that is, "average" consumers) for the "undeserved" billions reaped by producers. Moreover, by 1977 no one was naive enough to assume that the implied financing mechanism for energy assistance—a hefty tax on the producing industry's surplus earnings—could be put in place. The Ninety-third and Ninety-fourth Congresses had already grappled in vain with efforts to hitch windfall taxes onto deregulation plans for crude oil. In the Ninety-fifth Congress, most members had despaired of pursuing the formula in connection with oil-pricing reform, and the possibility was scarcely mentioned during the natural gas debate.

The Perpetual Debate

A final characteristic of the natural gas controversy, which frustrated any prompt and satisfactory resolution, was the duration of the debate. The natural gas issue was, as James Schlesinger put it, American energy policy's "Thirty Years' War."[103] The opposing armies had fired their first salvos before World War II and then fought fierce engagements at frequent intervals ever since.

THE BURDEN OF HISTORY. The Natural Gas Act of 1938 charged the Federal Power Commission with regulating transport of gas across state lines. Since then proposals to elaborate or restructure federal gas regulations had been presented and voted upon in the House and Senate chambers more than a dozen times. The gas bills considered by congressional committees, but that went no farther, are too numerous to keep track of. In 1950 and again in 1956, both houses of Congress adopted legislation guaranteeing most gas producers, as distinct from transmission companies, exemption from the Federal Power Commission's jurisdiction, only to provoke storms of protest from interests favoring wider

103. *New York Times*, May 25, 1978.

federal regulatory authority. In both cases, the legislation met with presidential vetoes.

The questions that divided Congress in 1977–78—such as the market power of large producers, the capacity of market pricing to alleviate shortages, and the relative costs and distributional effects of alternative pricing methods—were the identical points over which the legislators had clashed decades before. The contemporary antagonists addressed each other in similar terms and from the same seats as the preceding generation of disputants. Adlai E. Stevenson III, Democrat of Illinois, for example, spoke in the tradition of Paul H. Douglas, the earlier Illinois Democrat who had battled tirelessly against exemptions from price controls. Lloyd Bentsen, a leader in the deregulation movement, had inherited the baton brandished previously by a long line of senators from Texas, including Lyndon B. Johnson. Edward M. Kennedy recalled in both style and substance his elder brother. Barry M. Goldwater now sounded a lot like Barry M. Goldwater then.

Even the concerns about OPEC and inflation had been heard long before 1977. These issues had been prominent in the perennial strife over gas and oil decontrol plans that attracted renewed interest throughout the Nixon and Ford administrations. Anyone perusing, say, the Senate Energy Committee's hearings on gas-pricing legislation in June 1977 would sense that Senator Jackson's panel was covering ground already well trod by the Senate Commerce Committee under Warren Magnuson, Democrat of Washington, during its exhaustive hearings between October 1973 and April 1974. Indeed, the Carter energy program was mostly an outgrowth of prior congressional deliberations—contrary to the idea, apparently held by some, that Schlesinger's Energy Policy and Planning team had drawn its designs out of thin air, or had lifted them wholesale from the Ford Foundation's 1974 energy report, *A Time to Choose*. Especially on the House side, key committees had compiled long records dealing with precisely the sorts of policies assimilated later in the National Energy Plan. The administration's proposed utility rate reforms, for example, bore a definite resemblance to a bill drafted in 1976 by the Subcommittee on Energy and Power after extensive hearings on the subject. As suggested earlier, large parts of the plan's section on gas pricing—the notion of placing intrastate sales under federal controls, for instance—were reminiscent of a measure fashioned in the Interstate and Foreign Commerce Committee and passed, also in 1976, by the full House. Finally, as if all the precedents and polemics of the past forty years were not enough, Congress spent an additional year and a half in limbo over the natural gas problem after receiving the initial Carter plan. "You have sat too long here for any good you have been doing; in the name of God, go." Those were Oliver Cromwell's words in his farewell speech to the Rump Parliament in 1653. They could just have easily been expressed by anybody awaiting the results of the natural gas conference in 1978.

THE PERILS OF PROLONGED DEBATE. A legislative marathon runs a convoluted route along which contestants stumble or get sidetracked. The longer the time spent talking, the greater the number of actors and new considerations that can intervene to entangle and delay matters. Several developments during the months of negotiations over the natural gas bill illustrate this process.

A week after the House-Senate conferees finally came to an agreement on the framework (though not yet the precise legislative wording) of the gas compromise, events suddenly took an unexpected turn: the Supreme Court, as it had at so many critical junctures in the past, entered the picture. On May 31, 1978, a verdict in the case of *Southland Royalty Co.* was handed down.[104] The case involved some gas fields in west Texas that had been leased to Gulf Oil, which had sold the gas in the interstate market, subject to certification by the Federal Power Commission. When Gulf's lease expired in 1975, Southland Royalty, the owner of the property, tried to enter into a new contract to sell the gas at higher prices in the intrastate market, where federal controls did not apply. The Court ruled, however, that a federal certificate for interstate sales could remain in effect even after the lease's expiration. Naturally, this decision threw a scare into the gas-producing region, as local royalty holders and producers became nervous that the *Southland* opinion might permit federal regulators to claim precedence over countless intrastate contracts on the grounds that gas from the same acreage had once been dedicated to interstate commerce. *Southland* gave the precarious gas conference a jolt. Some liberal converts to the gas compromise began asking whether the bill was still necessary, since perhaps the Federal Energy Regulatory Commission (formerly the Federal Power Commission) could now reach into the intrastate market and siphon off more gas for the interstate sector. Members apprehensive about what the commission might do insisted that a special clause designed to void the effect of the *Southland* case be written into the NGPA.

104. *California et al.* v. *Southland Royalty Co. et al.*, 436 U.S. 519 (1978).

There were other diversions in the spring of 1978. At one point, the Federal Energy Regulatory Commission announced it would discontinue the practice of allowing some gas pumped from the Outer Continental Shelf to enter intrastate markets. Henceforth, the commission ruled, all gas from the continental shelf would be dedicated to interstate pipelines, with or without the natural gas bill. Again, those representatives who looked to the gas bill as a statutory vehicle to rebuild interstate supplies wondered whether the need for new legislation had passed.

As the discussions droned on, the outlook for gas availability seemed to change. The four-year decline in net gas production began to bottom out in mid-1977. By 1978 drilling was at record levels, additions to proved reserves were up, and with average intrastate prices dropping appreciably, new commitments to the interstate market more than tripled the 1976 volumes.[105] Although the longer-term significance of these improvements was arguable, they tended to dissipate, for the time being, the air of crisis that had previously imparted a sense of urgency to reform of gas pricing.

Drawing Party Lines

As the colloquy on natural gas degenerated from reasoned discourse to a recitation of well-rehearsed scripts, the partisan character of congressional voting grew increasingly keen (see table 3-4 in appendix B to this chapter for the statistical correlation between party and congressional votes over time). Glancing back at, say, the producer exemption bills passed by Congress some thirty-five years earlier, what stands out is the degree to which the votes cut across party lines. For instance, in March 1950, when the House carried the exemption bill written by Representative Oren Harris, Democrat of Arkansas, a narrow majority of Democrats, 116 to 97, voted against it; the Republicans voted 79 to 57 in favor. By 1977 the divisions followed party lines much more closely. The tally on the Krueger-Brown amendment, defeated in the House in August 1977, showed 72 Democrats joining 127 Republicans in support of decontrol, while 210 Democrats and 17 Republicans opposed it. A similar pattern evolved in the Senate. By the time the roll was called on the second Pearson-Bentsen bill in October 1977, a lopsided majority

105. *Congressional Record* (September 19, 1978), p. 29978. By early 1978, average intrastate gas prices had slid to $1.75 per mcf, as some state markets began working off spot surpluses. *Congressional Quarterly Weekly Report*, vol. 36 (September 16, 1978), p. 2454.

among Democrats rejected deregulation, but the Republicans were almost unanimously behind it.

Conclusions

The Natural Gas Policy Act was only one part of the 1978 National Energy Act, whose supposed cornerstone was conservation. An assortment of programs packed into the omnibus legislation—including insulation credits, energy audits, loans for solar energy systems, incentives for small hydropower projects, taxes on gas-guzzling cars, weatherization grants, and boiler-fuel restrictions—were intended to shrink the waste of scarce heating fuels. But no cluster of energy-saving measures could have served the goal of conservation better than a decision to sweep away price controls, not only on oil but also on natural gas—the one move Congress proved unable to make in 1978. Instead an elaborate compromise on decontrol was fashioned, which postponed the process needlessly and dragged regulatory inefficiencies well into the 1980s.

The political struggle accompanying the passage of the Natural Gas Policy Act inspired varying interpretations. Renditions ranged from bizarre conspiracy theories centering on crafty oil and gas "titans" to the notions that Congress was transfixed by conflicts between narrow constituent interests, that it simply answered a public outcry against higher gas prices, or even that the final gas bill was little more than a presidential blunder. But, more than any of these things, the grand compromise signified an attempted fusion between disparate views of how the government should put natural gas markets back in working order.

To the Republicans and their Democratic allies in gas-rich states, the postembargo era of rising petroleum prices was finally an ideal time to pull the federal government out of the natural gas business. Deregulation would permit gas prices to move toward oil equivalency, thus uncorking huge supplies that would otherwise remain bottled up for lack of drilling incentives. There were similarities with the line adopted by deregulators during the oil-pricing controversy: the main point of decontrol was boosting output; better demand restraint would also clear the market, but this bonus received less attention.

Although overconsumption of gas was at least as much a problem as the declining rate of reserve additions in the mid-1970s, the supply side of the natural gas equation dominated discussion for several reasons. First, to harp on wasteful overuse of gas amid persisting shortages risked sounding callous toward small consumers. Second, the public, for all its restiveness, seemed more interested in deregulation if the term did not imply primarily the suppression of demand through steeper heating bills. Also, the volume of gas resources to be tapped at higher prices was potentially dazzling, even if no one could say just how high those prices had to go to do the job. But perhaps most important, the proponents of decontrol were in the habit of thinking about energy price policy largely as a production issue, not as a mechanism for conservation.

The opponents of decontrol, overwhelmingly Democrats, had their own arsenal of explanations for why more regulation, rather than less, was in order. If the problem of pricing policy was how to release a greater gas supply, the first step was not to free the marketplace, but to rid it of at least two perceived flaws: the price disparity of the dual gas market, which discouraged producers from selling their product out of state; and the alleged propensity of producers to hold back gas at current prices to fetch a heftier return on it at some future date. The first defect led to the idea that prices ought to be capped uniformly for the intrastate as well as the interstate sector, the second, to the idea that a legally firm ceiling would deter, once and for all, the urge to withhold.

Most Democratic congressmen were inclined to believe that the main consequence of market pricing would not be to procure a lot more gas for consumers, but to force them to pay unjustified rents to producers: regardless of their activities or economic contributions, cautioned Carter's National Energy Plan, producers would pocket the enhanced value of gas fields appreciating in an uncontrolled market.[106] This matter was not new. For years regulators had argued that the natural gas industry was not sufficiently competitive to ensure that buyers would face a fee for gas based on prevalent costs of production. With the ascendancy of OPEC in the 1970s, however, considerable impetus was added to the theory that phony prices would prevail in an unregulated domestic oil and gas economy. Gas rates would shadow international petroleum prices, which were widely regarded as the whims of a cartel. The thrust of the Democratic party's rhetoric seemed to be that chilly consumers would watch big oil reap windfalls while an idle government witnessed the robbery without coming to the aid of the victims.

As in the confrontation over oil pricing, the course of the natural gas debate tended to calcify opposing positions. Again, if the object of

106. Executive Office of the President, *National Energy Plan*, p. 50.

market pricing was to enable the nation to produce its way out of the energy doldrums of the 1970s, it became relevant to ask, how and when? Plenty of quantitative answers estimating the price levels, regulatory conditions, and time frames needed to meet supply requirements were pressed into the hands of policymakers. However, the technical data seemed so often inconsistent, speculative, or patently politicized that the result was not so much to edify lawmakers as to split them further along party lines. Division solidified between those confident that the producing industry could make good the promised supply increases and those who suspected it wouldn't.

Other uncertainties had the same effect. The full extent of OPEC's grip on global energy prices, the actual comportment of the gas industry, the facts about decontrol's likely economic impact, and even the final verdict of public opinion were interpreted in different ways, mostly depending on the partisan loyalties of the interpreters.

Finally, 1977–78 was hardly the opening act of the natural gas drama; the debate was only another episode in a repetitious passion play that had been running in Washington for about forty years.

Torn between members who trusted that the productive stimulus of deregulated market prices would put an end to natural gas shortages and an equally avid body of legislators who insisted that deregulation was socially irresponsible, Congress found it difficult—in fact almost impossible—to have it both ways. What middle ground could be discovered under the circumstances was likely to represent a murky legislative twilight zone, repugnant to purists of both persuasions. That is why the process of reaching a final settlement aroused such sustained and unusual opposition, and why the settlement itself became a phenomenally complicated piece of legislation.

Recent Developments

The Natural Gas Policy Act seemed destined for a short life. The delicate nature of the compromise, the thinness of its margin of passage, and the congressional rancor it stirred appeared to presage amendments and even repeal. Yet just the opposite occurred: after 1978 the striking feature of the regulatory regime became its remarkable political immunity to reform. Even when the Reagan administration took over in 1981 with a good understanding of what was wrong with the law, and an earnest desire to step up the pace of deregulation, progress proved to be impossible.

Throughout 1981 congressional energies were deliberately absorbed in other business. The White House chose to defer the natural gas question, calculating that this contentious issue could easily overload the legislative circuits and drain precious political capital at a time when the president was pushing his economic program. But other forces also were already at work, building a configuration of interests that would thwart positive changes in the law.

The New Interest Group Melee

After 1978, calls for total price deregulation on an accelerated basis came primarily from larger oil companies that owned lots of old gas (wells drilled before 1977) forever regulated under the existing arrangement. Large industrial users of gas with low-priority status in the event of renewed rationing also favored complete decontrol because they reckoned it would assure them steady supplies. Before 1978 these lobbies had presented a common front with other segments of the natural gas industry—independent producers, pipelines, and utilities—but that unity had crumbled. Many independents were specializing in lifting deep gas or new gas, which commanded handsome prices under the natural gas bill's variegated rate structure. Such firms had little to gain, and in some cases a great deal to lose, by reshuffling the law's stacked deck: a freer market would probably equilibrate the prices of all gas categories, pushing prices up on older vintages but down on some newer ones.

At the same time, pipeline companies were now bickering with producers and with one another. Some pipelines, chiefly the intrastates with no cheap-gas cushions, favored proposals to broaden decontrol. But most were content to leave the NGPA's pricing schedules alone. They recommended separate legislation to facilitate the abrogation of onerous contracts, such as those with indefinite escalators and extensive take-or-pay requirements on high-priced gas. Spokesmen for the carriers maintained that contract cancellations would remove the leading cause of disorderly price spurts being experienced on some systems and would defuse the time bomb ticking to a possible price explosion upon decontrol of new gas in 1985. Though pipeline companies had an interest in "marketing out" of expensive contracts (overpriced gas was becoming harder to sell among end users who could convert to alternate fuels), producers tended to oppose the idea because they thought widespread contract revisions would create uncertainty and financial disarray in field markets.[107] This concern was echoed by representatives of the country's most important life insurance companies and by banks that were counting on the long-term revenues from extant contracts for repayment of the huge outstanding loans floated to oil- and gas-drilling firms.[108]

Finally, at the receiving end of the distribution chain, gas utilities were forming an unusual alliance with consumer organizations clamoring for drastic measures to tighten the NGPA.[109] The sudden rate hikes that followed the second oil shock had set off angry outbursts from consumer groups, especially in regions long accustomed to rigidly controlled gas prices. One group, the Citizens/Labor Energy Coalition, which had been inconsequential in 1977–78, had mushroomed into a far-reaching, well-organized protest movement four years later. The energy coalition and its affiliates sought an extension of the NGPA's controls past 1985, an interim overall price freeze, and punitive regulations on "imprudent" pipelines that had entered into costly gas contracts and passed the higher charges through to local distributors. Uncharacteristically, many local distribution companies had started to think along the same lines. A few years earlier these companies had fretted about supply shortfalls rather than prices; now they worried that the unanticipated rate increases of the 1980s were driving big industrial customers to switch fuels, that states and municipalities were moving to deny utility cost passthroughs, and that it could become increasingly difficult to make collections from a growing number of consumers in arrears on their utility bills. Some utilities blamed pipelines and their customers for careless contracts, for passing on high fixed costs from excess capacity, and for inflating wellhead prices through their monopsonistic access to field markets. So, these utilities and their ratepayers wanted the legal option to use pipelines as contract carriers—that is, to bypass the middlemen by purchasing gas directly from producers and then contracting with pipelines only to transport it.

107. *Congressional Quarterly Weekly Report*, vol. 41 (April 23, 1983), p. 796.

108. When legislation permitting contract invalidations eventually came to a vote in the Senate during November 1983, these financial institutions mounted an intense lobbying campaign against the measure. Andy Paztor, "Reagan's Gas Decontrol Bill Is Meeting Opposition by Some Big Banks, Insurers," *Wall Street Journal*, November 1, 1983.

109. *Congressional Quarterly Weekly Report*, vol. 41 (April 23, 1983), p. 796. Some utilities drummed up consumer complaints by attaching notices to monthly utility bills, which warned of price increases with decontrol.

The Reagan Administration Enters the Fray

To wade back into the regulatory swamp of the Natural Gas Policy Act in search of a sound legislative revision that would accommodate so many different demands was treacherous enough. But to try it in an election year, while the president's economic policy wobbled through a grueling recession, would be folly. Reagan's promised gas initiative was delayed again, through 1982. A House subcommittee held exploratory hearings on the natural gas problem, as the Senate Committee on Energy and Natural Resources had done the year before, and members of Congress introduced dozens of bills dealing with various aspects, but no action was taken.

In February 1983, however, the administration came up with a plan that appeared, at first glance, to offer an ingenious window to decontrol while guaranteeing safety for consumers and providing advantages for other apprehensive parties. The proposal, in a nutshell, was to deregulate old as well as new gas, but subject to an overall price cap and a ban on automatic pipeline passthroughs of price increases above inflation until 1986. In the meantime, more flexibility would be imposed on contractual arrangements by limiting take-or-pay provisions, by prodding producers and transmission companies to market out of their current contracts, and by creating incentives for competitive direct purchase of gas through contract carriage.

Yet when the Senate Energy Committee took up the administration's package in April, it found itself splintered on almost every detail, even though the panel was Republican controlled and loaded with producer-state members (theoretically, an ideal audience for the market approach embodied in the bill). The administration had hoped that, at a minimum, senators from producing states would rally behind the scheme, conceding the sections on contract reform to pave the way for deregulation. But even these normally cohesive members were no longer fellow travelers. Where they stood depended largely on what sorts of gas their producer-constituents sold. Sellers stuck with large old-gas reserves were prepared to accept revised contracts; indeed, some were anxious to initiate renegotiations in hopes of drawing higher prices, as the proposed bill permitted. But in states where producers had invested heavily in new-gas wells, operators often had little or no reason to break existing agreements. In fact these producers feared that the new legislation might enable pipeline companies to annul contracts to obtain lower field prices.

As for legislators representing nonproducing states, their reaction was predictably more pusillanimous than it would have been if service curtailments had still been wracking consumers in the fashion of the 1970s. Some fled from the administration-endorsed bill because they were still trembling from a genuine groundswell of local complaints about heating costs. Others looked after constituents who were luxuriating in disproportionate volumes of old gas. And most found it hard to believe Energy Secretary Donald P. Hodel's prognosis that deregulation would significantly reduce average residential gas costs.[110]

Even seemingly innocuous provisions, which did not agitate producer and consumer interests so directly, turned into sticking points. Chairman James A. McClure had wished to clear contract carriage, for instance, in one or two markup sessions. But under attack from the American Gas Association and the Interstate Natural Gas Association, which were speaking for major pipelines, the committee spent weeks haggling over it. Even the committee's original supporters of contract carriage began worrying that industrial load instability might develop on some distribution systems if it became too easy for big end users, as well as utility companies, to start shopping for their needs directly in a spot market.[111] Although the following fall, McClure finally managed to take a bill to the floor—"The Natural Gas Policy Act Amendments of 1983," comparable in most important respects to the administration's initial submission[112]—support for it in his committee was so lukewarm it was reported without recommendation. With only a threadbare coalition backing it, the measure was crushed by the full Senate, 67 to 28, shortly after its introduction.

Meanwhile in the House, John D. Dingell, now chairman of the

110. The Department of Energy's prediction that prices would fall assumed continued softening of world crude-oil prices. *Congressional Quarterly Weekly Report*, vol. 41 (March 5, 1983), p. 446. This assessment was contradicted by an Energy Information Administration report, which estimated that deregulation in 1985 would drive residential gas prices up by 6 percent. *National Journal*, vol. 15 (May 28, 1983), p. 1134. Secretary Hodel was also undercut by a Congressional Budget Office study forecasting consistently higher gas prices under the administration's plan than under existing law. Andy Paztor, "Senate Shelves Decontrol Bill for Natural Gas," *Wall Street Journal*, November 4, 1983.

111. *Congressional Quarterly Weekly Report*, vol. 41 (May 14, 1983), p. 941.

112. The main difference was that the eventual Senate bill (S. 1715) contained more elaborate provisions for gradually adjusting the price of gas under designated contracts either downward, for high-cost gas, or upward, for old gas, during the transition to a free market. For a neat summary and comparison of these and other recent natural gas bills, see *Natural Gas Proposals, 1983, 98 Congress, 1 Session* (Washington, D.C.: American Enterprise Institute, 1983).

Energy and Commerce Committee, had vowed that efforts to rush deregulation would only "occur over my dead body."[113] A bill relaxing price controls on additional yields from enhanced recovery in old fields had narrowly passed the Energy Subcommittee on Fossil and Synthetic Fuels. Technically, the subcommittee proposal only modified, but did not eliminate, the NGPA's exclusion of old gas from decontrol, since, unlike the Senate version, it did not propose to "ramp up" the price of old gas already flowing. Nevertheless, Dingell gaveled it down in full committee, and by the end of 1983, appeared to leave open only one possible alteration of existing law: tighter controls, for a longer period.

Congressional Action in 1984

Congressional activity on natural gas sputtered in 1984, despite the fact that the House Energy Committee did not quit work after efforts in the Senate reached a standstill. With Chairman Dingell and Representative Philip R. Sharp, Democrat of Indiana, masterminding things, the committee forged ahead with amendments designed to toughen the natural gas statute by setting ceilings on price escalators for all gas from 1985 to 1987 and by reaffirming a proscription on deregulation of any old gas.

The Dingell-Sharp formula never came before the full House. Apart from consumer representatives, few were pleased with its contents. The leading producers were outraged. One of their top lobbyists declared that "this legislation, if enacted, would essentially return natural gas pricing to the Stone Age."[114] Independents condemned the lengthening of controls, plus language in the bill granting pipelines the power to terminate contracts on high-cost gas. Banks and insurers objected on similar grounds. The pipeline companies were also uneasy. They appreciated proposed drastic reductions of takes on take-or-pay clauses (reductions that producers denounced), but shuddered at the pipeline imprudency tests that the bill empowered the Federal Energy Regulatory Commission to administer. Such dissension all but precluded serious consideration by the House. And even if House passage had been possible, the Republican Senate would have dragged its feet rather than go to conference with Dingell-Sharp.

---

113. *Congressional Quarterly Weekly Report*, vol. 40 (January 16, 1982), p. 79.
114. *Capital Energy Letter*, vol. 524 (April 9, 1984), p. 4.

Conclusion

The natural gas spectacle has moved off center stage. What began in 1982 as an important legislative attempt to let market forces smooth the distortions of the Natural Gas Policy Act ended up with more talk of tinkering with controls, or of leaving the existing ones in place. In 1984, further efforts to speed up the schedule of decontrol appeared unlikely. Administration energy officials and an apparent majority of the Senate seemed resigned to the status quo, citing several considerations: signs that a significant number of gas contracts were being renegotiated voluntarily; recent indications of steady price reductions in some previously volatile gas categories; reduced public pressure for action; and perhaps above all, fear that another push for legislation, in a presidential election year with a short legislative calendar, could result in a silly quick fix, worse than current law.

To some extent, the post-1978 congressional wrangle over gas pricing has displayed roughly the same political cleavage that shaped the Natural Gas Policy Act: once again, the more conservative Senate toyed with deregulatory options while the more liberal House drifted toward stiffer regulation. But for the most part, the complexion of the natural gas contest has changed since the NGPA's rules took effect. The 1978 act spawned a much more factious set of economic and geographic interests, including not only more potent consumer organizations but also powerful clients within the natural gas business itself. Indeed, the new factionalism of the 1980s has enhanced the importance of special interest rivalries as an influence on gas policy—and above all, as a source of policy paralysis. It has also tended to loosen the partisan blocs that squared off in the 1970s. For the first time since the 1950s, fairly bipartisan groupings, both for and against continued price controls, could be identified in Congress.[115] Nonetheless, had it not been for the ideological end game of 1977–78, the strange present phase of natural gas politics would not have unfolded.

Appendix A: Logit Analysis of Congressional Voting Patterns

In table 3-1, logit models are used to analyze the importance of state energy attributes as determinants of congressional votes on the Natural

115. For example, some errant Republicans in Congress were in the forefront of the campaign for recontrol in 1983. Senator Nancy L. Kassebaum, Republican of Kansas, introduced a bill to freeze prices, very much along the lines proposed by the Citizens/Labor

Gas Policy Act. What stands out is how few of the estimated coefficients in the logit equations are significant—and how the few that are significant are not consistently so across the two roll calls. Interestingly, a disjuncture between producing and consuming state interests emerges more sharply in the House than in the Senate. Evidently, where the major net consuming states carried more weight, a larger percentage of representatives appreciated the fact that the compromise legislation would funnel more regulated old gas into these areas; thus net gas consumption was linked more tightly to support for the NGPA.[116] Still, the net consumption variable is the only local energy variable with a demonstrable impact in the House equation; how members of Congress voted was not consistently a function of other presumably vital determinants such as state gas curtailments and state gas prices. Moreover, the cleavage between states that were net consumers of gas and states that produced more gas than they consumed might seem unexpectedly weak in the Senate vote. In the upper chamber, after all, small producing states held seats in excess of their share of the population, and if senators from these states had voted against the gas act uniformly, a more significant coefficient for net consumption would have resulted for the Senate's roll call as well.

No doubt, one explanation for such results was simply that the NGPA, being a compromise between antithetical House and Senate formulations, made numerous concessions to both camps, which, although adding to the bill's intricacy, enticed a number of legislators into defecting from the opposition. The special treatment given Alaskan gas is a good illustration. The act carefully exempted the transportation costs of Prudhoe Bay gas from incremental pricing, thus allowing the projected Alaska gas pipeline to pass these costs onto all end users. This exception would help the project's sponsors obtain financing, hence ensuring early completion. It also attracted the votes of Alaska's senators, as well as the state's sole House member, all of whom had previously been committed to the producer state bloc. Small but significant fissures were also created elsewhere in the producing region. The NGPA's special prices

Energy Coalition.

116. Per capita consumption of natural gas and per capita production of this fuel are directly and powerfully linked: $r = .84$ ($p < .001$). Clearly, where gas is abundant and easy to deliver, it is heavily used. The intercorrelation is so strong that consumption and production cannot be entered separately into the same logit equations without rendering inefficient estimates from one variable or the other. Net consumption avoids the problem of multicollinearity, accounting for both factors by taking the differential between them.

Table 3-1. *The Natural Gas Policy Act of 1978: Logit Analysis of State Energy Attributes as Determinants of Congressional Votes*[a]

Item	House[b] H. Res. 1434 Oct. 13, 1978 (413 votes)	Senate[c] H.R. 5289 Sept. 27, 1978 (99 votes)
Net consumption of natural gas per capita[d]	2.1283* (3.603)	1.7330 (1.779)
Coal production per capita	13.7448 (1.144)	10.0834 (0.884)
Natural gas curtailments per capita	27.8498 (1.362)	21.8946 (0.846)
Average price of natural gas (residential)	0.0029 (1.311)	0.0069* (2.060)
Average price of electricity (residential)	−0.0002 (1.039)	−0.0002 (0.788)
Party affiliation	3.9400* (9.438)	0.5577 (1.224)
Chi-squared	198.45	13.53

Sources: *House and Senate votes: Congressional Quarterly Weekly Report,* vol. 36 (October 21, 1978), pp. 3092–93; vol. 36 (September 30, 1978), p. 2709; *gas prices, production, and consumption:* American Gas Association, *Gas Facts: 1977 Data* (Arlington, Va.: American Gas Association, 1978), pp. 26, 27, 67, 72, 116; *electricity prices:* U.S. Department of Energy, Energy Information Administration, *State Energy Fuel Prices by Major Economic Sector from 1960 through 1977* (Washington, D.C.: Department of Energy, 1979), table B-1, pp. 95–96; *coal production:* National Coal Association, *Coal Facts* (Washington, D.C.: National Coal Association, 1979), p. 80 (figures are for thousands of net tons of bituminous coal produced in 1977, standardized by 1970 U.S. Census of Population); and *gas curtailments:* Federal Power Commission, *State-by-State Summary of Gas Curtailments* (Washington, D.C.: Federal Power Commission, 1977), pp. 5–8, figures are for winter 1976–77 (breakdowns for Maryland, Virginia, Idaho, Washington, and Oregon were provided directly by state public service commissions or local gas utilities in those service areas).

*$p < .05$.

a. Upper figures in each column are the estimated logit coefficients. Figures in parentheses are t-statistics. Data for the first five independent variables in the equations are aggregated by states. The sixth, party affiliation, is a dummy specified: 1 = Democrat; 0 = Republican. The dichotomous dependent variables are specified: 1 = a vote for the NGPA; 0 = a vote against the NGPA.

b. The key House vote on the NGPA conference report came on a procedural motion (see footnote 35).

c. The Senate's final vote adopting the NGPA conference report is the decisive roll call shown here.

d. Net consumption signifies consumption minus production.

for new and deep gas, for instance, managed to divide the New Mexico and Kansas delegations. Senators Pete V. Domenici and James B. Pearson, for example, wound up voting for the compromise.

The maze of bargaining and logrolling enmeshed both the House and Senate. But the Senate became the site of some of the most intense individual negotiations and settlements. Consequently, it became especially hard to detect systematic patterns in the final Senate vote. Here, even the influence of party was blunted, as Republican senators were carved up almost evenly (seventeen yeas against twenty nays) and more than a third of the Democrats voting dissented. In the House, by contrast, there was much stronger evidence of party-line voting in the critical roll call of October 13. The extremely narrow margin of that vote, in which the

Republicans chose to mount their last stand against the gas bill, contributed to the vote's more manifestly partisan character, as suggested by the significance of the House's party-affiliation coefficient in table 3-1.

Localism—the bidding and trading for local advantages—had limits. Congressional delegations in many parts of the country were divided, not only because separate deals had been struck with numerous members, but also because many legislators were unable to agree about the best interests of their respective states or regions.

For example, a contingent that purportedly had discerned where its bread was buttered was the coal-producing states. Yet in both roll calls in table 3-1, the coefficients for levels of state coal production and votes on the natural gas bill are positive but not significant. Coal production, as a predictor, is weak not just because there were too few coal-producing states to generate robust statistics, but also because there was considerable disunity among representatives from the leading producing states. In the Senate, for instance, if one takes the eight most important states, which together produced over 80 percent of the nation's coal in 1977, ten senators voted for the NGPA, but six voted against it.

Not surprisingly, since neither the Krueger-Brown nor the Pearson-Bentsen substitutes were compromise measures fashioned by a conference committee, the logit coefficients for local energy variables in table 3-2 are more substantial than those in table 3-1. Significantly, for example, votes for deregulation in the House equation are inversely related to electric rates as well as net gas consumption.[117] But these differences are not the most notable aspect of table 3-2. The most impressive aspect is now the importance of party in both equations: counted in percentages of votes predicted by the logit models, the entry of party affiliation contributes much more than half of the correct predictions on the Senate side as well as on the House side. Unless the models control for party, in other words, they explain a relatively small share of congressmen's votes on those roll calls that put positions on gas decontrol to a real test. (The equations in table 3-2, reestimated without the party variable, are tabulated fully in table 3-3.)

Other supposedly vital factors—the local residential retail price of natural gas, for instance—continued to show rather mild effects on voting behavior. If, as is customarily assumed, the states with higher delivered prices for gas had opposed deregulation cohesively, because of

---

117. Electricity rates can be sensitive to gas pricing in areas in which natural gas is used as a generator fuel, typically for peakload power plants.

Table 3-2. *Natural Gas Deregulation Bills in 1977: Logit Analysis of State Energy Attributes as Determinants of Congressional Votes*[a]

Item	House[b] H.R. 8444 Aug. 3, 1977 (426 votes)	Senate[c] S. 2104 Oct. 4, 1977 (96 votes)
Net consumption of natural gas	−5.3132*	−21.1125
per capita[d]	(4.860)	(1.485)
Coal production per capita	−27.2863*	20.1204
	(2.143)	(0.755)
Natural gas curtailments	−2.5663	88.7133*
per capita	(0.114)	(2.239)
Average price of natural gas	−0.0048	−0.0035
(residential)	(1.872)	(0.591)
Average price of electricity	−0.0006*	−0.0008
(residential)	(3.579)	(1.810)
Party affiliation	−3.7390*	−4.6555*
	(10.955)	(4.845)
Chi-squared	245.95	74.09
Percentage of votes predicted correctly[e]	70.10	71.70
Percentage of votes predicted correctly (party affiliation omitted)[f]	25.10	30.40

Sources: *House and Senate votes: Congressional Quarterly Weekly Report*, vol. 35 (August 6, 1977), pp. 1686–87; vol 35 (October 8, 1977), p. 2172; *gas prices, production, and consumption:* American Gas Association, *Gas Facts: 1977 Data*, pp. 26, 27, 67, 72, 116; *electricity prices:* U.S. Department of Energy, *State Energy Fuel Prices by Major Economic Sector from 1960 through 1977*, table B-1, pp. 95–96; *coal production:* National Coal Association, *Coal Facts*, p. 80 (figures are for thousands of net tons of bituminous coal produced in 1977, standardized by 1970 U.S. Census of Population); and *gas curtailments:* Federal Power Commission, *State-by-State Summary of Gas Curtailments*, pp. 5–8, figures are for winter 1976–77 (Breakdowns for Maryland, Virginia, Idaho, Washington, and Oregon were provided directly by state public service commissions or local gas utilities in those service areas.)

*$p < .05$.

a. Upper figures in each column are the estimated logit coefficients. Figures in parentheses are t-statistics. Data for the first five independent variables in the equations are aggregated by states. The sixth, party affiliation, is a dummy specified: 1 = Democrat; 0 = Republican. The dichotomous dependent variables are specified: 1 = a vote for decontrol; 0 = a vote against decontrol.

b. The vote analyzed is the decisive division on the Krueger-Brown bill (an amendment to H.R. 8444).

c. The vote is the final roll call on the Pearson-Bentsen amendment (H.R. 5289 amending S. 2104).

d. Net consumption signifies consumption minus production.

e. These are the normalized percentages of prodecontrol votes predicted by the above models (that is, the percentages after subtracting the percentages that would be predicted in a model that had no explanatory variables, other than a constant): $\hat{p} - p_o / 1 - p_o$, where $\hat{p}$ is the overall percentage of correct predictions in the equation, and p_o is the percentage of predictions in an equation with no explanatory variables other than a constant.

f. The normalized percentages of prodecontrol votes predicted by the same models, excluding party affiliation as an explanatory variable. See table 3-3 for the tabulated logit coefficients and t-tests.

sensitivity to further price increases, a desire to keep consumers from getting "ripped off," or other such considerations, one would expect the average residential gas price to yield more significant coefficients in both the Krueger-Brown and Pearson-Bentsen divisions. Apparently, senators and representatives from states with higher retail prices exhibited some tendency to resist the even steeper prices foreseen under decontrol, but aberrant cases rendered the pattern relatively unsystematic.

Table 3-3. *Natural Gas Deregulation Bills in 1977: Logit Analysis of State Energy Attributes as Determinants of Congressional Votes*[a]

Item	House[b] H.R. 8444 Aug. 3, 1977 (426 votes)	Senate[c] S. 2104 Oct. 4, 1977 (96 votes)
Net consumption of natural gas per capita[d]	−3.1291* (3.388)	−12.7280 (1.799)
Coal production per capita	−18.9985 (1.852)	1.1840 (0.055)
Natural gas curtailments per capita	−0.6958 (0.041)	46.1119 (1.397)
Average price of natural gas (residential)	−0.0035 (1.916)	−0.0032 (1.073)
Average price of electricity (residential)	−0.0004* (2.726)	−0.0002 (0.712)
Chi-squared	50.16	26.42
Percentage of votes predicted correctly[e]	25.10	30.40

Sources: *House and Senate votes: Congressional Quarterly Weekly Report*, vol. 35 (August 6, 1977), pp. 1686–87; vol. 35 (October 8, 1977), p. 2172; *gas prices, production, and consumption:* American Gas Association, *Gas Facts: 1977 Data*, pp. 26, 27, 67, 72, 116; *electricity prices:* U.S. Department of Energy, *State Energy Fuel Prices by Major Economic Sector from 1960 through 1977*, table B-1, pp. 95–96; *coal production:* National Coal Association, *Coal Facts*, p. 80 (figures are for thousands of net tons of bituminous coal produced in 1977, standardized by 1970 U.S. Census of Population); and *gas curtailments:* Federal Power Commission, *State-by-State Summary of Gas Curtailments*, pp. 5–8, figures are for winter 1976–77 (breakdowns for Maryland, Virginia, Idaho, Washington, and Oregon were provided directly by state public service commissions or local gas utilities in those service areas).
*p < .05.

a. Upper figures in each column are the estimated logit coefficients. Figures in parentheses are t-statistics. Data for the independent variables in the equations are aggregated by states. The dichotomous dependent variables are specified: 1 = a vote for decontrol; 0 = a vote against decontrol.
b. The vote analyzed is the decisive division on the Krueger-Brown bill (an amendment to H.R. 8444).
c. The vote is the final roll call on the Pearson-Bentsen amendment (H.R. 5289 amending S. 2104).
d. Net consumption signifies consumption minus production.
e. These are the normalized percentages of prodecontrol votes predicted by the above models (that is, the percentages after subtracting the percentages that would be predicted in a model that had no explanatory variables, other than a constant): $\hat{p} - p_O / 1 - p_O$ where $\hat{p}$ is the overall percentage of correct predictions in the equation, and p_O is the percentage of predictions in an equation with no explanatory variables other than a constant.

Similarly, states suffering severe gas curtailments, with attendant unemployment, might be expected to fear continued shortages and thus to opt for decontrol as a means of ensuring adequate supplies. In reality, this logic appeared to prevail in the Senate, but not in the House, where curtailments were, if anything, negatively associated with votes to decontrol.

Appendix B: Correlations between Party Affiliation and Congressional Voting over Time

The partisan collision during the natural gas fight of 1977–78 had come to reflect real differences between congressional liberals and conservatives. Party differences on the gas issue had grown increasingly intense over the years (table 3-4).

Table 3-4. *Natural Gas Deregulation Bills, 1950–77: Party as a Correlate in Congressional Votes*[a]

Legislation	House	Senate
S. 1498 Kerr-Thomas bill March 29, 1950 (82 votes)		−.21
H.R. 1758 Harris bill March 31, 1950 (350 votes)	−.12	
H.R. 6645 Harris bill July 28, 1955 (412 votes)	−.26*	
H.R. 6645 Harris-Fulbright bill February 6, 1956 (91 votes)		−.21
Buckley amendment to S. 2776 December 19, 1973 (88 votes)		−.57*
Pearson-Bentsen substitute for S. 2310 October 22, 1975 (91 votes)		−.57*
Krueger substitute for H.R. 9464 February 5, 1976 (402 votes)	−.53*	
Krueger-Brown-Wirth amendment to H.R. 8444 August 3, 1977 (426 votes)	−.59*	
Pearson-Bentsen amendment to S. 2104 October 4, 1977 (96 votes)		−.63*

Sources: *Congressional Quarterly Almanac*, vol. 6 (1950), pp. 714–15, 22; vol. 11 (1955), pp. 162–63; vol. 12 (1956), p. 151; vol. 29 (1973), p. 93-S; *Congressional Quarterly Weekly Report*, vol. 33 (October 25, 1975), p. 2289; vol. 34 (February 7, 1976), pp. 293–94; vol. 35 (December 31, 1977), p. 2694.

*$p < .01$ (two-tailed test).

a. The first four roll calls involved bills exempting producers from the Federal Power Commission's jurisdiction; the last five were proposals to decontrol the price of new gas (variously defined). Dependent variable: 1 = a vote for decontrol (or exemption); 0 = a vote against decontrol (or exemption). Independent variable: 1 = Democrat; 0 = Republican.

By 1977 congressional votes on natural gas were powerfully influenced by party labels, although the votes appear to have been decided even more basically by the closely related ideological orientations of members.[118] The votes of the Ninety-fifth Congress on its two strongest deregulation bills correlated impressively with the Americans for Democratic Action's rankings of members along a liberal-conservative scale: for Krueger-Brown in the House the simple correlation was $r = −.74$ ($p < .001$); for Pearson-Bentsen in the Senate, it was $r = −.76$ ($p < .001$). Consistently, representatives and senators with conservative records favored decontrol; those with more liberal ones rejected it.

118. Because of the extremely high intercorrelation between party and the measure of ideological orientation used, the index by the Americans for Democratic Action, ideology could not be incorporated along with party in the various logit equations presented earlier.

CHAPTER FOUR

Revision of Electric Utility Rates

GENERATION of electricity consumes one-third of the nation's energy. No other sector, not even transportation, takes so large a share. Part of the reason, of course, is that production of electric power is inherently fuel intensive; for every Btu-equivalent of power derived, three Btus are cast off as thermal losses in the conversion of primary fuels. Robust demand, however, has been the main force behind the prodigious commitment of energy resources to power generation. Demand, in turn, has tracked prices. Roughly until the oil boycott in 1973, consumption grew an average of 7 percent a year, spurred by electric tariffs that had fallen steadily.[1] When prices began turning up in the early 1970s, the increase in demand slid to less than half that annual rate.[2] Despite the slower growth, electricity consumption since the embargo climbed faster than overall energy usage, and for a while, much faster than GNP.[3] To trim consumption further, prices would have to move considerably higher than they already have. For all the furor that accompanied the rising

1. Because of scale economies and technological progress, the cost of electric power to consumers rose far more slowly than the cost of all other types of energy. Thus from the mid-1930s to roughly the mid-1970s, the average annual electricity consumption rate of 7 percent was nearly double the average annual growth in total energy consumption. Richard B. Mancke, *Squeaking By: U.S. Energy Policy Since the Embargo* (Columbia University Press, 1976), p. 137.

2. Then, with the onset of prolonged economic recession, demand for electricity shrank to a 1.7 percent annual increase in 1980, a 0.3 percent increase in 1981, and a net decrease of 2.3 percent in 1982. Peter Stoler, "Pulling the Nuclear Plug," *Time* (February 13, 1984), p. 37.

3. U.S. Department of Energy, *DOE's Role in Restoring the Financial Health of the Electric Utility Industry* (Washington, D.C.: Department of Energy, 1981), p. 5.

electric rates of the mid- and late 1970s, the residential retail price of electricity per kilowatt-hour actually rose from 2.4 cents to 2.9 cents (constant 1972 dollars) during the period 1973–78. That amounts to a 21 percent increase, which was less than half the period's rate of inflation.[4] In the early 1980s prices climbed more dramatically. Nonetheless, on average, electricity has been priced well below its would-be marginal price.[5]

It is often argued that because electricity is such a versatile form of energy, its widening utilization enhances the overall productive efficiency of the economy. Electrification during the 1910s, 1920s, and 1930s greatly improved manufacturing productivity.[6] In more recent years, however, the availability of underpriced power has led to misapplications that will be carried forward for decades. Between 1970 and 1980, for example, the percentage of electrically heated homes in the United States rose from 8 percent to 18 percent; two of every five new homes being built were all-electric.[7] While energy-saving heat pumps were installed in many units, more than half were still being fitted with inefficient resistance heaters.[8] Meanwhile, industrial firms, taking all their power from utility grids, shunned opportunities to cogenerate electricity by tapping waste process heat. After 1950, the share of electricity cogenerated in industry declined by almost three-quarters as reliance on relatively inexpensive purchased power displaced in-house systems.[9] In

4. Hans H. Landsberg and others, *Energy: The Next Twenty Years* (Ballinger Publishing Company for the Ford Foundation, 1979), p. 142.

5. Average electric rates are estimated to be 66.6 percent of the actual marginal price of electricity for industrial users and 76.6 percent for residential consumers (1980 dollars per million Btus). No other energy carrier, except natural gas, exhibits a wider gap. John H. Gibbons and William U. Chandler, *Energy: The Conservation Revolution* (New York: Plenum Press, 1981), p. 140.

6. National Research Council of the National Academy of Sciences, *Energy in Transition, 1985–2010: Final Report of the Committee on Nuclear and Alternative Energy Systems* (W.H. Freeman, 1980), p. 106.

7. Robert Reinhold, "American Way of Housing Changing às Number and Costs of Units Increase," *New York Times*, April 20, 1982; and Ann Pelham, *Energy Policy*, 2d ed. (Washington, D.C.: CQ Press, 1981), pp. 10–11.

8. Electric heat pumps for space heating deliver three times more heat than do resistance heaters per unit of electricity consumed. National Research Council, *Energy in Transition*, pp. 90–91.

9. Thirty percent of industry's electricity needs were met by cogeneration in the 1920s. Today, only 4 percent of industrial electricity is provided by on-site generation. *Status of Federal Energy Conservation Programs*, Hearings before the Subcommittee on Energy Conservation and Regulation of the Senate Committee on Energy and Natural Resources, 95 Cong. 1 sess. (Government Printing Office, 1977), pt. 1, p. 183; and Barnaby J. Feder,

the commercial sector, average energy use per square foot doubled for typical post-1950 office buildings. New York City's World Trade Center towers require about as much electricity, eighty megawatts, as the entire city of Schenectady, a community of 100,000 people.[10] Mechanical space conditioning of hermetically sealed interiors became standard design, irrespective of site, orientation, or geographic location. Investment decisions like these might have seemed economical when the real costs of providing electricity were still going down, as a result of economies of scale, technological refinements, or other conditions. But today such investments represent a questionable allocation of resources, induced by the practice of pricing electric power below its replacement cost.

Traditionally, electric rates have embodied the average cost over time of generating and distributing electricity, rather than the marginal cost of producing additional quantities when added demands arise on a system. Although the reasons for this are numerous, the main one is fairly simple. Historically, the electric utility industry was characterized by decreasing costs to scale. Under these conditions, adding capacity could lower unit costs to consumers, but prices set equal to the long-run marginal expense of the additional equipment used were unlikely to cover total production costs for the power companies. To enable the industry to recover its full costs, plus earn a fair profit, state public service commissions customarily permitted the utilities they regulated to incorporate the huge sunk costs of existing installations, the "rolled in" average of past and present capital investments, in rate base calculations. To spread this overhead as broadly as possible, electric tariffs were crafted to attract patronage, widening the base from which revenues would be collected. Forms of price discrimination were approved, such as the practice of offering volume discounts to big industrial customers on the theory that, without promotional pricing, these users, with their relatively high elasticity of demand for electricity, might take their business elsewhere.[11] The typical rate design took the form of the so-called declining block schedule, in which the average price charged any class of customers would decrease as a step function of quantity consumed.

After 1970, the expense of building electric plants and of supplying

"Cogeneration of Energy," *New York Times*, April 1, 1982.

10. Richard G. Stein, *Energy and Architecture* (Anchor Press/Doubleday, 1977), pp. 59, 60, 65.

11. Diana E. Sander, "The Price of Energy," *Annual Review of Energy*, vol. 1 (Palo Alto, Calif.: Annual Reviews Inc., 1976), p. 410.

their boiler fuels began escalating so rapidly that new investments in productive facilities ceased to procure economies. Thus in many parts of the country the price of electricity, still based on a utility's embedded assets at original interest and depreciation rates, began understating substantially the costs of churning out additional kilowatts. Despite growing awareness that continued underpricing of electricity stimulates demand —which exacts a heavy toll on scarce capital, environmental quality, and primary energy sources—the old rate structures, originally aimed at promoting sales, have not proven easy to dismantle.

Rate Modernization

Growing peak demand, unaffordable capital requirements, and higher operating expenditures prompted utility companies to deluge regulatory authorities with requests for rate increases. In response, some states began devising novel price systems, designed to reflect more accurately the rising incremental costs of production. In particular, the new approaches developed in New York, Wisconsin, and California drew national attention, and in 1975 Congress authorized a series of experiments in twelve other states, sponsored by the Federal Energy Administration. Congressional concern with rate reform mounted during the ensuing years as a complex alliance of interests coalesced around the issue. Federal energy officials began identifying possibilities for substantial fuel savings; environmentalists spotted in rate revisions a chance to curb construction of superfluous power stations; and consumer groups saw opportunities to shift the burden of higher electric bills onto nonresidential users.[12] Various legislative proposals, intended to accelerate the diffusion of innovations among the states, were introduced in 1976 and 1977, culminating with passage of the Public Utility Regulatory Policies Act (PURPA), as part of the National Energy Act in 1978.

No binding national standards for electricity pricing were mandated under the PURPA. But the law did require all state public utility commissions to consider the use of marginal-cost studies in future ratemaking proceedings. State regulators were also required to consider,

12. Another constituency that played a role in awakening early congressional interest in electric rate reform was the suppliers of competing fuels (oil jobbers, for example), who were afraid that the continued promotional pricing of electricity would cut more deeply into heating fuel markets. Interview with Robert R. Nordhaus, former chief counsel, House Committee on Interstate and Foreign Commerce, Washington, D.C., October 20, 1981.

presumably on the strength of these detailed cost-of-service data, re-placing the prevalent declining block tariffs with progressively scaled, time-differentiated rate structures that would track daily and seasonal load cycles.

The Reform Rationale

In general, usage of electricity fluctuates markedly by time of day and time of year. Most of the recent demand growth experienced by utilities has occurred in peak periods—mid-summer afternoons, for ex-ample, when millions of air conditioners are simultaneously switched on. While total consumption of electricity after 1973 increased an average of only 3 percent annually, peak consumption has grown much faster—6.5 percent in 1980, for instance.[13] If it were possible to store electrical energy in large quantities, peak requirements could be met simply by holding enough electricity in reserve to accommodate the added loads. Without such storage technology, utilities are forced to put extra gener-ating units on line when supplying peak power. The actual cost of this surge on the margin (the peak) has exceeded, often by as much as six to eight times, the average (around-the-clock) cost of providing power.[14]

Any big expansion of electrical generating facilities uses more energy inputs. The energy needs and costs of peaking and cycling units, however, are especially high.[15] Capacity to serve system peaks lies idle much of the time, tying up precious capital. In the interest of holding down this fixed cost, utilities tend to commission relatively small com-bustion turbines, typically oil or gas fired, for peak operation. These in-stallations require a lower capital investment, but they achieve much less thermal efficiency than the system's larger baseload generators do.[16] Early in the legislative debate leading to the PURPA, it was noted that

13. H. L. Culbreath, "An Overview of the Financial Difficulties of the Electric Utility Industry and Their Impact on the Funding of Necessary Future Construction," Statement before the Subcommittee on Energy Conservation and Power of the House Committee on Energy and Commerce, 97 Cong. 1 sess., April 6, 1981, p. 3.

14. Landsberg and others, *Energy: The Next Twenty Years*, p. 141.

15. Typically, baseload stations have capacity factors (that is, actual total output of a plant divided by the total output that would be obtained if the plant were operating at full capacity 100 percent of the time) of nearly 70 to 80 percent, while peakload units have average capacity factors of about 20 percent. Don E. Kash and others, *Our Energy Future: The Role of Research, Development, and Demonstration in Reaching a National Con-sensus on Energy Supply* (University of Oklahoma Press, 1976), pp. 263–64.

16. Edward Berlin, Charles J. Cicchetti, and William J. Gillen, *Perspectives on Power: A Study of the Regulation and Pricing of Electric Power* (Ballinger, 1974), p. 30.

nationwide these plants, running only 25 percent of the time or less, used an average of 22 percent more fuel for each kilowatt-hour generated than did baseload stations operating 50 percent or more of the time.[17]

The need for peak capacity, despite its relatively intensive use of energy, is partially unavoidable. Nothing is likely to change the propensity of people to turn their air conditioners on in August rather than February, or of housewives to cook the family meal on electric ranges at supper time rather than midnight. But peak power has also been greatly oversold by traditional pricing procedures, electric rates that charge an average fee unrelated to time of use, or that frequently charge lower-than-average fees in tail blocks of volumes consumed, even when the consumption occurs at or near peak hours. Seasonal rates and time-of-day rates would combat this perversity. Their price signals would encourage conservation in at least two ways. First, where demand was discretionary, much of it would shift to off-peak periods, improving the load factors of more efficient baseload plants. Second, where a shift was not feasible, average customers would acquire a strong incentive to consume less or to conserve energy by installing heat pumps, insulation, solar hot-water heaters, and the like. Large industrial users would begin to revive an old idea with vast energy-saving potential, cogeneration.[18]

The Response in the States

So far no clear picture has emerged as to how much progress has occurred in reorganizing electric rate structures in the United States. Under the PURPA, state public utility commissions were obligated to reach determinations regarding the act's provisions for rate design by November 1981. However, even if every state commission had rushed to adopt the proposed changes, large portions of the electric power industry

17. *Public Utility Rate Proposals of President Carter's Energy Program*, Hearings before the Subcommittee on Energy Conservation and Regulation of the Senate Committee on Energy and Natural Resources, 95 Cong. 1 sess. (GPO, 1978), pt. 1, p. 241. Seventy-six percent of the kilowatt-hours generated from plants with capacity factors of 25 percent or less were derived from oil and natural gas. Ibid., p. 205.

18. About 40 percent of industrial energy is used to produce low-pressure steam. This represents about 14 percent of total energy consumed in the U.S. economy. By recycling waste steam, cogeneration needs about half the additional fuel required by the most efficient single-purpose utility plant. National Research Council, *Energy in Transition*, p. 97. The aggregate potential energy savings are so enormous that with existing technology some experts estimate that cogeneration could provide about as much net new electricity as the economy will need by the year 2000. Robert H. Williams, "Industrial Cogeneration," *Annual Review of Energy*, vol. 3 (Palo Alto, Calif.: Annual Reviews Inc., 1976), p. 353.

would probably remain untouched. Worried about administrative costs, among many other concerns, the authors of the PURPA confined the law's coverage to utilities whose retail sales exceeded 500 million kilowatt-hours. Smaller investor-owned companies, municipal power corporations, and rural electric cooperatives were exempted. Furthermore, approximately 10 percent of the nation's installed electric capacity is federally owned. The government-run power administrations—Bonneville, Alaska, Southwestern, Southeastern, and the Tennessee Valley Authority (TVA)—fall outside the jurisdictions of state regulatory agencies. In principle the same PURPA guidelines extend both to large nonregulated power systems (for example, the TVA) and to private utilities regulated by state commissions. In reality these separate sectors are not equally pliant. The TVA, for example, operates under an independent congressional charge—to "promote and encourage the fullest possible use of electric light and power . . . at the lowest possible rates."[19] That mandate is at odds with the spirit of the PURPA's retail rate recommendations.

THE PURPA PROCEEDINGS. In any case, as the November 1981 deadline drew near, only a few states had moved from mere consideration of the substantive policy objectives expressed in the PURPA to a stage of extensive implementation. Rate cases in which the act's various recommended rate standards were under review dragged on. The General Accounting Office, in a report issued during September 1981, disclosed that this process of examining, either case by case or generically, the appropriateness of alternative pricing methods, such as declining blocks, seasonal tariffs, and time-of-day rates, had been completed for only about a quarter of all the electric utilities covered by the law.[20] More current data, collected by the National Association of Regulatory Utility Commissioners (NARUC), suggest that PURPA rate proceedings have now been concluded for a much greater percentage of utilities.[21]

Net results, however, remain murky. The NARUC, for instance, concluded that over half of the utilities in its most recent (1982) survey had been ordered to implement PURPA policy for declining block rates. But not only are thirteen states missing from the survey, a closer look at the

19. S. David Freeman, *Energy: The New Era* (Walker and Company, 1974), p. 162.
20. U.S. General Accounting Office, *Burdensome and Unnecessary Reporting Requirements of the Public Utility Regulatory Policies Act Need to Be Changed* (Washington, D.C.: General Accounting Office, 1981), p. 7.
21. Paul Rodgers and Charles D. Gray, *Second Report on State Commission Progress under the Public Utility Regulatory Policies Act of 1978* (Washington, D.C.: National Association of Regulatory Utility Commissioners [NARUC], 1982).

outcomes, revealed in the questionnaires that were returned, tells a more complicated story.[22] Many state utility commissions duly considered the problem of declining block rates, "implemented" the legislation's procedural requirements in their deliberations, and then opted to retain the rates. Often the state commissions cited cost justifications or concern over the potential impact on customers.[23] Illinois, Indiana, Minnesota, New York, North Dakota, Ohio, Oklahoma, Pennsylvania, and Wyoming were among the states that resolved key rate cases in this fashion. Similarly, the NARUC reported that orders adopting the utility act's seasonal rate criteria were being carried out by over a third of the utilities surveyed, but some states included in this estimate had only studied seasonal rate options in particular rate cases as required by the legislation; they had not directed the utilities concerned to put any of the rates into effect. Other states did effect the rates, but only for limited classes of customers. In South Carolina, for example, Duke Power Company was reported as having implemented the PURPA seasonal rate standard. It had, but just by offering seasonal rates to residential customers and introducing such rates in only 352 of 288,881 residences served by the utility.

TIME-OF-USE RATES. Seasonal tariffs are blunt instruments for purposes of peakload pricing. Seasonal weather conditions, hence electrical loads, seldom recur with exactly the same length or intensity from year to year. In certain locations, seasonally adjusted pricing may be wholly inapplicable. It is not surprising, for example, that the Florida Public Service Commission and the Public Utilities Commission of Hawaii flatly rejected PURPA exhortations regarding seasonal rates; the year-round climates of these states vary slightly or not at all. Time-of-day rates, on the other hand, are more sensitive to load oscillations; electricity is metered hour by hour, and customers are charged accordingly. As of 1982, how widespread were time-of-day rates among the large regulated utilities in each state? It was possible to estimate these frequencies with reasonable accuracy by piecing together information from three sources: the NARUC questionnaires mentioned earlier; the National Regulatory Research Institute's bulletins, which have monitored

22. The following analysis is based on a review of the raw survey instruments. I am grateful to Charles D. Gray, assistant general counsel of the NARUC, for making these indispensable data available.

23. On other kinds of ambiguous state determinations, see David Silverstone, *The Public Utility Regulatory Policies Act (PURPA): Promise, Performance, and Prologue*, PURPA Paper 7 (Washington, D.C.: Environmental Action Foundation, 1981), pp. 6–7.

state rate revision activities on a quarterly basis; and interviews with officials of public utility commissions in several states.[24] In ten states, over
90 percent of the big local utilities offered some form of time-of-day
tariffs to one or more customer classes; in seventeen states, over half of
the companies offered such rates; in thirty-two states, less than half did;
and in thirteen of these states, none did.

These data reveal nothing about whether the operative time-of-day
tariffs were based on marginal-cost computations. My sense is that few
were.[25] A 1982 survey conducted by National Economic Research Associates, Inc., found that utilities in only sixteen states actively measured
marginal or incremental costs for each customer class in rate setting.[26]
Even in New York, in the watershed case of *Long Island Lighting Co.*
(1976), where time-of-day pricing was first imposed on a sizable scale, the
final ratio of peak to off-peak prices was set at 4:1—nowhere near the 20:1
differential dictated by a strict marginal-cost analysis.[27] Moreover, the data say nothing about the extent of time-of-day rate coverage among customer classes and within them. On this score, perhaps the best recent
evidence comes from a study by EBASCO Business Consulting Company
in New York City, which sampled 132 leading electric utilities around the
country during the fall of 1981. The EBASCO survey discovered that only
6.0 percent of the industrial customers, 0.25 percent of the commercial
customers, and 0.11 percent of the residential customers served by the utilities were on time-of-day rates.[28]

24. The dependent variable, time-of-day rate implementation by state, is defined as the
percentage of each state's large (that is, PURPA-covered) investor-owned utilities reported
as having implemented some form of time-of-use rate design (optional or mandatory), for
one or more classes of customers, as of May 1982 (the completion date of the last
NARUC survey). The definition of PURPA-covered companies is found in *Federal Register*, vol. 45 (December 24, 1980), pp. 85386–97. In addition to the NARUC survey data
just cited, the National Regulatory Research Institute *Bulletins* (Columbus, Ohio: NRRI)
of July 1980 through October 1982 were reviewed, and telephone interviews with public
utility commission personnel were conducted to fill in gaps or clarify the data for the following states: Alabama, Delaware, Georgia, Indiana, Kansas, Kentucky, Louisiana, Maine,
Massachusetts, Mississippi, New Jersey, North Dakota, Ohio, Oklahoma, Oregon, Rhode
Island, South Dakota, Texas, Utah, Vermont, Virginia, and West Virginia.

25. Interview with Seth Margoshes, Lehman Brothers Kuhn Loeb, Inc., New York,
December 13, 1982.

26. National Association of Regulatory Utility Commissioners, *1981 Annual Report on
Utility and Carrier Regulation*, p. 649.

27. Douglas D. Anderson, *Regulatory Politics and Electric Utilities: A Case Study in
Political Economy* (Boston: Auburn House Publishing Company, 1981), pp. 128–30.

28. EBASCO Business Consulting Company, *Time-of-Day Rate Survey* (New York:
EBASCO, May 1982), p. 1.

Interest Groups

The stand taken by large industrial customers and the skepticism of the electric power industry have obstructed the process of restructuring utility rates. These, at least, are the impediments cited most frequently by embattled reformers.

Industrial Clients

Not unexpectedly, in state regulatory proceedings, and in clashes over the federal role in utility pricing, no lobby has resisted rate revision more steadfastly than the business interests that consume electricity in bulk, for example, automakers, aluminum manufacturers, chemical companies, steel mills, rubber factories, and phosphate mines. Their defense of traditional block discounts rests mostly on the variability in distribution costs associated with different customer classes. Residential and commercial consumers often require extensive, costly distribution networks and transformers that convert high voltage power to low voltage. Big industrial users are less diffuse and frequently can take power directly from transmission lines at full strength. These economies are often important. Whether they are large enough to offset the marginal costs of added generating capacity that bulk users may impose on utility systems—that is, large enough to justify preferential rates on a total, long-term, cost-of-service basis—is a lot more debatable in most instances. But firms with a stake in keeping their volume discounts have an obvious means of doing so: threatening to abandon or avoid the states (or utility market areas) where industrial declining blocks are being inverted.

Utilities

Rate reform troubles many utilities as well. Fewer utilities these days find it easy to increase their allowable incomes by expanding their rate bases. To make expansions worthwhile, the fair rates of return permitted by state regulatory bodies have to exceed the costs of new construction and operation, and increasingly, those rates no longer do. But that doesn't mean that every power company has stopped contemplating growth. During the legislative hearings on the PURPA, utility executives trooped before congressional committees asserting repeatedly that the overriding concern of the industry was to attract investors and raise funds for new plants. Few errors could be worse than "failure to recognize the substantial need for major increases in conventional sources of electric generation," the president of Carolina Power and Light Company suggested to the House Commerce Subcommittee on Energy and Power.[29] At these hearings, utility companies stressed projected capital requirements, estimated at about $850 billion by the early 1990s according to a spokesman for Commonwealth Edison of Chicago.[30] The risk of overbuilding capacity in the face of slower consumption was barely mentioned.

Power companies accustomed to growth, and still searching for ways to resume growing, have difficulty appreciating the virtues of pricing policies whose principal aims are to improve utilization of existing facilities and to reduce the need for additional ones. Moreover, a thorough restructuring of extant rate schedules, especially if federally enforced, entails a lengthy administrative process in which interim rate adjustments and investment plans may be greatly delayed. What these companies want is not to rethink their rate structures, but rather to attain three conditions: less regulatory lag in licensing new projects and in obtaining simple rate hikes under existing pricing procedures; permission from regulators to include in rate bases all investments associated with construction work in progress; and more government subsidies.[31] In 1981, for example, the electric utilities asked for more tax breaks, such as increased dividend exclusion, liberalized depreciation schedules, and tax deductions for decommissioning nuclear plants and handling spent fuel. They also wanted tax-exempt bond financing for a long list of eligible investments, extended investment credits, and elimination of withholding taxes on interest payments to foreign bondholders.[32]

For many utilities, expansion is out of the question for the foreseeable future, and their managers and stockholders know it. But these firms, some of which are now staggering financially with excess capacity, may be even less receptive to new rate designs that encourage conservation and cogeneration. Costly underutilization of their present capital

29. Sherwood H. Smith, Jr., President of Carolina Power and Light Company, Raleigh, North Carolina, "Statement on Behalf of the Edison Electric Institute on Electric Ratemaking Aspects of H.R. 6831 and H.R. 6660," before the Subcommittee on Energy Conservation and Power of the House Committee on Interstate and Foreign Commerce, 95 Cong. 1 sess., May 23, 1977, pp. 1–2. At Senate hearings, Smith's testimony was similar. *Public Utility Rate Proposals*, Hearings, pt. 2, pp. 125, 127.

30. *Public Utility Rate Proposals*, Hearings, pt. 2, p. 36.

31. *Public Utility Rate Proposals*, Hearings, pt. 2, pp. 62–63, 272.

32. Culbreath, "An Overview of the Financial Difficulties of the Electric Utility Industry," pp. 15–16.

equipment can only get worse if demand is further reduced and important customers are lost.[33]

The angst of the utilities became most intense when, as in the mid-1970s, Congress entertained the notion of setting stringent federal ratemaking rules. With the blessings of the Carter administration, the House of Representatives in 1977 had sought to impose standards that restricted declining block rates, required time-of-use pricing where cost effective, and directed the Federal Power Commission to review compliances. That this plan was rejected in favor of the looser, voluntary guidelines eventually framed for the PURPA resulted in no small part from a lobbying blitz orchestrated by the National Association of Electric Companies and the Edison Electric Institute. In the critical last stages of the negotiations that produced the Public Utility Regulatory Policies Act, these trade groups brought about forty top executives to Washington to demand key revisions in the draft legislation.[34] A senior Department of Energy official, who had closely observed the bargaining sessions in the PURPA conference committee during the fall of 1978, recalled that a dozen representatives of the utility companies were present at all times.[35] Simultaneously, the utility companies were stirring up their constituents in the hinterlands. Columbus and Southern Ohio Electric Company informed its shareholders that the proposal pending in Congress threatened free enterprise; the president of Mississippi Power and Light wrote to the mayors in the company's service area that the proposal threatened the survival of the United States as a free nation.[36]

"The upshot of all this," reported the trade journal *Electrical World,* "was that utilities succeeded in persuading a majority of conferees not to sign the conference report until the staff authors made some eleventh-hour changes."[37] The changes were significant. Among them was new language removing any doubt that the bill would, at best, merely oblige states and utilities to explore possible rate innovations and to follow certain procedures such as holding public hearings before making determinations. The discretion of the state regulatory authorities would be

33. Barry Commoner, *The Politics of Energy* (Alfred A. Knopf, 1979), pp. 70–71.

34. *Electrical Week*, October 2, 1977, p. 1.

35. Interview with Howard Perry, director of the Office of Utility Systems, Economic Regulatory Administration, U.S. Department of Energy, Washington, D.C., October 6, 1981.

36. Kent Whitney, "Senate Trashes Rate Reform," *Power Line*, vol. 3 (October 1977), p. 6; and Alden Meyer, *A Ratepayer's Guide to PURPA* (Washington, D.C.: Environmental Action Foundation, 1979), p. 6.

37. *Electrical Week*, October 23, 1978, p. 7.

preserved. They would not be forced to modify rate structures.[38]

Obstructionism in Perspective

Stronger federal legislation might have sped the pace of electric rate modernization in the states. But the private utilities and their large clients, who battered such legislation in 1978, were not the only force deterring rate reform. Arrayed against more aggressive alternatives to the PURPA were not just the Edison Electric Institute and the Electricity Consumers Resource Council (the main trade association of the big industrial buyers), but also the state public service commissions and, interestingly, the great majority of publicly owned power systems.[39] These public agencies feared a loss of autonomy, especially the loss of autonomous authority to keep soothing their clients with the lowest possible rates.

States that revamp their electric tariffs to better reflect replacement costs may find themselves at a competitive disadvantage in attracting or maintaining an electricity-intensive economic base. However, it is highly improbable that large numbers of states can be intimidated by the limited assortment of firms that the Electricity Consumers Resource Council represents. Only a few industries count electricity costs as a large share of the total cost of doing business and thus a decisive locational consideration.[40] Moreover, since energy costs are an important component of the expense of generating electricity, prices for electricity will continue to vary geographically regardless of local pricing policies. Surely, no remodeled rate structure can alter the fact that fuel costs for hydroelectric projects are essentially zero. But fuel constitutes about 45

38. Ibid.

39. The American Public Power Association, representing publicly owned utilities, repeatedly voiced its opposition to federally mandated rate standards (unless the standards applied exclusively to private utilities). *Public Power Weekly Newsletter*, May 30, 1977, p. 2. The National Association of Regulatory Utility Commissioners, speaking for state utility regulators, was correspondingly hostile to federal standards. Interview with Paul Rodgers, administrative director and general counsel, NARUC, Washington, D.C., September 28, 1981. However, some key members of prominent public utility commissions, such as those of Ohio and New York, dissented from this position. "NARUC Guarding States' Rights," *Weekly Energy Report*, vol. 4 (April 5, 1976), p. 14. Reportedly, the nonregulated, publicly owned power companies and rural electric cooperatives often have been even less responsive to the PURPA's guidelines than have investor-owned companies. Meyer, *Ratepayer's Guide to PURPA*, p. 9.

40. Interview with Jay B. Kennedy, executive director, Electricity Consumers Resource Council, Washington, D.C., October 1, 1981; and interview with Robert C. Dolan, Edison Electric Institute, Washington, D.C., October 1, 1981.

percent of generating costs for many oil- or coal-fired plants, substantially increasing the price paid for power. Given a choice, firms in quest of low prices will migrate to areas with abundant hydropower, irrespective of nuances in rate designs. In sum, although the threat of industrial relocation can inhibit rate reform in some places, the extent of the problem is frequently overstated.

Utilities have not uniformly eschewed innovation. Indeed, in a number of leading states the initiatives of major utility companies have been more noteworthy than the activities of the public utility commissions. For instance, four of Virginia's largest companies—Appalachian Power, Delmarva Power and Light, Potomac Edison, and Potomac Electric and Power—had begun offering seasonal rates long before the state's regulatory authority promoted such tariffs in 1982 and 1983 as a matter of general policy following PURPA proceedings. In Ohio some utilities, Dayton Power and Light Company, for example, have come before the public utility commission requesting that the commission order mandatory time-of-use rates.[41] In New York the cooperation of key utilities—Long Island Lighting, Consolidated Edison, and Central Hudson, among others—was credited with facilitating enormously the New York Public Service Commission's landmark rate cases in the mid-1970s.[42] And in Vermont, one of the state's two main power companies, Central Vermont Public Service Corporation, initiated retail rate and load management experiments before these novelties were pioneered virtually anywhere else in the country.[43]

Which utilities are disposed to rearrange their rate structures? As one might expect, the more inventive firms tend to be those experiencing increasingly skewed load cycles. In these circumstances, company managers are more likely to choose realistically between options: either to run more energy-guzzling peakload plants at great expense or to try peak-shaving price systems that may yield substantial savings in capital and operating costs. In my survey of time-of-day pricing among states, the percentages of utilities that had introduced these new price schedules as of 1982 varied closely with one factor, the price of residual fuel oil.[44]

41. Telephone interview with Doug Maag, Ohio Public Utility Commission, January 23, 1983.

42. Dennis P. Carrigan, "The Great Electricity Pricing Debate," *Public Utilities Fortnightly*, vol. 110 (August 19, 1982), p. 19.

43. Anne Cassin, "Electric Utility Rate Reform in Vermont" (University of Vermont, Department of Political Science, Fall 1979).

44. $r = .52$ ($p < .001$). The dependent variable is my survey of time-of-day rate implementation, discussed earlier. The independent variable is the 1977 retail price per barrel of

That is, time-of-day tariffs are most common where big utilities carry extensive peak capacity, powered by costly residual oil (a fuel used for peaking units).[45] In short, where immediate market conditions create strong incentives, inertia in rate reform is more easily overcome. Sometimes the utilities themselves lead the way.

Public Opinion

Public opinion, more than the utility industry, is the natural antagonist of any policy that would truly lift electric tariffs to the level of marginal costs. Few commodities evoke keener public reactions to price increases than does electricity. In growing numbers, Americans think their electricity bills are exorbitant: the proportion in national surveys who felt their rates were too high climbed from 23 percent in 1969 to 54 percent in 1981.[46] At times, as in a 1975 study by Opinion Research Corporation, majorities opine, erroneously, that electric rates have risen more than the prices of other energy sources, or, also erroneously, that electricity prices have "increased a great deal more than the cost of most other things," as disclosed in a 1979 sample by the Roper Organization.[47]

The shrinking percentage of persons who believe that their rates are still fair, only 27 percent in a 1982 poll, seems to be connected with two perceptions.[48] First, more than with other forms of energy, there is uncertainty that electricity usage can be conveniently reduced in response to higher prices.[49] Although wasteful consumption of gasoline, for ex-

residual fuel oil reported by state in U.S. Department of Energy, Energy Information Administration, *State Energy Fuel Prices by Major Economic Sector from 1960 through 1977* (Washington, D.C.: DOE, 1979), pp. 83–84.

45. Except for nuclear installations, the main component of increased costs per kilowatt-hour has been fuel; oil-fired plants incurred much larger price increases than did coal plants or gas units (at least until the 1980s). *Congressional Quarterly Weekly Report*, vol. 35 (March 26, 1977), p. 545.

46. Cambridge Reports, Inc., *American Attitudes toward Energy Issues and the Electric Utility Industry* (Washington, D.C.: Edison Electric Institute, 1982), p. 56.

47. Barbara Farhar and others, *Public Opinion about Energy: A Literature Review* (Golden, Colo.: Solar Energy Research Institute, 1979), p. 88; and *Roper Reports*, 79–7 (July 1979).

48. Cambridge Reports, Inc., *American Attitudes toward Energy Issues*, p. xiii.

49. Farhar and others, *Public Opinion about Energy*, pp. B-35, 88. The public perception seemed inconsistent with the empirical work of economists, who had found evidence of a strong price elasticity of demand for electric power even in studies before 1973. See, for example, J. W. Wilson, "Residential Demand for Electricity," *Quarterly Review of Economics and Business*, vol. 11 (Spring 1971), pp. 7–22; T. D. Mount, L. D.

ample, is widely acknowledged, few feel the same is true of electric power. Second, most consumers have become convinced that utilities, like oil companies, make too much profit. The percentages that held this view rose steadily, from 36 percent in 1976 to 51 percent by 1982.[50]

Attitudes on Rates

Because most people seem to feel that management of electrical demand through the price system is neither feasible nor fair, specific load-managing rate proposals draw little public assent. Polls indicate scant support for peakload pricing.[51] Granted, the observed lack of enthusiasm may be partly an artifact of the polling instruments employed. A Roper poll in 1976, for instance, reported that 74 percent of respondents opposed a plan that would monitor home electric meters so that electricity used during peak daytime hours would cost substantially more.[52] What this survey didn't mention was that under time-of-day schedules electricity used during off-peak hours might cost appreciably less. But even when the pricing questions are posed in a balanced fashion, there is only guarded approval of innovative rates. A poll taken in early 1983 found that only 17 percent of Americans strongly approve of time-of-day tariffs (although 38 percent said they approved somewhat), even though a majority of the respondents admitted they would probably change their use patterns to take advantage of lower off-peak rates.[53]

Implications

These citizen attitudes shed light on the tendency of many electric companies, state regulators, and federal lawmakers to approach utility rate issues with extreme caution. Nevertheless, as with views on oil and gas pricing, nuances in the public's disposition can lead policymakers down divergent trails. In 1977, for instance, Congress meshed two very different legislative schemes to produce the PURPA: a House bill that

---

Chapman, and T. J. Tyrrell, "Electricity Demand in the United States: An Econometric Analysis," in Michael S. Macrakis, ed., *Energy: Demand, Conservation, and Industrial Problems* (MIT Press, 1974), pp. 318–29; L. D. Taylor, "The Demand for Electricity: A Survey," *Bell Journal of Economics*, vol. 6 (Spring 1975).

50. Cambridge Reports, Inc., *American Attitudes toward Energy Issues*, p. 66.

51. Barbara C. Farhar and others, "Public Opinion about Energy," *Annual Review of Energy*, vol. 5 (Palo Alto, Calif.: Annual Reviews Inc., 1980), p. 3.

52. *Roper Reports*, 76-6 (June 1976).

53. Edison Electric Institute, *Quarterly Public Opinion Review*, First Quarter (Washington, D.C., 1983).

placed federal requirements on local retail rate setting and a Senate version that sought little more than to reaffirm the regulatory independence of the states.

Some House members felt sure that, potentially at least, their alternative conformed to popular preferences. Sustaining this inference was, first of all, the fact that ratepayers had begun to question increasingly the benefits of generating plant expansions, particularly if the plants were nuclear. Although misgivings about atomic energy swelled in the aftermath of the Three Mile Island disaster, national surveys detected mounting concern well before the accident. Gallup started reporting in 1976 that a plurality of respondents, 40 percent, favored cutting back the operation of reactors until their safety could be improved.[54] Later, the political message conveyed by a CBS News/*New York Times* poll was even more explicit: 43 percent said they were "likely to vote for someone who would stop construction of more nuclear power plants."[55] Nuclear power was in disrepute, yet in several sections of the country other options were limited if one assumed that utility systems had to keep growing. Proponents of new rate designs reasoned that one way to undo the Gordian knot was to slash through it: revise the assumptions about utility growth by altering the relative prices that determine growth. To make this possible, however, the rules of the ratemaking game would have to change, and that required new federal laws.

The popular notion that power companies reap excessive profits may prompt diverse policy responses. The main one, of course, is to do nothing that would increase prices, and hence profitability. But another is the possibility of devising rate structures that recapture any excess returns and distribute the benefits widely among average consumers. New rate structures may entail more elaborate government regulation of the utility industry, not less. But in this energy sector, public support of government regulation runs uniquely broad and deep. Considerably more Americans say that the industry serves the public poorly than well,[56] and distinct majorities endorse government control of price and profit levels.[57] Even if direct federal coercion may be less acceptable, indirect exertions, by way of federally backed citizen participation in local rate decisions, seem widely regarded as

54. *Gallup Opinion Index*, Report 174 (January 1980), p. 21.

55. CBS News/*New York Times* poll, June 1979.

56. Cambridge Reports, Inc., *American Attitudes toward Energy Issues*, p. 40. In this May 1982 survey, 36 percent said the electric light and power industry "is trying to serve the public well," but 48 percent said it "is not trying to serve the public well."

57. Ibid., pp. 118–19.

good ideas, perhaps because many people are under the impression that such participation will effect lower rates.[58] Regulatory reform proposals, such as the bill that passed the House in 1977, have been influenced conspicuously by these sorts of sentiments.

Localism

Price policy for electricity is conditioned by regional diversity. In the Southwest, for example, demand for power has risen 7 percent annually, propelled by economic and demographic growth.[59] The pressure on utilities to expand has not been limited to peak requirements; baseload facilities are being strained by burgeoning industrial sales, on top of extensive irrigation hookups, that drain power in heavy, continuous loads. The generating stations of some Texas power companies run at nearly full capability, twenty-four hours a day. With these load characteristics, time-of-day pricing makes no sense; there is no place to shift the load during the daily cycle. Moreover, since much of the region's installed capacity is gas fired, and recent natural gas prices have climbed much faster than the price of nearby western coal, the long-run marginal costs of replacing plants with coal-burning equipment may turn out to be lower than the near-term average costs of production. In these cases, electric rates based on marginal cost would force producers to operate at a loss.

In parts of the Frost Belt, peakload pricing has not caught on either, but for different reasons. Here demand growth, even in seasonal peaks, dropped so sharply after 1973 that many systems were left with gaping reserve margins (as much as 30 percent in the Northeast and much of the Midwest). Saddled with overcapacity, these utilities have lagged in conservation-related activities. Fuel mix as well as capacity margins influence a utility's interest in managing demand through rate schedules.[60] Although studies indicate that time-of-day rates, if more widely adopted in New England, could induce a greater load response there than in any other section of the country, the region's utilities cannot be sure that a big shift of electrical usage from peaks to valleys in their load curves is

58. Ibid., pp. 121, 127.
59. U.S. Department of Energy, Energy Information Administration, "EIA Annual Report on Monthly Comparisons of Peak Demand and Energy for Load—1976 to 1979," *Energy Data Report* (Washington, D.C.: DOE, 1980), p. 4.
60. Gerald S. Bower and Mark R. Berg, "The Changing Environment for Electric Power Generation: Portrait of a Transition," *Public Utilities Fortnightly*, vol. 110 (July 22, 1982), pp. 27–28.

worthwhile.[61] A great deal of baseload as well as peak capacity in the Northeast is still oil fired. Moving demand from one set of oil-burning installations to another may not reduce costs appreciably, even if it improves a system's overall load factor.

Utilities with heavier than average baseload dependence on coal, nuclear power, or hydropower, all of which have fairly low operating costs, may be more active in load control programs, whether through pricing methods or other devices. Yet in the region where baseload power is least expensive, the Northwest, one finds the greatest gap between prevailing electric rates and marginal capacity costs associated with the crests of electrical loads. A large portion of the Northwest's electric power is supplied by the federal government's hydrostations. Most potential sites for hydropower, however, have been fully developed. Increasingly, incremental generating needs will have to be met by new steam-generated plants, whose operating costs per kilowatt-hour are three to four times higher than the average price being charged. State regulators in the area are not eager to approve revised rate structures that, if based on such costs at the margin, would hit ratepayers with 400 percent increases in utility bills.[62] Thus, when the National Regulatory Research Institute closely analyzed the rate schedules of leading electric utilities in the state of Washington about 1979, it found that the rates and charges of the utilities appeared unrelated to costs of service; that the rates were much lower than estimated marginal costs, and thus users of electrical services in the state were overconsuming energy; and that these conditions were fairly typical.[63]

An implication of the variability in local circumstances is that flexibility in rate setting is desirable, but uniform standards are not. When the Senate refused to go along with the House-approved regulatory scheme of 1977, this point was reiterated ad nauseam. As the Senate Energy Committee explained,

At present, the state regulatory agencies rather than the federal government possess the expertise to conduct the detailed costing and demand studies required to implement rate structure revision. Moreover, the committee recognized that rate structures must reflect the individual needs and local peculiarities of each

61. Harlan D. Platt, "Some Implications of Cancelled Construction Plans," *Public Utilities Fortnightly,* vol. 110 (August 19, 1982), p. 28.

62. James L. Sweeney, "Energy Regulation—Solution or Problem?" in *Options for U.S. Energy Policy* (San Francisco: Institute for Contemporary Studies, 1977), p. 192.

63. National Regulatory Research Institute, *Review of Rate Structures for Washington Investor Owned Electric Utilities* (Columbus, Ohio: NRRI, 1979), pp. i–vi.

utility's service area; an appropriate rate design for Hawaii will not be appropriate for Idaho.[64]

The senators urged a limited, advisory-type federal role, like that ultimately authorized in the PURPA, rather than the more coercive approach envisaged by the House and backed by the Carter administration.

Inevitably, though, tension arises between the need for local discretion in ratemaking and the presumption that local reform should be spurred by federal involvement. This difficulty was not resolved satisfactorily in the PURPA. Indeed, the act is so mindful of local preferences and peculiarities, and the mechanisms by which public service commissions and utilities can be encouraged to achieve the law's broader aims are so feeble, that one wonders whether the record of rate reform among states today would differ significantly if the PURPA had never become law. In some of the places where rate innovation has languished, the law's toothlessness has been part of the trouble.

The unwillingness of the Senate to countenance federal legislation any less voluntaristic than the PURPA also reflected local pressures in a direct sense: key members of the Committee on Energy and Natural Resources (the Senate unit with jurisdiction over electric power regulation) represented states where big changes in rate structures were either impracticable or politically explosive. Almost a quarter of the committee membership, including the chairman, Henry M. Jackson, Democrat of Washington, hailed from the Northwest. Lobbyists did not let Jackson and his colleagues forget that, particularly in states in the Northwest such as Washington, marginal-cost pricing of electricity risked triggering steep rate increases and fury among constituents.

The same concerns had restrained Jackson's predecessor, Warren G. Magnuson. As chairman of the old Committee on Commerce, Senator Magnuson had presided over utility rate reform hearings in 1976, a year before the issue was passed to Energy and Natural Resources. In the end, recalled a lobbyist close to the scene, all proposals before the Commerce Committee were shelved, for fear of "rocking the boat" in areas like the Northwest.[65]

Eight other senators, for a total of exactly two-thirds of the Energy Committee, came from states in the West, many of which were charac-

64. Quoted in Ross D. Ain, "PURPA: Federal Energy Policy Impacting on the State Regulatory Domain," *Public Utilities Fortnightly*, vol. 104 (October 11, 1979), p. 72.

65. Interview with Martin H. Rogol, former chief lobbyist for Public Citizen, Washington, D.C., October 1, 1981.

terized by electrical generating sectors similar to that just described for the Southwest. Had a few more of the committee's seats gone to senators from areas with conditions favorable to rate reorganization and with better track records (for example, New York or Wisconsin), it is conceivable that the PURPA might have been strengthened.

Policy Management

American governmental institutions pose stumbling blocks to change in utility pricing. Critics sometimes contend, for instance, that the unitary regimes of West European countries such as France, where peakload pricing has been national policy for years, can move more aggressively to revamp electric rates. But federalism in the United States complicates things.

The States

Ratemaking is largely a local responsibility. The competency of the state regulatory commissions varies drastically. If the federal government intrudes to lessen disparities among them, or to appropriate their customary functions, disputes about states' rights flare up. Even the PURPA's innocuous form of federal participation has been challenged. In a suit brought in 1979, Mississippi charged that the legislation violated the Tenth Amendment. Although the act was ultimately upheld by the Supreme Court (*FERC* v. *Mississippi*, June 1, 1982), its constitutionality lay in limbo for nearly four years, during which several states delayed hearings on the law's retail rate guidelines pending resolution of the issue.

CONTROL BY THE PUBLIC UTILITY COMMISSIONS. Proponents of federal interference in local retail rate decisions usually note that too many utility commissions are scarcely in a position to be "laboratories for experimentation." Often understaffed and underfunded, some of these authorities cannot even complete the elaborate cost-of-service studies that must precede alternative rate-setting strategies.[66] As one member of the North Carolina Utilities Commission told a House energy panel not long ago: "If left totally to the states, a significant number of state commissions will, due to lack of both financial resources and adequate staff, be unable to continue the evaluation and consideration of new rate forms

66. Philip Mause, "Price Regulations and Energy Policy," in Hans H. Landsberg, ed., *Selected Studies on Energy* (Ballinger, 1980), p. 145.

and load management techniques."[67] Moreover, some commissions are highly politicized bodies, whose members are elected instead of appointed, serve short terms, and regard their posts primarily as springboards to higher offices. These agencies, it is argued, are susceptible to capture by powerful clients opposed to revised rates. Large local businesses, for instance, can deliver campaign contributions alongside their familiar pitch for favorable electric rates to help the state's business climate.

Organizational attributes of more professional commissions can pose difficulties as well. The staffs, typically trained as utility engineers, not economists, have had to undergo a slow and often frustrating reeducation. They must switch from conventional methods of cost accounting (the fairly simple routine of averaging embedded costs that can be readily verified by examining each power company's books) to the more complex methodologies associated with marginal-cost pricing.[68] When Professor Alfred Kahn, one of the nation's leading authorities on regulatory economics, became chairman of the New York Public Service Commission, he began work by patiently tutoring agency personnel in the application of economic theory and marginal analysis.[69] But commissions that resemble New York's are not typical, and ones headed by men or women of Kahn's stature are rarer still.

FEDERAL INTERVENTION. If these problems are widespread, more vigorous federal supervision might be justified, in the same way it has been justified in other realms previously reserved to the states, for example, air quality regulation. In fact, the Clean Air Act, leaving administrative responsibility to the states but under minimum performance standards enforceable by the Environmental Protection Agency, was explicitly the model invoked by utility rate reformers in the Carter administration and the House in 1977.[70] Yet encroachment upon the domain of the states in utility ratemaking seems to provoke unusually strenuous objections. Bizarre theories pop up, reminiscent of old "dual-federalist" doctrine, for example, suggesting that the federal government has a legitimate regulatory role to play in utility wholesale commerce and pricing, but not in retail transactions. Governors, state commission officials, and conserva-

67. *Inside FERC*, March 9, 1981, p. 4.
68. Interview with Harvey Reed, chief of Economic and Finance Branch, Office of Utility Systems, Economic Regulatory Administration, U.S. Department of Energy, Washington, D.C., September 24, 1981; Anderson, *Regulatory Politics and Electric Utilities*, p. 100.
69. Ibid., chap. 4.
70. Interview with Robert R. Nordhaus, October 20, 1981.

tive legislators decry the federal government's usurpation of responsibilities traditionally left to the states.[71] Even representatives and senators who do not normally hurl principled arguments against *étatist* remedies have regarded federal regulation of electric retail rates as off limits. Senator Jackson, for example, maintained that to trespass here, as the House proposed in 1977, was a terrible mistake, and Senator J. Bennett Johnston, Jr., Democrat of Louisiana, labeled federal involvement radical.[72]

But why would federal entry be considered radical or terrible? The answer lies deeper than that divergent interpretations of constitutional law are possible, or that states' rights are traditional. Perhaps nothing provides a better clue than what took place on October 5, 1977, in the midst of the congressional debate on the PURPA.[73] On that occasion, the same Senate majority that theorized at length about the prerogatives of state regulators suddenly paused to adopt a floor amendment that made a mockery of them. The measure, which passed comfortably on a vote of 57–36 but was later deleted in conference, called for each regulated utility to offer special below-cost rates, so-called lifeline rates, to elderly residential consumers. The states were forbidden to approve any rate schedules that violated that requirement.[74] At the Constitutional Convention in 1787, James Wilson of Pennsylvania wondered whether the Senate would legislate "for *men*, or for the imaginary beings called *States*?"[75] On October 5, the answer was clear: Whatever else the lifeline amendment signified, it implied a subsidy to a large bloc of voters, at no cost to the U.S. Treasury. Rhetoric notwithstanding, when such opportunities arise, senators can trench on state authority just as casually as House members do. That the Senate invoked state sovereignty to reject other forms of federally ordained electric rate modification (for example, the ban on declining blocks proposed in the Carter energy plan) was not inconsistent with this political impulse. In other proposals, the Senate detected perils that the House did not fully fathom, namely, that the proposed changes could portend not pork for constituents, but much higher costs.[76]

71. *Congressional Record* (August 1, 1977), p. 25912.
72. Pelham, *Energy Policy*, p. 62; and *Congressional Quarterly Weekly Report*, vol. 35 (September 17, 1977), p. 1990.
73. Ain, "PURPA," p. 72.
74. Senator Gary Hart, Democrat of Colorado, amendment to S. 2114, October 5, 1977, in *Congressional Quarterly Weekly Report*, vol. 35 (October 8, 1977), p. 2173.
75. Charles C. Tansill, ed., *Documents Illustrative of the Formation of the Union of American States* (GPO, 1927), p. 307.
76. Interview with Daniel A. Dreyfus, former deputy staff director, Senate Committee

Federalism, then, creates more than constitutional difficulties for national price policy on electric power. It provides a convenient vehicle in which Congress can, if it chooses, bypass controversial decisions. As with other contentious issues (benefit levels for welfare recipients is a classic illustration), the political heat of electric rate reform can be deflected by letting the problem rest at the local level. The Carter utility rate bill in 1977 could have raised "holy hell all across the country," sensed Colorado Senator Floyd Haskell, a liberal Democrat on the Energy Committee.[77] Why assume the blame for raising holy hell (that is, raising prices) by getting Congress into the business of setting rates, especially if that unpleasantness could be left with the states? That, concluded Senator Dale Bumpers, Democrat of Arkansas, was "just the whole ball game as far as the Senate was concerned."[78]

Finally, state control over ratemaking poses a dilemma: although rate revision has lagged in enough states to cast serious doubt on the effectiveness of the PURPA, it has also progressed widely enough to mute talk of enacting bolder federal measures. Opponents of new legislation, or even of a more assertive federal role along avenues already available under the utility act, can cite accomplishments of one sort or another in most states. For example, although pricing by time of day has had limited success thus far, seasonal rates are now common. Also, there is no question that many states have begun to flatten selectively their declining block tariffs, even though only a few states have banned them outright.[79] The public debate about electric rate policy has thus reached something of an impasse. Reformers see a need for further federal steps because they find their glass half empty. But detractors reply that, thanks to state initiatives, the glass is already half full.

The National Level: President Carter's Plan

The problem of electricity pricing was simmering in Congress well before Jimmy Carter became president. His administration, however, brought the issue to a boil in 1977 by making it a prominent ingredient

---

on Energy and Natural Resources, Washington, D.C., September 29, 1981. As Dreyfus explained, the fear in the Senate was that every senator "would have his picture on the monthly utility bill" if the House version were adopted.

77. *Congressional Quarterly Weekly Report*, vol. 35 (October 22, 1977), p. 2234.

78. Ibid., p. 2234.

79. Lehman Brothers Kuhn Loeb, Inc., Public Utility Regulatory Analysis Service, *Load Management Report* (July 1, 1980); and Irwin M. Stelzer, "The Electric Utilities Face the Next Twenty Years," in Landsberg, ed., *Selected Studies on Energy*, p. 141.

of the National Energy Plan. With congressional attention focused on rate reform as never before, the moment seemed ripe for far-reaching legislation. Yet the program that eventually emerged, the Public Utility Regulatory Policies Act, was not only a compromise but "a mere shadow of what it could have been," as Senator Howard M. Metzenbaum of Ohio protested.[80] As with the natural gas compromise, critics did not hesitate to fault the administration for what happened. And up to a point, they were right.

PROBLEMS WITH THE NATIONAL ENERGY PLAN. Like other key provisions of the proposed National Energy Act, the original section dealing with utility rates rankled skeptics more than it needed to. Particularly offensive to them was the enforcement mechanism through which the bill's mandatory ratemaking standards were to be secured. State public service commissions were to report biannually on their implementation efforts. Wherever compliance was found inadequate, the Federal Energy Administration would assume direct regulatory control over the utilities concerned. The "administrator" was also empowered to proscribe, through federal court injunctions, any interim rate relief, even to cover increased fuel costs, for such utilities until the requisite price-design policies were in place. These sanctions sent power company executives into a frenzy. Their grievances were aired loudly during Senate hearings on the bill. Twice-yearly reviews of state rate decisions by the Federal Energy Administration could prolong regulatory proceedings indefinitely; the volume of litigation would bulge, especially since cases could now be snarled up in federal courts as well as state courts; and the prohibition on timely rate increases "without a hearing, at the caprice of a single Federal official in Washington" was, to quote an outraged vice-president of one major midwestern utility, a "bone-crusher" that would jeopardize the industry's financial viability.[81] The Senate Energy Committee listened and grew fretful. Upon defeating the Carter plan, the majority's report stressed that "the potential uncertainty and delays accompanying federal regulation threatened to have an adverse impact on the financial health of the utility industry which outweighed the projected savings in capital expenditures claimed by supporters of the administration's proposal."[82]

80. Quoted in *Electrical Week*, October 16, 1978, p. 7.

81. The financial fears were underscored by various Wall Street witnesses at the Senate hearings. *Public Utility Rate Proposals*, Hearings, pt. 2, pp. 2–4, 14, 45, 269, 272–73.

82. Excerpted in Ain, "PURPA," p. 72. See also *Congressional Record* (October 5,

The National Energy Plan also expected utilities to undertake too many exploits at once.[83] To arrest the use of imported fuels under industrial boilers, the plan included a massive coal conversion program. Through heavy taxes and regulations, it called for the early retirement of billions of dollars' worth of oil- and gas-burning equipment and its replacement with new coal-fired facilities at an estimated cost of about $50 billion by the early 1990s. This ambitious venture raised an obvious question: could the utility industry, already straining for investment capital, pay to retrofit existing installations for coal combustion while sailing into the uncharted waters of federally enforced electric rate policy?[84] Industry representatives argued that coal conversion, hence the nation's pursuit of energy independence, required a stable regulatory environment. At a minimum, there should be no federal administrator policing the scene with the power to deny essential rate adjustments.

Arguably, had fewer red herrings been dragged across the debate on the Carter legislative initiatives, the administration's basic goal, federal advancement of rate innovation, could have received more support. But the president's numerous proposals had been formulated in haste. Parts of the National Energy Plan appeared to invite controversy where it might have been avoided. The sheer bulk of the overall menu made much of it hard for Congress to digest. This was especially true in the Senate, where a new committee, Energy and Natural Resources, faced issues such as electric rate reform for the first time.[85] In the House, by contrast, jurisdiction over this question remained with the Committee on Interstate and Foreign Commerce, whose Energy and Power Subcommittee had studied the problem, and drafted legislation dealing with it, as early as 1975.

Swamped with other items in the National Energy Act, and bogged down for months on the natural gas bill, the Senate Energy Committee was incapable of devoting to electricity pricing the time and labor it deserved. Although the panel's Subcommittee on Energy Conservation and Regulation did hold five intensive days of hearings on the subject in

---

1977), p. 32393.

83. Interview with Robert C. Dolan, Edison Electric Institute, Washington, D.C., October 1, 1981.

84. See, for example, the testimony of Con Ed Chairman Charles F. Luce, *Public Utility Rate Proposals*, Hearings, pt. 2, pp. 19–20.

85. Interview with Ross D. Ain, former associate general counsel of the Federal Energy Regulatory Commission and staff member of the House Committee on Interstate and Foreign Commerce, Washington, D.C., October 2, 1981.

1977, Senator Johnston, who chaired the proceedings, felt he and his colleagues were not doing it justice. "I do not think we know enough about this legislation to legislate responsibly," Johnston said. "I think it is irresponsible, frankly, to try to cover this territory in this period of time, when we have had only scant hours of testimony on it."[86]

THE ADMINISTRATION'S ROLE REASSESSED. Still and all, the Carter administration's profile in the legislative history of the PURPA was lower than commonly understood. The utility bill that the House sent to conference in the fall of 1977 was not, strictly speaking, the president's but an administration-backed substitute that bore the distinctive stamp of Representative John D. Dingell's (Democrat of Michigan) Commerce Subcommittee on Energy and Power. Similarities existed between the Dingell bill and the administration's original submission; both contained directives for mandatory rate design. The overlap was not surprising. Several ex-Commerce Committee staffers had joined the Energy Policy and Planning Office to work on the National Energy Plan. Robert R. Nordhaus, for instance, formerly the Commerce Committee's counsel and the primary draftsman of that committee's utility legislation in 1976, had signed on with the Schlesinger task force to write the administration's proposal.

But the two renditions also exhibited salient differences. The House version had softer edges. In particular, it did not prescribe continuous federal oversight by an enlarged bureaucracy armed with the power to preempt state authorities. Instead, the House measure envisioned a decentralized process, relying heavily on citizen participation in retail regulatory decisions. Ratepayers were to gain a statutory right to intervene in state proceedings, as well as the right to obtain judicial review. Under certain conditions, utilities could be required to compensate consumer intervenors for reasonable costs, such as attorney's fees, expert witness fees, and fees incurred in court appeals. Consumer groups would also receive aid through new federal grants. The bill did require public utility commissions to file progress reports with the Federal Power Commission (FPC) every two years. But the FPC's recourse against utilities that failed to comply with the law's rate standards was limited to the courts. The bill excluded the preemptive power that the administration had initially conferred on the Federal Energy Administration. By handing enforcement functions to the Federal Power Commission, the House chose an administrative agency that would probably leave the states wide lat-

86. *Public Utility Rate Proposals*, Hearings, pt. 2, p. 11.

itude in fixing rates; in Senate testimony at the time, FPC Chairman Richard L. Dunham questioned the wisdom of setting federal standards for retail rates, and he praised the independent activities going on in the states.[87]

All this rendered the Commerce Committee's strategem somewhat more palatable than the administration's. But not palatable enough, evidently, since Senate conferees gutted the core of it anyway. Congressional squeamishness toward federally mandated rate reform was probably heightened when the president, as in April 1977, presented the lawmakers with an awkward legislative formula. Resistance persisted, however, even after significant parts of the formula were recast.

The PURPA and the Failure of Federal Rate Reform

On the Senate side all bills comparable to the House Commerce Committee's were brushed aside. But in the House of Representatives the committee's proposal slipped through. This success in the House provides insights into the political currents that shaped the Public Utility Regulatory Policies Act.

The rate reform bill had been swept along in the torrent of other energy measures that rushed through the lower chamber in August 1977. Speaker Thomas P. O'Neill, Jr., had set the National Energy Act's various components on a fast track. Coordinating legislative activity through a specially constituted Ad Hoc Energy Committee, the House leadership had also managed to combine all the components, including the utility legislation, into a single, comprehensive package upon which the whole House would vote. Hostile lobbies had difficulty gaining access under these conditions. In the Senate, on the other hand, the National Energy Plan was sliced up into separate bills. Opposition there had more time to get organized and more bends in the road from which to ambush provisions. Once the utility measure had nestled its way into the Ad Hoc Committee's omnibus bill, passage by the full House was achieved largely by rigging the parliamentary rules to limit debate and disabling amendments. But to reach the Ad Hoc Committee, the legislation needed full Commerce Committee approval first.

FORMATIVE INFLUENCES. A nucleus of Commerce Committee members had studied utility-pricing problems for several years[88] and had grown con-

---

87. *Public Utility Rate Proposals*, Hearings, pt. 1, pp. 253, 260.
88. The following account is reconstructed largely from interviews with key actors close to the legislative process at the time: David J. Bardin, former deputy administrator, Federal

fident that important efficiencies could be attained through new rate systems.[89] From this group's standpoint, federal sponsorship of such systems was hardly a reckless foray into *terra incognita*, as the Senate Energy Committee was very much afraid, but a rational application of proven economic instruments to advance important national goals, such as the conservation of energy. The faction that viewed the issue in these terms, however, could not have prevailed without allies. Paradoxically, consumer advocates, with dubious credentials as pragmatic policymakers in other energy price debates, were the main group to enter the coalition. Thus, many of the congressmen who wanted pricing reform for electric power were the same politicians who deplored it (that is, who defended the regulatory status quo) for crude oil and natural gas.

A basic distinction enabled outspoken opponents of gas and oil decontrol—Anthony J. Moffett of Connecticut, Richard L. Ottinger of New York, Philip R. Sharp of Indiana, among numerous other liberal Democrats seated on House Commerce—to rally behind the proposed federal shake-up of electric retail rates. Unlike proposals to price other fuels at their commodity value, a policy relating electricity rates to marginal costs did not imply deregulation. Imaginably, what it could imply was new opportunities for regulators to manipulate prices and profits to

---

Energy Administration, Washington, D.C., September 28, 1981; Benjamin S. Cooper, staff, Senate Committee on Energy and Natural Resources, Washington, D.C., September 29, 1981; Daniel A. Dreyfus, September 29, 1981; Martin H. Rogol, October 1, 1981; Ross D. Ain, October 2, 1981; Howard Perry, October 6, 1981; and Robert R. Nordhaus, October 20, 1981.

89. Contrary to the allegations of some of the opponents of rate reform, there was considerable evidence available to Congress about the demand-managing effects of alternative rate structures. Preliminary findings from the fifteen electric-rate demonstration projects sponsored by the Federal Energy Administration, involving about 18,000 customers, indicated that the total amount of energy used by consumers on time-of-day rates, when compared with that of users on standard declining blocks, fell significantly during peak periods. For residential customers, the effective reduction in peak period consumption ranged from 15 to 30 percent in most projects. Douglas Bauer and Alan S. Hirshberg, "Improving the Efficiency of Electricity Generation and Usage," in John C. Sawhill, ed., *Energy Conservation and Public Policy* (Prentice-Hall, 1979), p. 162. And at least fifteen other states were engaged in small-scale, time-of-day rate experiments in 1977. Anderson, *Regulatory Politics and Electric Utilities*, pp. 82–83. As early as 1974, at least thirteen states had taken action to flatten the declining block rates of some of their utilities. Berlin, Cicchetti, and Gillen, *Perspectives on Power*, p. 66. Finally, over twenty years, there had been extensive experience with peakload pricing in a number of European countries and in Japan. Jan Paul Action, Bridger M. Mitchell, and Willard G. Manning, Jr., *European Industrial Response to Peak-Load Pricing of Electricity, with Implications for U.S. Energy Policy*, Paper P-5929 (Santa Monica, Calif.: Rand Corp., 1978), pp. 2–3; Bridger M. Mitchell, *Peak-Load Pricing: European Lessons for U.S. Energy Policy* (Ballinger, 1978).

the advantage of small consumers. The opportunities included, but were not limited to, the possibility that marginal-cost pricing would curtail future capacity expansions and thus stabilize rates in the long term. Where tariffs based on marginal costs would run above existing rates, regulatory authorities might be pressured into sparing the residential class and, presumably through inversion of declining blocks, inflicting all the pain on large industrial and commercial users. Above all, since rates of return remained tightly controlled, higher prices would bring no wind-falls to electricity producers. Instead, because public utility commissions were required by law to hold utility revenues to "fair" levels, producers could be forced to offset the excess receipts collected from higher rates among bulk users by lowering rates for small customers, low-income groups, or the elderly.[90]

Thus an energy conservation bill garnished abundantly with consumer protection provisions, or more accurately, with possibilities for income transfers, evolved in the House. Public utility commissions were directed to restructure rates to reflect the full cost of serving each customer class. But in another section, this stipulation was relaxed to make room for lifeline tariffs: nothing was to prevent a state or utility from fixing lower than cost-based rates "for the essential needs of residential electric consumers."[91] In other words, while commercial customers and industrials would see prices pegged to the true cost of providing them with power, residential users became eligible for subsidized prices that might bear no relation to cost of service.[92] Partly to increase the likelihood that precisely these sorts of arrangements would catch on in the states, and partly because public opinion strongly supported the idea, the legislation emphasized direct consumer representation in local rate cases, with compulsion by the Federal Power Commission as a last resort.

A program that might offer relief for small ratepayers was likely to interest liberals in both houses of Congress. The Senate vote of October 5 on lifeline pricing suggested that, at least on the floor, the upper

90. The central problem with prices based on marginal costs is that under current circumstances they are likely to yield revenues greater than those allowed by state utility commissions to achieve a fair rate of return on historical costs. Paul L. Joskow, "Electric Utility Rate Structures in the United States: Some Recent Developments," in Werner Sichel, ed., *Public Utility Rate Making in an Energy Conscious Environment* (Boulder, Colo.: Westview Press, 1979), p. 11.

91. H.R. 8444, H. Rept. 95–543, "Part V: Public Utilities Regulatory Policies," 95 Cong. 1 sess., p. 183.

92. Daniel Silverstone, *Conservation, Efficiency, Equity: The PURPA Purposes*, PURPA Paper 2 (Washington, D.C.: Environmental Action Foundation, 1979), p. 9.

chamber could be as venturesome as the House in turning utility rate designs into redistributional tools. But in the House Commerce Committee, unlike the Senate Energy Committee, consumer advocates were more numerous, more militant, and at least in this instance, less risk averse. Ralph Nader's organization, Public Citizen (whose chief lobbyist, Martin Rogol, played a major part in molding the House bill), rated almost a quarter of the Commerce membership higher than 90 on its pro-consumer scale of 1 to 100.[93] Only two of the eighteen Senate Energy members scored that high. John D. Dingell, the Energy and Power Subcommittee's formidable chief, rather than Harley O. Staggers, the committee's nominal chairman, piloted the Commerce Committee through its deliberations on utility pricing. The Nader group had given an 89 rating to Dingell, compared with a 16 to Bennett Johnston, whose subcommittee was writing the bill's Senate counterpart.

House passage of Dingell's bill, basically unamended, put him and the administration in a fairly strong position to haggle with the Senate in conference. Lots of concessions were won, yet on the central question of whether to instate any mandatory retail rate standards, however minimal, the House conferees backed down. One could argue that they had no choice. At the outset of the conference committee's sessions, Senator Johnston laid down his side's views in unmistakable terms: "On that essential point, of federal standards federally enforced, the Senate is simply not going to yield."[94] But there was more to the capitulation than just the fact that Johnston's "essential point" sounded nonnegotiable. The House gave in because, on almost everything else, the senators were prepared to be generous. In particular, they promptly went along with the main elements of the participatory ratemaking process that the House bill envisaged: direct advocacy of specified rate revisions by citizen intervenors, wearing a new mantle of legitimacy (the opportunity to intervene as a federally guaranteed "matter of right") and wielding new means with which to defray the cost (compensation by the government, the utilities, or both).

Consumer groups were jubilant. The outcome was hailed as an over-

93. Michael Barone, Grant Ujifusa, and Douglas Mathews, *The Almanac of American Politics, 1978* (E. P. Dutton, 1977). Martin H. Rogol, Public Citizen's key lobbyist at the time, attested emphatically that this difference in the politics of the members was the single most important distinction between the House and Senate committees legislating on utility rates, and that more than anything else, it accounted for their antithetical legislative products. Interview with Martin H. Rogol, October 1, 1981.

94. *Congressional Quarterly Weekly Report*, vol. 35 (November 19, 1977), p. 2447.

whelming success that for the first time equipped reformers with an effective means of forcing restructured rates.[95] "The compromise bill," one organization proclaimed confidently, "depends upon active local groups —not federal enforcement—for utility reform. New laws have been formulated that will increase the clout and financial resources of local utility organizations. With the aid of these new powers, local groups will be able to achieve long-sought-after changes."[96] Whether by design or by chance, the Senate negotiators had hit upon exactly the right side-payment to offer the principal clientele of the rate reform campaign in the House. The accord on intervenor funding seemed to leave some of Dingell's associates so satisfied that they more or less quit dickering and simply declared victory.[97] Dingell was reportedly "a little ticked off" at the way the House and the administration left the bargaining table,[98] but on this occasion his displeasure made little difference. The framework of the Public Utility Regulatory Policies Act's Title I, "Retail Regulatory Policies for Electric Utilities," was now firmly in place.

IMPLEMENTATION. Those who were euphoric about the compromise bill did not foresee that without clear, compulsory rate design requirements, local groups could scarcely sway the regulatory policies of most states merely by obtaining the right and the money to introduce witnesses and information during rate hearings. It was true that the senators had agreed to provide for public, as well as private, intervenors; thus the Department of Energy got the same formal assurance that it could take part, even uninvited, as an advocate in state rate cases. But no one, including the energy department, was entitled to instruct the state utility commissions to do anything besides address ("consider") the act's optional rate standards.

Moreover, the scope of the whole operation was subject to the vagaries of annual budgetary appropriations. Considerable sums were authorized to fund a utility intervenors' bureau in the Department of Energy's Economic Regulatory Administration; an aid program for the state commissions initiating PURPA rate proceedings; and a grant system to state consumer affairs offices to support local activists. The

95. Kent Whitney, "Congress to Aid Rate Reform," *Power Line*, vol. 3 (December 1977), p. 5.

96. Ibid., p. 4.

97. Interview with Howard Perry, October 6, 1981. Despite public protestations, utilities were aware that any intervenors would need voluminous technical data on marginal-cost pricing to impress most public utility commissions. Interview with Robert C. Dolan, October 1, 1981.

98. *Electrical Week*, November 21, 1977, p. 2.

money spent, however, fell far short of the authorizations during the first two years of the PURPA, and by the third, it had dried up. Of an authorized $10 million in consumer grants for fiscal years 1979 and 1980, $4 million were appropriated. These and other federal expenditures for the administration of the utility act were terminated by the 1981 budget. By early fall of 1981, having participated in just fifteen cases, the Economic Regulatory Administration's intervenors' office had shut down, and its staff was dismissed or transferred elsewhere.

As for the PURPA's only remaining method of financing intervenors, eligibility for direct reimbursements from utilities, the provision proved too involved to operate on a significant scale. Compensatory settlements were ordered here and there. In 1979, for instance, consumer groups were especially proud of an award paid by Minnesota Power and Light Company to the Senior Citizen Coalition of Northeastern Minnesota. The group received $11,206 in compensation upon convincing the Minnesota Public Service Commission to disallow one of the company's rate requests.[99] But overall, the number of cases, and the size of the payments, remained paltry.

A few interested parties continued to be afraid of the PURPA, long after Congress had finished sanitizing it. The Electricity Consumers Resource Council (ELCON), the lobbying arm of the industrial electricity users, was one. "From a practical viewpoint," an ELCON representative still warned as late as November 1980, "voluntary guidelines packaged by the federal government with the promise of federal grant monies are virtually indistinguishable from mandatory regulations or mandatory guidelines."[100] Almost everybody else, however, knew this was nonsense. Voluntary guidelines could not be anything but voluntary, particularly after the grant monies vanished.[101] A lot of legislators took comfort in

99. Meyer, *Ratepayer's Guide to PURPA*, p. 21.

100. U.S. Department of Energy, Economic Regulatory Administration, *Comments of the Electricity Consumers Resource Council (ELCON) in Response to the ERA Notice of Proposed Voluntary Guidelines for the Cost of Service Standard under the Public Utility Regulatory Policies Act of 1978*, DOE Docket, ERA-R-80-29 (Washington, D.C.: DOE, 1980), p. 10.

101. Thus, Senator Dewey Bartlett, Republican of Oklahoma, sized up the legislation more accurately: "this bill will produce no energy whatsoever, though it may produce a great many energy lawyers and 'energy experts.' Because what the bill does is to enact a complicated set of procedures and laws whose avowed intention is to have almost no mandatory effect." Senator Clifford Hansen, Republican of Wyoming, was equally pointed: "I am puzzled at just what we think this bill will now accomplish. . . . We need substance, not symbolism, and this bill now provides little but symbolism." *Electrical Week*, October 16, 1978, p. 7.

that fact. On October 9, 1978, the Senate adopted the PURPA conference report on a vote of 76 to 13. The tally was so favorable because, while some senators were genuinely convinced that the legislation was valuable, many were also happy to be ingesting milktoast.

Political Convictions

Deep ideological taproots can be traced beneath the political thicket in which rate policy is entangled. Two rather different ideals are being sought. Fittingly, they are prominently on display in the preamble of the Public Utility Regulatory Policies Act: One purpose of the law is the "increased conservation of electric energy" and "increased efficiency in the use of facilities and resources by electric utilities"; another is the provision of "equitable retail rates for electric consumers."[102] Ultimately, the difficulty of restructuring electric rates to conserve energy derives from this juxtaposition.

Efficiency, Equity, and Marginal-Cost Pricing

Superficially, it may appear that the competing demands of efficiency and equity are easier to reconcile in pricing designs for electricity than in those for petroleum or natural gas. This mirage is so alluring that it often brings together strange bedfellows. Economists and conservationists, with no particular desire to protect energy consumers of any kind, logically assume that resources are more efficiently allocated when tariffs vary directly with the incremental costs of production, rather than inversely with the amount of electricity purchased, as in the declining block schedules that charge larger users less per kilowatt-hour than smaller ones. Meanwhile, in theory at least, egalitarians can rejoice because the flattened blocks would seem to remove price discrimination against hard-pressed ratepayers, especially the poor and the elderly.

Rate revisionists realize that current electricity prices tend to underassess incremental production costs, albeit not in all regions. Hence, simply switching to real marginal-cost-based rates could spell huge and sudden revenue surpluses for many electric companies. But the revisionists also know that with state commissions keeping a tight lid on utility earnings, these overcollections would never be analogous to the windfall profits of oil and gas producers upon decontrol. Presumably, utilities would not be permitted to recover the bounty resulting from any

102. Pub. L. 95-617 (November 9, 1978), 92 Stat., p. 3119.

gap between their approved rates of return and the revised prices. A likely solution to the so-called revenue gap, or revenue requirement, problem, as already noted, appears to be the lifeline rebate, subsidizing small customers with extra proceeds from large ones. Admittedly, the goal of tying prices consistently to marginal costs is compromised, since the lifeline beneficiaries receive a cut-rate customer charge (that is, a below-cost kilowatt-hour charge). Reformers, however, tend to shrug off the inconsistency by assuming that small users are seldom responsible for system load growth, and thus for the costs of incremental power generation.

In practice the solution is unsatisfactory. To begin with, small users can often contribute heavily to load growth. Between 1966 and 1976, for instance, residential consumption of electricity grew by an average of 7.8 percent a year, while industrial sales by utilities increased at a rate of 5.4 percent.[103] With increasing use of air conditioners, electric heating, and other comforts, residential peak demand rose by seventy-seven gigawatts, compared with forty-one gigawatts for commercial use and thirty-nine for industry.[104]

In the 1970s, when Congress was debating rate structures, the major industrial users generally scored few points in legislative testimony.[105] "The attention span of the members could not be measured in weeks or days or hours, but in *minutes*," recalled Jay Kennedy, ELCON's chief lobbyist.[106] But the evidence they presented comparing demand characteristics by customer classes was too startling to be ignored; its impact, at least in the Senate Energy Committee, was devastating. Rates restructured to reduce charges for residential consumers, even for subclasses of such consumers, could scarcely yield energy savings if these households were adding to system peaks as much, if not more, than any other category of users.[107] If schemes to overhaul electric rates can subvert conservation, they are self-defeating. This effect enhances neither their intrinsic worth nor their political prospects. In part, the House-passed utility plan of 1977 was denigrated in the Senate because "it was never perceived as an energy conservation program over here," Benjamin S. Cooper, a key Energy Committee aide, emphasized in an interview.[108]

103. "A Broadside from EEI," *Weekly Energy Report*, vol. 4 (April 5, 1976), p. 13.
104. *Public Utility Rate Proposals*, Hearings, pt. 1, pp. 367, 519.
105. Interview with Ross D. Ain, October 2, 1981.
106. Interview with Jay B. Kennedy, October 1, 1981.
107. *Public Utility Rate Proposals*, Hearings, pt. 1, pp. 37, 502–03.
108. Interview with Benjamin S. Cooper, September 29, 1981.

The same sort of indictment is heard continually among state public service commissions, as they ponder the PURPA and the practicability of marginal-cost-based rates.

Inverting rates to favor households might be more defensible if it could be proven that these rates were genuinely equitable. No such proof emerges. Proponents of lifeline-type measures assert that the average price per kilowatt-hour paid by residential consumers has exceeded the price paid by commercial and industrial buyers—by as much as 64 percent, according to an estimate by the AFL-CIO a few years ago.[109] But the assertion overlooks the fact that it often costs utilities less to dispense power to a group of big commercial establishments and factories than to dispense it to thousands of scattered housing units—just as it costs, say, a milkman less to deliver four quarts of milk in a one-gallon container to a single large customer than four quarts in four containers to four different small customers.[110] Given this difference in distribution costs, a policy that indiscriminately sets unit prices for businesses above those of residences, or even requires parity between the two, could frequently create an injustice. Some businesses would find themselves getting billed more for their electrical service than it costs the utility to serve them.

Within the residential class, lifeline structures do not distinguish sensitively between households in real need of rate relief and the ratepaying population at large. Affluent consumers get subsidized along with poor families, just as they do under oil and gas price controls. Indeed, a wealthy household using electricity for space heating may be subsidized more than an impoverished one using fuel oil. Such flaws have caused the great majority of state utility commissions to think twice before mandating lifelines.

All but the most extreme lifeline proposals may not suffice to dissipate the surplus income arising from commercial-industrial tariffs that match marginal costs. The sheer size of the surplus that must be shed to remain within allowed revenue requirements is staggering for many utilities contemplating these tariffs. Not so long ago Commonwealth Edison of Chicago calculated that marginal-cost-based tariffs for commercial and industrial customers in its service area could have added $493

109. Statement on utility rate reform by AFL-CIO Executive Council, Bal Harbour, Florida, February 25, 1977.

110. Electricity Consumers Resource Council, *Profiles in Electricity Issues: Cost-of-Service Survey*, no. 6 (Washington, D.C.: ELCON, 1982), p. 1.

million to an expected $1,319 billion in revenues from these users.[111] To stay inside the Illinois Commerce Commission's approved total revenue limit, the company's rates for residential customers would have had to decline by two-thirds. Estimates submitted to the New York Public Service Commission by the state's giant utility, Consolidated Edison, were even more dismaying. If the company adopted strict marginal-cost rates for its larger customers, the change would produce about $650 million per year more than permitted by the commission even if residential customers were charged nothing.[112]

Consequently, the tendency among public utility commissions that want to depart from traditional price structures, without either authorizing much higher rates of return or literally giving away electricity to residential consumers, is to tinker with methods of computing costs. Variations in costing methodologies abound. Incremental costs of utility systems can be figured in several ways depending on the time frame chosen, the presence of excess or deficient capacity, the decision of whether to estimate costs on a company or pool basis, and the inclusion or exclusion of income taxes. The typical modification, however, consists of downgrading the full replacement value of generating facilities, fuel, transmission, or distribution by artistically blending marginal (future) with average (historic) cost measurements. An early and ingenious illustration of this type of formula, doctoring new time-of-use rates "to conform to the revenue constraint," was the much-admired *Long Island Lighting Company* case in New York.[113] More recent models are the Ohio rate decisions involving Dayton Power and Light Company and Cincinnati Gas and Electric. These cases are especially interesting because both of these utilities favored marginal-cost pricing but ended up with a solution in which marginal costs turned out to be equal to average costs.[114]

A Tax on Surplus Revenue?

Any correspondence between these manipulations and the dictates of economic theory is purely coincidental. The outcomes can be as arbitrary

111. *Public Utility Rate Proposals*, Hearings, pt. 1, pp. 46, 366.
112. Ibid., pp. 21, 27.
113. Thomas W. Keelin and Eugene N. Oatman, "Generating Capacity in U.S. Electric Utilities: How Much is Needed?" *Public Utilities Fortnightly*, vol. 110 (December 23, 1982), p. 144.
114. A. Scott Rothey and Samuel C. Randazzo, "Marginal Cost Electric Rate Making: Some Realities," *Public Utilities Fortnightly*, vol. 110 (July 8, 1982), p. 37.

as those from conventional cost-accounting techniques. So instead of fabricating a curious new stock of hybrid rate forms that still do not authentically incorporate the long-term costs to society of resupplying electricity, a more honest strategy might be for public utility commissions to abandon their traditional methods of regulating utility revenue allowances. Producer prices, according to this approach, would be elevated to the level of marginal costs for all classes of ratepayers. Then, to cushion the impact of the higher rates, a tax, much like the windfall profits tax on petroleum producers, could be levied on some share of the industry's inflated receipts.

But there are three reasons why such a seemingly neat resolution is not, and probably will never be, in the offing. First, basic institutional changes would be necessary in the regulatory roles of the state commissions. The commissions typically lack authority to tax and redistribute revenue directly, even though most of them can arrange rate structures to achieve what amounts to the same thing.[115] In many cases, longstanding state law would have to be junked.

Second, as should be clear by now, higher electric bills for all customer classes are not what the public, nor most utility activists, have in mind by reform. Consider the easy test: reaction to the more modest objective of flattening rates, but without necessarily boosting them up to equal marginal costs. When public utility commissions are urged to prohibit declining blocks, it is understood that the prohibition will affect large industrial and commercial users, the sectors that devour most of the nation's electricity.[116] But state regulators and wary federal lawmakers are soon made aware that a complete ban would also fall heavily on the millions of all-electric residential consumers, who soak up about a third of total residential electricity consumed. Thus, after the Nevada Public Service Commission attempted to increase impartially the rates in everyone's tail blocks by the same amount per kilowatt-hour, it was the residential users who "felt they had been induced to buy large homes with many electric appliances" who denounced the policy most harshly, compelling the commission to make adjustments.[117] Likewise, a backlash by electric heat customers against Connecticut's comprehensive flat-rate policy eventually forced that state to exempt these households

115. Berlin, Cicchetti, and Gillen, *Perspectives on Power*, p. 25.

116. Approximately 34 percent of the nation's electricity is consumed by residential users, about 24 percent by commercial customers, and 38 percent by industrials. *Congressional Quarterly Weekly Report*, vol. 35 (March 26, 1977), p. 544.

117. *Public Utility Rate Proposals*, Hearings, pt. 2, p. 243.

by putting them on a separate schedule. Similar episodes can be cited across the country.

To avoid angering consumers when pricing electricity uniformly at marginal cost, it would be imperative to guarantee that the utility tax would bite deeply into the industry's profits and then be fully rebated to the public. Therein lies the final pitfall. Any tax instrument that didn't repossess for average ratepayers at least as much utility income as is transferred implicitly under existing rate structures would probably be doomed from the start. The problem is not solely that no self-interested ratepayer will readily acquiesce to raw price increases. It is also that consumers and utility reformers shudder at the possibility that a tax might be a leaky vessel in which to siphon utility revenue. These groups think that somewhere in the process, the power companies might manage to widen their profit margins.

The anxiety about utility profits goes beyond distrust of natural monopolies. It also has to do with what critics suspect is a habitual urge in the electric industry: to expand capacity whenever rates of return improve.[118] Pronouncements by company managers about immutable, and fantastic, demand projections and capital requirements do little to quell the suspicion. Like oil companies, for which the central purpose of decontrolling petroleum prices was to put more drilling rigs in operation, the main virtue of rate increases, from the standpoint of some electricity producers, is still to finance additional electricity production, not to depress demand. This further explains why conservationist groups, such as the Environmental Defense Fund, which has led campaigns for peakload tariffs in several states, tend to affiliate with consumer lobbies pursuing contradictory pricing objectives, such as subsidized residential rates. The environmentalists can regard the compromise as a necessary expedient in their battle to hold the line against utility building programs. By inserting lifeline provisions into marginal-cost-based rate policies, the regulated revenue constraint on utilities can be kept intact, divesting the companies of any excess earnings that might otherwise go toward new plants.

Finally, the resolve of utility critics to keep utility profits low has been stiffened by the same consideration that hardened the opposition to de-

118. Despite the much lower growth rate for electricity demand during the period 1973–78, utilities continued to overbuild capacity until by 1980 the industry had about twice the reserve generating capacity considered necessary for a safety margin. See Walter A. Rosenbaum, *Energy, Politics and Public Policy* (Washington, D.C.: CQ Press, 1981), p. 210.

regulation of oil prices: public subsidies to the industry. This consideration, it is argued, has been lost in the continual cant about the financial punishment being meted out by unfriendly state and federal regulators. Thus, if regulators move to enforce, say, safety requirements for nuclear power stations (as the Nuclear Regulatory Commission did recently, fining one major New Jersey utility $850,000 for violations, and denying Illinois's Commonwealth Edison a license to operate its new Byron plant),[119] government actions are reported in the media as "a devastating blow" and "another nail in the coffin" of the financially depressed atomic plant operators.[120] The fact that the nuclear industry has received forms of government assistance, from research-and-development activities, to support for plant construction and insurance costs, to aid in fuel mining, milling, reprocessing, and cleanup, is infrequently mentioned.[121] (The only nondefense portions of the energy department's budget that the Reagan administration's fiscal 1983 budget did not propose to reduce were the nuclear energy programs.)[122]

Similarly, the erratic market for utility common stocks is regularly attributed to "the inhospitable regulatory climate" created by the public service commissions of several big states. However, wholesale prices for power sold to public utilities from federal dams and other federal generating projects are nothing if not hospitable.[123] The same goes for the widening array of federal tax preferences extended to the investor-owned electric companies. In 1979, private utilities paid $660 million in income taxes, deferring $1.25 billion through accelerated depreciation and claiming another $1.57 billion in credits.[124] More liberalized depreciation rates, exclusions on equity dividends, and other advantages introduced by the Economic Recovery Tax Act of 1981 gave electric utilities in 1982 about 42 percent of the tax expenditures claimed by energy-supply industries generally, and approximately 14 percent of all the benefits created by the act.[125]

119. Stoler, "Pulling the Nuclear Plug," pp. 34, 36.

120. *New York Times*, May 9, 1983.

121. Rosenbaum, *Energy, Politics and Public Policy,* pp. 42, 109–10, 166, 175–79, 181–84; Freeman, *Energy*, pp. 69, 172; and John F. O'Leary, "Nuclear Energy and Public Policy Issues," in Robert J. Kalter and William A. Vogely, eds., *Energy Supply and Government Policy* (Cornell University Press, 1976), pp. 242–43.

122. Conservation Foundation, *State of the Environment 1982* (Washington, D.C.: Conservation Foundation, 1982), pp. 393–94.

123. See Freeman, *Energy*, pp. 162, 293–94.

124. U.S. Department of Energy, *DOE's Role*, p. 8.

125. Conservation Foundation, *State of the Environment 1982*, p. 200.

In sum, full replacement-cost pricing of electric power is politically implausible if lurking within it is the risk of further wealth transfers from consumers to suppliers. Realistically, as every state public utility commissioner knows, a fail-safe mechanism for rebating the bonus that suppliers would gross is difficult to devise. It is hard enough to gain public consent for the new price policy under these circumstances. With taxpayers underwriting the electrical industry, it is harder still.

Conclusion

The need for improved electricity pricing looms large in the unfinished business of furthering the efficient utilization of energy in the United States. Ideally, national policy ought to pursue the same principle that was finally accepted in the pricing of crude oil: that each unit of energy cannot be sold for less than the cost of replacing it.

But progress is being stalled by a variety of obstacles. Heavy users of electric power have no interest in letting their volume discounts perish; their dissent cannot be wholly ignored by states competing for industry and jobs. Meanwhile, utilities have had trouble adapting to contemporary market conditions and novel economic roles. Still dedicated to promoting electrification, some power companies continue to chafe at the revolutionary notion of encouraging, rather than resisting, today's slower growth in electrical demand. Others recognize the new realities but fear that experimental rate designs (for example, time-of-use tariffs) might only widen their yawning capacity margins. Furthermore, public opinion furnishes no mandate for change—unless the change is in one direction, lowering consumer prices rather than increasing them. Even if these frustrations waned, great diversity among local electricity-generating sectors militates against general plans for rate revision. Local control is deemed appropriate, and regional representatives most partial to this tradition are well positioned politically to uphold it. That was one reason why the boldest attempt to introduce a federal policy for electric retail rates, the initiative lodged with the Carter administration's energy program, largely floundered. Another was that the chief policy entrepreneurs led unruly coalitions and committed some tactical errors to boot.

But intensifying these inhibitions, and contributing a few additional ones, is a more fundamental problem: the movement for electric rate innovation wavers under the weight of its own political contradictions. Some reformers seek to align energy prices more closely with final replacement costs, so that all users can properly compare the economic benefits of conserving energy with the net benefits of consuming it. Others, however, want the restructured prices to serve a more complex social goal: distributing welfare to small ratepayers at the expense of the electricity providers and their larger customers. Despite the popular appeal of rate breaks for modest consumers, the marriage of these dual aspirations is disharmonious. If, in the nature of things, large businesses were the only utility customers that overconsumed electricity, it might be easier to amalgamate the differing aims of rate reform. Energy could be conserved by billing the businesses at cost while assisting smaller users by billing them below cost. But more often than not, the crucial supposition that only big businesses overconsume is empirically baseless. So when ratemakers get down to cases, they become perplexed by requests to retract the old price schedules that are wasteful and discriminatory (declining blocks) only to put in their place new ones that are also wasteful and, to large clients, discriminatory (inverted blocks).

It is improbable that this hurdle can be cleared soon, since it is not likely that the reform ideals will be readily simplified. Hypothetically, instead of commingling within rate structures the separate objectives of energy efficiency and income maintenance, a better price system would charge everybody the replacement (marginal) costs of generating the power they take. In an independent procedure, there could be compensation for certain disadvantaged groups through energy stamps or cash payments, obtained if necessary from an explicit tax on producers.

But politically, such a scenario lacks charm. Although the concept of pricing electricity at marginal cost means different things to different people, to key actors in the ratemaking drama (such as the Senate Energy Committee's majority during the national debate of 1977 and the majority of state utility regulators in the local polemics continuing today) the concept is like Pandora's box; lift the lid and up fly utility prices and profits. To let prices soar, then to retrieve the excess profits by effective taxation, and finally to redistribute the enormous revenues fairly are big steps, fraught with political and administrative uncertainties.

Someday they may seem less hazardous, especially if there is diminished public pressure to keep utility earnings carefully regulated. But that pressure is not likely to subside as long as the industry is perceived to be subsidized and given to pouring too much of its treasure into capital investments that the marketplace rejects. Thus for the foreseeable future, Congress will be glad to leave the complexities of electricity pricing to the states. The state regulatory authorities, in turn, will continue to reason conservatively, as the Minnesota Public Service Commission did in a recent critique of comprehensive marginal costing. Unalloyed marginal cost-based rates, the Minnesota agency objected, "imply that the Commission should seek to accomplish one goal: economic efficiency." Ratemaking with "a single goal," the opinion continued, was not the agency's mission: "the Commission exists primarily to balance competing goals." And although economic efficiency is "important," it concluded, "so is a reasonable continuity of rates or the evolution of rates."[126]

126. U.S. Department of Energy, Economic Regulatory Administration, *Comments of the Electricity Consumers Resource Council*, p. 5 of appendix 2.

CHAPTER FIVE

Taxation of Gasoline

IF THE ENERGY-PRICING policies charted during the past decade had given freer rein to market forces, much of the passage to a sound national energy posture, based on conservation, would have been achieved by now. But, arguably, just decontrolling oil and gas, and restructuring utility rates would not have been enough to complete the transition. Even if these essential preconditions had been secured consummately and in timely fashion, a faulty market would persist, still skewing the quantities of energy demanded and supplied and diminishing the nation's energy efficiency. As discussed in the introduction of this book, magnifying the nominal prices of some fuels may be necessary to countervail the stimulative effects that other public policies have on energy consumption and to keep the momentum of conservation from flagging.

Public debate since the embargo has centered mostly on two ways of amplifying prices: imposing a tariff on imported oil, or levying a serious excise tax on gasoline. From the start, the second of these has had a good deal more to recommend it. Nevertheless, even as the energy crisis mounted, the United States remained the only leading industrial democracy to eschew significant increases in national motor fuel taxation. Heavy automotive fuel taxes had long been the norm in most of Western Europe. In 1973 regular gasoline was taxed the equivalent of $0.77 per gallon in France, $0.61 in Italy, $0.42 in the United Kingdom, and $1.09 in West Germany. When oil prices shot up after the embargo, these levies tended to reflect the change. By 1980 the tax on a gallon of regular gas had reached $1.19 in the United Kingdom; $1.23 in Germany; $1.68 in France; and a staggering $2.16 in Italy. Meanwhile, the average combined federal and state tax rate in the United States went from $0.12 to $0.14 a gallon.[1] To

1. Central Intelligence Agency data, reported in Ann Pelham, *Energy Policy*, 2d ed.

195

the extent that differences in pricing policy explain the sharp disparity between levels of energy utilization in the United States and the rest of the
industrialized world, this particular contrast is probably the most telling.

Federal policymakers have not been oblivious to the implications.
Higher gasoline taxes to spur conservation were considered in 1973 and
formally proposed in 1975, 1977, and 1980. In 1982 Congress finally
took action; a hike of $0.05 per gallon was approved.[2] As the first federal
increase in twenty-three years, this recent episode was widely hailed as a
political milestone. In reality, it signified less than that. The Surface
Transportation Assistance Act of 1983, in which the tax increase was
lodged, arrived on the national agenda amid some unusually helpful circumstances. The most remarkable thing about the legislation was not
that it passed under these conditions, but that despite them, it almost
didn't. A two-week filibuster by opponents nearly derailed the bill in the
Senate, and the measure also came close to losing in the House.[3] Such
fuss over a nickel ante would have bewildered European politicians and
motorists. In the United States, however, gasoline tax initiatives of all
shapes and sizes tend to suffocate in the acrimonious congressional
quarrels they always provoke. Enactment of the 1982 proposal was
something of an accident—one with rather long odds against being repeated at any time soon.

The tendency of Congress, with rare exceptions, to scorn the idea of
taxing gasoline is an intriguing political phenomenon with important implications for energy policy.

The Case for Gasoline Taxation

On some of the policy adjustments discussed in this book—oil-price deregulation, for example—a national consensus has finally been achieved.

(Washington, D.C.: CQ Press, 1981), p. 43. More recently, the combined average has inched
up as the states have raised their tax rates. In 1981, twenty-two states hiked their local gasoline levies. *New York Times*, December 22, 1981. Even with the $0.05 federal increment that
went into effect in April 1983, however, nowhere do American motorists pay a combined tax
of at least $0.25 cents per gallon.

2. The increase, part of the Surface Transportation Assistance Act, was passed by
Congress at the end of 1982, but signed into law in January 1983, with the tax hike not
scheduled to take effect until April 1983. References to the congressional action of 1982
and the act of 1983 refer to the same piece of legislation.

3. The decisive House vote on the tax was not the one for final passage, but the decision on a razor-thin margin of 197–194 to bring the measure to the floor under a
"closed" rule. *Congressional Quarterly Weekly Report*, vol. 40 (December 11, 1982), p.
2993.

For others, like utility rate revision, a coherent body of economic theory exists. Taxation of motor fuel, however, remains poorly understood.

The Gasoline Problem

America's use of fuel in surface transportation is a special case. Because of its uniqueness, imposing a tax on gasoline, to encourage conservation, makes more sense than applying a broad excise tax to petroleum.

TRANSPORTATION AND ENERGY: THE INTERNATIONAL COMPARISON. No other component of the American economy accounts for a larger part of the difference in energy use between the United States and other industrial nations than the transportation sector does.[4] A careful study by Resources for the Future in 1977 calculated that industrial energy utilization represented only 23 percent of the gap between the ratio of energy use to gross domestic product in the United States and that in other leading industrial nations.[5] Transformation losses added 15 percent, while households and commercial uses contributed 17 percent. The rest was entirely a result of transportation. If one peered into each of these sectors, moreover, the difference resulting from transportation loomed even larger. In the industrial contribution of 23 percent, energy and extractive industries, which constitute a large element in the American industrial mix, account for 16 percent. In other words, if these activities are excluded from the industrial base, the rest of American industry was responsible for only 7 percent of the variation in the ratio of energy use to gross domestic product.[6] In the household sector, the variance in space conditioning requirements matters most. About half of the space conditioning differential results from the prevalence of large, detached homes in the United States.[7] (On the whole, housing units in Western Europe and Japan are not better insulated than those in the United States.) To some degree, however, these housing attributes predominate in the United States because of the transportation system that services them: roads and automobiles. A different system, or one in which the costs of automobile travel were higher and the relative conve-

4. National Research Council of the National Academy of Sciences, *Energy in Transition, 1985–2010: Final Report of the Committee on Nuclear and Alternative Energy Systems* (W.H. Freeman, 1980), p. 109.

5. Joel Darmstadter, Joy Dunkerley, and Jack Alterman, *How Industrial Societies Use Energy: A Comparative Analysis* (Johns Hopkins University Press for Resources for the Future, 1977), pp. 70–71. The countries compared are the United States, Canada, the United Kingdom, France, West Germany, Italy, the Netherlands, Sweden, and Japan.

6. Ibid.

7. Ibid., pp. 47, 52, 66–67, 194.

nience lower, would probably alter residential patterns, moderating heat and electricity transmission losses through higher densities.[8] Thus, if its indirect influence on housing characteristics is factored in, transportation's effect is singularly important: it explains most of the divergence between American levels of energy consumption and those of other countries with which the United States is frequently compared.

EXPLAINING TRANSPORTATION'S IMPACT. Why is transportation extraordinarily energy intensive in the United States?[9] The size of the country and the need to ship bulk commodities, such as ores, grains, and coal, over long distances are not the primary reasons. If anything, the freight modal mix of the United States is more energy efficient than that of Western Europe because of the United States' large component of rail, pipeline, and waterborne traffic.[10] Size and distance do influence passenger miles journeyed, but less so than popularly supposed. More than 90 percent of all passenger miles are traveled by car, but most of the trips and total miles driven are attributable to urban, rather than intercity, driving.[11]

The fact that American cities are less densely settled than those of Japan or Europe is more significant. Greater urban densities support public transit patronage, which under compact land use patterns can be considerably more energy efficient than automotive transport. Density, however, is not a variable strictly exogenous to energy consumption in transportation. Mobility in urban areas with fewer inhabitants per square mile requires travel by automobile. But such areas also grow where highways are built, autos are widely owned and cheap to operate, and fewer public transit lines are provided or maintained to serve more concentrated development. Furthermore, much greater efficiency can be

8. I am not suggesting that higher motor fuels costs would bring enormous numbers of inhabitants back from the suburbs to central cities. Population densities within cities and within suburbs, however, would almost certainly increase. See Kenneth A. Small, "Energy Scarcity and Urban Development Patterns," Working Paper (Princeton University, Department of Economics, February 1980), especially p. 39.

9. Energy used in transportation, almost entirely from oil, has accounted for approximately one-quarter of all energy consumption in the United States in recent years. Private passenger vehicles contribute roughly half of the transportation sector's demand. Sam H. Schurr and others, *Energy in America's Future: The Choices before Us* (Johns Hopkins University Press for Resources for the Future, 1979), pp. 143–44.

10. Darmstadter and others, *How Industrial Societies Use Energy*, pp. 100, 191.

11. Fifty-eight percent of all auto travel takes place on urban streets; more than half of all trips taken are five miles or less; the average household makes 3.8 auto trips per day; and only a third of auto use includes getting to and from work. Robert F. Hemphill, Jr., "Energy Conservation in the Transportation Sector," in John C. Sawhill, ed., *Energy Conservation and Public Policy* (Prentice-Hall, 1979), p. 87.

achieved even with a relatively dispersed population. For example, Swedish gasoline consumption per passenger mile has been only 60 percent of what it is in the United States, despite comparable density and living standards.[12]

For several reasons Americans pour into transportation more than half of all the oil they consume, but the Europeans and Japanese allot less than 30 percent.[13] Americans own more cars per capita, and, despite the growth of automobile imports, from 15.2 percent of the market in 1970 to 27.8 percent in 1982, the preponderance of cars purchased are domestically produced. The fuel-efficiency level of new American-made cars remains on average almost 25 percent lower than the level of the foreign car fleet—and was, lamentably, farther away from matching the import average in 1983 than it was in 1979.[14] Finally, regardless of where they live, American motorists drive two to three times as many miles annually as the Japanese and Europeans.[15] Whatever else has fed these phenomena, a series of market malfunctions, some abetted by government policies, bears a share of the blame.

DISTORTIONS. When the energy crisis exploded in 1973, the nation suddenly became conscious of a costly blunder: the automobiles rolling off American assembly lines were averaging fewer miles per gallon (13.1 mpg) than the vehicles built in 1960 (14.3 mpg).[16] Despite the impending domestic oil and gas shrinkages, not to mention potential inroads by foreign competitors, U.S. auto manufacturers kept plying the domestic market with products whose size, weight, horsepower, and gadgetry bore little resemblance to those of the rapidly expanding automotive industries abroad.[17]

12. Lee Schipper, "Energy Use and Conservation in Industrialized Countries," in Sawhill, ed., *Energy Conservation and Public Policy*, p. 59. See also Lee Schipper, "Raising the Productivity of Energy Utilization," *Annual Review of Energy*, vol. 1 (Palo Alto, Calif.: Annual Reviews, Inc., 1976), p. 460.

13. Darmstadter and others, *How Industrial Societies Use Energy*, p. 171.

14. Calculated from data in Motor Vehicle Manufacturers Association, *MVMA Data Digest Relating to Motor Vehicles and Public Policy Issues: A Compilation Condensed from Government and Published Private Sector Sources* (Washington, D.C.: Motor Vehicle Manufacturers Association of the United States, 1983), table 3-8. If overall automobile fleets, that is, new and old on-road models, are used for comparison, American passenger cars still averaged almost 50 percent more fuel per passenger mile than European and Japanese cars. National Research Council, *Energy in Transition*, p. 109.

15. Darmstadter and others, *How Industrial Societies Use Energy*, p. 74.

16. Pelham, *Energy Policy*, p. 9.

17. By 1975, three-quarters of all General Motors cars, for example, had air conditioning. Automatic transmissions (estimated to decrease gasoline mileage by at least 10

Yet Detroit was supplying what American consumers wanted. Except for a brief surge in sales of domestic subcompacts in 1974–75, buyers continued to drift back to larger vehicles until 1979, when the same pattern began all over again.[18] The taste for large cars is not an American peculiarity, nor, as is sometimes alleged, a national obsession with convenience or prestige. Opinion surveys regularly suggest that consumers everywhere prefer big cars chiefly for reasons of safety.[19] But, if that is true, why is the revealed preference seemingly stronger among American motorists than among consumers in other countries? The prominence of huge, powerful vehicles on U.S. highways imposes an externality on anyone driving a smaller car. Bluntly stated, nobody wants to be at the wheel of a 2,200-pound Chevette that collides with a 5,100-pound Buick. But more important, why sacrifice safety, and comfort and status to boot, if the cost of running the Buick continues to be relatively affordable? In large measure, American consumers behave as they do because motor fuel in the United States remains comparatively inexpensive.

Gasoline is not the only form of energy whose cost has been traditionally lower in the United States than in Europe or Japan.[20] But, with the possible exception of natural gas, no other fuel has been as economical in comparative terms as gasoline. This was true even before the advent of domestic petroleum price regulations, and before the oil embargo set off a new round of sharp gasoline tax increases throughout Western Europe. In 1970, oil and electric power in the leading European countries and Japan were, respectively, about 40 and 55 percent more expensive than in the United States on average. Gasoline, on the other hand, was 190 percent more expensive.[21] After the embargo, the special case of gasoline became even more unusual. By 1974, for example, Swedish electricity rates per kilowatt-hour were similar to the American average. Prices for heating oil were only 16 percent cheaper for small

percent) had become standard equipment. Denis Hayes, *Energy: The Case for Conservation* (Washington, D.C.: Worldwatch Institute, 1976), pp. 7, 26.

18. Pelham, *Energy Policy*, p. 59; and *New York Times*, June 7, 1982.

19. Daniel Yergin, "Politics and Gasoline Consumption," in Daniel Yergin, ed., *The Dependence Dilemma: Gasoline Consumption and America's Security* (Harvard University, Center for International Affairs, 1980), pp. 81–82.

20. Energy prices in the United States have remained lower since 1953 than those in the eight other nations in the study by Resources for the Future. Joy Dunkerley, *Trends in Energy Use in Industrial Societies: An Overview* (Washington, D.C.: Resources for the Future, 1980), pp. 55–57.

21. Darmstadter and others, *How Industrial Societies Use Energy*, pp. 176–77.

customers in the United States.[22] But gasoline in Sweden still stood 157 percent above the U.S. price. Through most of the 1970s, not only did the cost of gasoline in America fall increasingly out of line with levels abroad; it dropped relative to other fuels domestically.[23] While the real price of heating oil rose, the real price of gasoline was lower in 1978 than it was in 1972.[24] More than anything else, the relative cost of gasoline is the root cause of the type of automobile preferred and produced in the United States. The low price also determines how much these cars are used. Around 1950, the average American spent about twenty-five minutes per day in an automobile. In the mid-1960s, the average reached forty minutes per day. In the 1970s, a whole hour became the norm.[25]

That most of the international contrast in gasoline prices reflects differing rates of sales taxation is well known. Less often grasped is the fact that base prices and consumption levels in the United States are not just natural occurrences. Pricing regulations in the 1970s seemed especially effective in controlling the relative price of gasoline, which helps explain the digressing domestic price paths of gasoline and distillate fuel oil just noted. Swollen demand, thanks to price controls in the 1970s, was scarcely balanced by the meager federal and state excises, whose effective rates were being eroded by inflation and by income tax deductions.[26] At the same time, other costs to consumers who use gasoline—or who acquire and operate automobiles—have been kept low. Consumers deduct the interest on car payments from income taxes. More than 70 percent of the time, these payments go toward the purchase of domestically manufactured vehicles whose fuel-efficiency average compares unfavorably with that of imports, but whose market since 1981 has been partially secured by quotas on Japanese competitors.[27]

22. National Research Council, *Energy in Transition*, p. xxi.

23. Schurr and others, *Energy in America's Future*, p. 95; between 1978 and 1981, the price of gasoline rose 50.6 percent more than overall consumer prices in the United States, causing the volume of gasoline consumed per dollar of GNP to fall by 15 percent. The price of heating oil, however, rose by 76 percent relative to consumer prices during the same period, inducing a 22 percent drop in consumption per dollar of GNP. Joint Committee on Taxation, *Taxes on Energy Consumption*, Committee Print, prepared for the Senate Finance Committee, 97 Cong. 2 sess. (Government Printing Office, 1982), p. 9.

24. Dunkerley, *Trends in Energy Use in Industrial Societies*, pp. 58–59.

25. Cited in Yergin, ed., *Dependence Dilemma*, pp. 64–65.

26. Thus, in the period 1974–78, the real price of gasoline declined by 11 percent, so that the real price at the pump in January 1979 was the same as in 1960—below what it had been in the 1950s. Daniel Yergin, "America in the Strait of Stringency," in Daniel Yergin and Martin Hillenbrand, eds., *Global Insecurity: A Strategy for Energy and Economic Renewal* (Houghton Mifflin, 1982), p. 126.

27. The "voluntary" export restraints on Japanese autos were imposed in 1981 and finally

The motorists then drive on interstate highways financed by a special trust fund and exempted from local property taxes.[28] General revenues, not just user fees, usually help pay for maintenance, law enforcement, and other expenses related to these facilities. Without tolls steep enough to ration access, side effects such as congestion, smog, and noise compound, inflicting penalties on more people than merely the ones immediately responsible. One study of Los Angeles estimated that motorists who drive during rush hours and periods of bad air pollution pass on $1 billion annually in external costs of this sort.[29] Finally, the incentives to overutilize automobiles at the expense of other transportation modes are fortified by a raft of government programs that shape American urban land use. Federal Housing Administration and Veterans' Administration mortgage guarantees, covering one-fourth of all new single-family homes in the postwar period; tax deductions for mortgage interest; and depreciation allowances that favor investment in new dwellings rather than renovation of older ones are examples. Dependence on automobiles is also encouraged by tax exemptions for development bonds to finance suburban industrial parks, federal grants-in-aid for new community infrastructures, roads in outlying areas, and, of course, traditional local zoning and subdivision ordinances that discourage cluster developments better linked to transit lines.[30]

Fuel Economy Regulations

A gasoline tax is not the only means of compensating for the residual effects of market distortions, but one thing seems increasingly clear: direct regulation is not an equally effective remedy, at least judging from the results of the automobile fuel-economy standards enacted under the Energy Policy and Conservation Act of 1975 in lieu of a tax measure.

---

relaxed in 1985.

28. Inasmuch as excises on motor fuel are earmarked for highway improvements above a level that taxpayers would choose to support from general revenue, the use to which these fees are put may make automotive transportation more attractive relative to other modes and therefore may increase motor fuel consumption. Committee on Energy Taxation, Assembly of Behavioral and Social Sciences, *Energy Taxation: An Analysis of Selected Taxes* (Washington, D.C.: National Academy of Science, 1980), p. 62. If urban mass transit systems had been financed by a similar mass transit trust fund, they would have competed with highways for resources on a more equal basis.

29. Ward Elliott, "Hidden Costs, Hidden Subsidies: The Case for Road Use Charges in Los Angeles," Working Paper (Claremont Men's College, Institute of State and Local Government, February 1975).

30. See Roger J. Vaughan, Anthony H. Pascal, and Mary E. Vaiana, *The Urban Impact of Federal Policies*, vol. 1 (Santa Monica, Calif.: Rand Corp., 1981), pp. 13–16.

The fuel efficiency of each new fleet of American automobiles seems to vary with the world price of oil, not just the strictures of federal mileage policy. In the 1980s, as in the 1970s, movement toward fuel-economic vehicles accelerated in the immediate aftermath of a price shock. But as prices slipped down during ensuing gluts, consumers were back in dealers' showrooms snapping up larger, less economical models. Thus, in March of 1982, compacts and subcompacts constituted 53 percent of domestic new-car sales. A year later, these economy cars were down to 38 percent.[31] The recent revival of demand for traditional large and intermediate models led Ford and General Motors to notify the federal government that they did not expect to meet the fleet-average standard of 26 mpg in the 1983 model year. They would only attain averages of about 24 mpg.[32]

Granted, certified levels of 24 mpg on new-car fleets are a far cry from the 14 mpg recorded in 1974. Yet a full accounting of the regulatory program's net benefits must extend beyond this type of felicitous but limited comparison. In fact, federal regulations have manipulated the market haphazardly, failing to address various flaws and even adding some new ones.

For example, the delay in setting stringent standards for light trucks and vans, as distinct from average automobiles, created difficulties when sales of these vehicles leapt to over 25 percent of the market in the late 1970s.[33] Because the vans and pickups were lasting longer, were averaging only about ten miles to the gallon, and were being used 80 percent of the time for personal and recreational transportation (not business), they lowered the true overall gas-economy average of the passenger vehicle fleet.[34] Moreover, since the government standards left the price of gasoline unchanged,

31. N. R. Kleinfield, "A Comeback for the Big Car: Cheaper Gas, Safety Cited," *New York Times*, May 4, 1983.

32. *Newsweek* (June 27, 1983), p. 70. According to a consumer survey by J. D. Power and Associates, only 15 percent of the car buyers at the beginning of 1983 considered fuel economy the most important factor in the selection of a new car. In 1980 the figure was 30 percent. John Holusha, "Buyers Return to Bigger Cars: Less Stress on Saving Gas," *New York Times*, January 25, 1983.

33. Daniel Yergin, "Conservation: The Key Energy Source," in Robert Stobaugh and Daniel Yergin, eds., *Energy Future: Report of the Energy Project at the Harvard Business School* (Random House, 1979), p. 152.

34. Schurr and others, *Energy in America's Future*, p. 153; and Frank von Hippel, "Forty Miles a Gallon by 1995 at the Very Least: Why the U.S. Needs a New Automotive Fuel Economy Goal," in Yergin, ed., *Dependence Dilemma*, pp. 94–95. Current regulations, however, call for fuel-economy ratings of 21 mpg for light trucks in the 1985 model year. *New York Times*, December 10, 1980.

but added to the expense of buying new cars, turnover in the total fleet slowed somewhat, leaving more old gas-guzzlers on the road longer.[35] The bottom line at the end of the decade was that fuel efficiency for the whole on-road fleet—regulated cars, unregulated trucks, and older vehicles—was a paltry 0.21 mpg better than in 1973.[36] Additionally, fuel-economy regulations entail long lead times before delivering the vast energy savings that are theoretically possible. The regulations attain savings only through replacement of the auto fleet, a slow process in which only 6 percent to 8 percent of all cars are scrapped in any one year. In the meantime, no constructive impact is made on the amount of driving, unlike the effect of a tax, which exploits the substitution possibilities of driving less, or differently, as well as driving a smaller car. In fact, with stable or declining gasoline prices, the mandatory fuel-economy program reduces the marginal cost of driving, enabling people with smaller cars to drive more.[37]

Further, during the time it takes to implement the regulatory scheme, its directives and the tastes of consumers may conflict. Manufacturers then get mixed signals. The auto industry was forced to start retooling after 1975. It proceeded with some reluctance.[38] With consumers still favoring big cars, Detroit's natural inclination was to meet initial targets with minimal design modifications. Consequently, when the market made a sudden and dramatic shift in 1980, at least two of the leading automakers found themselves wedged into obsolete plants and product lines. The seeds were thus sown for additional government involvement. First, Chrysler Corporation ran to Congress for $1.5 billion in loan guarantees. Then the whole industry, including the United Automobile Workers, clamored for and got trade restrictions on Japanese imports.

Imaginably, the plight of the American automobile industry, and the pressure for government programs to bail it out, could have abated if Congress in 1975 had chosen to tax gasoline and deregulate petroleum prices,

35. The Congressional Budget Office estimated that the Energy Policy and Conservation Act's fuel-economy regulations would increase the average price of new cars by $400 to $600. Alan A. Altshuler, *The Urban Transportation System: Politics and Policy Innovation* (MIT Press, 1979), p. 139. The regulations could cause automobile companies to take smaller markups (sometimes losses) on smaller cars and higher markups on larger cars, thereby working to reduce demand for larger models. The recent surge in demand for big cars, however, raises questions about the extent of this effect.

36. David Stockman, "Needed: A Dual Resurrection?" *Journal of Energy and Development*, vol. 5 (Spring 1980), pp. 176–77.

37. John R. Meyer and Jose A. Goméz-Ibañez, *Autos, Transit, and Cities* (Harvard University Press, 1981), p. 146; and Hans H. Landsberg and others, *Energy: The Next Twenty Years* (Ballinger Publishing Company for the Ford Foundation, 1979), p. 133.

38. Von Hippel, "Forty Miles a Gallon," in Yergin, ed., *Dependence Dilemma*, p. 91.

instead of attempting to mandate automotive fuel-efficiency levels. Abolition of subsidized gasoline consumption would have prevented the periodic market rejections of subcompacts that have frustrated company efforts to make intelligent, long-range investment decisions. Finally, while fuel-economy standards (and excise taxes on inefficient new models, such as the gas-guzzler levy adopted in 1978) may have slowed purchases of new cars, a gasoline tax would have helped speed the replacement of less efficient, older vehicles with newer, more efficient ones.[39]

Gasoline Tax versus Oil Tariff

The most frequently discussed alternative to increased gasoline taxation is a tariff on oil imports. Unless the main policy objective is to protect domestic oil producers from foreign competition, it is hard to understand why policymakers continue to express interest in an oil tariff. Its drawbacks are manifold and only reinforce the arguments in favor of taxing gasoline instead.

For one thing, in the context of soft prices for crude oil, a substantial import fee levied by the world's leading oil importer might close down additional productive capacity outside the Persian Gulf, possibly leaving the United States with a larger proportion of imports from insecure sources. To be sure, more stable foreign suppliers—like Mexico, Venezuela, and Canada—could be exempted from the fee. But the United States would then be left with a tariff that exempted most of the oil imported. Per barrel of oil conserved, only the most extreme gasoline tax proposals run a comparable risk of tampering recklessly with the brittle international petroleum market.[40]

Assuming it were not riddled with exemptions, a tariff would back out foreign oil by a combination of reduced domestic demand and stimulated

39. Of course, because of their lead in manufacturing subcompacts, Japanese automakers might have gained an even larger share of the domestic market, thus heightening protectionist demands from the American automobile industry. However, unless these demands were heeded more closely, the added competition, coming at an earlier stage, might have hastened the adjustment of U.S. manufacturers to the production of highly fuel-efficient cars.

40. Arguably, a suitable tax directed at gasoline can provide benefits for energy security with greater precision than a general oil tariff. Heavy gasoline consumption in the United States has made American refineries more dependent on a lighter, lower-sulfur crude oil mix than the average in the world oil market. The preferred crude grades are not only more expensive; they often come from producing areas that are the least stable politically. Alvin L. Alm, William Colglazier, and Barbara Kates-Garnick, "Coping with Interruptions," in David E. Deese and Joseph S. Nye, eds., *Energy and Security* (Ballinger, 1981), p. 332.

domestic production.[41] This raises a second concern: should domestic oil companies receive, as they did throughout the 1960s, the subsidy provided by trade protection? The dilemma does not arise with an increase in the national gasoline tax, which does not shelter the oil industry and contribute to renewed protectionism.

The gas tax would also be environmentally benign. Indeed, by reducing combustion of motor fuel, it would curb a leading source of air pollution.[42] A tariff, on the other hand, would reduce pollution by cutting consumption but could also increase it by stimulating domestic energy development projects and by expanding the use of coal (since relative prices under an oil-import fee would favor coal).

It is often asserted that the main virtue of an import duty over a motor fuel levy is that the duty promotes conservation across all petroleum products and among all users, but the motor fuel levy is too narrowly based. To recommend an excise tax on motor fuel exclusively would seem inconsistent with the need of energy conservation to be comprehensive. Moreover, the asymmetry, or narrow focus, of such a tax might seem less equitable.

These objections oversimplify the issue. It is desirable to differentiate carefully between market-determined and market-correcting distributions of incentives. There is no a priori imperative that the two be identical. The purpose of a consumption tax on energy is to offset identifiable imperfections or biases built into the marketplace, often because of other government policies. Yet the sectors that exhibit these defects, not the whole economy indiscriminately, ought to be the target of the tax. A case can be made that the pattern of fuel consumption in transportation calls for remedial tax policy. But other sectors—for example, industrial use of energy, where the most impressive savings are being realized through existing price pressures[43]—should be excluded. Moreover, an across-the-board surcharge on oil, unlike a tax limited to

41. Arthur W. Wright, "Energy Independence: Insuring Against Disruptions of Supply," in *Options for U.S. Energy Policy* (San Francisco: Institute for Contemporary Studies, 1977), p. 54; and James M. Griffin, *Energy Conservation in the OECD: 1980 to 2000* (Ballinger, 1979), p. 279.

42. Combustion of gasoline is the number one source of carbon monoxide, hydrocarbon, and nitrogen oxides. Harry W. Richardson, *Economic Aspects of the Energy Crisis* (Lexington Books, 1975), p. 151.

43. The bright spot in conservation unquestionably has been American industry. While energy usage in other sectors of the economy was increasing, industrial use of energy declined by 9.2 percent between 1973 and 1981, even as production rose by 20 percent. Joint Committee, *Taxes on Energy Consumption*, p. 9.

gasoline, would probably risk worse inflationary consequences,[44] and could put U.S. industry at a further disadvantage in the face of foreign competition.

It is wrong to assume that since an oil tariff's coverage is broader than that of a gasoline excise, the tariff is fairer.[45] Geographically, the incidence of a tariff would slant sharply onto the Northeast, where oil products heat homes and power electric generators and industrial machinery, as well as motor vehicles. A gasoline tax would be felt more acutely by persons living in rural areas, where distances are great and where alternative means of transportation are limited. Yet, critics of the tax, who stress this inequity, often seem to overlook at least two considerations. The first is elementary: the United States is an urban nation. Although per capita rates of gasoline usage inevitably run higher in rural areas, most gasoline is consumed where most people live—in metropolitan areas. (Close to 60 percent of all automobile travel takes place on city streets, with over half of all the trips covering less than six miles.)[46] The bulk of a gasoline tax would be paid by residents of cities and suburbs. Second, although the burden per capita would fall more heavily on low-density states, particularly in the West, this uneven impact is partially balanced by the fact that many of these states have long enjoyed lower prices for other forms of energy, specifically natural gas and electricity.[47]

44. An across-the-board price increase on petroleum could ripple out more widely through industrial wage settlements than a price increase confined to the single commodity, gasoline. Interview with Charles L. Schultze, former chairman of the Council of Economic Advisers, Washington, D.C., October 23, 1981.

45. Besides the points that follow, at least one other concern about equity must be mentioned: an oil tariff would almost certainly generate political pressure for new rules and programs to correct discriminatory incidence among refiners. Refineries awash with "untaxed" domestic crude would quickly gain a competitive edge over refineries dependent on imports (at least in the short run). The latter firms would then demand compensatory regulations, probably bringing back something analogous to the infamous "entitlements" program allocating crude oil during the 1970s. Clyde H. Farnsworth, "Oil Import Fee," *New York Times*, April 8, 1982.

46. Robert F. Hemphill, Jr., "Energy Conservation in the Transportation Sector," in Sawhill, ed., *Energy Conservation and Public Policy*, p. 87; and William U. Chandler and Holly L. Gwin, "Gasoline Consumption in the Era of Confrontation," in Yergin, ed., *Dependence Dilemma*, p. 111.

47. The statistical relationships are clear. States with high levels of population per square mile have tended to pay higher average prices for natural gas ($r = .43$, $p < .01$) and, even more markedly, higher average electric rates ($r = .66$ and $r = .67$, $p < .001$, for the residential and industrial customer classes, respectively). Computed using population density counts reported in the Bureau of the Census, *County and City Data Book, 1977*

In its incidence across income groups, a gasoline tax compares even more favorably on grounds of equity. Gasoline consumption, like energy use generally, is a direct function of household income. Indeed, the correlation is particularly strong for gasoline, since usage of this fuel depends entirely on automobile ownership and vehicle miles traveled, both of which are very closely related to income.[48] Put another way, while nearly everyone lives in a housing unit, and makes use of a furnace, a hot-water heater, and certain basic electrical appliances, autos are owned and driven extensively only by persons that can afford them. Half of the poor don't drive, and those who do, drive only about half as much as the national average.[49] Because relatively little gasoline is consumed at the lower rungs of the economic ladder and much more at the upper end, low-income households spend a smaller proportion of their income on gasoline than they spend on other essential fuels.[50] Families in the lowest income quintile still spend, as a percentage of income, about twice as much on gasoline as families in the top quintile, but the lower-income families pay four times as much for heating oil.[51]

Contrast the distributional impacts of a $10.00-per-barrel oil-import fee and a $0.20-per-gallon tax on gasoline, both of which were reputed to save comparable amounts of oil and to raise roughly the same amounts of direct revenue.[52] Average consumption of petroleum deriva-

---

(GPO, 1977), table 1, p. 2; gas prices reported in American Gas Association, *Gas Facts 1980* (Arlington, Va.: American Gas Association, 1981), pp. 25, 120–21; and electricity prices per kilowatt-hour reported in U.S. Department of Energy, Energy Information Administration, *State Energy Fuel Prices by Major Economic Sector from 1960 through 1977* (Washington, D.C.: Department of Energy, 1979), pp. 95–96, 99–100. (Prices are for 1975.)

48. Income is much more closely related to the demand for gasoline than to the demand for, say, electricity and natural gas. Douglas R. Bohi, *Analyzing Demand Behavior: A Study of Energy Elasticities* (Johns Hopkins University Press for Resources for the Future, 1981), p. 126.

49. Hans H. Landsberg and Joseph M. Dukert, *High Energy Costs: Uneven, Unfair, Unavoidable?* (Johns Hopkins University Press for Resources for the Future, 1981), p. 29.

50. Fifteen percent of the population buys 45 percent of all gasoline sold. Daniel Yergin, "Flexibility in Auto Use?" in Yergin, ed., *Dependence Dilemma*, p. 66.

51. Congressional Budget Office, "Oil Import Tariffs: Alternative Scenarios and Their Effects," Staff Working Paper (Washington, D.C.: CBO, 1982), p. 16.

52. The eventual conservation and revenue effects of various energy taxes are hard to predict precisely. For gasoline taxation, estimates of the extended price elasticity of gasoline demand have traditionally clustered around −0.7. This figure may be low, since most of the familiar elasticity studies use sample data from a period of relatively flat energy prices—that is, data that typically predate the effects of post-1979 price ranges. Bohi, *Analyzing Demand Behavior*, pp. 116–17. For oil tariffs, special problems arise with as-

tives, such as distillate fuel, kerosene, and liquid petroleum gas, which would go up in price with an import fee on crude oil, varies less with income than does average consumption of gasoline. Thus the net effect of the tariff is to leave poor households somewhat worse off, and richer ones noticeably better off, than under the gasoline tax. The tariff would cost the average household with an income under $5,000 at least $10.00 more per year than the gasoline tax, but it would cost households with incomes over $25,000 an average of at least $16.00 less annually than the gasoline tax.[53] Marginal redistributive effects of this sort ought not become the prime criteria for choosing among energy tax alternatives. Such effects are mentioned only because the common perception seems to be that a gasoline excise is the most inequitable type of energy tax.

---

sumptions about incidence: if overseas producers were to absorb a significant income loss from a tariff, its burden on domestic consumers would be much lighter, resulting in less conservation and less government revenue. Also, as already stressed, much would depend on how many foreign suppliers were exempted. Assuming that overseas suppliers would absorb one-third of an import fee of $10.00 per barrel, the Congressional Budget Office has estimated that this fee (if it had been levied starting in 1982) would gross directly about $19.6 billion during fiscal 1984. Extrapolating on the basis of the effect of a fee of $5.00 per barrel (which is the tariff CBO analyzes in greater detail), the CBO study would suggest that a $10.00 fee ought to knock oil consumption down by approximately 400,000 barrels per day. Congressional Budget Office, "Oil Import Tariffs," pp. ii, 6. The best available forecasts of fuel savings and revenue yields from higher gasoline taxes assume a tax of $0.50 per gallon. John H. Gibbons, director of the Congressional Office of Technology Assessment, and a colleague have estimated an annual reduction of 700,000 to 1 million barrels of oil per day, and $50 billion in revenues annually, from such a tax. John H. Gibbons and William U. Chandler, *Energy: The Conservation Revolution* (New York: Plenum Press, 1981), p. 239. Based on these calculations, a $0.20 gas tax would save between 320,000 and 400,000 barrels of oil daily and earn revenues of about $20 billion a year.

53. These conservative estimates are based on the following data sources: gasoline consumption per income class: U.S. Department of Energy, Energy Information Administration, *Residential Energy Consumption Survey: Consumption Patterns of Household Vehicles, June 1979 to December 1980*, DOE/EIA-0319 (Washington, D.C.: DOE, 1982), p. 27 (income figures are for 1977); *households per income class* (averaged estimates using three sources): Bureau of the Census, *Current Population Reports: Money Income of Households in the United States* (GPO, 1979), p. 3; U.S. Department of Energy, Energy Information Administration, *Residential Energy Consumption Survey: 1979–1980 Consumption and Expenditures*, part 1, National Data, DOE/EIA-0262/1 (Washington, D.C.: DOE, 1981), p. 13 (income figures are for 1978); and U.S. Department of Energy, "Residential Energy Consumption Survey: Housing Characteristics 1980," unpublished data. For heating oil, kerosene, and liquid petroleum gas consumption per income class: U.S. Department of Energy, *Residential Energy Consumption Survey: 1979–1980 Consumption and Expenditures*, p. 13. For the estimated cost impact of a $10-per-barrel oil-import fee: Congressional Budget Office, "Oil Import Tariffs," p. 11.

Interest Groups

If gasoline taxation is sensible, why does Congress agonize over it?

Few, if any, organized interests have reason to lobby for this type of energy tax, but many have reason to attack it. Notice, once again, the key distinction between a gasoline levy and an oil tariff: the tariff shelters the nonmultinational portion of the petroleum industry. Under certain conditions, domestic oil producers not only welcome the protection but actively campaign for it, as they did in the successful drive for import restrictions throughout the 1950s. Even when the oil industry deems trade barriers inexpedient, tariffs may gain favor with suppliers of competing fuels. At congressional hearings on energy tax proposals in 1982, for example, some segments of the natural gas industry expressed guarded support for the reimposition of oil-import fees.[54] The National Coal Association revealed its preference by objecting only to the proposals that would have an impact on coal operators, a "Btu tax" or a comprehensive ad valorem tax.[55] (Higher fees for petroleum can enlarge the market for natural gas and coal.)

A gasoline tax lacks allies among energy producers of any kind. Perforce, the cross elasticity of demand between gasoline and other fuels is zero: automobile engines cannot be hooked to natural gas pipelines, nor can they run on chunks of coal. Hence, the tax offers coal and natural gas companies no real opportunity to improve their market shares. As far as the petroleum business is concerned, slack demand for its principal refined product is a bad thing. Others think so too. Alongside the sullen gasoline sellers stand throngs of sympathizers. Road contractors and engineers; taxicab companies and motorboat manufacturers; truckers and farmers; and automakers and the United Auto Workers oppose the gas tax. State highway departments and state legislatures, which fear the loss of revenue from tolls and from state gas taxes if gasoline demand

54. American Gas Association, "Summary of Principal Points on Energy Taxes," Hearings before the Subcommittee on Energy and Agricultural Taxation of the Senate Finance Committee, 97 Cong. 1 sess., June 9, 1982, p. 1.

55. R. E. Samples, chairman of the Board of Directors, National Coal Association, "Statement on Energy Tax Options," Hearings before the Subcommittee on Energy and Agricultural Taxation of the Senate Finance Committee, 97 Cong. 1 sess., June 9, 1982. On coal's past support for oil tariffs: Craufurd D. Goodwin, "Truman Administration Policies toward Particular Energy Sources," in Craufurd D. Goodwin, ed., *Energy Policy in Perspective: Today's Problems, Yesterday's Solutions* (Brookings, 1981), p. 87.

drops, fight the tax. Indeed, in the United States, except for foreign car dealerships, public transit authorities, and commuter railroads, it is not easy to identify any constituency willing to endorse higher motor fuel taxes. The broader coalition behind the nickel tax increase of 1982 was a special case, partially facilitated by the fact that the increment was small and earmarked primarily for nondeferrable highway repairs.

When European political systems debate these taxes, the lineup looks different. Excluding nuclear power, most European economies lack large, domestic energy-producing sectors. Washington can be besieged by armies of indigenous oil men roaming the Capitol's corridors whenever the government contemplates any tax on their merchandise. Paris or Stockholm can't. Nor are there likely to be members of the Swedish or French parliaments whose election campaigns are bankrolled by energy interests in the style to which many U.S. senators and representatives are accustomed. (Of the millions donated by business political action committees in the congressional races of 1982, approximately $1 of every $4 was given by oil and gas industry groups.)[56] Where important energy industries do exist, petroleum production is either a negligible part of the mix or a fairly recent development. The Germans and Dutch, for instance, possess significant domestic fossil fuel reserves. But the dominant industries are coal and natural gas, neither of which stands to lose from higher petroleum-based excise taxes. Even Britain's oil industry, which is now sizable, has been a fledgling political force compared with the coal miners. In part, taxes levied on gasoline and other oil products in the United Kingdom stem historically from protectionism, originating in the 1950s and 1960s, when imports of cheap Arabian crude began to undercut the British coal market.

Further, while gasoline taxation in Europe faces fewer foes, it also mobilizes more powerful friends. The immediate beneficiaries of motor fuel taxation are principally the public transit systems, passenger railroads, and airlines (if the tax does not fall heavily on jet fuel). Not only do these enterprises prosper from the substitution effect of high automotive travel costs, they are often nationally run industries, financed significantly by the tax and well situated institutionally to grab a large hunk of the revenue. Is there an American analogue? State and local transportation agencies in the United States requested, and received, large doses of federal funds during the 1970s, as did the federally operated railway, Amtrak. But unlike the entrenched transport bureau-

56. *New York Times*, July 18, 1982.

cracies of most European central governments, the American intergovernmental lobby has not steadily sought subsidization through a higher national gasoline excise. If anything, the states dread federal usurpation of sales taxation—an issue that, by definition, does not arise in the unitary regimes abroad.

Still, the pattern of pressure groups cannot account for all cross-national differences in fuel tax policies. The kinds of factions that assail such tax measures in the United States do have at least some parallels in other industrial nations.

INTEREST GROUPS ABROAD. There is no reason to believe, for example, that French agricultural confederations, a potent force in French politics, relish a gasoline levy of $1.70 per gallon any more than American farm associations would.

Italy and France are not countries that produce crude oil domestically. But they do have large-scale refining operations. As of 1978, for instance, domestic refining capacity in both these countries not only exceeded that of the other West European nations, but also represented a sizable combined volume even in comparison with North America (382,875 versus 938,605 million metric tons annually).[57] All the same, gasoline is taxed more heavily in Italy and France than practically anywhere else in the free world. Is one to infer that the substantial Italian and French refining interests are politically inert? Or haven't these European refiners figured out what refiners in Houston or Port Arthur know—that under normal market conditions, profits tend to go down when gasoline taxes go up?

Not unlike the American states, the Canadian provinces and, to a lesser degree, the West German *Länder* sacrifice potential tax receipts whenever the federal government decides to enlarge its take. Yet federalism has not precluded higher national tax shares in those countries. In Germany, motor fuel taxation is a constitutional prerogative of the central authorities. But part of the *mineralölsteuer* that motorists pay at the pump reflects the general value-added tax, the apportionment of which has been a continual source of strife among the states and between the states and the government in Bonn. Federal preemption of provincial tax bases has proven controversial in Canada. Even so, at least prior to April 1983, Ottawa managed to tax gasoline at a level more than double the U.S. federal rate.

57. Giovanni Altieri, *Risparmio e fabbisogno energetico* (Roma: Editrice Sindacale Italiana, 1980), p. 90.

Private automotive industries are also politically salient in Japan, Italy, and West Germany. Before their export industries became preeminent, the car manufacturers in these countries had every incentive to reckon, much like their American brethren, that lower national fuel costs would encourage domestic sales. Yet taxes on motor fuels in Italy, West Germany, and Japan kept going up, even as the companies strove to expand their native markets.

Maybe American interest groups are more adept at foiling gasoline tax increases. Perhaps General Motors is mightier than FIAT in Italy or Nissan in Japan; or perhaps the National Council of Farmer Cooperatives is more resourceful than the French National Federation of Unions of Agricultural Producers; or maybe Texas looms larger in American politics than Alberta in the energy politics of Canada. Few knowledgeable students of comparative government, however, would cheerfully concede these propositions.

THE DOMESTIC OIL LOBBY. The importance imputed to veto groups in the politics of motor fuel taxation should not be exaggerated. When interviewed, members of Congress and their staffs seldom cite the oil industry, for instance, as the leading factor in the failure of gasoline tax bills, despite the scores of political action committees affiliated with oil and gas interests that have mushroomed and contributed massively to the campaigns of House and Senate candidates in recent years. To understand why, it is helpful to remember, first of all, that a higher gasoline levy was not blocked in 1982, when the oil lobby had recovered some of its old clout in Congress, but the tax was prevented in 1975 and 1977. That happened just when oil companies were nothing if not pariahs on Capitol Hill, and before they had learned how to turn the 1974 campaign finance reforms to good advantage.[58] As much as the proposals to tax gasoline may have vexed the industry, petroleum producers saved most of their ammunition for the bloodier battles that raged contemporaneously—the showdowns over oil-price deregulation in 1975, natural gas in 1977, and excess-profits taxation in 1980. Most important, no oil firm's lobbying effort could account for the kinds of congressional majorities that have balked at gasoline taxes, majorities often so lopsided and broad based as to conjoin the industry's perennial apologists with its worst assailants. When the Senate joined the House in routing President

58. Between 1975 and 1980 the number of oil company political action committees and the dollar amounts they donated to congressional races increased about tenfold. See Pelham, *Energy Policy*, pp. 124–25.

Carter's plan for a surcharge of $0.10 per gallon in the summer of 1980, the sixty-eight senators on the winning side included not only James A. McClure, Republican of Idaho, and Russell B. Long, Democrat of Louisiana, but also Edward M. Kennedy, Democrat of Massachusetts, and Henry M. Jackson, Democrat of Washington.

AUTOMOBILE MANUFACTURERS. The motor vehicle manufacturers have disagreed with one another on the matter of gasoline tax increases. Some auto industry spokesmen testified against the major tax measure advanced by the House Ways and Means Committee in 1975. At the same time, the Motor Vehicle Manufacturers Association issued a policy statement acquiescing, though in highly qualified language, to "an additional tax on gasoline and special motor fuels for the limited time required to effect greater energy conservation."[59] No auto industry representative was on record as opposing higher gasoline charges at legislative hearings on energy taxes held in 1977, 1980, or 1982.

One reason why the industry's stance is not always clear is that marketing strategies among the Big Three have differed. When Chrysler Corporation finally committed itself to producing small cars, it proceeded more aggressively than Ford or General Motors. By 1982, Chrysler accounted for 25 percent of the compact cars sold, even though the company's share of the total U.S. automobile sales was only 10 percent. To buttress demand for its products and deepen its overall market penetration, Chrysler has repeatedly endorsed higher gasoline prices through taxes.[60]

Like the oil companies, the auto manufacturers have had to fight on other fronts deemed more vital. In 1975 and 1977, for example, their chief preoccupation was to ward off tax legislation aimed at placing stiff penalties on new cars with below-average fuel-economy ratings. Why the automakers were much more worried about these gas-guzzler tax schemes than about proposed taxes on fuel is not hard to guess: any significant tax on the front-end purchase price of energy-consuming equipment is more likely to hurt sales directly than is a fee that merely raises the operating cost of the equipment.

HIGHWAY CLIENTS. Certain special interests battle gasoline tax proposals with great regularity. One of these groups is the Highway Users

59. Motor Vehicle Manufacturers Association, *National Energy Policy and Passenger Car Fuel Economy* (Washington, D.C.: Motor Vehicle Manufacturers Association of the United States, Inc., 1975), p. 1.

60. John Holusha, "Buyers Return to Bigger Cars," *New York Times*, January 25, 1983.

Federation, an organization with thousands of members, a $3 million annual budget, and well-staffed headquarters in downtown Washington.[61] The federation's corporate membership ranges from car rental companies, trucking firms, and rubber corporations to advertising agencies and ice cream manufacturers. Despite the group's diversity, it manages to deliver a consistent message whenever energy tax issues are raised in Congress: federal gasoline taxes are harmful unless they add up to just a few pennies per gallon, dedicated entirely to the highway trust fund.

Other interests that voice particularly loud objections when there is talk of taxing automotive fuels are, naturally, the organizations representing gasoline vendors. In 1981, when the Department of Transportation first recommended a token boost in the federal tax to pay largely for essential repairs on the interstate system, some of these fuel retailers associations still demurred.

The really big antitax lobby, however, is one about which political pundits seldom write: the service industries associated with travel and tourism. Almost every congressional district bulges with motels, fast-food chains, shopping centers, and countless other roadside businesses for whom patronage by motorists—and, at bottom, existence of cheap gasoline—is the lifeblood. Congressmen listen when the Travel and Tourism Government Affairs Policy Council describes itself as speaking for a $190 billion retail industry, of which small businesses constitute 99 percent. The industry ranks as one of the top employers in at least thirty-five states.[62] Constituencies so ubiquitous undoubtedly help broaden the congressional opposition to gasoline taxation.

But many members of Congress stand ready to bury gas tax legislation whether they hear from these interest groups or not. Consider what happened in the spring of 1980. President Carter had attempted to impose a $4.60-per-barrel oil-import fee. Its entire cost was to be loaded onto a single petroleum product, gasoline, hence representing the functional equivalent of a $0.10 per gallon increase in the federal gasoline tax. Overwhelmingly, the House of Representatives defeated the higher fee on gasoline. Most members were disposed to vote down the fee regardless of

61. Highway Users Federation, *Report to Members, 1981–1982* (Washington, D.C.: Highway Users Federation, 1982), p. 21.

62. William D. Toohey, vice-chairman, Travel and Tourism Government Affairs Policy Council, "Statement Opposing Various Energy Tax Revenue Options," presented before the Subcommittee on Energy and Agricultural Taxation of the Senate Finance Committee, 97 Cong. 1 sess., June 9, 1982, p. 1.

whether they received campaign gifts from the American Hotel and Motel Association, the National Association of Truck Stop Operators, the National Restaurant Association, and a host of other intensely interested parties. In fact, using figures for a sample of twenty key political action committees in the travel-tourism and gasoline-retail businesses, it was possible to estimate statistically how much the votes of representatives on this issue might have been related to the dollars they received from these highly salient lobbies.[63] Not surprisingly, the average of contributions to opponents of the proposed fee did exceed the average among the president's supporters, but the difference ($498 to $420 per member) was too narrow to be significant.[64]

Public Opinion

Between 1973 and 1980, the crisis years for energy policymakers, the House of Representatives voted several times on federal gasoline tax legislation (table 5-1). The steady, widespread opposition strongly suggests that the American electorate has communicated its distaste for gasoline tax measures in no uncertain terms.

Public opinion on the issue has been extremely well defined over the years—much more so than in reference to other energy-pricing questions, such as deregulation of oil and natural gas. A review of survey results of the 1970s would find that respondents in almost every published poll objected to higher taxes on gasoline by margins of 2 to 1 or better, regardless of how slight the mentioned increase and irrespective of whether the questionnaires were administered during the peaks or troughs of energy shortages.[65] The only digressions from the pattern occurred when questions were worded so as to promise full rebates of the tax revenues. Then, as one Harris survey reported, tolerance toward a $0.10 tax rose to 35 percent, and disapproval dropped to 56 percent.[66]

63. House member 1979–80 campaign contribution data for the sample of twenty political action committees were compiled from Federal Election Commission statistics by the campaign finance analysts of Common Cause, Washington, D.C., June 22, 1982.

64. The difference between the means was only significant statistically at the .10 level (n = 369). The roll call analyzed was the House vote on whether to override President Carter's veto of a congressional resolution disapproving the imposition of a $0.10-per-gallon surcharge on gasoline by way of an oil-import fee, June 5, 1980. *Congressional Quarterly Almanac*, vol. 36 (1980), pp. 82-H, 83-H.

65. For a thorough summary of the polling data, see the compendium prepared for the U.S. Department of Energy by Barbara C. Farhar and others, *Public Opinion about Energy: A Literature Review* (Golden, Colo.: Solar Energy Research Institute, 1979), p. 117.

66. *Harris Survey*, December 1974.

Table 5-1. *House Votes on Gasoline Tax Legislation, 1973–80*

Legislation	For	Against
Amendment to H.R. 6860, to increase the federal tax by $0.20 per gallon on a standby basis (June 11, 1975)	72	345
Amendment to H.R. 6860, to increase the federal tax by $0.03 per gallon (June 11, 1975)	187	209
Amendment to H.R. 8444, to increase the federal tax by $0.05 per gallon (August 4, 1977)	82	339
Amendment to H.R. 8444, to increase the federal tax by $0.04 per gallon (August 4, 1977)	52	370
H.R. 7428, to add a $0.10-per-gallon fee through an oil tariff tilted onto gasoline (June 5, 1980)	34	335

Sources: *Congressional Quarterly Weekly Report*, vol. 33 (June 11, 1975), pp. 1262–63; vol. 35 (August 6, 1977), pp. 1690–91; and vol. 38 (June 7, 1980), pp. 1604–05.

Are Americans Unique?

The fact that gas taxes are so repugnant to the American public might be all that is needed to know to explain their dismal legislative history, were it not for an obvious question. When it comes to taxing automotive fuel, are the views of U.S. voters really unlike those of citizens in other western democracies whose legislatures are equally representative but still reach very different decisions? Judging from the available data on the likes and dislikes of taxpayers elsewhere, American attitudes are not atypical. When the French were polled on the subject by the Gallup organization in 1974, a resounding 87 percent disapproved of the government increasing the cost of gasoline to conserve fuel.[67] The same year, a Gallup poll in Great Britain found 68 percent opposed to any increase in the national value-added tax on petrol.[68] Along somewhat similar lines, a sample of Canadian drivers in 1979 discovered that 72 percent preferred other methods of conserving gasoline, including strict rationing, over "increasing the price until people used less."[69] But these

67. George H. Gallup, *The Gallup International Public Opinion Polls: France 1939, 1944–1975*, vol. 2 (Random House, 1976), pp. 1072–73.

68. George H. Gallup, *The Gallup International Public Opinion Polls: Great Britain 1937–1975*, vol. 2 (Random House, 1976), p. 1318.

69. See Survey Research Consultants International, Inc., *Index to International Public*

sorts of sentiments did not stop the French and British governments from hiking gasoline prices through taxes after 1973 and did not prevent the Canadian federal rate from climbing appreciably in recent years.

One could posit that public hostility toward gasoline taxes impresses American congressmen more than it influences legislators in other countries. Imaginably, the opinion polls are discounted in France and Britain because elected officials there are convinced that high gasoline excises entail fewer sacrifices, but American lawmakers view economical gasoline as a vital necessity that, like food, should be almost tax exempt.

Detracting somewhat from this thesis is an enigma: on one hand, a great deal of congressional rhetoric characterizes gasoline as an essential commodity; any major taxation of it could amount to a form of cruel and unusual punishment. On the other, the debate over the years has ceased to have, as its central point of contention, the question of whether demand for gasoline is highly elastic.

Even if price controls in the mid-1970s tended to blur signs that U.S. motorists would react to higher fuel costs by altering their driving habits, numerous surveys had identified a potentially powerful response. Time and again, huge majorities indicated that higher prices were not only effective but more effective than anything else in reducing gasoline consumption.[70] In addition, reduced driving was cited as one of the most likely reactions to rising energy prices, far more common than, say, insulating one's home, or even turning off lights.[71] Most interestingly, a majority of drivers admitted it would be possible to cut back on their use of cars with little trouble. In fact, when Gallup queried a sample of mo-

---

Opinion, 1979–80 (Westport, Conn.: Greenwood Press, 1981), p. 48.

70. On the perceived effectiveness of gasoline taxes, see the data cited in Joe W. Russell, Jr., *Economic Disincentives for Energy Conservation* (Ballinger, 1979), p. 75.

71. The public consistently mentions residential conservation measures as the preferred method of saving energy, well ahead of reduced driving. Farhar and others, *Public Opinion about Energy*, p. 117. Yet when asked which actions are actually taken to save energy, reduced driving is cited more frequently than most residential conservation steps. Thus in a CBS News/*New York Times* poll in July 1977, respondents were presented with lists of possible options to conserve energy assuming that "the cost of energy continues to go up." Sixty-four percent said they would most likely "cut down on the amount of driving," and 50 percent said they were likely to insulate their homes "more than . . . now." Similarly, a Harris survey in October 1975 found that 51 percent reported they had "cut back driving" in the face of higher energy prices, but 23 percent said they had "improved home insulation" and 43 percent mentioned using "electrical appliances less often." *Harris Survey*, November 1975. Gallup found that "reduced driving" was cited more frequently than "turned off lights" in at least two surveys: *Gallup Opinion Index*, Report 149 (December 1977), p. 22; and Report 164 (March 1979), p. 17.

torists in August 1979 about the feasibility of giving up driving one day each week, these were the marginals: 2 percent didn't know; 14 percent claimed it would be fairly difficult; 22 percent, very difficult; and 62 percent, not very difficult.[72] Sometimes the issue was framed in more drastic terms. "Suppose you had to reduce the number of miles you drove by one-fourth. How difficult would it be for you to meet this requirement?" A plurality, 40 percent, still answered "not at all difficult."[73] In sum, what the available survey data seem to show is that less use of fuel is widely expected under rising prices and that a majority of drivers do not appear to equate significantly diminished gasoline usage with hardship. At a minimum, these perceptions seem to belie a banal interpretation of gasoline politics—one, for example, picturing long-suffering American motorists beseeching their government to avoid any energy policy that might constrict automotive travel.

How much more onerous the marginal cost of a gasoline price hike might be to Americans compared with citizens of other countries (and how readily Congress can regard inexpensive gasoline as more indispensable to Americans) is not easy to ascertain. U.S. households allot a larger share of their budgets to gasoline than do the Europeans and Japanese.[74] This might suggest that the burden to Americans is heavier; after all, the high level of U.S. motor-fuel consumption is owed in part to inadequate public transportation in much of the nation and to the decentralized structure of American metropolitan areas, which necessitate extensive use of automobiles. Yet, while gasoline is the most prominent type of energy expenditure, to which U.S. consumers devote a larger share of their budgets than consumers in Japan and Europe, it is not the only type. Americans spend more on almost every other kind of energy purchase as well.[75] The basis of the difference in each instance is not merely that Americans "need" to allocate their resources in this manner as much as that the prices of energy, and of most energy-using consumer durables, have tended to be lower in the United States. This encourages the substitution of energy and energy-consuming items for other goods in the consumer shopping basket.[76]

72. *Gallup Opinion Index*, Report 170 (September 1979), p. 22.
73. *Gallup Opinion Index*, Report 140 (March 1977), p. 2.
74. Eberhard Meller, "The Equity Issue in Europe and Japan," in Hans H. Landsberg, ed., *High Energy Costs: Assessing the Burden* (Washington, D.C.: Resources for the Future, 1982), p. 338.
75. Darmstadter and others, *How Industrial Societies Use Energy*, p. 182.
76. Ibid., pp. 57, 59, 171, 178, 180, 182.

Whatever their objective needs, of course, it is still possible that American consumers complain more frequently to their elected representatives than foreigners do when the price of gasoline jumps. One reason for this is simple: the United States has almost as many registered automobiles as there are adults in the country. In 1981, population per car was 1.8 in the United States; the European runner-up, Switzerland, had a ratio of 2.5 persons per car.[77] Since vehicle owners are the group with the keenest interest in keeping down automotive operating costs, and since ownership is so extensive in the United States, the public outcry against a heavy gasoline tax increase can be especially pervasive and intense. Politically, the impact may be magnified because voter turnouts in the United States are lower than in European countries and Japan, and because voter participation is a function of socioeconomic status, which, in turn, is closely correlated with automobile ownership. In political systems where turnouts are much higher, nonmotorists are likely to figure more importantly in the active electorate.

Fairness

But American attitudes about gasoline taxation may be touching a sensitive political nerve in another sense. A clue to it may be found in the curious fact that throughout the 1970s solid majorities said they preferred gas rationing to taxes as a means of limiting consumption.[78] Citizens professed greater willingness to put up with the practical inconvenience, the red tape, and the strict curtailments associated with administered rations than to pay moderately higher prices at the pump. In the spring of 1978 Gallup asked a national sample to pick between a rationing program that would have required drivers to limit severely (that is, by one-quarter) the miles they drove and a tax that would have added twenty-five cents to the cost of a gallon of gas. The outcome was astonishing: only 20 percent chose the tax.[79] Why do people react this way? The answer is not that gullible motorists have been duped into believing that rationing ultimately costs them less than a tax. Rather, it has to do with a perception that rationing is somehow fair, but fuel taxes are unfair.[80] "It's that pop-

77. Motor Vehicle Manufacturers Association, *Facts and Figures 1983* (Washington, D.C.: Motor Vehicle Manufacturers Association of the United States, Inc., 1983), pp. 36–37.

78. See, for instance, *Harris Survey*, September 1973; and CBS News/*New York Times* poll, July 1977 and June 1979.

79. *Gallup Opinion Index*, Report 157 (August 1978), p. 30.

80. CBS News/*New York Times* poll, August 1977.

ulism again," explained one congressman in a lengthy interview. "It's just the idea that it is a regressive kind of a national sales tax that is particularly hard on the little guy, who drives up to the pump and has to pay just as much as the rich guy, who drives up in his Lincoln Continental or Cadillac."[81] The congressman was in a position to know. He was former Representative John B. Anderson, Republican of Illinois, whose outspoken advocacy of a serious gasoline tax increase during the 1980 election proved politically disastrous.

Localism

"If this tax is enacted, we will be requiring the people of the heartland of America to carry this burden on both shoulders. It is unfair; it is inequitable; it is grossly discriminatory against the . . . people of this country who do not have access to public transportation."[82] The voice ringing through the House chamber was that of Democrat William V. Alexander of Arkansas, urging his fellow legislators to shred the gasoline tax plan that had come before Congress during the summer of 1975. Similar perorations could be heard every other year that Congress took up gas tax legislation. And each time, dozens of representatives from the heartland of America would chime in behind a flood of negative votes. That rural representatives would react this way was understandable. As Representative Alexander asked, "Did you ever hear of anybody catching a subway in Osceola, Arkansas, or a bus in Bugtussle, Oklahoma?"[83]

Less well known is the fact that there were representatives from places like Boston (where lots of people catch buses and subways) who also behaved as if their constituents were living in Bugtussle. The vast hinterlands of the South and West have traditionally fought gasoline taxation, but to a remarkable degree, so have the extensively urban states of the Northeast.[84]

81. Interview with former Congressman John B. Anderson, Republican of Illinois, Washington, D.C., May 12, 1982.
82. *Congressional Record* (June 11, 1975), p. 18435.
83. Ibid.
84. Representatives elected from central city districts are somewhat more likely to vote for gasoline tax increases than are representatives from suburban and rural districts. But the striking fact is that a great many of these urban representatives—even those from high-density areas in the oldest central cities, with relatively developed public transit systems—still tend to oppose higher gasoline taxes. Consider the second vote of August 4, 1977, on a bill that would have raised the federal gas tax by only $0.04. In Boston, the only congressmen whose districts lay in the central city proper (the Massachusetts Ninth

The constancy of this geopolitical profile, as reflected in congressional voting, constrains the capacity of state characteristics to explain votes. The results of a statistical analysis for the five House roll calls cited earlier, plus the key House vote on the Surface Transportation Assistance Act in 1982, generally confirm the expected tendency of members from urban states to lean less solidly against higher gas taxes (see table 5-2 in the appendix to this chapter). But the pattern is weaker than commonly supposed. Several other state attributes, such as per capita consumption of gasoline, local gasoline price levels, and local excise tax rates, appear to predict even fewer votes. As in other energy roll calls analyzed throughout this book, the party affiliations of members of Congress remain a consistently significant predictor, but even this final factor is less powerful here than in the oil and gas deregulation decisions examined earlier.

By and large, congressional resistance to gasoline taxation has not been confined to particular states or regions; it is a national phenomenon. Two explanations for this have already been offered: the public is antagonistic toward such taxes, and hostile commercial interests are pervasive at the grass-roots level.

A third has to do with the logrolling that permeates congressional decisionmaking on energy tax policies. When Congress considers gasoline taxation, it usually does so with other options waiting in the wings. Comparisons are made with broader-based proposals that spread the incidence more evenly across petroleum-refined products, as an oil tariff or general oil excise tax would. Potentially, local preferences among these alternatives will differ markedly. Western representatives will oppose motor fuel taxes most adamantly. (Extensive automobile travel is unavoidable in those sections of the country that are thinly or newly settled. Where homes are heated with natural gas and where oil is used less frequently to generate electric power, a widely distributed tax has a milder impact per revenue dollar raised than a charge falling entirely on the one fuel that these areas consume voraciously.) Eastern representatives, especially those from populous urban states, are more inclined to

---

District, held at the time by Democratic Representative Joe Moakley) voted against the tax. Of the fifteen members from New York City who voted on the bill, six supported the tax, but the rest opposed it. Philadelphia's four representatives were split, two for, and two against. Chicago's seven-member delegation cast two yeas and five nays. And so it went, in city after city. Naturally, if one looked at the roll calls that were more lopsided (the one held on June 5, 1980, for example), one would find urban representatives voting against gasoline tax increases in even greater proportions.

accept a tax on automotive fuel than they are to accept a general tariff or excise on oil, the derivatives of which are applied in these states to a wider range of needs. But in practice, these latent regional schisms often do not show up clearly in voting blocs for a simple reason: Congress has typically managed to avoid an either-or choice between the options by rejecting both. A bargain is struck: representatives from the Northeast gain the allies they need to stave off tariffs by joining the rest of the House in repelling gasoline tax increases. This happened in 1975 and again in 1980, when the coalitions that beat back gasoline levies were more or less the same majorities that repulsed oil-import fees.

There is, however, another reason for the breadth of the coalitions. Teaming up with members from rural or low-density areas who have a direct interest in holding down the cost of automotive fuel are representatives who disapprove of gasoline taxation on philosophical grounds. Liberals say the tax is regressive, and conservatives say its revenues would only nourish big government.

Policy Management

Increased taxation of gasoline requires extraordinary circumstances to succeed. The necessary conditions finally came together in 1982. It is useful to contrast the earlier fiascoes with this intermission in the usual performance. The comparison raises a question about gasoline tax politics that this book has asked, in one form or another, about all other energy-pricing debates: how much do policy outcomes depend on the vicissitudes of political leadership? The following four cases, presented in chronological order, contain some answers.

The Ways and Means Committee Plan of 1975

Raising federal taxes on motor fuels first came under serious discussion in late 1973, when the Nixon administration was casting about for techniques to relieve worsening oil shortages. The White House never chose to submit legislation along these lines during either the Nixon or Ford years, despite the views of prominent administration officials, such as Treasury Secretary George P. Shultz and Council of Economic Advisers Chairman Herbert Stein under Nixon, and John C. Sawhill, the first Federal Energy Administration chief under Ford.[85] Even so, the

85. Neil de Marchi, "Energy Policy under Nixon: Mainly Putting Out Fires"; and

early flirtations with the concept had been educational for some members of Congress, most notably Albert C. Ullman, Democrat of Oregon, the new House Ways and Means chairman.

Originally unsympathetic to a gas tax, Ullman had become increasingly impressed by estimates of its conservation potential. (As early as November 1973, Deputy Treasury Secretary William Simon had predicted that each $0.10 boost in the gasoline tax would reduce consumption by 7 percent and that a $0.30 tax would chop demand down by 1 million barrels of oil daily.)[86] So when Congress finally fell to preparing a comprehensive energy program at the beginning of 1975, and the Ways and Means Committee assumed the task of writing much of it, Ullman was determined to insert as a central feature a bold increase in the tax on motor fuels.

The tax bill that evolved in Ullman's panel in 1975 underwent a profound metamorphosis between first draft and final version. Originally, it had looked as though the lawmakers might recommend an increase of $0.10 per gallon starting in 1976, rising as high as $0.50 in the ensuing four or five years. But as the markup process dragged on over several months, the initial $0.10 hike was successively lowered to $0.07, $0.05, and then $0.03, while the maximum tax in the out years fell to $0.40, $0.37, and even less later. In June 1975, when the completed bill was unfurled, it proposed a $0.03 spike at the outset, followed by a conditional $0.20 increase that would be levied in $0.05 increments only if gasoline consumption in subsequent years topped an arbitrary baseline set in 1973.[87]

The tax had shrunk in size but not in complexity. Exemptions galore were worked in—for local governments and nonprofit institutions, farmers and taxicab operators, airplanes and diesels, and a variety of others. Moreover, after the initial $0.03 increase, most of the revenue from any additional increment was to be refunded.[88] (Everybody was allotted a quota of forty gallons of gas per month, on which a 100 percent credit could be taken against individual income taxes. Persons using fuel for business or trade could claim an added 50 percent credit on taxed gasoline above the monthly allotment.) Also, although the gas tax would

Thomas H. Tietenberg, *Energy Planning and Policy: The Political Economy of Project Independence* (Lexington Books, 1976), p. 87.

86. *Congressional Quarterly Weekly Report*, vol. 31 (December 1, 1973), p. 3141.
87. *Congressional Quarterly Almanac*, vol. 31 (1975), p. 213.
88. *Congressional Quarterly Weekly Report*, vol. 33 (May 17, 1975), p. 1018.

soon reduce energy demand, at least if the full $0.23 per gallon were phased in promptly, it alone no longer sufficed to achieve even half the Ways and Means Committee's goal of cutting American oil consumption by more than 2 million barrels a day by 1985. Consequently, the committee's attention turned toward auxiliary conservation measures, the most notable of which was a schedule of mandatory fuel-economy standards for new car fleets, with graduated tax penalties for enforcement.

One needn't go much further to notice that the legislation now lacked elegance. Its contents were potentially redundant. A steeper gasoline tax would have rendered the section on fuel economy and gas-guzzlers unnecessary. On the other hand, the weakened tax, which in extremis would only have started to inch above $0.03 per gallon after nearly two years, permitted skeptics to suggest that the tax might not procure energy savings greatly in excess of what the other provisions promised.[89]

Ullman's critics were quick to spot the muddle and to rain derision on his bill because of it. Representative Barber B. Conable, Republican of New York, an experienced hand on Ways and Means, was characteristically candid on the subject. The "emerging bill," Conable wrote in his personal journal, "looks increasingly as though it were put together by a bunch of incompetents." The committee was "trying to shovel as many feathers up into the air as possible."[90]

Given the choice, there wasn't much doubt about which feathers the full House would shoot down and which ones it would decide to wear. In a series of votes on June 11 and 12, the gasoline tax was blown away, the auto mileage standards were kept, and the gas-guzzler penalties were exchanged for a more innocuous system of civil fines. The mileage regulations enforced by fines were regarded by the United Auto Workers and by some of the automobile companies, as well as by most politicians, as a fairly painless way of subduing gasoline demand. But many members of Congress conjectured, rightly or wrongly, that the Ways and Means bill, as it now stood, might conserve almost as much energy if the gas tax were stricken as it would if the tax stayed in.[91]

89. *Congressional Record* (June 11, 1975), p. 18443; and (June 10, 1975), pp. 18021, 18045.

90. Interview with Representative Barber B. Conable, Jr., Republican of New York, Washington, D.C., May 20, 1982.

91. Their hunch received support from the staff of the Joint Committee on Internal Revenue and Taxation, which estimated energy savings of about 2 million barrels of oil daily under the Ullman bill stripped of its gasoline levy. *Congressional Quarterly Weekly*

Redundancy was just one of the bill's flaws. Straining to prove that the gas tax was not meant to raise new revenue for the federal Treasury, Congress took great care to arrange that the proceeds would bounce back swiftly to the public. But for every member of the House placated by the rebate formula, four seemed to be disgusted by it. Rural representatives remonstrated that the bill failed to offer larger tax credits for country folk than for city folk. Suburban representatives, almost all of whose constituents were car owners, fumed at the idea that the whole population, and not merely licensed drivers, would be eligible for credits. In the words of Representative Stewart B. McKinney, Republican of Connecticut, and elected from one of the nation's wealthiest suburban counties, a "basic problem" with the legislation was that it signified "a form of income redistribution in that those who buy gasoline—including those who must buy it—would be giving up to $100 a year to the 20 percent of the population which does not hold a driver's license."[92] Others felt that the framers were wrong to suppose that the public would accept a rebated levy much more readily than a straight tax. According to these dissidents, the logic of sending money to Washington, only to have it returned minus a postage fee, as Senator Russell B. Long once quipped, escaped the average citizen. (Lore has it that Senator Dale L. Bumpers, Democrat of Arkansas, once asked his local barber how he would feel if the government were to tax gasoline, reimburse most of the revenue, but keep five cents on the gallon. The barber reflected for an instant, reached into his pocket, handed the senator a nickel, and replied, "There, now, ain't that a whole lot simpler?")[93] Still others recognized that the goals of conserving energy and of rapidly recycling tax dollars were not necessarily compatible. The gasoline excise would curb demand for one fuel, but the rebates might lift consumption of another.[94] What would prevent people from using their gas tax refunds to buy more air conditioning, or more diesel-powered recreational vehicles, or more heated outdoor Jacuzzis?

Report, vol. 33 (June 28, 1975), p. 1384. A month earlier, the Joint Committee staff had imputed about half of the bill's savings of 2.1 million barrels a day to its gasoline tax component. *Congressional Quarterly Weekly Report*, vol. 33 (May 17, 1975), pp. 1018, 1019.

92. *Congressional Record* (June 10, 1975), p. 18046.

93. Interview with Benjamin Cooper, minority staff, Senate Committee on Energy and Natural Resources, Washington, D.C., September 29, 1981.

94. Interview with Paul Oösterhuis, former staff member, Joint Committee on Taxation, Washington, D.C., October 13, 1981.

The worst thing about the Ways and Means Committee's construct was that it furnished the decor for an energy policy without first laying the necessary building blocks—namely, a foundation of domestic petroleum prices anchored to world market levels. As stressed in chapter 2, the failure of the Ways and Means Committee to draft a windfall profits tax as an integral part of its energy bill in 1975 made it all but impossible for other legislative committees to push ahead with decontrol of oil prices.[95] The omission also barred a possible bipartisan compromise. President Ford might have consented to a gasoline tax, in lieu of the oil-import fees and general excises he had recommended, in exchange for phased decontrol from the Democratic Congress.[96] Ways and Means could have stood on solid ground if it had prescribed a tax on gasoline to supplement the deregulated price of oil. Instead, the committee ambled into legislative quicksand, trying to attach a tax to a regulated base price. The chosen formulation was not just awkward intellectually; it was a mistake politically. Few liberal Democrats could be counted on to vote for a consumption tax of any kind, particularly during a recession. As for Republicans and oil-state Democrats, none would ever support an energy tax summoned as a stand-in for deregulated oil prices. But conceivably, Ullman could have enlisted the Ford administration's cooperation in nudging a bloc of Republicans and centrist Democrats toward a gas tax if it had been coupled inextricably with a timetable for the removal of price controls.

Why was the gasoline tax legislation of 1975 so poorly packaged? Frail and fractionated institutional leadership was part of the problem. As noted in chapter 2, Ullman was new to the chair of the reorganized Ways and Means Committee. Wary of violating jurisdictional boundaries, he postponed action on a windfall profits tax measure pending the outcome of the House Interstate and Foreign Commerce Committee's decisions on oil-price regulations. At the same time, eager to assert his committee's prerogatives, Ullman rebuffed suggestions by other Democratic leaders in the House that he subordinate his panel's deliberations to a special ad hoc committee that would oversee all energy legislation then split among several consignees. A supervisory committee, like the one created by Speaker Thomas P. O'Neill, Jr., to expedite President Carter's energy initiative two years later, might have better coordinated

95. *Congressional Quarterly Weekly Report*, vol. 33 (May 10, 1975), p. 961.

96. Interview with Frank Zarb, former head of the Federal Energy Administration, New York City, November 24, 1981.

the activities of Ways and Means with those of the Commerce Committee. Possibly, a provision for a windfall profits tax could have been coaxed out of Ways and Means to complement some sort of graduated deregulation plan from Commerce. Instead, the two units followed separate itineraries and ultracautious strategies. In doing so, the authors of the 1975 gasoline tax proposal lost sight of the fundamental verities of legislating any type of energy tax in the mid-1970s: there could never be a tax on motor fuel, or on other fuels, without decontrol, and there could be no decontrol without a levy on windfall profits.

These linkages were not lost for want of consultations between Congress and the executive branch. During the critical months of March and April 1975, when it still appeared that the Ways and Means Committee could pave the way to oil-price deregulation by readying an excess profits tax, Ullman met frequently with Ford's emissary, Frank Zarb, the new head of the Federal Energy Administration. Midway through these conversations Zarb expressed a belief that "60 percent agreement" had been reached.[97] It also became known that Zarb was prepared to take a tax on gasoline if Ways and Means members were willing to align more of their thinking on energy policy with that of the president. But accords made between Zarb and Ullman carried little weight. The chairman's word could never be backed by solid assurances that the other actors, with whom he shared power, would not dissent.[98] The resurgent House Democratic Caucus, which had recently managed to depose several senior committee heads, stood ready to repudiate any compromise that strayed too close to the administration's position. Even when Ullman wasn't feeling "the hot breath of the caucus on his neck," as Representative William E. Frenzel, Republican of Minnesota, put it, his own Ways and Means cohorts were rebellious.[99] And who could tell what the outcome would be of the floating crap game going on simultaneously in the House Commerce Committee, in whose hands the future of domestic oil-price policy rested as well? As much as Ullman may have wanted an agreement, the White House despaired of trying to reach one with him. "You can't look to anybody in a leadership position in the House today to deliver on energy. They can make a personal commitment, but they can't follow through," observed White House congres-

97. *Congressional Quarterly Weekly Report*, vol. 33 (March 22, 1975), pp. 580–81.

98. Interview with Albert C. Ullman, Washington, D.C., October 21, 1981.

99. *Congressional Quarterly Weekly Report*, vol. 33 (June 28, 1975), p. 1345; and vol. 33 (March 15, 1975), pp. 511, 516.

sional liaison, Douglas Bennett.[100] The gasoline tax plan of 1975 might have fared somewhat better on the House floor if it had arrived with the president's blessing. But a presidential nod, if obtainable at all, could not be gotten without serious bargaining between people capable of assuming risks and honoring commitments. The leadership of the House Ways and Means Committee, to whom fell the responsibility but not the power to undertake such negotiations, was unable to clasp the opportunity.

Other aspects of the 1975 legislation reflected governmental fragmentation. In part, the bill's rebate system, for instance, was the predictable outgrowth of time-honored intramural rivalries over the disposition of tax dollars. Ways and Means could have chosen to turn over more of the gasoline tax earnings to general revenue. But that would have cast the tax writers in the unpleasant role of being mere fund raisers, while other institutions—chiefly the appropriations committees—would get the happier task of spending the money.[101] Another way to avoid this situation was to set all the funds aside for prespecified purposes. If the tax stayed at $0.03 or so, there was an established receptacle into which receipts could pour—the highway trust fund. But to earmark the entire income stream from higher tax rates (for example, $0.23 per gallon) in this manner was sure to drive the traditional guardians of the budgetary process—the congressional budget and appropriations units, along with the Office of Management and Budget—into vigorous opposition. To duck such difficulties and to serve other objectives deemed critical at the time, such as buoying disposable income during a recession, the gasoline tax was made to resemble a fiscal Ping-Pong game. People would pay the tax, and then the government would promptly bat back more than 80 percent of the proceeds.[102]

The Carter Legislation of 1977

Two years after the demise of the Ways and Means bill, several gasoline tax measures came up in Congress again, this time hitched to the Carter administration's mammoth energy plan. Although most of the Carter National Energy Plan passed the House of Representatives intact

100. *Congressional Quarterly Weekly Report*, vol. 33 (June 28, 1975), p. 1345.

101. James W. Wetzler, "Energy Excise Taxes as Substitutes for Income Taxes," *National Tax Journal*, vol. 33 (September 1980), pp. 324–25.

102. *Congressional Record* (June 11, 1975), p. 18448.

during the summer of 1977, the main gasoline tax proposal never even got out of committee. Defective design damaged its prospects.

Several aspects were reminiscent of the ill-fated Ways and Means scheme of 1975. The tax was to be levied on a standby basis in annual increments of $0.05. (The increments would take effect only if gasoline consumption during previous calendar years exceeded targets set by the government.) Although the cumulative amount of the tax could have reached a higher limit than in 1975, $0.50 instead of $0.23, the phase-in process was tortuous. The first $0.05 installment was not scheduled to begin before 1979, so that the $0.50 maximum, if ever attained, would not have come until the end of the 1980s. As for the revenue collected, all was to be rebated progressively through the federal income tax system. Persons not paying income taxes were to receive direct payments.

In part, the formulation ran aground on the same sorts of shoals struck earlier. The tax was so gently tapered that its conservation effect appeared too remote and uncertain. Congress squirmed at the thought of jolting constituents with a hefty, one-shot price increase, but it also winced at a series of $0.05 nuisance taxes, piling up year after year. Because the drawn-out process would only yield substantial gasoline savings years later, it was necessary once again to rely on supplemental measures. As in 1975, a gas-guzzler tax was proposed alongside the motor fuel tax, handing Congress a golden opportunity to shrug off the latter, adopt the former, and still congratulate itself for having acted to reduce fuel consumption. In addition, the mechanism for refunding revenue provoked many of the same squabbles experienced before, except that this time the public bickering took place in the executive branch as well as on Capitol Hill. At one point, for instance, Secretary of Transportation Brock Adams showed up at a Ways and Means Committee hearing with a recommendation that about $6 billion of the tax's initial yield be spent on road repairs, transit improvements, and energy research, instead of being returned directly to consumers. Adams claimed he had cleared his suggestion with the White House, even though press secretary Jody Powell insisted that the president had not changed his commitment to full rebates.[103]

Finally, the gas tax fell victim to the political undertow agitated by the sheer corpulence of the National Energy Plan. When the House Ways and Means Committee began work on its portions of the agenda in April 1977, it confronted in addition to the gasoline tax bill, five bulky

103. *Congressional Quarterly Weekly Report*, vol. 35 (May 21, 1977), p. 955.

pieces of tax legislation called up by the National Energy Plan. Inevitably, some of the cargo flopped overboard as the administration ran back and forth among a dozen congressional committees, attempting to batten down the plan's multiple segments. Although the president had vowed to fight, "down to the last vote," for the gasoline levy, the administration seemed almost resigned when Ways and Means voted in June to scuttle it, 27–10.[104]

The committee members felt that, for all the entrées served by the National Energy Plan, there was scarcely a morsel with which to entice a coalition for gasoline taxation. Price controls on natural gas and crude oil were not scheduled for early retirement under the plan. Thus, there was no possibility of swapping decontrol of these fuels for any aid from Republicans and western-state delegations in passing a gasoline tax. At the same time, the plan's proposed crude oil equalization tax implied much higher energy costs for the oil-consuming Northeast, stiffening that region's opposition to further energy price increases, including any from a gasoline excise. Of course, if the equalization tax had been a mere bargaining chip, to be traded in for support of the gas tax, representatives from the Northeast might have worked harder to keep the gas tax alive. The equalization tax, however, was a keystone of the National Energy Plan, not a secondary item to barter away.

To comprehend why the Carter gasoline tax took the form it did, one must remember an earlier observation about the roots of the National Energy Plan. It was no coincidence that the 1977 standby tax bore similarities to the 1975 rendition. Much of the energy plan was a collage of prior congressional initiatives, partly because the new administration assumed that familiar formulas would reassure party regulars in Congress, and partly because the White House task force that drafted the plan was staffed with former congressional aides who, under a grueling deadline, proceeded to warm over old legislative recipes.[105] The trouble with all this attention to precedent was that entire sections were robbed of two highly desirable properties: originality and simplicity. Maybe a few brave warriors, bloodied in the 1975 fray, were flattered to find their intricate gasoline scheme substantially resurrected and were willing to

104. Richard Corrigan, "Energy Package Goes to the House," *National Journal*, vol. 9 (July 30, 1977), p. 1198.

105. On the practical politics of gas tax designs, however, there was remarkably little consultation between administration energy planners and Ways and Means Committee members or staff. Interview with Robert Leonard, majority staff, House Ways and Means Committee, Washington, D.C., October 15, 1981.

charge forth with it again. But the vast majority of Ways and Means members, including the chairman, remembered 1975 as a humiliation not to be repeated. Further, with lots of other particulars in the energy plan beckoning for the committee's energies, it was better to avoid getting mired again in controversy over a gasoline tax.

Would the reception have been warmer if the Carter administration had sent up fresh wine in new bottles? Two stripped-down substitutes—with no standby, no delayed fuse, and no rebates—did reach the House chamber in August 1977. One was a $0.04 maximum surtax quickly slapped together by senior members of the Ad Hoc Energy Committee after the original Carter bill had died in Ways and Means. Income from this levy would be earmarked for a variety of ends, ranging from energy research and a strategic petroleum reserve to assistance for local car-pooling projects. Another was an amendment offered spontaneously by Representative James J. Howard, Democrat of New Jersey, then chairman of the Public Works Subcommittee on Surface Transportation. Instead of spreading revenues among several programs, as the Ad Hoc Committee proposed, Howard's measure was to raise the gasoline tax rate by $0.05 and spend half the money on highways, the other half on transit systems. In successive votes on August 4, the full House demolished both these alternatives.

Although these setbacks suggested that no tax, no matter how petite and tidy, could have won the hearts and minds of the House in 1977, the proposals were hardly optimal tests of what was possible. Both initiatives were mismanaged. The Ad Hoc Energy Committee, for instance, advertised its $0.04 impost as an energy tax. Measured against the initial Carter proposal, this invited ridicule. To pretend that the National Energy Plan's energy conservation objectives could still be achieved after the original gasoline tax was whittled down from $0.50 to just $0.04 per gallon was preposterous. At the same time, many representatives felt that the Howard amendment, which emphasized transportation requirements rather than energy goals, had no business hitting the House floor unexpectedly during a debate on energy policy.[106] When the administration suddenly decided to back this bill, made by a subcommittee chairman who was not even involved in the drafting of the energy

106. *Congressional Quarterly Weekly Report*, vol. 35 (August 6, 1977), p. 1628. In the words of Congressman Robert C. Eckhardt, Democrat of Texas, "I don't think there is any rational connection between energy conservation and increasing the cost of gasoline by five cents."

package, the majority leadership was dismayed, and everybody else was confused.

Conceivably, a straightforward gasoline tax could have made more headway than these late arrivals did, if, from start to finish, it had been presented emphatically as a top policy priority and a badly needed source of revenue. Such a presentation, however, demanded more than political finesse. It required, at a minimum, a different political context, with wider recognition that a serious national problem existed, an acknowledged need for revenues, and a simplification of the legislative agenda. But even the last condition, a simpler energy plan, was not entirely in the president's power to arrange. No plan could look clean and compact if energy price controls remained in effect. Barriers, like the Energy Policy and Conservation Act of 1975, ensured that they would.

The Carter Gasoline Fee of 1980

Early in 1980 the Carter White House renewed its interest in a gasoline levy. The second oil shock, whose severity was not unrelated to surging American demand for motor fuel in the late 1970s, was still fresh on the minds of energy planners. A second energy program, advancing the deregulation of crude-oil prices and committing the federal government to large-scale synthetic fuels development, was in the works. Administration officials wanted a conservation tax to round it out. But the administration and supportive Democratic leaders in Congress had other motives as well. For the first time, gasoline excise revenue was viewed as grist for the budget process: it offered an opportunity to help balance the budget and perhaps make possible a significant income tax reduction.

Recalling the congressional debacles three years before, however, strategists were not anxious to request specific legislation for a tax on gasoline. It might have been feasible to ask for an affirmative decision by Congress, had the administration proposed it as a quid pro quo for oil deregulation. But in 1980, a trade of this type could not be organized for two reasons. In the first place, the president had chosen, courageously, to let the Energy Policy and Conservation Act's price controls end after 1979. Second, by permitting decontrol to commence unconditionally, the president put pressure on Congress to pass a windfall profits tax. Now the legislators would have to enact one, or take the blame for any jump in oil company profits after controls expired. The administration decided, therefore, to arrive at the gasoline tax circuitously, employing executive authority under the Trade Expansion Act of 1962 to set import fees. The stratagem was to impose a $4.62 surcharge on each barrel of imported oil, and then, by administrative means, pass this fee through to consumers as a dime-a-gallon increase at the gasoline pump.

On March 14, the executive order was announced. The uproar that ensued took the administration and the congressional leadership by surprise. Republicans jumped at the chance to characterize Carter's action as political chicanery, intended to set the stage for an election-year tax cut. Election-conscious Democrats saw an opportunity to strike a blow for consumers by going on record against the fee. Custodians of congressional prerogative protested "a policy of having the president impose taxes on the American people" in a matter "that ought to be the determination of Congress."[107] Legalists chided the president for overstepping his statutory powers. The Trade Expansion Act, they argued, empowered the president to order quotas or fees on imported oil generally, but did not allow him to raise the price of particular products, such as gasoline, that might be partly or completely refined from domestic oil.[108] Western representatives noted that gasoline prices had already risen by $0.60 a gallon in the last year and concluded that drivers "have conserved about as much as they can."[109] Northeastern representatives, concerned about heating-oil prices, feared that administrative procedures might fail to tilt the tariff exclusively onto gasoline. Marathon Oil Company and the independent gasoline dealers association joined consumer groups filing suit against the energy department in federal court.

The Trade Expansion Act had been amended, giving Congress authority to block new import fees or quotas by passing a joint resolution of disapproval. The president retained the right to veto the resolution, but then the legislature, by a two-thirds vote of both houses, could overrule him. Between mid-May and the first week of June, this unlikely script was in fact played out. On June 5 and 6, Congress overrode the president 335–34 in the House and 68–10 in the Senate. Not only was this count far in excess of the two-thirds needed to kill the fee; it was the first override of a veto by a Democratic president since 1952, when Harry S. Truman was in office.

Again, one can question the way the tax venture was handled. The politically charged atmosphere of an election year was no time to con-

107. *Congressional Quarterly Weekly Report*, vol. 38 (June 7, 1980), p. 1540.
108. *Congressional Quarterly Weekly Report*, vol. 38 (May 17, 1980), p. 1308.
109. *Congressional Quarterly Weekly Report*, vol. 38 (June 7, 1980), p. 1540.

front Congress and the public with an administered fuel cost increase. The notion of acting unilaterally, by executive fiat, was bound to roil Congress, and even to raise issues of law. (In the suit against the fee, Federal District Judge Aubrey E. Robinson, Jr., ruled that the president had exceeded his authority.)[110] The hidden agenda in this instance—the application of gas tax revenue for budget balancing—hindered rather than helped Carter's effort. At the time, the prospective federal deficit was not sobering enough to whet a congressional appetite for the estimated $12.6 billion in annual revenues that the fee would bring in. Consequently, this bonanza smacked too brazenly of a ploy to finance preelection income tax relief. Stressing that the primary purpose of the fee was still to save energy did little good. As Representative Edward J. Markey, Democrat of Massachusetts, said to Energy Secretary Charles W. Duncan, Jr., during hearings before the Ways and Means Trade Subcommittee in April: "You are generating revenues and justifying it under the shibboleth of conservation—it is nothing more than a fig leaf to disguise a [budgetary] program. . . . You ought to be called the secretary of taxation."[111]

Yet, no critique of the administration's tactics can fully explain the extremity of the drubbing that the proposed tax took. More than any other congressional uprising in recent years, the votes of June 5 and 6 betrayed the presidency's weakness in the interlude between Watergate and the 1980 election. Few other episodes also revealed more starkly the degree of disarray in the Democratic party. Beset by an unremitting foreign policy crisis (the American hostages in Iran) and by relentless challenges not only from outside his party (by the GOP's top presidential contender) but also from within it (Senator Kennedy's dogged drive for the Democratic nomination), Carter spent the last year of his tenure fighting for survival. What fealty the "outsider in Washington"[112] ever enjoyed among rank-and-file Democrats in Congress had long since evaporated. The influence of Democratic congressional leaders was so slender among average members in the harsh political glare of the 1980 campaign, that disorderly majorities moved at will to embarrass their party's incumbent president, its leadership, and perhaps themselves, just months before the nation was to go to the polls.

110. *Congressional Quarterly Weekly Report*, vol. 38 (May 17, 1980), p. 1307.
111. *Congressional Quarterly Weekly Report*, vol. 38 (April 26, 1980), p. 1144.
112. Jimmy Carter, *Keeping Faith: Memoirs of a President* (Bantam Books, 1982), p. 63.

The Surface Transportation Assistance Act of 1983

On April 1, 1983, after a stalemate that lasted nearly a quarter century, the federal government began adding $0.05 to its $0.04-per-gallon gasoline tax. By contrasting the history of the earlier legislative attempts to increase the gas tax with the 1983 success, key catalysts that finally enabled the federal government to act can be discerned.

For one thing, given the bountiful state of the world oil supply and the modest scale of the proposed tax increase, motorists were not likely to notice any immediate change in fuel prices after the law took effect. Although even smaller surtaxes of $0.03 and $0.04 had been advanced unsuccessfully in 1975 and 1977, in 1982, crude and refined-product prices were tumbling rapidly, not just stabilizing as they did in 1975–77. These market conditions pretty much guaranteed that the extra nickel levied after April 1 would not be passed on to consumers quickly. Technically, the federal gasoline levy is not a sales tax automatically tacked onto prices at the filling-station pump, but a tax on firms that sell gas to retailers, oil companies, middlemen, and service station operators, who are likely to absorb a substantial portion of the increase through reduced profit margins.

It was also understood from the start of the legislative proceedings that at least 80 percent of the surtax's revenue would be spent on emergency road repairs, through the highway trust fund. In the early 1980s, deterioration of the nation's transportation infrastructure had begun to alarm a broad spectrum of interests. Public officials at all levels, as well as user groups such as the American Automobile Association and the American Trucking Associations, were concerned. All parties seemed to agree that at least 10 percent of the interstate system needed immediate resurfacing and that basic maintenance of older bridges and other facilities could not be deferred any longer.[113] On account of inflation and the stationary federal tax rate for gasoline, the highway trust fund was disbursing more than it collected.[114] Everyone recognized that the fund's income would soon need supplementing. Of course, there had been almost as many potholes on the country's highways in 1980, when Pres-

113. Ernest Hoesendoeph, "Saving the Interstate Highways," *New York Times*, May 9, 1982.
114. Ernest Hoesendoeph, "Questions and Answers on Administration's Plan," *New York Times*, December 5, 1982.

ident Carter sought a $0.10 gasoline fee, as there were in 1982. But a dime's worth of tax was more daunting than a nickel, and more important, the proposed revenues from Carter's plan had not been earmarked for highways. The Howard bill of 1977 did propose to funnel a $0.05 boost into transportation projects, but alarm then about the condition of the nation's highways had not yet swelled much beyond Congressman Howard's subcommittee.

In 1982–83, the consensus for road restoration coincided with the worst spell of unemployment since 1941. In the Democratic party, murmurs of reviving New Deal-style projects for the unemployed were becoming audible, after having been stilled temporarily by the Reagan landslide of 1980. Party leaders in the Democratically controlled House of Representatives sighted an opportunity: highway rebuilding could double as a jobs program. The gasoline tax initiative of 1975 had also come during a period of relatively high unemployment. But because the income from this scheme was not designated for highway repairs, nor for other public works, the proposal was much more vulnerable to charges of being fiscally procyclical in the midst of a serious recession.

The jobless rate reached a postwar high of 10.8 percent late in November 1982, just in time for the midterm elections, costing the Republican party twenty-six seats in the House and a near-loss of its majority in the Senate. The message to Republican survivors was clear: they too would have to show more interest in creating jobs. On November 22, Senate Majority Leader Howard H. Baker, Jr., Republican of Tennessee, announced that he intended to work closely with Speaker O'Neill, and the rest of the Democratic leadership, to fashion an emergency highway and jobs bill in a special session of the Ninety-seventh Congress. The groundswell of concern about unemployment was so strong, that Republican congressional leaders vowed to move ahead with a bipartisan plan whether the White House approved or not. The 1975 and 1977 bouts over gasoline taxation were different. Those clashes were somewhat more partisan, with some Democratic leaders sponsoring the tax bills, while the Republicans attacked them.

Conditions in the legislature were also auspicious for the passage of the 1983 tax. For instance, because action on the legislation was scheduled during a lame-duck session, the only unpleasant feature of the transportation assistance act—the tax to finance it—could be decided by a Congress that had just finished an election campaign. Consequently, a number of members, who were retiring (voluntarily or not) at the end of the term, could vote for the tax provision without the usual jitters about constituents' reaction.

The administration also rose to the challenge of backing the new tax. President Reagan, after a brief delay, threw his support behind the measure. Although a bill embodying both a tax hike and a new unemployment relief program seemed at odds with the Reagan administration's professed fiscal policies, the designation of funds for the transportation sector allowed the president to label the package a user fee. He could then declare it consistent with the administration's market-oriented approach to the utilization of public facilities.[115] The gasoline tax that Congress had considered in 1975 was, like this one, congressionally initiated. Unlike this one, however, it had never received a presidential endorsement.

Furthermore, in the critical last stages of the legislative process, the White House did more than wish the bill well; it pushed hard for it. To crack the Senate filibuster only hours before adjournment, loyal senators who had already left town for Christmas were flown back to Washington on military aircraft and rushed to the Capitol in police cars with lights flashing and sirens wailing in time for the cloture vote. The president had an immediate incentive. A group of Senate Democrats was poised to submit a much more ambitious and expensive jobs program, to be paid for by rescinding the 10 percent federal income tax reduction scheduled for July 1983. To defuse this threat to the administration's basic economic policy, the White House thought it prudent to embrace some form of jobs legislation in 1982, even if only a symbolic facsimile.[116]

And by 1982, the time had come to contemplate new taxes, despite the continuing recession. With the Treasury hemorrhaging from the big tax cut of 1981 and the protracted economic slump, and with the administration's massive defense buildup under way, the nation suddenly found itself staring at projected out-year federal deficits of $200 to $300 billion. In Congress the specter of such radical fiscal disequilibrium was sending shivers through Republican ranks. The chairmen of the Senate Finance and Senate Budget Committees were openly advocating higher

115. *New York Times*, November 12, 1982; and Martin Tolchin, "O'Neill and Baker to Seek Tax to Aid Road Repair Plan," *New York Times*, November 23, 1982.

116. The transportation assistance act was expected to create just 320,000 construction jobs, an optimistic figure according to many economists, including Martin Feldstein, the administration's own Council of Economic Advisers chairman. "Public Works Certainly Not without Critics," *National Journal*, vol. 14 (November 27, 1982), p. 2020; and *Wall Street Journal*, December 2, 1982.

taxes, not just spending cuts, to close the fiscal gap. At least outside the Oval Office, the same sentiment was spreading within the administration. Doubts about supply-side orthodoxy mounted in the Council of Economic Advisers and in the Office of Management and Budget (where a year earlier, director David Stockman had described the 1981 tax cut as a Trojan horse).[117] The chairman of the Federal Reserve Board, Paul Volcker, and other top economic policymakers were calling for passage of a gasoline tax increase. The 1982 gas tax legislation cannot be interpreted as an important deficit-trimming measure, however. Against a revenue shortfall of $200 billion, $5 billion a year generated by the tax was a drop in the bucket. Nonetheless, the tax was regarded as a step in the right direction, especially in the short term, before the states would have to be reimbursed for their outlays. The highway trust fund could rapidly accumulate an appreciable sum of ready cash, available to the Treasury at favorable interest rates compared with the cost of tapping capital in the credit market. Substantial deficits had also plagued the federal government in earlier times. Carter, for example, inherited a 1976 deficit of $66 billion, and in 1980 he briefly considered a gasoline levy to help balance the budget. But 1982 was unique; it was one of the few times since World War II that political leaders of both parties concluded that the government was famished for revenue.

Adoption of the bill, especially in the House, was eased by larding the legislation with "domestic content" (buy American) provisions that appealed to representatives from depressed industrial districts. One amendment, for instance, stipulated that cement, steel, and manufactured products used in federally assisted transportation improvements be American made.

Finally, the gasoline tax's chief sponsors engineered something of a "palace coup," to borrow President Reagan's phrase.[118] Exertions by Baker and O'Neill greased the skids in the legislative branch, but masterminding the plot even earlier was Drew Lewis, the secretary of transportation. Having launched his own campaign to raise motor fuel taxes and other highway-related charges shortly after his appointment in 1981, Lewis rallied various lobbies behind him. The generally seductive envelope in which the tax plan and other recommendations were sealed was central to his success. The tax would be a mere $0.05 per gallon. Almost

---

117. See William Greider, "The Education of David Stockman," *Atlantic*, vol. 248 (December 1981), pp. 27–54.

118. *Congressional Quarterly Weekly Report*, vol. 40 (November 27, 1982), p. 2914.

all of it would go toward sprucing up highways, but just enough, approximately $1 billion, would be channeled to financially strapped cities for mass transit improvements. People would be put back to work on repairs and renovations that were long overdue. Highway safety would be enhanced. Although a report from the Department of Transportation suggested that better road maintenance could reduce fuel consumption, since poor road conditions were adding significantly to driving times, conservation of gasoline was never underlined as an objective of the tax increase.[119] By underplaying the energy-saving aspect of the new tax, Lewis and his allies skirted two political liabilities: an accusation that the government was conspiring to impose conservation by price and a challenge on the grounds that, if that was the real purpose, a nickel tax would accomplish very little.

So, well before congressional majorities grew excited about the issue, Lewis had foraged patiently for support from outside sources, as well as inside ones. The Associated General Contractors of America was, naturally, among the first groups to line up. Then came local officials—the National League of Cities and the U.S. Conference of Mayors. Although the Highway Users Federation was divided on the matter of diverting some highway trust fund monies to mass transit, and the American Automobile Association called this idea a perversion, both still joined the contented American Public Transit Association in backing the gasoline tax.[120] Meanwhile, the transit subsidy won the immediate cooperation of Representative Howard, now chairman of the full Public Works and Transportation Committee. The transportation secretary's powers of persuasion were also helpful in gaining early commitments from the chairmen of the two tax-writing committees, Representative Daniel D. Rostenkowski, Democrat of Illinois, and Senator Robert J. Dole, Republican of Kansas, and eventually from another key player, Ronald Reagan. Policy entrepreneurs of such caliber had been lacking in prior political collisions over gasoline taxes.

Conclusion

These case histories suggest that the feasibility of gasoline tax increases partly depends on how the governmental process is managed. Skillful direction, as occurred in 1982, improves the odds of a break-

---

119. *Congressional Quarterly Weekly Report*, vol. 40 (November 20, 1982), p. 2876.
120. *Congressional Quarterly Weekly Report*, vol. 40 (November 27, 1982), p. 2914.

through. Bad timing, poor salesmanship, or nearly total loss of political control, as in the cases prior to 1982, turns an arduous task into an impossible one.

But cleverness in handling the relevant political institutions is not the most important determinant of whether gas taxes fly or flop. When the federal levy finally went up in 1983, a variety of forces had contributed to the result. Not the least of these was a feeling, sufficiently widespread on both sides of the aisle, that the nation's taxes needed bolstering. European governments, with their proportionally larger public sectors, had turned to motor fuel excises to generate revenue long ago.[121] But in the United States this notion was a novel dimension in the recurring debate.

Despite it and other conducive circumstances, the tax hike of 1983 remained tiny by foreign standards, and still remarkably controversial. In fact, passage of the legislation had remained in doubt until the eleventh hour. A final factor, not adequately discussed thus far, had continued to complicate the issue: deep-seated ideological antipathy toward the taxation of gasoline.

Political Convictions

The recurrent congressional wrangling over gas taxes has not run along party lines as regularly as did the oil and gas deregulation disputes in the 1970s. The comparatively limited influence of party affiliation makes this plain (see table 5-2 in the appendix to this chapter). Democrats were, on the whole, somewhat more inclined to back higher gasoline levies than were Republicans. It is not hard to account for this rough tendency. Historically, most of the gasoline tax proposals were advanced by Democratic congressional leaders, or as occurred in 1977, endorsed by a Democratic president. Yet, in none of the roll calls analyzed in table 5-2, with the possible exception of the second vote on June 11, 1975, does party predict votes as well as in the key natural gas and oil-pricing divisions discussed earlier.[122] Ideolog-

121. Joel Darmstadter, "Conserving Energy: Issues, Opportunities, Prospects," *Journal of Energy and Development*, vol. 2 (Autumn 1976), p. 7.

122. Expressed in simple (Pearson) correlations, none of the gasoline tax roll calls (except for the second vote on June 11, 1975) yielded coefficients any greater than $r = .29$ when party affiliation (1 = Democrat, 0 = Republican) was correlated with votes. Correlating Americans for Democratic Action (ADA) ratings with the votes, the highest coefficient obtained was $r = .39$ (except, again, for the second roll call of June 11, 1975). These comparatively modest results stand in contrast to the much stronger Pearson correlation coefficients generated by party and ADA scores in the House divisions on oil and gas decontrol.

ical forces and factions in Congress were still at work, but they assumed rather different configurations.

In contrast to the deregulation decisions, congressional skittishness about taxing gasoline tends to span a wider range of political convictions. This is what generates the big antitax majorities. The debate in 1982 was the first in a long while when opposition was narrowed down somewhat to one end of the spectrum—chiefly the right wing of the GOP. Even so, the fringe group picked up enough help in the center and among liberals to keep the outcome close. Indeed, such is the swath cutting across party cleavages that it can take in even the far Right and Left, as in 1980, or often unite them into an identifiable coalition, dampening the capacity of Congress to align on simple partisan, or liberal versus conservative, dimensions. In the decisive House vote on the 1983 tax increase, for instance, 70 percent of the nays were cast by an assemblage of archconservatives and extreme liberals, defined here as members whose 1982 ratings on the Americans for Democratic Action (ADA) scale of 1 to 100 were either above 79 points or below 21 points.[123]

What brings together congressmen like Albert Lee Smith, Jr., Republican of Alabama (ADA score: 0), and Gerry E. Studds, Democrat of Massachusetts (ADA score: 100), or Jesse A. Helms, Republican of North Carolina (ADA score: 0), and Paul S. Sarbanes, Democrat of Maryland (ADA score: 95)?[124]

The Conservative View

To conservatives, the supposed virtue of the taxation of motor fuel is also its defect: it raises so much revenue so quickly and dependably that it invites the government to go on a spending spree. Some conservative senators and representatives are leery of upping federal taxes in any form. For example, during Senate debate on the recent transportation assistance act, Mack Mattingly, the first popularly elected Republican

123. The critical vote came on adoption of the rule (H. Res. 620) permitting floor consideration of the bill. *Congressional Quarterly Weekly Report*, vol. 40 (December 11, 1982), pp. 3016–17.

124. Conservatives like Smith and liberals like Studds joined forces against H. Res. 620. In the 56–34 final Senate vote on H.R. 6211 (the transportation assistance act), which came on December 20, 1982, Sarbanes and Helms were among the strange bedfellows opposing the bill. *Congressional Quarterly Weekly Report*, vol. 40 (December 25, 1982), p. 3125. The ADA ratings shown are those for 1982, as reported in the *Christian Science Monitor*, October 27, 1982.

senator from Georgia, declared, "I am not sure there is ever an appropriate time to raise taxes short of war or some other overwhelming national need."[125] In the conservative view, highly visible, blunt, and effective forms of taxation seem to be particularly nettlesome. Granted, in 1982 a sufficient number of Republicans grew less dogmatic and helped squeeze the nickel gas tax through Congress, along with some other tax increases. Apprehension over mounting budget deficits, exacerbated by the recession-wracked economy at the time, brought a pause to their tax revolt. But an economic recovery gathering momentum in 1983 cast doubt on whether this new consent for "revenue enhancement" would continue or ebb. Realistically, Republicans as well as Democrats find it hard to duck the need for more money to stanch the government's persisting torrent of red ink. Whether the conservatives are prepared to be serious about making a meaningful downpayment against projected deficits, however, remains to be seen.

Apart from the high visibility of gasoline taxation, conservatives will probably remain uncomfortable with this revenue source for another reason: they interpose a restrictive conception of the national government's role vis-à-vis the states. According to Senator Donald L. Nickles, Republican of Oklahoma, the higher federal gasoline tax proposed in 1982 "takes away from the States their right to have control over their own excise taxes."[126]

The Liberal View

The creed on the Left is just as clear-cut: sales taxation on a widely used commodity is wrong. Uppermost in the liberal view is an ideal model of government tax policy: taxes should rise progressively with ability to pay. As the tax system has evolved, the prime sources of federal revenue—taxes on individual-earned income, wealth, corporate income, and payrolls—hardly approximate this standard admirably. But that doesn't deter most liberals from ruling out substitutes. Indeed, the less progressive the system's personal income, payroll, and estate taxes become, the more strongly some Democrats criticize excise tax alternatives. To Senator Donald W. Riegle of Michigan, for instance, the $0.05 gas levy of 1983 was doubly "unfair and unwise" in the wake of the 1981 tax act: "the Government will be extracting the gas tax with one

125. *Congressional Record*, daily edition (December 23, 1982), pp. S16062, S16063.
126. Ibid., p. S16045.

hand from low- and middle-income people, senior citizens, and others of modest circumstances, while, in mid-1983, the Government will be distributing a large tax cut to individuals of high income levels who neither deserve nor need this large personal tax cut."[127]

The hope that somehow, someday, the federal tax system can be purified captivates liberal Democrats. Although the Democrats in 1982–83 saw a need for more government revenue, most wanted to start obtaining it primarily by capping the third year of the Reagan tax reduction, rather than by inventing any additional modes of taxation. For once, many liberals did vote in favor of the last gas tax increase, but mostly because the bill was portrayed fortuitously as a chance to do something about the unacceptable unemployment rate in the fall of 1982.

Large increases in the federal automotive fuel tax cannot germinate easily in this ideological landscape. On one side, those who seek to shrink the public sector, or at least to transfer more of it from the national to the local level, prefer to avoid, if possible, a major new fount of federal funds. On the opposite side, those eager to fill the federal fisc with revenues collected equitably pursue their own elusive grail—to purge the tax code of loopholes and preferences for the rich—rather than make, in their opinion, a regressive system worse by fortifying it with a large energy consumption tax. Thus far, pragmatists caught in between these positions have not gained the upper hand. That they managed to snatch a minor victory from the jaws of defeat in late 1982 does not mean that a new ethos had dawned, only that under special conditions, modest deviations can occur.

Conclusions

If an argument can be made that some kind of energy tax is warranted to brace current price pressures, heavier taxation of automotive fuel ought to be considered seriously. The case for a higher gasoline tax is stronger than the much-discussed alternative of reerecting an oil tariff. Yet politically, a gasoline tax is the toughest of all energy conservation measures for American society to accept—tougher than crude-oil deregulation, natural gas de-

---

127. *Congressional Record*, daily edition (December 21, 1982), pp. S15896, S15897. Accordingly, during Senate debate on the transportation assistance act, Riegle proposed an amendment that would have exempted families earning $10,000 or less a year from the gasoline tax. Riegle's amendment was killed on a 50 to 42 vote. Interestingly, Republican senators voted 47 to 4 against it, but Democrats came down 38 to 3 in favor. *Congressional Quarterly Weekly Report*, vol. 40 (December 25, 1982), p. 3124.

control, or even new electric rates reflecting replacement costs. For better or worse, in this respect U.S. fuel-pricing policy will continue to stand alone among the major industrialized countries.

The futility of proposing major increases in gasoline taxes, and, at least until 1982, even of proposing minor ones, is harder to elucidate than the popular commentary on the topic might suggest. It seems likely, for instance, that organized interests inimical to higher fuel taxes reign more widely in the United States than in Western Europe or Japan. Also, nowhere is automobile ownership as widespread as in the United States—doubtless increasing the American electorate's affection for cheap gasoline and aggravating the animus toward any taxes that make gasoline more expensive.

Nevertheless, public opinion surveys in such countries as Britain and France, where automobiles are now omnipresent as well, offer no evidence that proposed increases in gasoline excise taxes go down much better with these Europeans. Maybe the American people harbor an especially intense intolerance of gasoline taxation. But if public opinion is the sole force setting comparative tax rates, it would have to follow that this intolerance is about 750 to 1,100 percent more intense in the United States than in Britain and France (roughly the difference in the levels of motor fuel levies between the United States and the two European counterparts in 1980). A discrepancy that great would be exceedingly mysterious—unless, of course, Americans believed their usage of gasoline to be inelastic, in which case stiffer tax rates might seem especially painful to absorb. But available domestic data do not appear to support that thesis. Rather, the data show that U.S. motorists acknowledge considerable leeway for reducing demand.

Up to a point, resistance to motor fuel taxes varies geographically. The lower a state's level of urbanization, the greater the per capita costs of such taxes, and hence, the more stubbornly the public opposes them. But congressional voting decisions only partly reflect this fact; urban representatives commonly close ranks with rural representatives against gasoline tax legislation.

Nor do the fortunes of gasoline tax bills depend primarily on the acuity or the political virtuosity of their authors. Several initiatives during the past decade were badly arranged, ill-suited to the rigors of steering controversial innovations through governmental bodies as splintered and spiny as the United States Congress was, especially in the 1970s. But one doubts that better leadership in 1975, 1977, or 1980

could have made all the difference between success and failure. Ultimately, a significant rise in the federal gasoline tax, regardless of how it
was polished and promoted, was never an idea whose time had come.

A big barrier to higher taxes on gasoline in the United States is ideological. The core of the issue is this: where gasoline taxation is steep, as
in most of Western Europe, the central justification for it has been the
need to support large, rapidly expanding government sectors. In some
countries, Italy for instance, this source of revenue is among those that
have grown most quickly and reliably. The same rationale for taxing
motor fuel has been missing in the United States, where the scope of
government remains comparatively limited and where the political philosophy of at least one of the country's two ruling parties holds, however
selectively, that the government's role should stay that way. Thus, when
Congress wrestles with gas tax proposals, the dispute is not just about
the unpopular impost; it is about what to do with all the proceeds.

Since 1981 worry over cavernous federal deficits has altered the
picture somewhat. For many policymakers the deficit has refocused attention on revenue requirements, while for others, the size of the deficit
has lent urgency to the task of chipping away at the size of the federal
government. In the fall of 1982, anxiety about deficits helped pull together a rare congressional majority in favor of raising the federal gasoline tax slightly. Substantial increments are unlikely to follow soon,
however. In the first place, budgetary concerns were but one of the
factors that lifted the 1982 legislation past its adversaries; various other
conditions combined momentarily to break the impasse. More basically,
although conservatives (and everybody else) are apprehensive about the
extreme fiscal imbalance foreseen for the later 1980s, too many still
appear to count on renewed economic growth, rather than the possibility
of bold new tax action, to help balance the government's books. A significant faction of opponents of a gas tax consists of inveterate opponents of
any new taxes, under practically any circumstances. These are the orthodox supply siders who, in the words of Representative Jack I. Kemp,
Republican of New York, have chosen not to "worship at the shrine of
the balanced budget,"[128] if the price for narrower deficits is the adoption
of substantial revenue measures. They are also the group whose parliamentary tactics came close to torpedoing the gasoline surtax of 1983.

Meanwhile, a great many liberals, for whom big government is less of

128. *Newsweek* (May 16, 1983), p. 30.

a curse, will continue to question the concept of a gasoline tax from another perspective. From their point of view, revenue infusions are essential to sustain social programs. But equally imperative is that the infusions be generated fairly. No comfort is taken from suggestions that an excise on automotive fuel may be no less fair to "the little guy" than many other elements of the extant tax system, or than some of the other tax plans under consideration. Liberals would reply that such arguments only prove how badly the system needs reform and that systematic reform is the first order of business.

Measured against the basic social goal of the Left—a much more equitable fiscal policy—gasoline taxation appears indisputably regressive. But why does this trouble America's liberal Democrats more than it evidently bothers the socialists, or social democrats, of Europe? No rigorous answer to that riddle can be developed here. The following hypothesis, however, ought to be explored: perhaps European conflicts over society's distribution of wealth tend to be fought, and maybe settled more obviously, on a separate battleground—the field of welfare policy. But in the United States, the Left has felt the need, or the urge, to address welfare issues wherever it can.

Appendix: Logit Analysis of Congressional Voting Patterns

In table 5-2, various determinants of congressional voting on gasoline tax bills are analyzed. As expected, support for the tax bills tends to vary with the level of urbanization among states. The logit coefficients for percent urban are consistently positive and statistically significant in four of the six roll calls modeled. Yet, judging from the comparatively meager explanatory strength of most of the equations, percent urban bears an attenuated relationship to the various votes. In varying degrees, the same holds for the remaining independent variables. Clearly, for instance, most legislators did not divide sharply on the basis of whether state gasoline prices and excises were already high or low; very few of the respective coefficients are significant. Nor did an anticipated inverse relation between per capita consumption of gasoline and support for tax increases show up consistently; four of the coefficients for consumption are negative, but only two of them are significant. Finally, although party affiliation consistently has an effect on gas-tax votes, it displays less predictive power here than in other energy roll calls analyzed elsewhere in this book. (To put the effects of the independent variables in

Table 5-2. Logit Analysis of State Energy Attributes as Determinants of House Votes on Gasoline Tax Bills[a]

Item	H.R. 6860 June 11, 1975 (417 votes)	H.R. 6860 June 11, 1975 (396 votes)	H.R. 8444 Aug. 4, 1977 (421 votes)	H.R. 8444 Aug. 4, 1977 (422 votes)	H.R. 7428[b] June 5, 1980 (369 votes)	H.R. 6211[c] Dec. 6, 1982 (391 votes)
Percent urban	0.0427* (3.626)	0.0218* (2.652)	0.0063 (0.805)	0.0310* (2.534)	0.0352 (1.803)	0.0210* (2.737)
Gasoline consumption per capita	0.7547 (0.448)	-3.6912* (2.295)	-0.0171 (0.296)	0.2946 (0.156)	-0.0023 (0.743)	-0.0107* (4.610)
Average retail price of gasoline	-0.0007 (0.877)	-0.0021* (2.833)	0.1956* (2.714)	0.1505 (1.661)	0.0113 (0.113)	0.0002 (0.286)
State gasoline sales tax	-0.0444* (2.519)	-0.0249 (1.657)	-0.0062 (0.434)	-0.0054 (0.281)	-13.4114 (0.634)	-0.0048 (0.628)
Party affiliation	2.1400* (4.429)	2.6065* (8.610)	2.2248* (5.023)	2.7620* (3.764)	47.4922 (0.000)	1.4156* (5.904)
Chi-squared	49.82	124.70	48.17	49.78	40.92	95.10

Sources: *House and Senate votes: Congressional Quarterly Weekly Report*, vol. 33 (June 11, 1975), pp. 1262–63; vol. 35 (August 6, 1977), pp. 1690–91; vol. 38 (June 7, 1980), pp. 1604–05; vol. 40 (December 11, 1982), pp. 3016–17. *Percent urban:* 1970 U.S. Census of Population, combining central city and suburban percentages by state, Michael Barone, Grant Ujifusa, and Douglas Mathews, *The Almanac of American Politics, 1976* (E. P. Dutton and Company, 1975); 1980 U.S. Census of Population, Michael Barone and Grant Ujifusa, *The Almanac of American Politics, 1982* (Washington, D.C.: Barone and Company, 1982); U.S. Bureau of the Census, *Statistical Abstract of the United States, 1981* (Government Printing Office, 1981), p. 12 (for the 1980 roll call); *gasoline consumption:* gallons sold 1975 and 1980, American Petroleum Institute, *Basic Petroleum Data Book*, vol. 2 (Washington, D.C.: American Petroleum Institute, 1982), table 9a; *gasoline prices:* Retail prices in 1975 and 1977, U.S. Department of Energy, Energy Information Administration, *State Energy Fuel Prices by Major Economic Sector from 1960 through 1977* (Washington, D.C.: DOE, 1979), pp. 93–94; and *state sales taxes:* U.S. Department of Energy, *State Energy Fuel Prices*, table C-2, p. 131.

*p < .05.

a. Upper figures are the estimated logit coefficients. Figures in parentheses are t-statistics. Data for the first four independent variables in the equations are aggregated by states. The fifth, party, is specified: 1 = Democrat; 0 = Republican. The dichotomous dependent variables are specified: 1 = a vote for a federal gasoline tax increase; 0 = a vote against a federal gasoline tax increase.

b. The vote here was on whether to override President Carter's veto of a congressional resolution disallowing the imposition of an oil-import fee.

c. The decisive vote in this case was on adoption of the rule (H. Res. 620) providing for floor consideration of the bill.

table 5-2 in perspective, compare the generally low chi-squared levels in the table with the much higher ones tabulated for the House roll calls analyzed in chapters 2 and 3.)[129]

129. Unlike the deregulation roll calls discussed in chapters 2 and 3, I have not reported percentages of votes correctly predicted for each of the models in table 5-2. To present such percentages here, where most of the tallies were extremely lopsided, would leave the thoroughly misleading impression that the various equations explain a very large proportion of overall votes. In fact, their estimates apply to small margins of votes. In this case, relative goodness of fit is measured more appropriately by a comparison of the chi-squared statistics.

CHAPTER SIX

Conclusion

THE PRIMACY of conservation in brightening America's energy future is no longer debatable, if it ever really was. Agreement on the general proposition is expressed routinely in the nation's political rhetoric. Crowning a decade in which Americans became conscious of energy waste, the Democratic party platform in 1980 proclaimed the efficient use of energy to be of "highest priority." Not to be outdone, Republican planks affirmed that "we must strive to maximize conservation."[1] Even discounting the facility with which avowals to maximize or to assign highest priority are tossed around in political oratory, this seemed like strong language, underscoring an apparent commitment to conservation as a vital, if not dominant, goal of national energy policy.

But the gulf between appearance and substance remained wide. Entering the 1980s, Americans had been served a full plate of new federal programs aimed at saving scarce fuels, yet on it were only some of the essentials needed to achieve maximum energy efficiency. The programmatic menu was long on regulatory standards, subsidies, advisory services, and standby plans, yet relatively short on basic pricing reforms. Although the remaining restraints on domestic crude oil prices were lifted in 1981 (an important energy-saving step, but one that came too late to help soften the disastrous second oil shock in 1979),[2] attempts to pry off controls on natural gas faltered in 1977 and again in 1983. De-

1. *Congressional Quarterly Almanac*, vol. 36 (1980), pp. 74-B, 110-B.
2. The process of decontrol began in June 1979 and, as noted earlier, achieved an appreciable reduction in the price differential between U.S. domestic and international crude oil acquisition costs by late 1980. Still, if decontrol had commenced five years earlier, U.S. oil imports would probably have been trimmed further by the end of the 1970s. Greater slack in the world oil market on the eve of the Iranian shutdown might have diminished its impact.

spite the remedial federal legislation enacted in 1978, outmoded utility rate structures continued to misprice electricity in many states. And in automotive transportation, where U.S. consumption of fuel seemed singularly excessive, price incentives to promote conservation were still applied too sparingly: policy has consisted of belated price deregulation, supplemented by a slight federal surtax on gasoline. In short, if by 1980 the political system had reached consensus on the need to conserve energy, it had just begun to implement the most effective methods.

Four Paradigms

The lag has some basis in four political facts of life that are, by now, familiar to all observers of the process of energy policymaking in the United States. Policies that pursue conservation by price lack widespread public support. They are also opposed by narrow economic interests. Local and regional dissension is often involved. Exceptional leadership is required to manage policymaking institutions beset by these and other pressures.

The Role of Interest Groups

Because some federal regulation of business serves the interests of the regulated industries, or of influential firms therein, it is sometimes assumed that this was true with the price-regulating policies that were devised for oil and natural gas in the 1970s. According to this interpretation, subsectors of the oil industry—most notably, petroleum product marketers and small refineries—were the engine propelling the 1975 Energy Policy and Conservation Act, which set price restrictions on every barrel of domestically produced oil. In the natural gas industry, the Natural Gas Policy Act of 1978 (NGPA) codified two dozen different price schedules for production, placing some gas in high categories and some in low ones. Some of the most vociferous critics at the time charged that the real winners in this complicated scheme were the big oil companies and that the hidden hand behind the legislation was theirs.

Such theories lack evidence. The regulatory framework for natural gas that remains in force today was not what the important producing firms, nor virtually any other part of the gas industry, had demanded in 1977–78. Indeed, the Natural Gas Policy Act's pricing apparatus, featuring indefinite controls on a large volume of gas, was adopted in place of much broader deregulation proposals backed uniformly by the industry and by a wide coalition of free-market adherents. Subsequently, the NGPA acquired a clientele that defended the statute against efforts to repeal or amend it to accelerate full decontrol. Disunity in the industry was partly responsible for the collapse of these efforts in 1983, despite a more conservative Congress than the one seated in 1978 and an administration ideologically dedicated to a market solution. To say that the natural gas bill created a set of vested interests, however, is not to conclude, *cui bono*, that these same interests wrote the law. In any event, the law's clients have never included the major oil and gas producers; ever since 1978, they have fought a losing battle to obtain new legislation. In sum, during 1977–78, after the issue was debated thoroughly, Congress could have chosen not to procrastinate with the decontrol of natural gas. The decision to spin another regulatory web instead was not inspired by lobbyists from any quarter of the oil and gas industry.

Industry groups played a different role in the development of federally managed petroleum prices. Independent refiners and fuel distributors in particular were a driving force in early congressional moves to legislate statutory price and allocation rules. But their influence was stronger on the Emergency Petroleum Allocation Act of 1973 (EPAA) than it was on the Energy Policy and Conservation Act of 1975 (EPCA), the law that established a much more comprehensive, and wasteful, regulatory program. The fashioning of the Energy Policy and Conservation Act cannot be regarded simply as a larger-scale replay of the successful lobbying campaign mounted by the EPAA's various patrons two years earlier. Even the political strength of the numerous "tin can" refineries, perhaps the best example of an interest group that reaped direct benefits from the regulatory setup, seemed reduced. When the EPCA came to a vote in Congress, the states in which most of the small refineries were situated voted against it.

Some business interests resist novel utility rates and oppose the imposition of energy taxes, such as ones that would significantly boost the retail price of gasoline. Industrial purchasers of electricity, and some electric companies, have a stake in traditional rate designs: bulk users profit from volume discounts and may threaten to vote with their feet if local regulators try to invert declining block tariffs. Utilities, in the business of selling electric power, are often reluctant to experiment with pricing arrangements that may constrict consumption or that might drive off important customers. The foes of major gasoline tax proposals seem even more powerful. Not only are they wide ranging; what is more important, they are largely unopposed.

Yet delays in policy innovation affecting electricity rates cannot be traced to the activities of business lobbies alone. Credible economic blackmail may hinder electric rate reform in a handful of states anxious to retain (or attract) a footloose industrial base with firms highly sensitive to local utility charges. But in most states, the industrial employers who are given to bluffing by threats to relocate are more numerous than those that would actually migrate in search of greener pastures. In locational decisions, electric rates are only one, usually small, factor among many in a complex equation. Likewise, every state public service commission that cites the risk of industrial flight is not necessarily genuinely intimidated by the prospect. Some seem to allude to it only as a pretext for maintaining conservative rate policies. Nor are utility companies invariably the guardians of such policies. Some important rate cases, in which principles of marginal-cost pricing were at least partially implemented, have had the strong support of the utilities involved.

Even when it comes to legislating a major national excise tax on automotive fuel, narrow "veto groups" are not the only obstacles, nor necessarily the main ones. Anyone viewing the often huge congressional majorities that defeat this energy-conserving tax would be hard pressed to account for them by plumbing the pattern of campaign contributions from political action committees or by studying any other form of lobbying activity by mobilized opponents. Further, anyone trying to fit interest group models to the politics of this issue cannot ignore the fact that the American political system has no monopoly on groups opposed to higher motor fuel taxes; other advanced pluralistic polities, with much steeper fees at the gas pump, know them too.

These observations are not meant to provide an exhaustive chronicle of the involvement of interest groups in the formation of American energy conservation policies. I have concentrated on those commercial interests about which theories or allegations of influence prevail. There are also nonbusiness lobbies engaged in the various disputes, most obviously, the consumer organizations. Even a detailed exploration of their participation, however, would not weaken the thrust of my argument. Organized pressure groups are not the central barriers to efficient energy pricing.

Much government energy policy purports to protect American consumers from exorbitant fuel costs. But it has tended to do so with or without the imprimatur of formal consumer-oriented lobbies.[3] I know of

3. See John E. Chubb, *Interest Groups and the Bureaucracy: The Politics of Energy*

no serious explanation of the past decade's oil regulations or of the recurring energy tax debates that points to the specific exertions of the Citizen/Labor Energy Coalition, the Consumer Federation of America, Energy Action, or any other consumer advocacy association. In 1978 consumer representatives were only frustrated bystanders watching a congressional conference committee finally unwrap the compromise on natural gas pricing. Even though the law postponed decontrol and included other putative safeguards for residential gas users, it also allowed higher prices for some supplies, a provision that drew angry denunciations from most consumer spokesmen.

By and large, though, organizations claiming to represent average energy consumers are more than spectators; usually they weigh in actively to uphold the regulatory status quo. The best recent example is the massive grass-roots drive led by the Citizen/Labor Energy Coalition against the Reagan administration's attempt to overturn the Natural Gas Policy Act. The coalition's formative influence on the NGPA had been trivial in 1978, but the pressure it brought against the Reagan initiative in 1983 helped ensure that the 1978 legislation would remain intact. Occasionally, however, organized consumers have been a force for change. For all its inconsistencies, the movement for electric rate reform, and for federal standards to further the process, gathered what momentum it did during the 1970s with the help of consumer advocates.

The record of flawed energy pricing cannot be reduced to simple accounts of obstructionism by consumer groups any better than to sinister narratives about predatory oil or gas producers, parasitic refiners, or stubborn utilities.

The Role of Public Opinion

In the conventional wisdom on energy politics, vigorous speculation about the supremacy of special interests appears alongside an equally common, but quite different, argument: that policymakers largely bow to prevailing public preferences. Ultimately, the energy-saving modes available to any democratic society are bounded by what citizens will accept. In the United States, attitudes are supposedly colored by encrusted patterns of prodigal energy usage, owing in large part to the historic abundance of natural resources. In such a culture, the public sets rigid limits on conservation: everybody applauds the goal as long as it

(Stanford University Press, 1983), pp. 167–72.

requires no sacrifice. Politicians supposedly share this frame of mind. Attuned to the electorate, political leaders shy away from measures that lean on the price system to slim down demand.

This formulation, in which stalemated price policies amount to little more than a reflex by election-conscious officials in response to the public's wish for easy energy, is an oversimplification. Issues such as the deregulation of natural gas do not boil down to a simple choice between burdening voters, by presenting them with higher energy prices in the marketplace, and ensuring them relative comfort, by offering them low-cost fuel, courtesy of government regulators. The final costs borne by consumers under the debated alternatives are not easily predicted and depend importantly on one's time horizon. If, for example, restrictions on the price of domestic crude oil had been phased out starting in 1975 rather than four years later, the average price of oil might have lurched upward at first, but then followed a smoother track later on. Similarly, if the lids on natural gas had come off in 1977, the initial price spike would have been sharper, but increases thereafter might well have been less jagged. Therefore, to learn that people prefer benefits to burdens is of limited help to elected representatives who need to know not only what the electorate wants, but precisely what to do about its wants. If Congress equivocates—mandating natural gas decontrol, but only half-way, and accepting oil decontrol, but belatedly—it is partly because most politicians, when in doubt, will choose to deflect or defer immediate costs. But many members of Congress also realize that the collective desire for affordable energy, although keen, provides no solid standard on which to base policy.

Further, while decisionmakers come under public pressure to restrain fuel bills, they are also made aware that chronic shortages are intolerable. They receive complaints when prices go up, but they also hear gripes if supplies diminish. In 1975, when Congress repeatedly rejected President Ford's plans for oil decontrol, no one could be sure that this was definitely what a majority of Americans preferred. Polls revealed that majorities objected to deregulation if its main consequence was higher prices, but that they approved of it if the likely result was a larger oil supply. When samples were told that the probable outcome would be a little of both—fewer shortages but higher prices—opinion was fairly bifurcated between those who favored continued price controls and those who either disagreed or were undecided.

Similar complications could be detected in popular sentiment on the decontrol of natural gas, at least before 1982. Even though gas is more commonly used for an essential purpose (heating) and its cost is a matter of extreme concern to consumers, national surveys during the crucial debate of 1977 did not always find that most people opposed deregulation. Again, much seemed to depend on whether citizens were led to believe that deregulation would imply increased availability or only painful price hikes. Congress was unable to agree on the meaning of the message. The House of Representatives took it to signify one thing, the Senate another. In the end, neither side was convinced that the final compromise managed to strike a proper balance between the public's dual demands. Although the Natural Gas Policy Act was supposed to offer the best of both worlds, by stabilizing prices and simultaneously creating incentives to boost production, few legislators were confident that this feat could be performed. Even fewer felt that the compromise represented a popular mandate. The formula was flogged into law despite pervasive doubts and reservations.

It is easier to notice a clear congruence between policy and public opinion when one examines the problem of gasoline taxation. The same intricacies that characterize attitudes on deregulation do not carry over. Popular opposition to a major federal tax on gasoline is unequivocal and therefore respected assiduously by Congress. Yet the congressional response is motivated by more than a uniquely American sensitivity to the cost of gasoline or intolerance toward constraints on freewheeling use of this fuel.

No aspect of America's energy price system is more peculiar, in comparison with other industrial countries, than the absence of a substantial national sales tax on gasoline. It is increasingly hard to believe, however, that the retail price of gasoline is held down in the United States and kept high elsewhere because Americans are fond of economical automotive fuel while everybody else is not. The United States is a nation of automobile owners; thus the societal preference for low-taxed motor fuel is especially broad. But the gap between American and European gasoline excise rates has remained so wide that one suspects there are other pieces to the puzzle. With the phenomenal growth of automobile ownership throughout Western Europe and Japan, opinion surveys abroad also suggest scant citizen support for ever-increasing petrol levies. It is often argued that U.S. motorists can make a special claim for cheap fuel: Americans are more dependent on cars. Even so, when polled, majorities in the United States have recognized that gasoline consumption can be moderated, and not just through improved vehicle mileage-economy, but also by significant reductions in automotive travel. The data do not indicate that most drivers see such moderation as a hardship. What seems to bother people is not just the privation, but also the method inducing it: a tax instead of some other rationing device.

In the muddy realm of electricity ratemaking, most utility customers say that their bills wind up being too high. Consumers call on government to exert more control over what providers charge. Less regulation is deemed out of the question in this sphere; scarcely anyone wonders whether, by underpricing electricity, regulatory bureaucracies might someday bring power outages, much as price controls aggravated gasoline and natural gas deficits. Though consumers appear to concede that demand for gasoline reacts flexibly to price, they seem to acknowledge less elasticity for electric power. Undeniably such attitudes constrain opportunities to conserve energy by redesigning rate schedules. Few states are able to speed toward a comprehensive rearrangement of prices that would distribute widely, among households as well as industrial and commercial customer classes, the true replacement costs of generating power.

But people's antipathy toward rate policies that might force small customers as well as large ones to pay the incremental cost of electricity is grounded in something besides material self-interest: as with gasoline excise taxation, but for a somewhat different reason, the public considers such price structures unfair. The prevalent impression that electric utilities, like oil companies, have collected unreasonable profits is at the heart of the problem. Without the working equivalent of a windfall tax on utility companies, authentic experimentation with marginal-cost pricing for all classes of users would often augment those profits. The prospect of this income transfer, not just the fact that higher charges would be a nuisance to ratepayers, keeps utility regulators from scrapping their customary rate-fixing practices.

In sum, to understand how diffuse interests as well as narrowly gauged ones relate to energy-pricing decisions, clichés must be avoided. The tendency is to assume that efficient approaches are precluded by a habitual, and faintly freakish, American impatience with policies that could crimp a fast and loose energy lifestyle. Americans do have a strong preference for energy bargains. But they are hardly alone in that respect, nor are they peculiarly prone to deny, ostrichlike, that it is necessary and possible to adjust to a world in which the energy bargain basement is running bare. Consequently, one should doubt that in every important instance policymakers in the United States are uniquely pressured by public opinion—hence by electoral imperatives—to coddle consumers by doctoring prices. If, owing to electoral pressures, the U.S. government had sought chiefly to pamper consumers by suppressing prices, how could congressional actions, such as the gasoline surtax of 1983, the repeal of percentage depletion in 1975, or the proposal for a crude oil equalization tax in 1977, have occurred? All these measures were known to increase the cost of fuel to consumers. The first two became law, while the equalization tax, which would have hoisted oil retail rates to world levels, passed the House of Representatives, in which proconsumer Democrats were indisputably the ruling majority.[4]

Even though rising energy costs of the 1970s were a novelty, and most Americans yearned for the good old days of steadier prices, the policy implications were never obvious. Many analysts have believed, with good reason, that the public's interest is not served by clamping controls on prices. Even in the complex case of electricity, the goal of rate stabilization need not entail perforce a vote of confidence for the existing regulatory regime. Traditional ratemaking has hardly provided a guarantee against mounting average utility charges. On the contrary, failure to reorganize the system could beget worse price spirals, as power companies scrounge for revenue, if not to finance more unnecessary expansions, then to cover the increasing operating costs of irregular utilization of capacity. In part, fuel price controls and conventional electric rate regulation have proven controversial because it has never been clear that these mechanisms offer an effective solution, much less the sole solution, to the public's yen for price stability. Because people are concerned with the availability of energy as well as its cost, the inexact science of matching policy to public preferences becomes even shakier.

What consistently slips into the dialogue about energy pricing is not only a popular desire for cheap fuel, but also a more unusual combination of collective beliefs. Prominent among them is distrust of the energy industry.[5] Domestic energy suppliers, be they oil companies,

4. There were two reasons for the passage of the crude oil equalization tax by the House. One was the early willingness to follow the newly inaugurated president, a cooperative spirit that drove most of the Carter National Energy Plan through the lower chamber in the summer of 1977. The other was that the tax was perceived to be a "fair" kind of price increase, because producers would not see profits from the higher prices. Interview with Nancy Mathews, majority staff, House Committee on Energy and Commerce, Washington, D.C., September 25, 1981.

5. During the 1979 oil crisis, for example, the oil companies were again prime targets

natural gas producers, or electric utilities, are forever suspected of price gouging. When they raise prices, more than consumer discomfort is at issue; the social legitimacy of the increases is in doubt. This propensity to perceive higher energy prices as a loss of the public's income to private profiteers is less marked in other cultures in which indigenous primary energy-producing sectors have a larger publicly owned component or are insignificant economically. But in the United States another, even more basic outlook complicates matters: paradoxically, the gigantic industry, in which Americans vest so little trust, is not fair game for nationalization or divestiture. The political agenda is influenced by a public perpetually agitated over energy rip-offs and, at the same time, unwilling to sanction steps that, drawbacks aside, could remove this apparent irritant once and for all. (Presumably, an advantage, probably the only advantage, of shifting energy corporations from private to public domains is that, by definition, it settles the question of "unearned" private profits.)[6]

For many politicians, therefore, recourse to a form of partial government tutelage, public regulation of private markets, befits this attitude. Others disagree, citing evidence that citizens seem more receptive to decontrol if it promises a prodigious energy supply. But whether this additional twist in popular tastes, high hopes for supply elasticity, provides the political impetus for pricing reform is far from certain. Arguably, it has only abetted a tendency to bog down discussion on how energy price and production levels interrelate, instead of airing the broader question of whether field-price and retail-rate regulations are energy efficient.

The Role of Localism

Although public attitudes at the national level are often too abstract or inconsistent to give explicit direction to conservation strategies, local preferences can have a more direct bearing. There is nothing ambiguous, for instance, about the antagonism of rural areas toward major federal

---

of suspicion by the American public. The Europeans, however, shrugged their shoulders. Richard E. Bissell, "The West in Concert: A Very Complex Score," in *Oil Diplomacy: The Atlantic Nations in the Oil Crisis of 1978–79* (Philadelphia: Foreign Policy Research Institute, 1980), p. 81.

6. See Aaron Wildavsky and Ellen Tenenbaum, *The Politics of Mistrust: Estimating American Oil and Gas Resources* (Beverly Hills, Calif.: Sage Publications, 1981), pp. 314–17.

gasoline tax proposals. In Congress, these bills founder partly because of the ability of rural states to compose a large opposition bloc.

Movement toward energy-sensitive utility rates is another process that depends importantly on local circumstances. Setting electric rates at full marginal cost is least feasible where the gap between existing and projected capacity costs is so great that switching from old (average-cost-based) techniques to new (incrementally based) ones could suddenly triple or quadruple electric bills. If the nation has lacked an effective federal policy to modernize electricity price structures, part of the reason is that key congressional committees dealing with the question have been ruled by representatives from states most leery of the economic and political hazards.

To an important degree, the political constituency underpinning oil and natural gas price controls has also been regionally centered: the non-producing Northeast and Midwest, into which these fuels have to be imported or transported at extra expense to end users, have always delivered the most votes against deregulation.

If fuel-conserving price policies often seem more contentious in the United States than in other societies, it is partly because America's regional diversity—in demography, resource endowments, and energy costs—adds another level of conflict: debate about the sectional distribution of wealth.

The clash of local interests is salient in energy price disputes, but it is not the whole sum and substance of them. Roll call votes in Congress constitute a reasonably convenient data base from which to measure the political effects of localism. In the various congressional showdowns reviewed in this book, the way that legislators positioned themselves on energy-pricing options usually bore a relation to conditions back home. Thus resistance to gasoline tax bills has varied somewhat with a state's degree of urbanization. Interest in regulating natural gas was linked with local net consumption of that fuel. Support for ceilings on petroleum prices differed importantly depending on whether a state consumed more oil than it produced, as well as on immediate energy price levels. But overall these and other geographic factors were not always vigorous predictors of how the members of Congress voted.

The reasons for this are complex. There are states, even entire regions, whose material interests in particular energy-pricing issues are so well defined that native policy lines can be marked out and followed with considerable consistency. Large parts of the country, however, have not shown such clarity of political purpose. The local balance sheets of perceived costs and benefits posed by policy choices are often fuzzy. In these areas politicians do not just act on instructions from constituents; they are forced to make judgments. The upshot is that legislative outcomes often amount to more than a summation of parochial pressures. Highly illustrative was the episode that has been widely interpreted, quite dubiously, as first and foremost an interregional fight: the natural gas battle of 1977–78. Although most representatives from the Northeast and Midwest fell in with the proregulation camp, in these regions and virtually everywhere else except the Southwest, many delegations were disunified. They were torn between differing assessments of whether market pricing could reduce the frequency of industrial gas interruptions and by it stem an exodus of industry to areas with reliable gas supplies, as well as combat higher utility passthroughs of fixed costs to residential gas users.

National attitudes do overshadow local concerns on some issues. Public discussion of gasoline taxation has this character. The congressional coalitions it generates are knitted together by more than favor trading between diverse geographic blocs (rural-urban, Western-Eastern, and the like). Contempt for the concept of a gas tax is a mass phenomenon, even though its intensity may vary according to local contexts.

Finally, while local constituents tug on the loyalties of lawmakers, so do party ties and even more basically, ideological leanings. An analysis of congressional roll calls shows that partisanship sometimes swamps the statistical relationships between voting behavior and local variables. In general, to find out why members of Congress vote as they do on the mainstays of a national energy conservation policy, like the deregulation of oil prices in 1975 and the decontrol of natural gas prices in 1977, it is useful to be familiar with the members' home states: local demographic profiles, levels of fossil fuel production and utilization, and energy price conditions facing users can be highly salient. But frequently it is still more important to know each congressman's "politics," whether he or she happens to be a Democrat or a Republican, or better, whether he or she is politically liberal, conservative, or something in between.[7]

7. The "politics" of congressmen, of course, are partly determined by electoral constituencies. Members of Congress vote as Democrats or Republicans (liberals or conservatives) in part because their districts generally, and their reelection constituencies specifically, tend to favor one party, or ideological direction, or the other. A congressman's party identification, or a standard measure of his or her ideological voting behavior (ADA ratings, for example), provides no sure guide to his or her personal political beliefs. See Richard T.

The Role of Policy Management

Wasteful energy pricing is just one of several domestic policy predicaments to have festered in recent decades. During the 1970s, energy was the headline-grabbing issue on which the U.S. government seemed to "drift, dawdle and debate forever" (as one of the period's beleaguered presidents lamented). But at least until the mid-1960s, similar phrases had characterized the progress on civil rights for blacks and the politics of federal health insurance for the elderly. Today those words could fairly describe the latest governmental quagmire: structural budget deficits and the fiscal woes of the nation's principal entitlement programs. Inertia on other fronts like these might suggest that what afflicts policymaking for energy conservation is really a larger pathology: periodic institutional immobilism.

SYSTEMIC COMPLEXITY. The American system is unique in the extent to which it disperses power. Constitutional checks and balances partition authority not only among the federal branches but also within them, and between the national government and the states. In the not-too-distant past centripetal forces, such as a stronger pair of political parties, a more centralized congressional committee structure, and a longer span of relatively solid presidencies, helped bridge the separation of powers and provided mechanisms for policy integration. But the decline of these integrating institutions distinguishes the modern political order. Longer spells of divided government have attended the erosion of parties in the electorate, as voters pay less attention to party labels and cast fewer straight tickets for the triad of national elective offices. The weakening of the committee hierarchies, following the 1974–76 reorganization in the House of Representatives, which stripped power from standing committee chairmen and bestowed more of it on a multitude of subcommittees, has deepened problems of legislative coordination and control.

Carson and Joe A. Oppenheimer, "A Method of Estimating the Personal Ideology of Political Representatives," *American Political Science Review*, vol. 78 (March 1984), pp. 163–78. But the question of whether the political convictions of members should be conceptualized as purely personal, constituent-inspired, or a combination of both, is not of central concern here. The more pertinent distinction is whether legislators acted exclusively as agents for parochial material interests, or often weighed and interpreted such interests through the perspective of broader partisan values, however derived. The thesis in this book is that the second process was often operating (except for delegates from a handful of major energy-producing states).

Last, a procession of shaken presidencies has sapped the system of a final catalyst, strong executive leadership.

To many political scientists, this last deficiency is especially troublesome. Just as policy paralysis can be aggravated by presidential incompetence, it can be alleviated by presidential skill. Energy policy is no exception. To advance potent incentives for energy conservation, greater political aplomb and agility are needed than some recent presidents have demonstrated. Aborted tenure in office (since 1960 no occupant of the Oval Office has yet managed to serve two full terms) has made the task more difficult. Complicated assignments, which may take longer than the three years between inauguration and the next presidential election year, may never be completed. Scandals and assassins' bullets have hurt the institution and have obviously contributed to the frequency of one-term administrations. But a more fundamental source of instability rests in the way presidential candidates are selected.

The selection procedure since 1968 has pushed most contenders into a quadrennial marathon: the long trail of primaries and caucuses. Since almost any aspirant sees a chance to win in this political crapshoot (provided he can field an efficient grass-roots organization in about forty states and can take the time to campaign indefatigably for at least a year or two), the temptation is great to contest an incumbent's renomination. (Ronald Reagan is the first incumbent president in twenty years who has had no primary challenge.) Thus, much of a president's initial time in office is spent skirting controversies that imaginable adversaries could exploit in future primary contests, or worse, desperately fighting off real challenges, as was true of two of the last three presidents. Finally, while the whole affair can overburden an experienced and qualified chief executive, it can also send to the White House a novice, less prepared to lead. James L. Sundquist has described the process and its perils.

There is no screening mechanism. A party's nominee for president now is someone who has been able to devote enough time to shaking hands in the early primary and caucus states and forming an effective get-out-the-vote organization there. . . . He may be an outsider to the national political process. . . . He may be a neophyte in dealing with complex issues of foreign relations and the domestic economy. He may be in no sense the natural leader of large and crucial elements in his own party. If elected, he may be a stranger to the people in Congress with whom he has to work, and he may have little sense of how to get along with them.[8]

8. James L. Sundquist, "Congress, the President, and the Crisis of Competence in Government," in Laurence C. Dodd and Bruce I. Oppenheimer, eds., *Congress Reconsidered*, 2d

As has been shown throughout this book, impoverished political leadership sometimes seemed to impair the formulation of effective energy-saving policies. During Jimmy Carter's presidency, for instance, the die was cast on natural gas pricing. Carter was the type of president that Sundquist described—"an outsider to the national political process" and "a stranger to the people in Congress." His administration's handling of the natural gas issue suffered from those handicaps and from attempts to overcompensate for them.

When oil deregulation should have commenced, in 1975, the tremors of Watergate were still resonating. Nixon's resignation had placed an unelected president in power. Ford confronted a mutinous Congress in which the political opposition held large majorities. And as a presidential candidate, he faced the prospect of a debilitating fight for his party's nomination. This was tough terrain on which to move a market solution to oil pricing. When the going got rough, Ford backed down.

Although the Ninety-fourth Congress succeeded in sinking the Ford administration's energy program, that Congress failed to enact an efficient pricing program of its own. The only congressionally initiated measure to embody the principle of conservation by price, a gasoline tax bill fashioned by the newly overhauled House Ways and Means Committee, fell far short of passage. Its prime sponsor, the panel's chairman, Albert C. Ullman, Democrat of Oregon, knew all along that "the toughest thing in the world is voting for a gasoline tax."[9] But his tremulous helmsmanship, buffeted by factionalism in Ways and Means and by committee jealousies over turf, added to the difficulty.

Subsequent proposals for a gasoline excise were also crippled by crises in leadership. The spectacular defeat of Carter's proposed $0.10 fee in 1980, for instance, revealed the depths to which the president's standing in Congress had fallen and exposed the powerlessness of Democratic congressional chiefs to maintain order in the party's ranks.

Three years earlier, the Carter administration had scuffled with the Senate over federal standards in electric rate regulation. On that occasion, executive influence over the legislative process would have been tenuous under the best of circumstances, since the president's proposed standards ran afoul of another institutional snare: responsibility for retail ratemaking lay traditionally with the states. The administration's tack with Congress and the specific treatment it contemplated for the utility industry and for

ed. (Washington, D.C.: CQ Press, 1981), p. 359.
  9. *Washington Post*, April 11, 1985.

state regulatory bodies also heightened political anxieties.

INSTITUTIONAL DISARRAY: HOW CONSEQUENTIAL? It may be tempting to paint the whole checkered history of energy-price reform in the United States as a sequence of institutional disorders and management problems. But there is another side to the story.

Divided party control of the legislative and executive branches did raise the odds against President Ford's winning congressional consent for oil decontrol. Nevertheless, a restoration of market pricing did not require explicit legislative approval; price ceilings could have disappeared automatically upon expiration of the authorizing statute, the Emergency Petroleum Allocation Act.[10] And although the Democratic Congress was ever poised to seek extensions of the act, the president had sufficient support to wield a decisive weapon against these attempts, the executive veto. The Ford administration could have held out for decontrol, even without working majorities in Congress. During the first half of 1975, recognition of this fact came close to giving the White House all the leverage it needed to force congressional acquiescence on a plan for phased deregulation.

Granted, the president's actions in the latter part of 1975, especially the eventual decision to relent and sign the Energy Policy and Conservation Act, are easier to depict as the path of least resistance, followed by a politically vulnerable administration. But even this portrayal needs qualification. The electoral calculus that eventually tipped Ford into signing extended price regulations was hotly debated within the administration. Opponents of the decision warned the president that capitulation on oil pricing could jeopardize his nomination. The immediate threat was Ronald Reagan's candidacy. Market freedom was a rallying cry in Reagan's bid to topple Ford, and the issue of oil regulation gave the challenger's campaign a lift, especially among restive western Republicans and disaffected conservatives in the party. That this subjected the administration to added political stress is undeniable. That it was what drove the president to make unsound energy choices, however, does not follow. On the contrary, other political strains aside, the internecine rivalry could have impelled Ford to make better policy, by persuading him to veto the Energy Policy and Conservation Act.[11]

10. The acknowledged disadvantage of the separation of powers, especially if compounded by split-party control, is that it can impede coherent policy leadership. Richard Neustadt, *Presidential Power: The Politics of Leaders from FDR to Carter* (John Wiley and Sons, 1960), p. 191. But in this case, the salience of this problem was debatable.
    11. Reagan had asserted that if he were president, he would veto the Energy Policy and

Whatever else snarled up the nation's energy legislation two years later, divided government could not be counted among the snags. When Jimmy Carter took office, his party's dominance of Congress approximated numerically that of Lyndon Johnson's "fabulous Eighty-ninth." However, Carter lacked Johnson's genius for harnessing the legislative power of the party's extraordinary majorities, and on some of the Carter administration's energy schemes (for example, the 1980 gasoline tax proposal), this weakness was unmistakable. But it is doubtful that another Democratic president, perhaps a more respected party insider, would have managed greater progress on energy pricing. Carter cast his lot with the traditional Democratic party position in the early rounds of the natural gas debate, but he was forced to edge away from it as the struggle wore on. The eventual compromise, which the president rescued rather adroitly, at least set a timetable for partial decontrol. Arguably, a stronger Democrat in the White House—someone more bound by party orthodoxy and more capable of governing the Democratic Senate as well as the House—would have secured, even more deftly, not the Natural Gas Policy Act, but a system of permanent, uncropped price controls.

Nor did the increasing frailty of the Carter presidency toward the end of its term keep the president from starting a phase out of oil price restraints, as the Energy Policy and Conservation Act permitted after May 1979. Despite the feverish attack by Senator Edward M. Kennedy in the 1980 presidential primaries (in which Kennedy campaigned against any cessation of petroleum price regulation), and despite the apprehensions of political advisers and party stalwarts in the administration, Carter began the process of decontrol that President Reagan completed in 1981.

For the most part, more imaginative leadership and even streamlined legislative procedures were not the lubricants that could have sufficed to unclog the governmental machinery to flush out of it stronger federal price policies for automotive fuel and for electric power. It was said in 1975, for instance, that if the deliberations of key congressional committees had been more disciplined and better coordinated, possibly through the integrative device of an ad hoc energy committee and closer supervision by the House speaker, the committee chairmen, and other pivotal policy managers, the House Ways and Means Committee's unpromising gasoline tax measure might have been encased in a sturdier legislative package, improving the chances for passage. Yet in 1977 a

Conservation Act.

special select committee was constituted to harmonize energy law-making, and this time, House leaders did run a tighter ship. To what effect? The select unit's proposed gasoline excise was crushed in a floor vote that closely resembled the one two years before. Meanwhile, the provision for a motor fuel levy in the president's National Energy Plan failed even to survive a Ways and Means markup. Admittedly, when a gasoline tax bill finally did clear Congress in 1982, it was engineered more shrewdly. But in that instance, many other helpful circumstances fell into place, and without them, the legislation would not have been possible.

Perhaps if state administration of utility ratemaking were less entrenched, and if Carter's legislative tacticians had been able to drive a harder bargain, the Senate Energy Committee in 1977 would not have discarded so summarily the idea of a firmer federal function in the Public Utility Regulatory Policies Act (PURPA). But even if this had happened—that is, even if the House version had prevailed, leaving a little less discretion to state regulatory authorities—the PURPA would have continued to dodge the prickly question: should utilities sell electricity to anyone for less than its replacement value? A complete and impartial federally enforced proscription of that practice was never in sight. The possibility had been thoroughly compromised from the outset, not in the Senate, but in the other body—by the original liberal coalition that had written the House bill.

In conclusion, although some of the twists and turns of the energy-pricing debate since 1973 might be ascribed directly to systemic impediments, specifically, to the limitations of political leaders and, more generally, to the fragmentation of power in American government, it is not clear that institutional bottlenecks were always the main constraints on policy.

Political Convictions

The preceding paradigms do not completely explain the politics of energy conservation in the United States. Shaping the political bedrock of conservation—the making of price policy—is more than the influence of lobbies, public opinion, localism, and styles of policy management. Intense political convictions collide over the issue, and they are central to an understanding of it. At the core of the oil and gas deregulation conflicts lie contrasting images of the role of government. One side prefers that policy be limited to rejuvenating the nation's energy-producing prowess by restoring market pricing; the other envisages a more elaborate social objective, that of reallocating in the name of economic justice the market's distribution of energy costs and benefits. At bottom, related themes flow through the energy tax dialogue. To liberals, the implications for distributive justice, and to conservatives, the proper balance of public and private power, inform the question of gasoline taxation. In the electric utility sector, public intervention is an accepted fact; governmental authority to set retail rates was affirmed in the states about eighty years ago. But the institutional locus of that authority, national or local, remains very much in tension, as does, more importantly, the final definition of the public purpose. If one aim of modern electric rate regulation is to encourage the efficient generation and usage of energy, another is to enhance distributive equity.

Because energy policy in America is an expression not only of disparate economic interests but also of competing ideas, deadlocks develop. Thus in the natural gas and oil-pricing battles of the 1970s, the opposing policy premises were so rigidly held, and often so evenly matched, that established programs proved excruciatingly difficult to reshape. Congress was split very much along party lines, between conservatives longing to "remove the throttles on energy production" and liberals in quest of "fairness."[12]

Ideological crosswinds begot irresolution in the other energy arenas too. Regulators, for example, have not found it simple to simulate full-market rates for electric power, by pricing electricity at its "real" commodity cost, while, with the same stroke, holding utility profits steady and dispensing what amounts to welfare benefits through below-market rates for designated consumer classes. Inasmuch as the public utility commissions, even after the PURPA's prodding, have failed to chalk up enough energy-saving dividends in new local rate designs, the fault lies in large measure with the twin goals imputed to the regulatory mission. The simultaneous attainment of economic efficiency and social equity, all within the tight radius of electric rate structures, is a tall order—indeed, often an impossible one.

As for fuel-saving tax measures, the chances are slim of legislating a European-style price disincentive to the overutilization of gasoline. Not only is there little or no active constituency for such a policy in the United States, but the option is choked off by a pincer-like onslaught from opposite ends of the partisan spectrum. To the Left, where the perennial grievance is that upper-income groups are not carrying their fair

12. William E. Simon, *A Time for Truth* (Berkley Books, 1978), p. 87.

share in taxes, another nonprogressive levy, especially on consumption of a vital commodity, adds insult to injury. At the same time, the Right has worried that if new, potentially copious sources of federal revenue are discovered, there is no telling what orgies of fiscal profligacy the big spenders could unleash.

Curiously, the ideological turbulence in energy pricing has seemed more marked and more apt to complicate policy in the United States than in much of Western Europe, where partisan discord and warring ideologies have been prominent historically. To make sense of this oddity, one must return to the roots of American political culture and trace the subtle doctrinal tensions in American party politics.

Political Culture

Remnants of classical liberalism—the virtues of self-reliance, the advantages of a market economy, the subordinate economic role of the state—frame American public philosophy. The possible sources of these beliefs in the nation's formative experience will continue to generate diverse historiography, but on this much few observers disagree: because American history bypassed a feudal stage, and hence largely avoided the convulsive class conflicts that sharpened competing social theories in Europe, political development in the United States has lacked Europe's ideological diversity.[13] Conspicuous by their absence are the European statist and corporatist traditions of both the Right and Left: the Tory brand of conservatism, a legacy of the feudal order predating liberalism, and a full-blown socialist movement, in a sense, the intellectual offshoot of both.[14] Instead, differing conceptions of government, although visible, are roughly confined to varying shades of the culture's preponderantly liberal ethos. Two basic implications follow.

First, where antique precedents for governmental *dirigism* are comparatively weak, and where rugged individualism is less tempered by collectivist values (or, in the tradition of Disraeli and Bismark, by paternalism), the national welfare state blossoms relatively late and assumes fairly restrained proportions.[15] The state acquires virtually no na-

13. The well-known exposition of this thesis is Louis Hartz's classic work, which was, in turn, substantially influenced by Alexis de Tocqueville's *Democracy in America*. Louis Hartz, *The Liberal Tradition in America: An Interpretation of American Political Thought Since the Revolution* (Harcourt, Brace and World, 1955).

14. See, for instance, Samuel H. Beer, *British Politics in the Collectivist Age* (Vintage Books, 1969), chap. 3.

15. See Arnold J. Heidenheimer, Hugh Heclo, and Carolyn Teich Adams, *Compar-

tionally owned industries and shares more power with independent local authorities. It also remains limited enough to finance itself without greatly diversifying the national tax system, that is, without adding on top of federal income taxation any major federal excise or value-added taxes. The state also develops a confusing patchwork of social programs whose costs mount, but whose overall coverage and adequacy continue to be perceived by critics as too restrictive or uneven.

Second, a compressed political spectrum, with an agenda spanning fewer permissible policy options, does not necessarily make the governmental process more serene, pragmatic, and, as Daniel J. Boorstin once contended, particularly free of political dogma.[16] On the contrary, the comparatively narrow philosophical band within which American political discourse ranges sometimes seems to put a finer edge on the partisan differences that do exist, imparting a distinctive sectarian intensity to some disputes. In these instances, the pragmatism that is the genius of American politics falters.

Few recent public issues have given this dynamic a clearer exhibition than have aspects of energy policy, especially during the 1970s. Far from becoming consensual ruminations about practical energy-saving methods, essential moves, such as the deregulation of oil and gas, were transformed into ideologically charged controversies, frequently pitting the great majority of Democrats against a great majority of Republicans in Congress. Even concerns that did not divide the parties quite so perfectly —the various gasoline tax bills and the tussles over utility rate standards —mobilized ideological coalitions that contributed to the fervor with which these questions have been debated. What was going on?

Ultimately, the politicization of the energy debates may well be magnified by the system's "mobilization of bias" in other relevant policy orbits. The unique attention to problems of equity in energy pricing may bear a relationship to the sorts of systemic settlements concerning, for example, the correctness of state ownership of industry and the uneasy

ative Public Policy: The Politics of Social Choice in Europe and America (St. Martin's Press, 1975), chap. 7; and Howard M. Leichter and Harrell R. Rodgers, Jr., *American Public Policy in a Comparative Context* (McGraw-Hill, 1984), chap. 2. Although social expenditures in the U.S. had moved up from 11 percent of the economy's total output of goods and services in 1960 to 21 percent by 1981, the OECD estimates that during the same interval, social outlays in the thirteen principal Western European economies reached 26.3 percent (from 14.5 percent in 1960). *New York Times*, February 19, 1984, p. 3.

16. Daniel J. Boorstin, *The Genius of American Politics* (University of Chicago Press, 1953), pp. 34–35.

status of redistributive policies. Thus, as suggested earlier, the crucial matter of private excess profits is bound to present a divisive dilemma where a national consensus has pretty much excluded the possibility of consigning energy production more extensively to the public sector. (I do not mean to conclude that nationalized energy industries are desirable for the sake of efficiency, only that the earnings of state-run enterprises cannot be characterized as a transfer of "rents" out of public hands.)[17] Also, traditional ambivalence about the legitimate scope of social policy increases the chances that schismatic welfare issues will spill into energy conservation decisions. Meanwhile, distrust of big government, or at least of centralized government, keeps puncturing fiscal arguments for a much higher national tax on gasoline consumption and inhibits any real federal encroachment on state control of electric ratemaking.

Politics and Markets

If energy pricing can detonate pitched battles between American liberals and conservatives, hence generally between Democrats and Republicans, as in the deregulation debates of the 1970s, it is not because either group contemplates extreme departures, like nationalization, from the market economy. Rather, hostilities flare in the context of shared, though far from identical, allegiances to it.[18]

Neither of the major political parties (not even the Democrats in the heyday of the New Deal or under the banner of William Jennings Bryan, whose early program appropriated elements of the truly radical Populist platform of 1892)[19] has ever proposed the sort of wholesale abandonment of private enterprise so common in Europe; there has been no public seizure of entire industrial sectors. Insofar as government cor-

---

17. The closest American counterparts to the governmental interests of European countries in their domestic energy sectors are the U.S. state governments in the leading energy-producing regions. Higher prices serve the revenue needs of these states through lucrative royalties and severance taxes, just as they do the government-held energy corporations (and treasuries) in nations such as Norway and Great Britain.

18. I owe several aspects of the argument being developed here to Shonfield's work of twenty years ago. Andrew Shonfield, *Modern Capitalism: The Changing Balance of Public and Private Power* (Oxford University Press, 1965), especially p. 298. More recently, a somewhat similar interpretation was advanced by David Vogel. See David Vogel, "The 'New' Social Regulation in Historical and Comparative Perspective," in Thomas K. McCraw, ed., *Regulation in Perspective: Historical Essays* (Harvard University Press, 1981), pp. 183–84.

19. The Populist platform, drafted at the Omaha convention of 1892, however, had called for public ownership and operation of railroads, telegraph, and telephones.

porations exist (scattered municipally owned utilities, the TVA, Veterans' Administration hospitals, Amtrak), the understanding has been that the experiments remain limited.[20] Amid contemporary caricatures that often seem to sketch Republicans as economic libertarians and Democrats as incorrigibly distrustful of the marketplace, it is easy to forget how frequently, in the perspective of history, roles were blurred if not reversed. Between the Civil War and roughly the end of the Korean War, the Democrats came closest to being the party of free trade. In the 1920s, their advocacy of supply-side tax reductions practically outdid that of Calvin Coolidge. And in the late 1970s, liberal Democrats in Congress and a Democratic administration led drives to deregulate the airline, trucking, railroad, and banking industries.[21]

So it is not too much to say that the squabbling parties have been less concerned with the fundamental legitimacy of market principles than with rival claims on them. Perhaps this makes their squabbles all the more zealous. In a sense, both Republicans and Democrats have invoked the same general scripture, various market solutions, but wrangle strenuously about the right interpretation, each side convinced that it knows more about what government ought to do to make markets function beneficently.

Thus the Democratic congressional majorities that defended energy price controls throughout the last decade did not think of themselves as betraying the market system; on the contrary, they spoke as if their regulatory interventions were merely ridding it of imperfections, securing the competitive environment, the price signals, and the distributional effects that a genuinely free system would generate. The Democratic legislators were troubled by the prospect of uncontrolled oil and gas prices greatly exceeding average costs of production, at least so long as OPEC retained the ability to set production quotas. The Democrats also feared the possibility that large, integrated firms might exploit conditions of taut supply and high prices to squeeze small competitors out of the industry, especially its refining and marketing operations. Regulations intended to redress these flaws were not deemed inconsistent with plans to decontrol prices in other economic sectors, airline fares, for example. On the contrary, what enabled Democrats to embark upon both courses with

20. In the nineteenth century, mixed corporations were fairly common at the state level, however. Shonfield, *Modern Capitalism*, p. 302.

21. Martha Derthick and Paul J. Quirk, *The Politics of Deregulation* (Brookings, 1985); and Alan Stone, *Regulation and Its Alternatives* (Washington, D.C.: CQ Press, 1982), pp. 250–52.

equal enthusiasm was that the policy objectives were thought to be more or less the same: to bring prices more nearly into line with supposed costs and to enhance the "competitive viability" of the industry in question.

The last point merits emphasis. Although their market-mending policies were intended to help consumers, many liberals also felt that they were upholding a time-honored tradition: coming to the aid of small business against corporate Goliaths. In reality, the degree of industrial concentration among oil and gas firms was modest compared with the structures of many other large American industries.[22] Nor was there a shred of evidence that concentration would be reduced, or competitive viability increased, by price controls.[23] Nonetheless, a kind of populist passion to affirm equal opportunity for small companies—what John Kenneth Galbraith has called the liberal "social nostalgia,"[24] harking all the way back to the Jeffersonian ancestry of the Democratic party— inspired the various price and allocation regulations of the 1970s. It also motivated a host of other energy determinations. Small outfits of all descriptions repeatedly received preferential treatment at the hands of the Democratically controlled Congress. Even minor independent producers —"Mom and Pop millionaires," as they are sometimes known in the business—could say they had "the small business syndrome going for us."[25] They gained partial exemptions from the 1975 repeal of the oil depletion allowance, from the 1980 windfall profits tax, and, in the case of stripper well operators, from lower-tier price lids in both the Energy Policy Conservation Act and the Natural Gas Policy Act.

But while liberals were satisfied that their exertions were cleansing blemished energy markets and improving the competitive fortunes of small firms, conservatives grew convinced that what had started out as emergency corrective action (in the form of short-term legislation such as the Emergency Petroleum Allocation Act) had turned into yet an-

22. See Richard B. Mancke, "Competition in the Petroleum Industry," in Patricia Maloney Markun, ed., *The Future of American Oil* (Washington, D.C.: American Petroleum Institute, 1976), pp. 97–132; and Jesse W. Markham, "Market Structure and Horizontal Divestiture of the Energy Companies," in Edward J. Mitchell, ed., *Horizontal Divestiture in the Oil Industry* (Washington, D.C.: American Enterprise Institute, 1978), pp. 21–27.

23. On the contrary, there were indications that price controls in the natural gas industry had forced significant numbers of minor independents to liquidate or merge with larger companies. *Consumer Energy Act of 1974*, Hearings before the Senate Committee on Commerce, 93 Cong. 2 sess. (Government Printing Office, 1974), p. 1561.

24. John Kenneth Galbraith, *The Liberal Hour* (Houghton Mifflin, 1960), p. 124.

25. *Congressional Quarterly Weekly Report*, vol. 33 (May 3, 1975), p. 941.

other potentially permanent public "strangulation" of a strategic private industry.[26]

Deviation

Where the ideological warfare is not between capitalism and collectivism, but between rival parties who in their own ways profess to prize the private economy, assertions of superior fidelity to it are a favorite tactic and an endless source of friction. Congressional advocates of energy deregulation would have liked nothing better than to anoint themselves original apostles of market freedom and pillory their adversaries as nonbelievers. But historically, the integrity of energy markets had been sufficiently compromised by liberals and conservatives alike to draw spirited accusations of heresy from either sect.[27]

Although conservative politicians now preached laissez-faire, the awkward truth was that key precedents for the governmental distortion of fuel pricing bore the fingerprints of Republican presidents. Certainly the seeds of the Emergency Petroleum Allocation Act, and eventually of the Energy Policy and Conservation Act, were planted by Nixon's general wage and price freeze in 1971. Well before that, the oil-import control program, the first direct federal manipulation of crude oil prices, had been inaugurated under President Dwight D. Eisenhower, who (despite noble intentions) also shared considerable responsibility for the permanence of federal natural gas controls, owing to his veto of the Harris-Fulbright gas bill in 1957.

In many respects, Republican energy programs contained the same impurity that Democrats had observed in Republican economic policies of earlier vintage: a tendency to exalt free enterprise, but then to employ the power of the federal government to protect or stimulate business for the sake of national industrial expansion or security. Hence, just as Republican administrations from Lincoln to Hoover had found room for massive tariff walls in between pledges to allow "the least possible Government entry into the economic field,"[28] the GOP's response to the

26. William E. Simon, *A Time for Truth*, p. 72.
27. See Joseph P. Kalt and Robert S. Stillman, "The Role of Governmental Incentives in Energy Production: An Historical Overview," *Annual Review of Energy*, vol. 5 (Palo Alto, Calif.: Annual Reviews Inc., 1980), pp. 6, 7.
28. Third annual message to Congress, December 8, 1931, in William Starr Myers, ed., *The State Papers and Other Public Writings of Herbert Hoover*, vol. 2 (Doubleday, Doran and Company, 1934), p. 44.

energy crisis strayed from strict faith in the hallowed magic of the invisible hand. Actually, in the interest of promoting domestic energy growth and of achieving "zero oil imports," a host of extra subsidies for producers were supported, along with new federal bureaucracies to administer them.[29] The Democrats of Bryan's day had denounced Republican tariffs for nurturing "monopoly under the pleas of protection."[30] Not long after, Woodrow Wilson had stood on the principle of unrestricted international commerce against a Republican Congress bent on raising trade barriers to new heights. A half century later, Republicans were stung by similar criticisms on energy policy. Liberals scolded the Ford administration for pursuing "an isolationist policy." "Energy independence," Senator Edward M. Kennedy protested, was "the illusion that we can withdraw from the global economy."[31] The administration was also taken to task for asking consumers to sink or swim amid turbulent market forces while large energy companies would ride them, buoyed by publicly subsidized flotation cushions.

The proderegulation partisans parried these charges by stressing that the price controls to which liberals had grown so attached were nothing if not quixotic efforts to insulate the domestic economy from international economic realities. In actuality the controls neither served the needs of consumers nor curbed the market power of multinational producers. But such rebuttals were slow to win converts. Most Democrats mistrusted them, insisting that these arguments came from a Republican party that had forfeited a right to speak authoritatively about "internal contradictions" in Democratic energy plans, or about its own alleged "greater reliance on competitive pricing."[32] As one liberal Democrat, Governor Michael Dukakis of Massachusetts, reckoned in defense of the Emergency Petroleum Allocation Act's entitlements program, others had been guilty of "playing with the price" of oil in the past, and now it was

29. The text of the Republican Project Independence report noted that "while zero imports is achievable, it is simply not warranted economically or politically." Yet, when President Nixon launched Project Independence in a November 1973 television address, he stated, "Let us set as our national goal . . . that by the end of this decade we will have developed the potential to meet our own energy needs without depending on any foreign sources." John L. Moore, ed., *Continuing Energy Crisis in America* (Washington, D.C.: CQ Press, 1975), p. 2.

30. Democratic platform of 1900, in Lewis L. Gould, *Reform and Regulation: American Politics, 1900–1916* (John Wiley and Sons, 1978), p. 18.

31. *Congressional Record* (October 8, 1975), p. 32175.

32. Senate Republican Policy Committee energy initiative, in *Congressional Quarterly Weekly Report*, vol. 35 (May 21, 1977), p. 958.

his side's turn to "be pardoned if we react in kind."[33]

In general, a plump record of federal interference in energy pricing, and especially of subventions conferred on energy businesses, all too often by political conservatives, tightened the grip on price restraints that liberals regarded as a way of evening the score. Oil and gas decontrol was not the only type of price reform thus resisted. Similar mistrust of the electric rate innovations that might appear to give power companies an opportunity for higher profits was augmented by the legacy of government subsidies to utilities. All governments, of course, actively promote their energy-producing industries, often regardless of the coloration of the parties in power. But in the United States, perhaps more than other countries, the process fuels controversy because it is not easily reconciled with the avowed American philosophy of economic freedom.

The Supply-Side Orientation

What has positioned the Republican party to the right of center in the course of modern American history is not a deeper deference to the foundations of the economic order, nor necessarily greater circumspection in the interposition of public policies that affect it. The Republican party desires a relationship between business and government that is aimed at building national wealth, with Republicans paying less attention than the Democrats usually do to the immediate distribution of the wealth. (Some leading Republicans have sought a different emphasis. Theodore Roosevelt, for example, came to believe that "the most pressing problems that confront the present century are not concerned with the material production of wealth, but with its distribution." To campaign in earnest with this view, however, he found it necessary to bolt the party.)[34] Generally, on the strength of the conviction that in time the fruits of capitalism trickle down generously to society as a whole, and that concentrations of wealth and economic power are difficult to reduce without undercutting the entrepreneurial incentives needed to bear the fruits in the first place, Republicans have seldom

33. Edward J. Mitchell, ed., *Energy: Regional Goals and the National Interest* (Washington, D.C.: American Enterprise Institute, 1976), p. 24.

34. See William A. Schambra, "The Roots of the American Public Philosophy," *Public Interest*, vol. 67 (Spring 1982), p. 44. On the post-1964 expulsion of the progressive wing of the Republican party, see William Schneider, "Democrats and Republicans, Liberals and Conservatives," in Seymour Martin Lipset, ed., *Party Coalitions in the 1980s* (San Francisco: Institute for Contemporary Studies, 1981), pp. 224–25.

been as suspicious as Democrats of bigness in business.[35] (On this point even the progressive wing of the GOP differed from Wilsonian Progressives.)[36] The Republicans have tended to be less comfortable than the majority of Democrats could be with greater governmental activism to relieve economic inequalities.

If, from time to time, the party would readily reconcile itself to a different kind of federal initiative—namely, public subsidies, even regulations, to foster industrial growth—it is because this sort of policy could appear to nourish, rather than stifle, the productive force of the private sector. Forms of promotionalism thus have been a theme unifying many Republican economic blueprints, from portions of the Economic Recovery Tax Act of 1981 to the towering tariffs shielding infant industries at the turn of the century, the railroad loans and land grants after the Civil War, the ancestral Whig programs for internal improvements, or going back to the very beginning, Alexander Hamilton's *Report on Manufactures*.[37]

For the most part, when thinking about energy price policy, Republicans, along with errant boll weevil Democrats, viewed government's mission in more or less the same fashion: chiefly as another exercise in promoting commercial development ("production, production, production," one thoughtful congressional critic quipped),[38] the benefits of which (abundant yields, oil security, gentler fuel bills) would eventually find their way to citizens at all levels. Accordingly, even the 1980 Republican platform, which trumpeted a revival of "maximum feasible choice and freedom in the marketplace for energy," spoke simultaneously of the continuing need for a coal conversion program, of government support for new energy-producing technologies, of federal efforts to encourage development of breeder reactors and the accelerated use of nuclear power, in sum, of "aggressively boosting," rather than

35. According to Hubert H. Humphrey, for instance, the government's mandate was unequivocal: "large concentrations of power should be broken up by government action." Hubert H. Humphrey, *The Cause is Mankind: A Liberal Program for Modern America* (Frederick A. Praeger, 1964), p. 14. It is hard to think of any Republican reformers, even among the trust-busting Progressives, who would have subscribed so absolutely to this view.

36. Perhaps more than anything else, this was what differentiated the economic doctrine of Theodore Roosevelt's "New Nationalism" from the "New Freedom" of Wilson and Brandeis. Gould, *Reform and Regulation*, pp. 143–44.

37. William Nisbet Chambers, *Political Parties in a New Nation: The American Experience, 1776–1809* (Oxford University Press, 1963), pp. 37–38.

38. Paul Tsongas, *The Road from Here: Liberalism and Realities in the 1980s* (Alfred A. Knopf, 1981), p. 54.

leaving exclusively to the market, the nation's energy supplies.[39]

Inasmuch as it complemented this orientation, price deregulation became a top priority. When deregulation had meant removing price floors as well as ceilings, it had not been such strict Republican gospel. One recalls far fewer cries of "let the marketplace prevail" and "get the government off the industry's back" in the earlier context of soft international oil prices, the 1950s and 1960s, when price-supporting import controls were in effect. Rather, many Republicans in Congress, along with Democratic allies from oil-producing states, warmed quickly to the position when world oil prices started surging in the early 1970s. Then, all of a sudden, the coalition sensed that a hands-off approach to pricing was propitious to the profitability, and hence the volume, of domestic energy exploration and extraction. By 1975 decontrol of domestic oil and natural gas had turned into a fiercely partisan affair, the Republican party's cause célèbre.

That conservative legislators were interested in deregulation largely as a production inducement, rather than a fuel-saving opportunity, did not mean they discounted conservation. Indeed, most seemed more confident and knowledgeable about the elasticity of energy demand than many liberals appeared to be. Moreover, the preoccupation with production was not just an idiosyncratic bias, to the exclusion of other contributing factors. It also touched an apparently responsive chord in public opinion, and, in the case of natural gas, it received encouragement from some impressive estimates of the future supply potential. Still, by championing decontrol of oil and gas almost exclusively from the supply side, its proponents clouded the terms of the public dialogue. Well into the 1980 presidential campaign (in which the successful Republican candidate predicted that "with decontrol, we could be producing enough oil to be self-sufficient in five years"),[40] congressional attention was riveted on how much energy might be pumped out by the market mechanism, rather than on what market pricing could also provide, a formidable brake on consumption.

Consequently, the policy process became extraordinarily polemical. Few things were more speculative than how production would respond to the lifting of price controls. As one frustrated participant in 1975 put it,

39. *Congressional Quarterly Almanac,* vol. 36 (1980), pp. 73-B, 74-B.

40. Daniel Yergin, "America in the Strait of Stringency," in Daniel Yergin and Martin Hillenbrand, eds., *Global Insecurity: A Strategy for Energy and Economical Renewal* (Houghton Mifflin, 1981), p. 102.

We are stumbling around in the dark for the right price for crude oil without any—I should emphasize—with absolutely no knowledge of the relationship between supply and price, with no objective insight into production costs, and with no hard estimates of economically recoverable reserves in light of current prices and technology.[41]

Inevitably, therefore, tendentious partisan theories gained currency, and what passed for empirical analysis seemed to embroider these theories rather than test them. If there were some fragmentary facts about supply elasticities in the mid-1970s, few appeared to support the contention that production, particularly of crude oil, would soar with deregulation. Even though "production is the first key issue on everyone's mind," shouted one of the most vocal liberal critics during a 1975 House debate, "there has been no consistent case made by anyone, inside or outside the oil industry, that production will be increased if prices rise . . . , or alternatively, that any increments will be anything more than so slight as to be virtually meaningless."[42] Based at least on the paltry domestic supply responses to oil-price increases at that time, Representative Andrew J. Maguire, Democrat of New Jersey, and his many fellow skeptics appeared to have a point.

Moreover, since production was indeed the first, and for the most part the only, issue on everyone's mind when deregulation was debated, the impracticality of other (nonmarket) techniques for clipping consumption was poorly understood, as were the likely macroeconomic effects of decontrol. Hence many liberals were able to cling rigidly to the fiction that somehow energy savings and efficiency could be accomplished without price incentives. This notion could not be shaken so long as deregulators failed to articulate the demand-side benefits of the policy they were prescribing.

Finally, in its zeal to spur production, the conservative coalition continued to vote for producers' tax preferences (the depletion allowance, for instance) even as it recommended a levy on windfall profits to accompany decontrol. Consequently, liberals suspected that the talk of windfall profits taxation was not serious and then pounced on the opportunity to lampoon their opposition as being in bed with oil barons.

Energy and Equity

It is a gross exaggeration to suggest, as some critics have, that Democrats became devotees of controls on energy prices because the party had

41. *Congressional Quarterly Weekly Report*, vol. 33 (May 24, 1975), p. 1067.
42. *Congressional Record* (July 15, 1975), p. 22761.

been captured in the 1970s by a new class of no-growth romantics or postindustrial Luddites repudiating the economic system. The party's stance actually conformed to a more conventional political instinct. The Democrats wanted to claim for themselves the reputation for being purveyors of prosperity and to keep fastening on the GOP, as they had done during the New Deal, public opprobrium for bringing bad times. Thus in the decisive oil-pricing battle, which happened to unfold during a serious recession, Democrats warned about decontrol's "astounding inflationary impact" and its potential for "economic disaster."[43] The Left seemed as convinced that continued controls were instrumental to reviving the flagging economy as the Right was sure that they posed an obstacle.[44]

But neither can one say that the main point of Democratic energy-pricing policy was just to nurse a stagnant economy back to health. For as much as Democrats shared with Republicans an interest in renewing economic growth, they did not have the same patience for the process by which its rewards would percolate to the average consumer. To conservatives, a rising tide could lift all boats, but to their opponents on the Left, the responsibility of government (as an outspoken liberal congressman described it) was "to recognize that concern for economic equity requires *a good deal more* than simply pumping up the GNP," since "people are not boats. The economy is not a tide. And an increase in GNP may occur in a way that leaves some people no better off than they were, while others find their condition worsening."[45]

Nothing in the American energy saga was more distinctive than the fact that Democrats did not reserve this warrant for the domain of social policy, but carried it squarely into the various pricing debates. Whatever else the regulation of energy prices was supposed to accomplish, many Democrats saw it as "the little guy's" last line of defense against rapacious oil companies and as a form of social insurance compensating for the regressive effects of rising fuel costs.[46] The tangled web of income support programs

43. *Congressional Quarterly Weekly Report*, vol. 33 (January 25, 1975), pp. 171, 178; and David E. Rosenbaum, "Democrats Fear Inflation from Oil Price Decontrol," *New York Times*, July 15, 1975.

44. See, for example, the floor speech of Senator Henry M. Jackson, Democrat of Washington, *Congressional Quarterly Weekly Report*, vol. 33 (February 22, 1975), p. 358.

45. Representative Barney Frank, Democrat of Massachusetts, "Is This a Dagger I See Before Me?" *Washington Post*, July 27, 1983. Emphasis added.

46. Subsidized energy pricing was not strictly an American invention, with no analogues abroad during the 1970s. Price controls on petroleum refined-products were tried in some other OECD countries such as France and Italy. See Horst Mendershausen, *Coping with the Oil Crisis: French and German Experiences* (Johns Hopkins University Press for Resources

was judged too porous and unreliable to afford enough protection, so supplemental safeguards had to be assembled. Had they been available, funds from new taxes on producer profits following decontrol could have helped shore up the social safety net. But until 1980, adoption of these tax measures, to say nothing of redistributive plans for their revenues, seemed so fraught with legislative uncertainties that a nervous congressional majority hung on to subsidized fuel pricing instead.

This presumption that the existing array of social transfer outlays did not suffice for "the common man" to cope with the energy crisis, later coupled with a growing sense that the federal tax structure wasn't giving him a fair shake either, prolonged the congressional attachment to price controls. It also animated liberal opposition to higher gasoline excises and spurred an interest in rate relief for small utility customers. Perhaps nowhere was the motif exemplified more openly than in the hearings on the Public Utility Regulatory Policies Act, during which liberals strove to mandate electric rate subsidies for at least one group they deemed disadvantaged: the elderly. At one point, Senator Clifford Hansen, Republican of Wyoming, asked Senator Gary Hart, a leading advocate of lifeline rate proposals before the Senate, the question that was very much on the minds of skeptical conservatives: why require energy rate regulators to perform income maintenance functions that were more suitably "the responsibility of the welfare agencies?"[47] The Colorado

---

for the Future, 1976), pp. 78–82. At one point, Sweden attempted to freeze its gasoline and diesel fuel prices. See International Energy Agency, *Energy Policies and Programmes of IFA Countries, 1979 Review* (Paris: Organization for Economic Cooperation and Development, 1980), p. 192. Natural gas prices were in effect in the Netherlands, whose Groningen fields produced about half of that nation's energy. Canada regulated her domestic crude oil prices more stringently than the United States did. Japan sheltered kerosene, Japan's key fuel for home heating, from the full effect of rising prices. Even Britain, which like West Germany, favored a strict free market approach to petroleum pricing, regulated domestic natural gas and electric power rates at below-replacement costs. See S.A. Van Vactor, "Energy Conservation in the OECD: Progress and Results," *Journal of Energy and Development*, vol. 3 (Spring 1978), pp. 247–48. Nonetheless, market pricing was eventually accepted more fully, smoothly, and rapidly in most of these countries than it was in the United States. In general, the best available comparative analysis of the practice of energy-price subsidization, and of relative concern with equity in bearing the burden of higher energy prices, suggests that the concern and the practice have been consistently less intense in Europe and Japan than in the United States. See Eberhard Meller, "The Equity Issue in Europe and Japan," in Hans H. Landsberg, ed., *High Energy Costs: Assessing the Burden* (Washington, D.C.: Resources for the Future, 1982), especially pp. 337, 340–43. See also Edward R. Fried, "Comments on 'The Equity Issues in Europe and Japan' " in Landsberg, ed., *High Energy Costs*, pp. 378–79.

47. *Public Utility Rate Proposals of President Carter's Energy Program*, Hearings before the Subcommittee on Energy Conservation and Regulation of the Senate Com-

Democrat's reply expressed the sentiment common among members of his party:

On the part of your question of why not leave it to established welfare-type agencies, that would be fine and good if they were, in fact, doing something about this problem. But, as I am sure you know from talking to senior citizens from Wyoming, this [fact of rising utility bills] is a substantial problem for older people in this country and there is no mechanism in our present welfare structure to account to them.

Now, if we increase the social security payments for increased energy costs or if we gave them energy stamps or something else, that is fine. But we aren't. In the meantime in the winters they are hard pressed to make ends meet. There are documented cases where senior citizens, who should be afforded dignity in our society, are eating dog food because they can't have an adequate diet and pay their energy bills at the same time.[48]

One wonders how a sophisticated lawmaker in the late 1970s, when federal social expenditures were nearing some $230 billion annually,[49] could opine that "welfare-type agencies" were not "doing something" to alleviate economic hardships. This much seems clear: there was more to the matter than mere posturing, demagoguery, or handwringing over anecdotes about dog food dinners. The way Democrats amalgamated energy policy with welfare policy ultimately reflected an old and uneasy outlook on the welfare structure: they were dissatisfied with it, but lacked the political muscle, the internal cohesion, and perhaps the resolve needed to overhaul it comprehensively.

In part it was as if the main thing about the social agenda legislated during the New Deal and the Great Society was not that both parties had since come to terms with much of it, or that the American welfare state, like all others, was now large and expensive, but rather that history had carved into institutional memories the ordeals of initial adoption. One might say, in other words, that the original schisms (such as the congressional division on the Social Security Act of 1935, in which 85 percent of House Democrats voted for the plan, while 99 percent of House Republicans stood against it, or the vote on Medicare in 1965, favored by 78 percent of the Democrats in the House, but opposed by 93 percent of the Republicans) had left deeper political imprints than the fact that a bipartisan consensus had later presided over major expansions

---

mittee on Energy and Natural Resources, 95 Cong. 1 sess. (GPO, 1977), pt. 1, p. 132.

48. Ibid.

49. Henry Aaron, "The Domestic Budget," in Joseph A. Pechman, ed., *Setting National Priorities: The 1980 Budget* (Brookings, 1979), p. 102.

of the established social security system. Add-ons to institutionalized components could come quite easily, but fresh debates on new programs could reopen old wounds, reminding liberals that enactment was historically grudging, except in instances of overwhelming liberal legislative dominance. By the late 1970s, even add-ons were no longer guaranteed easy votes; the taxes needed to finance them were beginning to pinch much more keenly.

In principle it might be preferable to deal separately with the two sides of the energy muddle by decoupling pricing decisions from compensatory subsidies. But new social spending to pay on a large scale for energy stamps, or other income supplements aimed at filling alleged gaps in existing social assistance provisions, was given increasingly long political odds. Hence the safer bet was to insert into energy-price management as many distributive adjustments as possible, satisfying supposed social needs through field-price restraints, utility rate manipulations, and vetoes on energy-saving excise taxes.

In part, as well, liberals looked to subsidized energy pricing to deliver the functional equivalent of a social service because they were simply not up to the task of addressing directly the various perceived inadequacies in extant social welfare programs. The piecemeal approach, providing welfare by proxy, so to speak, was a tactical expedient, but also a reflection of the Democratic party's own internal scissions and ultimate lack of programmatic clarity in the pursuit of social reform. The Democratic majorities in Congress could have disencumbered the politics of energy conservation if they had been wholly prepared to resolve questions of equity elsewhere, chiefly through welfare reform and federal tax policy. But these Democratic majorities often behaved ambivalently when genuine opportunities presented themselves. Thus, ironically, the ill-fated Family Assistance Plan in 1970 drew as many objections from Democrats as from conservatives in the GOP. Seven years later, when a Democratic president sent to a Democratic Congress another version of a guaranteed income plan, the "Program for Better Jobs and Income," the proposal fared no better. Although the political circumstances surrounding these outcomes were complex, societal attitudes were very much involved. The prevalent currents of opinion that have fed the stream of American politics generally were also running through the Democratic coalition itself: periodically, populist eagerness to "share our wealth" could flow into it,[50] but a steadier tributary was the civic

50. Franklin D. Roosevelt spoke openly, for example, of "stealing [Huey P.] Long's

culture's usual caution as to how much federal relief should be doled out, and to whom.[51]

By and large, that prudence, transcending party lines much of the time, has been a blessing: Democrats as well as Republicans have been able to appreciate Hamilton's concern that a consuming passion for affirmative public action to level social inequalities puts at grave risk both personal liberty and the national prosperity. But as the political decisions on energy conservation often attested, a hesitant spirit does not always simplify government policy when big tradeoffs are perceived to exist between equality and economic efficiency. For sometimes, the political hopes for enhancing efficiency rest not so much on realizing that "any sacrifice of either has to be justified as a necessary means of obtaining more of the other,"[52] as on recognition that requirements for social equity may have to be settled more explicitly, and if necessary, more generously, first.

---

thunder" by his proposed tax reforms in 1935. James L. Sundquist, *Dynamics of the Party System: Alignment and Realignment of Political Parties in the United States*, rev. ed. (Brookings, 1983), p. 212.

51. Lest it be assumed that the cautious disposition has always found expression in the Republican party alone, one might recall which president once intoned, "Federal aid . . . encourages the expectation of paternal care on the part of the Government and weakens the sturdiness of our national character." It was Grover Cleveland, a northern Democrat. Veto of Texas seed bill, February 16, 1887, in *1837–1908: Chronology, Documents, Bibliographical Aids* (Dobbs Ferry, N.Y.: Oceana Publications, 1968), p. 62.

52. Arthur M. Okun, *Equality and Efficiency: The Big Tradeoff* (Brookings, 1975), p. 88.

Index

286